# European Fair Trading Law
## The Unfair Commercial Practices Directive

GERAINT HOWELLS
*Lancaster University, UK*

HANS-W. MICKLITZ
*University of Bamberg, Germany*

THOMAS WILHELMSSON
*University of Helsinki, Finland*

ASHGATE

Published by
Ashgate Publishing Limited
Gower House
Croft Road
Aldershot
Hampshire GU11 3HR
England

Ashgate Publishing Company
Suite 420
101 Cherry Street
Burlington, VT 05401-4405
USA

Ashgate website: http://www.ashgate.com

**British Library Cataloguing in Publication Data**
Howells, Geraint G.
    European fair trading law : the Unfair Commercial Practices
    Directive. - (Markets and the law)
    1. European Union. Directive 2005/29/EC  2. Competition,
    Unfair - Law and legislation - European Union countries
    3. Restraint of trade - European Union countries 4. Consumer
    protection - European Union countries
    I. Title  II. Micklitz, Hans-W.  III. Wilhelmsson, Thomas, 1949-
    343.4'072

**Library of Congress Cataloging-in-Publication Data**
Howells, Geraint G.
    European fair trading law : the unfair commercial practices directive / by Geraint
Howells, Hans Micklitz, Thomas Wilhelmsson.
        p.  cm. (Markets and the law)
    Includes index.
    ISBN 0-7546-4589-4
    1. Competition, Unfair--European Union countries. 2.  Consumer protection--Law and
legislation--European Union countries. I. Micklitz, Hans-W. II. Wilhelmsson, Thomas,
1949- III. Title. IV. Series.

    KJE6536.H69 2006
    343.24'072--dc22

                                                                            2006012259

ISBN-10: 0-7546-4589-4
ISBN-13: 978-0-7546-4589-4

Printed and bound in Great Britain by MPG Books Ltd, Bodmin Cornwall.

# Markets and the Law

*Series Editor*:
Geraint Howells,
Lancaster University, UK

Markets and the Law is concerned with the way the law interacts with the market through regulation, self-regulation and the impact of private law regimes. It looks at the impact of regional and international organizations (eg EC and WTO) and many of the works adopt a comparative approach and/or appeal to an international audience. Examples of subjects covered include trade laws, intellectual property, sales law, insurance, consumer law, banking, financial markets, labour law, environmental law and social regulation affecting the market as well as competition law. The series includes texts covering a broad area, monographs on focused issues, and collections of essays dealing with particular themes.

*Other titles in the series*

**Information Rights and Obligations**
**A Challenge for Party Autonomy and Transactional Fairness**
*Edited by*
Geraint Howells, André Janssen and Reiner Schulze
ISBN 0 7546 2432 3

**Cyber Consumer Law and Unfair Trading Practices**
Cristina Coteanu
ISBN 0 7546 2417 X

**Consumer Protection Law**
Geraint Howells and Stephen Weatherill
ISBN 0 7546 2338 6 (Pbk)
ISBN 0 7546 2331 9 (Hbk)

**Personal Insolvency Law, Regulation and Policy**
David Milman
ISBN 0 7546 4302 6

# Contents

# Preface

The Unfair Commercial Practices Directive is one of the most significant pieces of legislation to emanate from Brussels in recent times. It seeks to introduce a European conception of fairness by introducing a general clause to cover all economic harm caused to consumers by unfair practices. Moreover, it seeks to adopt a maximal harmonisation approach that would for the most part prevent Member States from introducing stricter national laws.

The three authors have followed the development of this Directive closely and to varying degrees have more or less formally engaged in debates with the European legislator about what the scope and content of the Directive should have been. Now the European law is in place, we wanted to come together to produce a work which took stock of the evolution of European fair trading law, evaluated the Directive and assessed it in this wider European law context and gave some assistance to those grappling to implement the Directive and thereafter apply it.

This is neither a collection of essays nor a multi-authored work. We each took responsibility for distinct chapters and, whilst we discussed and compared notes, we allowed room for individual expressions of opinion. Whilst we agree on most aspects, there were some differences between us. Rather than always paper over these differences, we thought it would be more interesting, for the reader, to flag some of them up and explain why we take different approaches.

Every difference of opinion on legal interpretation depends to some extent on individual judgment, but we also suspect traits of our national legal experience remain with us when considering the Directive. This needs to be recognised as an important dimension of the European convergence process and either respected or techniques developed to overcome it (depending on one's perspective).

All three authors come from legal systems that have been or will be most profoundly affected by European fair trade law. Germany's very protective unfair competition laws, under which trader protection often masqueraded as consumer protection, have been uprooted by European free movement, misleading advertising and now the fairness standard in this Directive. Finland's strong tradition of consumer protection feels threatened by the more market-oriented philosophy that lies behind much of the Directive. The United Kingdom is familiar with such a robust approach, but will have to come to terms with a new style of regulation based on the use of general clauses.

This background explains some of our differences of opinion (or sometimes emphasis). The majority did not always result from the same traditions combining. For instance, the German contributor was more concerned to see the fairness doctrine in the Directive underpin the movement away from the previous draconian German conception of fairness and was wary in case over-protectionism crept in through arguments that the national rules being invoked fell outside the economic scope of the Directive. The other two were keener to emphasise that the Directive's conception of fairness only applied within its scope. By contrast the two continental scholars were fairly complimentary about the drafting of the Directive, admiring its structure of general clause, clauses on misleading and aggressive practices and blacklist of prohibited practices. The common lawyer still complained that the drafting left too many unanswered questions and sometimes caused difficulty in reconciling the rules with the stated policy objectives.

If we had involved colleagues from other traditions we might have had an even richer debate. However, our experience supports our decision to restrict cooperation to just three legal traditions. One thing on which we agree is that this would have been a better piece of legislation if it had not attempted to achieve maximal harmonisation. Our debates highlight to us the complexity of this area and the folly of attempting to impose a European model with little room for national flexibility.

Hopefully the reader will come away understanding the Directive and its context better. We cannot claim to offer answers to every question or even agreement on all answers, but even where we offer different opinions we hope the discussion throws some light on this complex area of European law which is certain to generate even greater complexity at the national level, both on implementation and afterwards when it has to be enforced.

Finally, we wish to acknowledge some institutions and people that have supported the writing of this book. The work of Thomas Wilhelmsson has been done within a research project funded by the Academy of Finland on 'Private Law in a Multicultural and Multilingual European Society (PriME)'. In addition, Wilhelmsson also wants to thank the Universities of Oslo and Bamberg for their hospitality, as he wrote the main parts of his contribution during stays at these institutions. All authors wish to record their thanks to Julie Prescott who helped prepare the manuscript for publication and to Ashgate, especially Alison Kirk, for their faith in this project.

Geraint Howells
Hans-W. Micklitz
Thomas Wilhelmsson
September, 2006

# List of Directives with Abbreviations

Directive 84/450/EC on the approximation of the laws, regulations and administrative provisions of the Member States concerning misleading advertising: OJ 1984 L250/17 (hereafter Misleading Advertising Directive).

Directive 85/577/EEC to protect the consumer in respect of contracts negotiated away from business premises: OJ 1985 L372/31 (hereafter Doorstep Selling Directive).

Directive 89/552/EEC concerning the pursuit of television broadcasting activities: OJ 1989 L298/23 as amended by OJ 1997 L202/60 (hereafter 'Television without Frontiers' Directive).

Directive 1993/13/EEC on unfair terms in consumer contracts: 1993 OJ 1993 L95/29 (hereafter Unfair Contract Terms Directive).

Directive 95/46/EC on the protection of individuals with regard to the processing of personal data and on the free movement of such data: OJ 1995 L281/31 (hereafter Data Protection Directive).

Directive 97/7/EC on the protection of consumers in respect of distance contracts: OJ 1997 L1444/19 (hereafter Distance Selling Directive).

Directive 97/55/EC amending Directive 84/450/EEC concerning misleading advertising so as to include comparative advertising: OJ 1997 L290/18 (hereafter Comparative Advertising Directive).

Directive 98/6/EC of the European Parliament and of the Council of 16 February 1998 on consumer protection in the indication of the prices of products offered to consumers: OJ 1980 L80/27 (hereafter the Price Indications Directive).

Directive 98/27/EC of the European Parliament and of the Council of 19 May 1998 on injunctions for the protection of consumers' interests: OJ 1998 L166/51 (hereafter the Consumer Injunctions Directive).

Directive 1999/44/EC on certain aspects of the sale of goods and associated guarantees: OJ 1999 L171/12 (hereafter the Consumer Sales Directive).

Directive 2000/13/EC on certain legal aspects of information society services, in particular electronic commerce, in the Internal Market: OJ 2000 L178/1 (hereafter Electronic Commerce Directive).

Directive 2000/43/EC implementing the principle of equal treatment between persons irrespective of racial or ethnic origin: OJ 2000 L180/82, see Article 3(1)(h) (hereafter Race Discrimination Directive).

Council Regulation (EC) No 44/2001 of 22 December 2000 on jurisdiction and the recognition and enforcement of judgments in civil and commercial matters: OJ 2001 L12/1 (hereafter Regulation on Jurisdiction and the Recognition and Enforcement of Judgments.

Directive 2002/58/EC concerning the processing of personal data and the protection of privacy in the electronic communications sector: OJ 2002 L201/37 (hereafter Privacy and Electronic Communications Directive).

Directive 2002/65/EC concerning the distance marketing of consumer financial services: OJ 2002 L271/16 (hereafter Distance Selling of Financial Services Directive).

Directive 2004/113/EC implementing the principle of equal treatment between men and women in the access to and supply of goods and services: OJ 2004 L373/37 (hereafter Sex Discrimination Directive).

Regulation (EC) No. 2006/2004 of the European Parliament and of the Council of 27 October 2004 on cooperation between national authorities responsible for the enforcement of consumer protection laws (the Regulation on consumer protection co-operation): OJ 2004 L364/1 (hereafter the Regulation on Consumer Protection Co-operation).

Directive 2005/29/EC concerning unfair business-to-consumer commercial practices in the internal market: OJ 2005 L149/22 (hereafter Unfair Commercial Practices Directive).

Proposal for a Council Regulation on the law applicable to non-contractual obligations (Rome II) COM [2003] 427 final (hereafter Rome II).

# Chapter 1

# Introduction

Geraint Howells

## a. Background

On 11 May 2005 the European Community adopted Directive 2005/29/EC concerning unfair business-to-consumer commercial practices in the internal market.[1] This introduces a general prohibition on unfair business-to-consumer commercial practices that is fleshed out by reference to the concepts of misleading and aggressive commercial practices and an annex listing practices considered unfair in all circumstances. The reference point for judging the fairness of a practice is the average consumer, building on the jurisprudence of the European Court of Justice; although this standard is adapted to take the interests of vulnerable consumers into account as considered appropriate. A controversial aspect of the Directive is its maximum harmonisation nature, by which is meant that Member States cannot, for reasons other than those specified in the Directive, restrict the freedom to provide services nor restrict the movement of goods for reasons falling within the field approximated by the Directive.

This book is concerned with explaining the Unfair Commercial Practices Directive, exploring the many ambiguities in its drafting and considering its implications for trading and consumer protection within Europe as well as the relationship between European and national trade practices law. Towards the end of this introductory chapter certain key features of the Directive will be set out in outline to prepare the reader for the detailed discussion later in the text. First, however, some background will be provided on the pre-existing national traditions of fair trade regulation; the EC rules that had already been developed in this area; and the preparatory process that led to the adoption of the Directive highlighting the major points of debate.

## b. The Traditions of Fair Trade Regulation within the Member States

We are fortunate in having some excellent studies outlining the laws of the Member States prior to the Directive that were commissioned by the EU as part of its background research whilst developing policy in this area. Two studies in particular warrant careful attention, that by the research institute VIEW on *The Feasibility of a*

---

1    OJ 2005 L149/22 (hereafter Unfair Commercial Practices Directive).

*General Legislative Framework on Fair Trading*[2] and another by Professors Reiner Schulze and Hans Schulte-Nölke providing an *Analysis of National Fairness Laws Aimed at Protecting Consumers in Relation to Commercial Practices.*[3] Since those studies the EU has been enlarged by the addition of ten new Member States and the Commission has arranged for the British Institute of International and Comparative Law to conduct a survey of the laws in those countries.[4] The Commission, when proposing a Directive harmonising this field, alleged that the laws of the Member States relating to unfair commercial practices showed marked differences which generated appreciable distortions of competition and obstacles to the smooth functioning of the internal market.[5]

*(i) Special regime for consumers?*

The interest of the Community in fair trading laws is long standing and as early as 1965 Eugen Ulmer wrote a comparative analysis of the then six Member States' laws.[6] He identified three sets of interests that can be protected by fair trading laws – competitors, consumers and the public at large. Fair trading laws may directly or indirectly protect one, two or all three of these interests. The national laws reflect a broad spectrum concerning the interests protected. By contrast the Directive focuses squarely on those fair trading rules that protect the consumer. It seeks to tackle unfair practices that distort the economic behaviour of consumers so that they take transactional decisions they would not otherwise have taken.

    The case for the Directive being extended to cover business-to-business disputes was pressed by some states whose laws already had that broader scope, but to no avail. Such broader laws seek to prevent businesses using unfair tactics to gain a competitive advantage; this is often reflected in the term unfair competition that is given to such laws. However, these fair trading/unfair competition laws have traditionally been conceptually different from general competition law principles which seek to prevent the abuse of market power. Unfair competition from the business perspective is connected to intellectual property law, especially trademarks and passing off actions. The public also has an interest in fair trading laws that promote taste and decency and appropriate standards of conduct. These are also

---

    2    Available at:http://europa.eu.int/comm/consumers/cons_int/safe_shop/fair_bus_pract/ green_pap_comm/studies/sur21_sum_en.pdf. This was coordinated by one of the present authors (H.-W. Micklitz) and will be referred to as the VIEW Study.

    3    Available at:http://europa.eu.int/comm/consumers/cons_int/safe_shop/fair_bus_pract/ green_pap_comm/studies/unfair_practices_en.pdf. Hereafter referred to as the Schulze and Schulte-Nölke Study.

    4    BIICL, *Unfair Commercial Practices – An analysis of the existing national rules, including case law, on unfair commercial practices between business and consumers in the New Member States and the possible resulting internal market barrier.*

    5    Recital 3.

    6    E. Ulmer, *Das Recht des unlauteren Wettbewerbs in den Mitgliedstaaten der Euroipäischen Wirtschaftsgemeoinschaft* (Munich: C.H. Beck Verlag, 1965).

outside the present Directive. Of course rules aimed at protecting consumers may have an indirect impact on competitors and the interest of the general public. Indeed one of the challenges for the consumer movement is to have the consumer voice heard more strongly in competition law debates.[7] Some people view this Unfair Commercial Practices Directive as providing a stimulus for the development of a more consumer-friendly competition policy.

To some extent whether Member States' pre-existing national laws focused on consumer protection or had a broader scope extending to competitors depended upon whether it adopted a general clause. Certainly those countries like the United Kingdom and Ireland that favoured punctual legislation tended to develop specific rules for consumers. That is not to say that in all European countries there are not specific rules aimed at protecting consumers, just that a general clause might be associated with broader objectives. Below we consider the extent to which those states that relied upon general clauses applied these to consumers as well as competitors. Many of these general clauses originated in the early part of the twentieth century when their aim was to protect traders from unfair competition. Consumer protection interests were grafted on to several of those statutes in the latter part of that century as consumer protection rose up the political agenda. A criticism is that some of these general clauses have failed adequately to integrate the consumer protection dimension.[8]

Several Member States had a single statute having common provisions for both commercial and consumer practices, although there may have been detailed differences between how the law applied to consumers and competitors. Examples of such laws include the Danish Marketing Practices Act, Swedish Marketing Act and the Austrian, German and Greek Acts against Unfair Competition.

The Belgian Act on Commercial Practices and Consumer Information contains within the same legislation two general clauses. One protects the interests of competitors; the other protects consumers. They are largely identical, only differing in the extent of the damage that needs to be proven.[9] Finland achieves the same bifurcation, but does so by adopting two separate pieces of legislation, the Consumer Protection Act and the Unfair Trade Practices Act.

Some countries have developed rules in their Civil Code to cover unfair competition. Thus unfair competition and advertising law in the Netherlands is derived from the basic provisions of the law of tort found in Article 6.162 of the *Burgerlijk Wetboek*. This rule applies in all situations, not just in actions between competitors, and has been the basis of the development of unfair competition law since a 1919 case extended the scope of the earlier rule to cover violations of accepted standards of morality and the care that has to be observed in the course of business.[10]

---

7   S. Weatherill, 'The Links between Competition and Consumer Protection' [2006] *Yearbook of Consumer Law* forthcoming.

8   VIEW Study, Executive Summary at 7–9.

9   Schulze and Schulte-Nölke Study, Belgium Report, at 4.

10   *Lindenbaum v Cohen* NJ 1919 Nr. 161, cited in VIEW Study, Vol. 3 at 172.

In Italy the *Codice Civile* contains a general clause on unfair competition, but this is mainly aimed at competitors and any consumer protection is only a by-product.[11] Likewise in France breaches of private law obligations in the *Code Civile* have given rise to the concept of unfair competition ('*concurrence déloyale*') which can only be invoked by competitors. Consumer protection rules are found in the *Code de la Consommation*.

Of the new accession states, the Czech Republic, Hungary, Poland[12] and Slovakia have general clauses covering both consumers and business. Estonia and Slovenia have two general clauses with a specific one for consumers. Lithuania has no special general clauses dealing with fair commercial practices, but is in the process of adopting a Law on Consumer Rights Protection which would include such a clause for consumers. Malta and Cyprus only have specific legislation, perhaps particularly in relation to Cyprus reflecting the common law influence.

### (ii) Use of general clause?

Most continental systems have used a general clause to control unfair commercial practices. The VIEW Study identified five different types of legal instrument.[13] The German law-influenced countries (Austria, Germany, Greece and Portugal) have a general clause based on '*bonos mores*' (against public morals). The former German law used the phrase '*guten Sitten*' which could be translated as honest market practices, whereas the new law of 2004 talks instead of unfair ('*unlauteren*') competition, but this was not intended to alter its core meaning. The civil law countries, like Belgium, Italy and Luxembourg use 'fair commercial practices' and it is even suggested this might reflect the practice in France.[14] The Nordic countries, such as Denmark, Finland and Sweden, prefer 'good market practices'. 'Unlawfulness' and 'fault' are the leitmotifs in the Netherlands and France respectively.

However, the VIEW study goes on to make the telling point that so long as there is some catch-all provision, then too much should not be read into its precise formulation. More precisely one might rephrase this to suggest that the wording of the general clause does not necessarily determine the content of the law, although it can have an influence on the content. This influence might be particularly strong where a long tradition is being changed, as is the case with German fair trading law under the influence of European law.[15] Such general clauses do not, however, always give a strong steer as to the content of the obligation. This is often more dependent upon the conception of competition on which the law is based and the manner in which it is enforced. We have already noted that many regimes started off based on

---

11  Article 2598. Schulze and Schulte-Nölke Study, Italian Report, at 2.

12  The Polish law does not allow individual consumers to bring individual actions.

13  Executive Summary, at 8.

14  *Ibid.*

15  This might explain why some German scholars seem to consider the new European-inspired general clause to have an impact even beyond the scope of the Directive.

a model of fair competition intended to protect competitors and this was extended to include consumer protection and matters of public interest. The more explicitly the consumer protection perspective is reflected in the law, the more likely it is that the content of the law will have a strong element of consumer protection. Equally where consumers and consumer protection agencies have the right to invoke the general clause and regularly do so the consumer protection element will be promoted.

Thus one might expect to, and indeed does, find strong consumer protection elements in Nordic law, where consumer protection has been embraced as an important element of marketing law and is enforced by well-resourced Consumer Ombudsmen. By contrast in a country like Italy where the rules are only intended to protect competitors, the consumer protection element tends to be weak.[16] Germany is an interesting example, for although consumers' associations can now bring collective actions, the emphasis is on cases brought by competitors and this is reflected in the case law, which has introduced many rules on fair trading, but still mainly from the business perspective. This lies at the heart of the debate about the scope of unfair competition law, for many of the rules can be viewed not so much as protecting consumers, but rather controls on competition by competitors, and the extent to which this is allowed in the internal market lies at the heart of European policy-making both in relation to the Unfair Commercial Practices Directive and the Sales Promotion Regulation that was proposed at the same time.[17]

*(iii) Consumer typology*

When applying the general clause a key element will be the consumer typology the legislature has in mind. Whether marketing is unfair or not may depend upon whose perspective it is judged from. It is now well known that consumer laws within Europe worked with a wide range of consumer images.[18] Marketing may be unfair if judged from the standpoint of the credulous, even if most consumers would be robust enough not to be affected by it. Germany was infamous, through successive cases referred to the European Court of Justice,[19] for judging practices against the standards of the gullible, although very often the beneficiary was a competitor rather

---

16 Although the *Cassazione civile*, sez. I, 11 August 2000, no. 10684 has said competition is unfair if it prevents consumers from making an informed and conscious choice.

17 See COM(2001) 546 final and revised proposal at COM(2002) 585 final. This is now likely to be abandoned: see Commission Communication, *Outcome of the screening of legislative proposals pending before the Legislator* COM(2005) 462 final.

18 T. Wilhelmsson, 'Consumer Images in East and West', in *Rechtseinheit oder Rechtsvielfalt in Europa? Rolle und Funktion des Verbaucherrechts in der EG unde den MOE–Staaten*, H.-W. Micklitz (ed.), (Baden-Baden: Nomos, 1996).

19 See inter alia Case C–315/1992 *Verband Sozialer Wettbewerb e.V. v Clinique Laboratoires SNC et Estée Lauder Cosmetics GmbH*, EC [1994] I–317; Case C–220/98 *Estée Lauder Cosmetics GmbH & Co OHG v Lancaster Group GmbH*, ECR [2000] 117; Case C–210/96 *Gut Springenheide GmbH and Rudolf Tusky v Oberkreisdirektor des Kreises Steinfurt – Amt für Lebensmittelüberwachung*, (1998) ECR I–4657.

than the injured consumer. Nordic advertising law tended to assume consumers read advertisements as a casual glancer, rather than considering every small detail.

By contrast, the United Kingdom courts, when assessing whether trade descriptions are misleading, have tried to assess conduct against the standard of the average consumer. Although there are some divergences in the case law it seems as though this will be robustly applied. The UK consumer is expected to read any claim in the context of all the information provided. Where there is ambiguity it is not sufficient that the consumer could have been misled, this must have been likely.[20] This is in fact in line with the Community law image of the consumer which has been described as supposing a 'well-informed and well-to-be–informed consumer'.[21] We shall see that the case law supporting this approach has been relied upon in the Unfair Commercial Practices Directive as the basis for the average consumer standard it adopts.[22]

### (iv) Strict liability?

In most systems liability for trade practices law is strict at least as regards regulatory controls through the administrative and criminal law or injunction procedures. This is certainly the case in common law countries where regulatory law tends to be strict in the sense of requiring no *mens rea*, only the commission of the *actus reus*. This is typically accompanied by a due diligence defence to give relief for the trader who has done everything reasonably possible to avoid the commission of the offence.[23] Many of the specific controls lay down prohibitions or requirements the mere breach of which gives rise to liability.

Above, it was noted that the general clauses rely on a variety of terms, such as *bonos more*, honest market practices, unfair competition, fair commercial practices, good market practices, unlawfulness and fault. Whilst fault and to some extent unlawfulness reflect different policies than strict liability, many of the other standards are compatible with strict liability. They are ways of setting standards against which conduct will be judged, but once that objective standard is not reached it will not be a defence to argue that the trader had tried his best or lacked the resources or expertise to meet the standard required by the law.

Where legal systems allow for claims for damages based on breach of trade practice law, it is more common for them to require some evidence of fault or negligence, although equally some regimes do allow for civil actions to be brought on the back of criminal claims (as in the *action civile* in France) or allow for the

---

20  *Doble v David Greig Ltd.*, [1972] 2 ALL ER 195, *Dixons v Barnett*, (1998) 153 JP 268 and *Bryan Roy Lewin v Purty Soft Drinks Ltd.*, [2004] EWHC 3119.

21  G. Howells and T. Wilhelmsson, *EC Consumer Law* (Aldershot: Dartmouth, 1997) at 316.

22  Such as cases cited in note 74.

23  It is a matter for debate whether this defence is compatible with EU rules that do not expressly provide for it, but it is submitted that this should be allowed as the expression of a national tradition: G. Howells and S. Weatherill, *Consumer Protection Law* (Aldershot: Ashgate, 2005) at 504.

possibility of compensation to be paid as part of the criminal procedure (as in the United Kingdom).

## (v) Civil/criminal law

Fair trading law lies on the cusp of civil and criminal law. In all systems some rules relating to fair trading will derive from civil law and others will have a more public/criminal law character. Perhaps the most important divide is between those countries who typically rely on private enforcement of a general clause, typified by Germany, and those that concentrate on public enforcement. According to national legal traditions this public enforcement might either be viewed as criminal law enforcement or be more administrative law in character. The Nordic Ombudsmen model is typical of this regulatory approach with an administrative law flavour, whilst under the common law model criminal statutes are enforced by public agencies, like trading standards officers. Also in France, for instance, the criminal law plays an important role under the supervision of the *Direction générale de la concurrence de la consommation de la répression des frauds* (DGCCRF). Indicative of the hybrid status of unfair commercial practices law is the increased reliance, under the influence of European law,[24] of the injunction brought by public bodies or consumer organisations.

## (vi) Sanctions

Injunctions are indeed a primary remedy for breach of unfair commercial practices law. When brought by a competitor, the state or consumer organisation, the first aim is often to stop the unfair practice before it causes harm or any further harm. The injunction can be a private law remedy to prevent infringement of private rights or be prescribed by statute. For example, in the Nordic countries the Ombudsman, if unable to obtain a voluntary undertaking from the trader, will typically seek a prohibition order; whilst in the United Kingdom the trading standards officers or Office of Fair Trading will try to obtain undertakings from the trader not to engage in unlawful conduct or go to court for an enforcement order to that effect. As noted there has been an increased use of injunctions based on the EC Consumer Injunctions Directive.

Very often general clauses will also support a claim for damages. This may be a vital concern for consumers who have been harmed by an unfair practice. One exception in this respect is Sweden where damages can only be obtained for breach of specific provisions, not the general clause. Of course it may well be that unfair commercial practices can give rise to an independent right to damages due to the breach of some other contractual or non-contractual obligation.

---

24 Directive 98/27/EC of the European Parliament and of the Council of 19 May 1998 on injunctions for the protection of consumers' interests: OJ 1998 L166/51 (hereafter the Consumer Injunctions Directive).

Some countries do rely on the criminal law to enforce consumer protection law. The United Kingdom is a prime example. Yet these laws are often described as being regulatory offences and not criminal in the true sense.[25] Although prison sentences might be theoretically available for such offences, they are rarely handed down. Fines, often of low order, are usually imposed. In some countries, like the Nordic states, the non-penal nature of the offence is recognised by describing them as administrative fines.

### (vii) Soft law

There is increasing pressure at both the national and European level to take advantage of soft law, through institutions like codes of conduct.[26] This is viewed as a modern form of regulation. The extent to which such rules are in practice relevant throughout the Community in relation to unfair commercial practices varies greatly.[27] One sector where soft law is very influential is advertising, most countries having self-regulatory institutions inspired by the Advertising Code of the International Chamber of Commerce. But even in this sector one finds that in Germany, for instance, there is no general Advertising Code and the *Deutscher Werberat* has only developed codes of conduct concerning advertising with and addressed to children, alcohol, discrimination and advertising with politicians. Also in certain financial service sectors, such as banking and insurance, there is a greater tendency amongst the Member States to rely on self-regulation.

Nevertheless, there are many countries, including France and Germany, where at least outside the field of advertising, there is little tradition of self-regulation of commercial practices. The United Kingdom is often held up as the Member State with the strongest tradition of self-regulation in this area. This was because the Office of Fair Trading had been given an obligation to encourage trade associations to adopt codes of practice and over forty had been generated. However, there was a certain exaggeration about the practical impact of such codes. The Office of Fair Trading found that many were not very effective[28] and it has introduced new rules for approving codes which few codes seem likely to meet in the near future.[29] In the Nordic countries the guidelines generated by the Ombudsmen are of great practical importance. Although soft law instruments, these guidelines are often not strictly self-regulatory as they are developed by or with the involvement of the Ombudsmen.

---

25   G. Howells and S. Weatherill, *Consumer Protection Law* 2nd edn (Ashgate, 2005) Chapter 11.

26   See Chapter 7.

27   See Schulze and Schulte-Nölke Study, at 21–2.

28   *Voluntary Codes of Practice* (OFT, 1996).

29   Section 8 Enterprise Act 2002, see Howells and Weatherill, *op.cit.*, at 586–591.

## c. The Community Acquis

*(i) Negative harmonisation*

The Community has from its earliest times had a lot of dealings with fair trading laws, for challenges to national fair trading laws are central to many of the cases concerning the free movement of goods and services. The allegation has often been that national fair trading rules infringe Article 28 (goods) and Article 49 (services), because they are sometimes (not too well disguised) barriers to trade that cannot be justified by reference to valid objectives like consumer protection. Actually the free movement rules do not merely catch disguised protectionism but, as the European Court of Justice said in *Procureur du Roi v Benoit and Gustave Dassonville*,[30] 'All trading rules enacted by Member States which are capable of hindering, directly or indirectly, actually or potentially, intra-Community trade are to be considered as measures having an effect equivalent to quantitative restrictions'.

This gave European law a lot of scope to intervene and strike down or require modifications to national fair trading laws that impeded the internal market project. If Europe could have used this negative harmonisation to remove all problematic national fair trading rules there would in theory have been no need for the present Directive. This Directive is needed because European free movement law also includes limitations on the extent to which free movement can be used as a justification for the removal of national legislation. These limitations will be discussed shortly, but first an important caveat to the *Dassonville* approach must be studied.

As it came to be interpreted, *Dassonville* meant that if a rule could be shown to lead to reduced sales of imports then it would be contrary to European Law even if it had an identical impact on domestic goods. The Sunday Trading cases are the archetypal example of this and the Court finally realised it was going beyond what was needed to open up the internal market if it scrutinised such 'local' laws. Therefore in *Criminal proceedings against Bernard Keck and Daniel Mithouard*[31] the Court held that:

> contrary to what has previously been decided, the application to products from other Member States of national provisions restricting or prohibiting certain selling arrangements is not such as to hinder directly or indirectly, actually or potentially, trade between Member States within the meaning of the *Dassonville* judgment, so long as those provisions apply to all relevant traders operating within the national territory and so long as they affect in the same manner, in law and in fact, the marketing of domestic products and of those from other Member States.

This takes outside of Article 28 national rules relating to 'certain selling arrangements'. This is not the place to go into all the details of the *Keck* proviso, but it should be noted that rules which concern the goods themselves, such as labelling requirements,

---

30   Case 8/74 [1974] ECR 837.
31   Joined cases C–267/91 and C–268/91 [1993] ECR I–6097.

will continue to be within the scope of Article 28.[32] Furthermore, *Keck* only exempts those rules whose nature is not 'such as to prevent their [the goods] access to the market or to impede access any more than it impedes access of domestic products'. It is also unclear whether the *Keck* proviso applies to services.[33]

Nevertheless, *Keck* does place certain rules relating to selling arrangements outside the control of European law. If these rules really do not impede access to the market more for imported than for domestic products it could legitimately be argued that these rules should be outside the domain of European internal market law, including positive harmonisation. Of course if European law has a more positive agenda to force a certain type of approach to fair trading, then it might want to go further and address issues that impede access to the market equally for domestic and imported goods. There are signs that Europe does have such an agenda – most obviously this was evident in the proposed Sales Promotion Regulation.[34] This would certainly have involved recognising that the scope for positive regulation is broader than that for negative regulation. Of course once Europe has competence on internal market grounds it is free to develop policy choices as to the form of regulation that best fits the problems at hand.[35] However, that is a different matter from saying that Europe should be able to regulate matters that do not affect the internal market. Such powers require express Treaty provisions, which so far are lacking in the field of consumer protection.[36] It is questionable whether the internal market can be used to justify legislation on issues that *Keck* leaves to the Member States because by implication such matters do not impede access to markets. But such niceties are often forgotten in the rush to legislate.

Despite *Keck*, Article 28 allows Europe plenty of scope to use negative harmonisation as a way of equalising unfair commercial practices law. The need

---

32 See, for example, Case C–315/92 *Verband Sozialer Wettbewerb e.V. v Clinique Laboratoires SNC and Estée Lauder Cosmetics GmbH*, [1994] ECR I–317; Case C–470/93 *Verein gegen Unwesen in Handel und Gewerbe Kölne e.V. v Mars GmbH*, [1995] ECR I– 1923; Case C–210/96 *Gut Springenheide GmbH and Rudolf Tusky v Oberkreisdirektor des Kreises Steinfurt – Amt für Lebensmittelüberwachung*, [1998] ECR I–4657; Case C–220/98 *Estée Lauder Cosmetics GmbH v Lancaster Group GmbH*, [2000] ECR I–117. For discussion, M. Radeideh, *Fair Trading in EC Law* (Groningen: Europa, 2005) at 68–82, N. Reich, 'The "November Revolution" of the European Court of Justice: Keck, Meng and Audi Revisited' (1994) 31 *Common Market Law Review* 459 and S. Weatherill, 'After Keck: Some Thoughts on how to Clarify the Clarification' (1996) 33 *CMLR* 885.

33 Radeideh, *ibid.*, at 80–81.

34 It has already been noted that this is likely to be abandoned.

35 This was even confirmed by the European Court of Justice when it struck down the Tobacco Advertising Directive: see Case C–376/98 *Germany v European Parliament and another supported by France and other, interveners*, [2000] ECR I–8419 and Case C–74/99 *R v Secretary of State for Health and others, ex parte Imperial Tobacco Ltd. and others*, [2000] ECR I–8599.

36 The current powers in Article 153 give only limited scope. For a call for their enhancement see H.-W. Micklitz, N. Reich and S. Weatherill, 'EU Treaty Revision and Consumer Protection' (2004) 27 *Journal of Consumer Policy* 367.

for the present Directive is explained by those rules that continue to allow Member States to retain such laws for valid reasons. These are found in Article 30 for goods which allows prohibitions or restrictions on grounds of public morality, public policy or public security; the protection of health and life of humans, animals or plants; the protection of national treasures possessing artistic, historic or archaeological value; or the protection of industrial and commercial property. Certainly some of these may impact on unfair commercial practices, but more directly relevant to consumer protection issues is the judgment in *Rewe–Zentrale AG v Bundesmonopolverwaltung für Branntwein* (Cassis de Dijon)[37] that:

> Obstacles to movement within the Community resulting from disparities between the national laws relating to the marketing of the products in question must be accepted in so far as those provisions may be recognised as being necessary in order to satisfy mandatory requirements relating in particular to the effectiveness of fiscal supervision, the protection of public health, the fairness of commercial transactions and the defence of the consumer.

The European Court of Justice has on a number of occasions recognised consumer protection as a valid reason for upholding national fair trading laws. In *Oosthoek's Uitgeversmaatschappij*[38] a Dutch law that placed restrictions on free gifts schemes was upheld as it was accepted that free gifts could mislead consumers as to the true value of products. Similarly in *R. Buet and Educational Business Services (EBS) v Ministère Public*[39] a French prohibition on the doorstep canvassing of educational material was upheld with the Court taking note that such educational materials were often targeted at vulnerable consumers who needed special protection. In the field of service, in *Alpine Investments BV v Minister van Financien*[40]a Dutch ban on the 'cold-calling' of financial services was upheld. It seems that consumer protection may only have been relevant in so far as the impact on consumer protection indirectly justified a rule aimed at safeguarding the reputation of the Dutch financial markets. However, the Court's view that consumer protection in other Member States was not a concern for the Dutch authorities may have been influenced by the fact that the case concerned a ban on business canvassing from the Netherlands to other Member States and so no direct issues of consumer protection were raised. It is clear that consumer protection can justify the maintenance or introduction of some national laws concerning unfair commercial practices. Of course any such justification only permits a rule which is proportionate to the justification and adopts the means that are the least restrictive of trade.

---

37  Case 120/78 [1979] ECR 649.
38  Case 286/81 [1982] ECR 4575.
39  Case 382/87 [1989] ECR 1235.
40  Case C–384/93 [1995] ECR I–1141.

## *(ii) Legislative competence*

Free movement rules can remove national rules that unduly impede cross-border trade, subject to the *Keck* proviso, but cannot do away with national rules that serve a legitimate consumer protection function. The existence of these national protective rules explains in part why Europe sees it as important to create a positive integration process. If there are legitimate concerns these should be addressed in a harmonised European manner in order to remove any remaining barriers to trade.

Equally Europe is called upon to strengthen consumer protection,[41] offer a high level of consumer protection,[42] and internal market-justified laws should take as a base a high level of protection.[43] Arguably this forms the basis for a positive integration approach for European fair trading legislation that applies not only to situations where the protected national rules are being replaced, but also where negative harmonisation has removed national rules. There may be a theoretical problem in including situations where national rules have been removed. Admittedly it can appear tautologous to argue that a national rule has no objective justification and then seek to address the same concern through European legislation. However, it is certainly the case that the European Court of Justice has held that contractual rules, for example on the sale of goods, do not have an impact on the internal market[44] and yet a Directive on the sale of goods has been adopted without challenge to its legal base.[45] By analogy this would allow positive integration in areas excluded from review under Article 28 by the *Keck* proviso. It is then an easy step to suggest that European law can address issues that can no longer be legitimately addressed at the national level. The argument would be that whilst such national rules should not be allowed to stand in the way of the establishment of the internal market, nevertheless a harmonised approach to these matters will not affect cross-border trade and might be justified to enhance confidence in the internal market. Often this same result can be achieved in an indirect way by arguing that laws addressing legitimate internal market concerns will also have spill-over effects requiring a broader range of issues to be addressed. In other words the positive integration agenda of Europe can be broader than addressing only those issues left after negative harmonisation has had its toll on national law.

However, there are limits to this. In the consumer field the constitutional provisions are very circumscribed. Article 153 sets out the powers in relation to consumer protection, but for the most part these are limited.[46] Only one significant piece of consumer legislation has been based on Article 153; the Price Indications

---

41   Article 3(t) Treaty establishing the European Community (hereafter EC Treaty).

42   Article 153(1) EC Treaty.

43   Article 95(3) EC Treaty.

44   Case C–339/89 *Alsthom Atlantique SA v Compagnie Construction Mechanique Sulzer SA*, [1991] ECR I–107.

45   Directive 1999/44/EC on certain aspects of the sale of goods and associated guarantees: OJ 1999 L171/12 (hereafter the Consumer Sales Directive).

46   See H.-W. Micklitz, N. Reich and S. Weatherill, 'EU Treaty Revision and Consumer Protection' (2004) 27 *Journal of Consumer Policy* 367.

Directive.[47] The rest rely on Article 95, the internal market clause. In *Germany v European Parliament*[48] the European Court was unwilling to accept that the Community had a general regulatory power. Measures must first be justified in terms of the internal market power for which it is necessary to show either that Community law is needed to promote the four freedoms (free movement of goods, services, persons and capital) by eliminating barriers to trade or to prevent distortions of competition. It is also possible to act to prevent possible future obstacles to trade resulting from disparate responses emerging from the Member States. However, once the internal market justification can be established the Community has a degree of freedom to determine at what standard the rules are pitched and indeed should be guided by the principle that a high standard of consumer protection should be achieved.

Clearly therefore the Community has power to act to harmonise those national rules that survive scrutiny under the Treaty's free movement provisions, probably can address issues excluded from scrutiny by *Keck* and possibly can even consider legislating on matters at the European level that European law has removed from the national legal systems. In the context of a broad horizontal piece of legislation such as the Unfair Commercial Practices Directive, these intricacies are likely to be less crucial. Once it is accepted that a general clause is the best approach to deal with some matters that are clearly justified by Article 95, then it is self-evident that it will have to cover a range of other matters as well, which may have less of an internal market dimension. It has not been Europe's way, at least until recently, to focus exclusively on rules for cross-border sales or only those dimensions of the problem that starkly raise European concerns.

### (iii) Positive regulation before the Unfair Commercial Practices Directive

Before turning our attention fully to the Unfair Commercial Practices Directive it is useful to note both what Europe had already done in this broad field and what underlying policy it was developing. Prior to the Unfair Commercial Practices Directive, the most significant piece of horizontal European legislation in this field was the Misleading Advertising Directive,[49] which was later extended to cover comparative advertising.[50] This was of course narrower in only covering advertising

---

47 Directive 98/6/EC on consumer protection in the indication of the prices offered to consumers: OJ 1980 L80/27 (hereafter the Price Indications Directive).

48 Case C–376/98 *Germany v European Parliament and another supported by France and other, interveners*, [2000] ECR I–8419 and Case C–74/99 *R v Secretary of State for Health and others, ex parte Imperial Tobacco Ltd. and others* [2000] ECR I–8599.

49 Directive 84/450/EC on the approximation of the laws, regulations and administrative provisions of the Member States concerning misleading advertising: OJ 1984 L250/17 (hereafter Misleading Advertising Directive).

50 Directive 97/55/EC amending Directive 84/450/EEC concerning misleading advertising so as to include comparative advertising: OJ 1997 L290/18 (hereafter Comparative Advertising Directive).

and only controlling advertisements which were misleading. Nevertheless it placed within the European *acquis* the concept of misleading practices which the present Directive builds upon.

In fact the Commission had been more ambitious in their earlier proposals. In the 1960s following the Ulmer study[51] on unfair competition, there was an intense debate during which the Commission shifted its focus on to consumer protection. It explained in its first preliminary Programme for Consumer Protection and Information Policy of 1975: 'practices which were once regarded in many countries as unfair solely in terms of competition between producers (misleading advertising, for example) are now also considered from the point of view of relations between producers and consumers.'[52]

Its 1978 proposal covered not only misleading advertising, but also unfair advertising. This was defined as:

> any advertising which (a) casts discredit on another person by improper reference to his nationality, origin, private life or good name, or (b) injures or is likely to injure the commercial reputation of another person by false statements or defamatory comments concerning his firm, goods or services, or (c) appeals to sentiments of fear, or promotes social or religious discrimination, or (d) clearly infringes the principle of the social, economic and cultural equality of the sexes, or (e) exploits the trust, credulity or lack of experience of a consumer, or influences or is likely to influence a consumer or the public in general in any other improper manner.[53]

It has been commented that this is less a definition than an enumeration of examples that was meant to be exhaustive,[54] albeit if some phrases such as 'any other improper manner' could be given a broad interpretation. It is also surprisingly different from the concept of unfairness in the present Directive. Whilst appealing to sentiments of fear and exploiting the trust, credulity or lack of experience of consumers or other improper influence are clearly echoes of the concept of aggressive practices in the Directive, and false statements and defamatory comments are probably also within the scope of the Directive, the others emphasise equality. Although these practices undoubtedly are contrary to professional diligence, we shall see that there also needs to be a distortion of the economic behaviour of consumers, which it might be hard to establish with respect to equality; although, we shall also suggest that this economic behaviour test is difficult to reconcile with many instances of aggressive practices, which the Directive is clearly intended to encompass.[55] Nevertheless this earlier link between fairness and equality is illuminating for it highlights the absence of such concerns from the face of the present Directive. It may be that the Commission was aware that discrimination in access to goods and services is now regulated in

---

51  Ulmer, *op.cit.*
52  OJ 1975 C92/1 at 7.
53  OJ 1978 C70/4, amendment in OJ 1979 C194/3.
54  Radeideh, *op.cit.*, at 111.
55  See Chapter 6(b)(ii).

other Directives dealing with race[56] and sex discrimination,[57] but it might have been useful to underline that such commercial practices were unfair and it is unfortunate that at the very least no cross reference was made to the discrimination Directives. Indeed it should be noted that the Sex Discrimination Directive expressly excludes advertising from its scope of application.[58]

The Data Protection Directives are another important form of horizontal legislation that impacts on unfair commercial practices, in particular with respect to unfair means of communicating with consumers.[59] We have already noted that there is a Directive regulating the price indications on products. The formulation of the obligations in that Directive seems to exclude its application to services.[60]

Some of the most important Directives are vertical regulations applying to particular selling techniques. There are Directives on doorstep selling,[61] distance selling[62] and the distance selling of financial services.[63] These typically provide the consumer with a right of cancellation. This is a self-enforcing remedy available to consumers for a short period should they regret the transaction. There is no need to give reasons for the cancellation. Obviously it would assist where unfair commercial practices had induced the contract. The distance selling directives in particular focus on requiring the consumer to be provided with key information and also address other matters such as the appropriate means of communicating with consumers. Similar rules are developed and adapted for the internet in the Electronic Commerce Directive.[64] The 'Television without Frontiers' Directive has specific rules on advertising.[65] In

---

56  Council Directive 2000/43/EC implementing the principle of equal treatment between persons irrespective of racial or ethnic origin: OJ 2000 L180/82, see Article 3(1)(h) (hereafter Race Discrimination Directive).

57  Council Directive 2004/113/EC implementing the principle of equal treatment between men and women in the access to and supply of goods and services: OJ 2004 L373/37 (hereafter Sex Discrimination Directive).

58  Article 3(3).

59  See Directive 95/46/EC on the protection of individuals with regard to the processing of personal data and on the free movement of such data: OJ 1995 L281/31 (hereafter Date Protection Directive) and Directive 2002/58/EC concerning the processing of personal data and the protection of privacy in the electronic communications sector: OJ 1997 L24/1 (hereafter Privacy and Electronic Communications Directive).

60  Radeideh, *op.cit.*, at 122.

61  Directive 85/577/EEC to protect the consumer in respect of contracts negotiated away from business premises: OJ 1985 L372/31 (hereafter Doorstep Selling Directive).

62  Directive 97/7/EC on the protection of consumers in respect of distance contracts: OJ 1997 L1444/19 (hereafter Distance Selling Directive).

63  Directive 2002/65/EC concerning the distance marketing of consumer financial services: OJ 2002 L271/16 (hereafter Distance Selling of Financial Services Directive).

64  Directive 2000/13/EC on certain legal aspects of information society services, in particular electronic commerce, in the Internal Market: OJ 2000 L178/1 (hereafter Electronic Commerce Directive).

65  Directive 89/552/EEC concerning the pursuit of television broadcasting activities: OJ 1989 L298/23 as amended by OJ 1997 L202/60 (hereafter 'Television without Frontiers'

addition there are numerous product-specific regulations at the European level with some relevance to unfair commercial practices, especially as regards information and labelling requirements covering areas such as food, cosmetics, pharmaceuticals, tobacco, consumer credit, investment services, insurance, package holidays and timeshares.[66]

### (iv) Community policy

Throughout the development of EC unfair commercial practices law, both by the European Court of Justice and in the secondary legislation, it is evident that there is a strong emphasis on the provision of information being a good thing,[67] and an effective means of the consumer protecting himself.[68] Indeed some occasions when the Court has been willing to uphold national rules can be interpreted as support for national rules aimed at making the bargain transparent.[69] Indeed this emphasis on information and transparency is carried through into the Unfair Commercial Practices Directive, where one of the innovative measures concerns misleading omissions. However, a crucial counterbalance to these obligations to inform has been the development of a robust consumer image against which consumer behaviour with respect to that information and consumer practices generally can be judged. This can usefully be traced through the case law both interpreting the Misleading Advertising Directive and under Article 28. Much of this resulted from challenges to the protective German unfair competition laws. In fact the two lines of case law come together in so far as in the comparative advertising case of *Pippig Augenoptik GmbH v Hartlauer Handelsgesellschaft mbH*[70] the Court adopted the stance in the free movement case of *Estée Lauder Cosmetics GmbH v Lancaster Group GmbH*,[71] that the court should consider the 'average individual who is reasonably well informed and reasonably observant and circumspect'.

*Pippig Augenoptik* concerned comparative advertising where the European Court of Justice has been reluctant to introduce restrictions on the flow of information through such advertising. In *Toshiba Europe GmbH v Katun Germany GmbH*[72] the use of a trademark in comparative advertising for photocopier spare parts and consumables was not considered misleading as the Court noted it was aimed at traders who would understand what was being offered. Similarly the

---

Directive).

66  See Radeideh, *op.cit.*, at 145–174.

67  See the hostility to national laws restricting the provision of information in Case C–362/88 *GB–Inno–BM v Confédératon du commerce luxembourgois*, [1990] ECR I–667.

68  S. Weatherill, 'The Role of the Informed Consumer in European Community Law and Policy' (1994) 2 *Consum LJ* 49.

69  See Radeideh, *op.cit.*, at 47 citing *Oosthoek*.

70  Case C–44/01 [2003] ECR I–3095.

71  Case C–220/98 [2000] ECR I–117.

72  Case C–112/99 [2001] ECR I–7945.

Court promoted parallel imports in *Criminal proceedings against X ('Nissan')*[73] by holding it was not misleading to describe an imported car as new, despite it having been registered for import purposes and being of a lower specification than the local French cars. In reaching this conclusion the Court assumed that 'the consumer who goes to a parallel importer … is perfectly well aware that he is using a particular sales network with its specific features. The sale and purchase of cars, unlike other goods, is normally preceded, moreover, by a certain amount of negotiation in order to establish precisely the characteristics of the product.' Thus we can see the kernel of a European conception of fairness. A fairly robust attitude to consumers, but a willingness to consider exactly who the practice is directed at. In these misleading and comparative advertising cases the consumers were experienced and knowledgeable target groups, but in *Oosthoek* and *Buet* the Court showed itself to be sensitive to the needs of vulnerable consumers. This should not be overlooked when reading the case law on free movement which was explicitly referred to when developing the concept of the average consumer within the present Directive.[74] Also it must be remembered that in the free movement cases the Court was reacting to some pretty draconian German national law that had more to do with competitor protection than consumer protection. Even within that jurisprudence we find some signs that the Court is willing to take account of the particular circumstances. This is not to deny that the Court's jurisprudence is pretty hardnosed,[75] and that one might prefer a more generous approach to consumer protection which sees the vulnerable consumer as less of an aberration and accepts that we are all vulnerable to some degree.[76] But it does mean that one should not read the jurisprudence too pessimistically and believe the Court is always hostile to consumer protection.

Indeed when one looks at the cases on free movement one cannot really disagree with the Court's assessment that in many of the cases which it has had to deal with free movement should trump protectionism. Reasonable consumers are not really interested where a trademark was registered,[77] do not believe the extra chocolate in a Mars bar whose wrapper indicated '+10 per cent' was related to the size of the

---

73  Case C–373/90 [1992] ECR I–131.

74  The Proposal COM(2003) 356 final at para. 35 refers to Case C–315/1992 *Verband Sozialer Wettbewerb e.V. v Clinique Laboratoires SNC et Estée Lauder Cosmetics GmbH*, ECR [1994] I–317 and Case C–210/96 *Gut Springenheide GmbH and Rudolf Tusky v Oberkreisdirektor des Kreises Steinfurt – Amt für Lebensmittelüberwachung*, (1998) ECR I–4657.

75  As applauded by J. Stuyck, 'European Consumer Law after the Treaty of Amsterdam: Consumer Policy in or beyond the Internal Market' (2000) 37 *CMLR* 367.

76  G. Howells and T. Wilhelmsson, 'EC Consumer Law – Has it Come of Age?' (2003) 28 *ELR* 370 and G. Howells, 'The Potential and Limits of Consumer Empowerment by Information' (2005) 32 *Journal of Law and Society* 349.

77  Case C–238/89 *Pall Corp. v P.J. Dahlhausen & Co.*, [1990] ECR I–4827.

printing of the offer,[78] would not believe 'Clinique' had medicinal properties,[79] or that a lifting cream would have identical effects to surgery.[80] Indeed only very few consumers would argue that they need protection from such offers. When confronted with a more marginal question, as in *Gut Springenheide GmbH*, the Court was more circumspect. The case involved eggs packed under the description 'six grain – ten fresh eggs' when the six varieties only accounted for 60 per cent of the feed. Faced with the blunt question of whether the standard should be that of the average or casual consumer, the European Court clearly directed the national court 'must take into account the presumed expectations which it evokes in an average consumer who is reasonably well-informed and reasonably observant and circumspect'. Although it emphasised that courts should usually make this assessment for themselves it did not:

> preclude the possibility that, where the national court has particular difficulty in assessing the misleading nature of the statement or description in question, it may have recourse, under the conditions laid down by its own national law, to a consumer research poll or an expert's report as guidance for its judgment.

This scope for national diversity and sensitivity to the actual expectations of particular target groups of consumers is well exemplified by the approach of the Court in *Estée Lauder Cosmetics GmbH v Lancaster Group GmbH* which is worth quoting at some length:

> In order to apply that [*Gut Springenheide* average consumer] test to the present case, several considerations must be borne in mind. In particular, it must be determined whether social, cultural or linguistic factors may justify the term 'lifting', used in connection with a firming cream, meaning something different to the German consumer as opposed to consumers in other Member States, or whether the instructions for the use of the product are in themselves sufficient to make it quite clear that its effects are short-lived, thus neutralising any conclusion to the contrary that might be derived from the word 'lifting'.

> Although, at first sight, the average consumer – reasonably well informed and reasonably observant and circumspect – ought not to expect a cream whose name incorporates the term 'lifting' to produce enduring effects, it nevertheless remains for the national court to determine, in the light of all the relevant factors, whether that is the position in this case.

> In the absence of any provisions of Community law on this matter, it is for the national court – which may consider it necessary to commission an expert opinion or a survey of public opinion in order to clarify whether or not a promotional description or statement is misleading – to determine, in the light of its own national law, the percentage of consumers

---

78 Case C–470/93 *Verein gegen Unwesen in Handel und Gewerbe Kölne e.V. v Mars GmbH*, [1995] ECR I–1923.

79 Case C–315/1992 *Verband Sozialer Wettbewerb e.V. v Clinique Laboratoires SNC et Estée Lauder Cosmetics GmbH*, [1994] ECR I–317.

80 Case C–220/98 *Estée Lauder Cosmetics GmbH v Lancaster Group GmbH*, [2000] ECR I–117.

misled by that description or statement which would appear to it sufficiently significant to justify prohibiting its use.

Indeed such a sensitivity to local circumstances had been shown by Advocate General Gulmann in *Verband Sozialer Wettbewerb eV v Clinique Laboratoires SNC et Estée Lauder Cosmetics GmbH*[81] and, although not followed by the Court on that occasion, had resonated in the decision in *Fratelli Graffione SNC v Ditta Fransa*[82] that it was possible because of linguistic, cultural and social differences between the Member States that a trademark which is not liable to mislead a consumer in one Member State may be liable to do so in another. This time is was a preliminary reference from Italy (for a change) as to whether the name 'Cotonelle' could be prohibited because it might mislead consumers into believing the product contained cotton. The Court accepted that this was possible.

Thus prior to the Unfair Commercial Practices Directive, European law had taken a rather market orientated approach to consumer protection. It favoured information disclosure and expected this to be used by consumers in a reasonable manner. But it was not above accepting that certain consumers were vulnerable, judging the practice against its target audience and taking into account linguistic, social and cultural factors. Often this produced sensible results, but the headlines were for a very liberal, in the sense of market orientated, consumer protection. One of the struggles we shall note in the debate surrounding the adoption of the Directive was whether these headlines would be concretised in a caricatured form of the average consumer in the Directive.

### d. The Preparation of the Directive and Major Points of Debate

The prospect of a general Directive on unfair commercial practices came on to the agenda with the *Green Paper on EU Consumer Protection*.[83] Despite its broad title it really focused in on trade practices law and canvassed opinion on whether future European interventions should continue to be by punctual specific regulations (like the ideas that were developing around sales promotions) or whether a framework Directive should be adopted. Even at this early stage the tone made it obvious that the Commission had ambitions for a general Directive and this was confirmed in the *Follow-up Communication on EU Consumer Law*.[84] This concentrated on the form such a general framework Directive should adopt and it was clear that it would be based on a general clause and limited to business-to-consumer contracts. Some Member States favoured extending it to allow businesses to challenge unfair practices of competitors, but the Commission did not want to go that far.

---

81  Case C–315/1992 ECR [1994] I–317.
82  Case C–313/94 [1996] ECR I–6039.
83  COM(2001) 531 final.
84  COM(2002) 531 final.

On 18 June 2003 the Commission adopted a proposal for a Directive concerning unfair business-to-consumer practices in the internal market.[85] The structure of the Directive closely resembles that of the Proposal. At the same time the Commission also proposed a Regulation on Sale Promotion,[86] which would have forced a greater liberalisation of the sales promotions allowed in Member States. It was strange for these two initiatives to have come forward at the same time from two different branches of the Commission. DG SANCO promoted the Unfair Commercial Practices Directive, whereas DG Markt is promoting the Sales Promotion Regulation as part of its services strategy. It was unfortunate in many respects that the two projects were not better coordinated, for whilst the Green Paper on Consumer Protection tried to open a debate on the nature of European regulation, the Regulation would dictate directly the form of regulation in a major area of European fair trading law. Indeed if it were ever adopted the nature of unfair commercial practices protection for matters within its scope would have to be re-evaluated.

The Sales Promotion Regulation has, however, proven to be very controversial, little progress has been made and it now looks likely to be abandoned. By contrast, given the broad ambitions of the Directive, the different national traditions in this field and the complex nature of the law and practice in this area, the Unfair Commercial Practices proposal made relatively brisk progress through the political decision-making process. A political agreement was reached in Competitiveness Council on 18 May 2004 with a common position being agreed on 15 November 2004.[87] The Directive was adopted at the Competitiveness Council 7 March 2005 and *Directive 2005/29/EC concerning business-to-consumer commercial practices in the internal market and amending Council Directive 84/450/EEC, Directives 97/7/EC, 98/27/EC and 2002/65/EC of the European Parliament and of the Council and Regulation (EC) No 2006/2004 of the European Parliament and of the Council (Unfair Commercial Practices Directive)* was published in the Official Journal on 11 June 2005.[88]

The major debates during the adoption process concerned the unfairness standard (average consumer and transactional decision test); the maximum harmonisation standard; the extent of the blacklist in the annex and the role of codes of conduct. These topics will be considered in more detail in subsequent chapters, but it is useful to comment on some of these issues and how they were addressed during the adoption of the Directive.

### (i) Unfairness standard

The initial proposal had contained a definition of average consumer as meaning 'the consumer who is reasonably well-informed and reasonably observant and

---

85   COM(2003) 356 final.

86   COM(2001) 546 final and revised proposal at COM(2002) 585 final. As stated above this is likely to be abandoned.

87   OJ 2005 C38/E/1.

88   OJ 2005 L149/22.

circumspect'.[89] This was removed and the Common Position simply referred to the jurisprudence of the European Court of Justice in the recitals. This was expanded on in the final version to include in the recital wording lifted from the jurisprudence, namely that the average consumer is 'reasonably well-informed and reasonably observant and circumspect, taking into account social, cultural and linguistic factors, as interpreted by the Court of Justice'.[90] There was a desire not to include a precise definition so as to allow jurisprudence to develop. Equally consumer advocates were keen to include reference to social, cultural and linguistic factors to reflect the nuanced approach of the Court and to prevent the impression that European law uncritically assumed that everyone was always able to process information correctly and not be misled.

A transactional decision requirement was built into the unfairness standard to underline that the test related to economic considerations. Consumer groups had concerns about the impact of this requirement on the need to establish causation between the practice and consumer detriment and also because there were difficulties in applying it to some situations where either unfair practices did not affect a transactional decision (for instance, when consumers ignored aggressive practices) or there was no opportunity for consumers to make a transactional decision (such as post-contractual removal of services by a trader). These concerns were not so much addressed as said not to be real concerns in practice. The transactional decision test is not thought to be a very high hurdle for consumers; we wait to see if the courts take a similar approach.

### (ii) Maximum harmonisation

Article 4 of the Directive is the internal market clause, which simply states: 'Member States shall neither restrict the freedom to provide services nor restrict the free movement of goods for reasons falling within the field approximated by this Directive'.

The original proposal had preceded this with a statement that traders shall only comply with the national provisions, falling within the field approximated by this Directive, of the Member States in which they are established. This was removed, apparently as a concession to those with concerns about this maximum harmonisation approach; but this was a rather pyrrhic victory, for it was only removed on the understanding that it was not needed to achieve maximum harmonisation. With it also went the obligation on Member States to ensure compliance, but hopefully this is covered by the general enforcement provisions. However, the amended version does at least have the merit of allowing the authorities in the state where the practice occurs of enforcing its laws. The earlier version would have forced them to rely on the authorities of the country of origin. The complicated issues surrounding the extent and effect of maximum harmonisation are explored more thoroughly in Chapter 2.

---

89  Article 2(b).
90  Recital 18.

The Commission refused to discuss the maximum harmonisation principle. In the end it became clear that they had heard the arguments against it, rejected them and it was a waste of time debating the issue. Those who disagree with the policy might suggest that the Commission could come to rue their refusal to take counsel on this fundamental policy issue. This is an area of law that is too complex to be resolved simply by a newly formulated general clause and it might prove difficult to achieve true uniformity of interpretation and application. The Commission was even unwilling to introduce any safeguard clause allowing Member States to react to plug clear loopholes that might emerge.

National laws within the scope of the Directive will have to be reviewed and brought into line with its rules, unless they fall within specific exemptions such as those contract law rules concerning validity, formation and effect;[91] jurisdiction;[92] health and safety rules;[93] financial services;[94] the regulated professions;[95] fine metals[96] and laws based on minimum harmonisation clauses in other EC Directives[97] or subject to a more specific Community rule.[98] Otherwise more protective rules will have to be outside the scope of the Directive: so competitors can be afforded higher protection than consumers! Arguably Recital 7 gives Member States some wriggle room, as it allows Member States to continue to regulate for taste and decency, and its example of solicitations in the street suggests a broad understanding of the scope of taste and decency.

*(iii) Blacklist*

With the policy of maximum harmonisation set firm, the advice to the consumer lobby was to focus on the Annex I of commercial practices which are considered unfair in all circumstances. The original proposal listed 28 practices, which in the final version was extended to 31. Whereas some of these are straightforward, others touch complex issues such as pyramid selling,[99] and one might wonder whether there is a need for more detailed rules than are found in the Annex I. Also the matters listed appear to be a rather rag bag collection of unfair practices. Although they are listed under two headings for misleading and aggressive practices, it is not even clear that all the practices are listed under the appropriate heading and in some cases one might question whether they all are indeed examples of misleading and aggressive practices. Some seem to be simply objectionable practices that have simply been listed with little attention being paid to defining the underlying policy for the prohibition.

---

91  Article 3(2).
92  Article 3(7).
93  Article 3(3).
94  Article 3(9).
95  Article 3(8).
96  Article 3(10).
97  Article 3(5).
98  Article 3(4).
99  Item 14.

## (iv) Codes of conduct

The background papers had discussed the possibility of creating structures to provide non-binding guidance on the application of the general clause, but this never figured in the discussions from the time of the first proposal. It is true that the Directive takes some limited steps to encourage the use of codes and the Explanatory Memorandum to the first proposal notes that codes can be taken into account in assessing whether there has been a breach,[100] but even here the Commission became less ambitious. In the *Follow-up Communication on EU Consumer Law*[101] the Commission had been enthusiastic about the development of European-wide codes. This enthusiasm waned, presumably, because it saw little prospect of many meaningful European codes being adopted. The Commission had even been willing to canvass the idea of their endorsing codes which would then carry a presumption of conformity with the Directive. This idea was quickly dropped.

## (v) Enforcement

Perhaps surprisingly, given that effective enforcement of consumer protection rules is one of the three key objectives in the Commission's *Consumer Policy Strategy*[102] there was relatively little discussion of enforcement during the progress of the Directive. Too many big discussions on the nature of the general clause and maximum harmonisation no doubt tended to overshadow practical enforcement concerns. However, the language used, with references to prohibitions and penalties, certainly seems to suggest that the Commission had in mind criminal and or administrative controls, especially as the Directive also includes the now familiar European technique of requiring that injunction procedures be available. The Directive in no way seems to require that damages be available for breach, but equally it does not seem to prevent Member States from introducing such a remedy.

## e. Outline of the Directive

The Unfair Commercial Practices Directive regulates unfair commercial practices harming consumers' economic interests (Article 1). Article 2 provides a raft of definitions, while Article 3 delimits the scope of the Directive. Article 4 is the internal market (maximum harmonisation) clause. The meat of the Directive lies in Articles 5–9. Article 5 sets out the general unfairness test, Article 6 specifies this for misleading actions, Article 7 for misleading omissions (with Annex II listing those community provisions setting out rules for advertising and commercial communication which are regarded as material) and Articles 8–9 for aggressive commercial practices. These are supplemented by a list of practices that are always

---

100 *Op.cit.*, at para. 74.
101 *Op.cit.*, at para. 29.
102 COM(2002) 205 final.

considered unfair in Annex I. Codes of conduct are addressed in Article 10. Articles 11–13 deal with enforcement issues, including rules on the substantiation of claims. Articles 15–16 deal with consequential amendments to other Directives. Articles 17–20 deal with some other procedural matters considered below.

### f. Revision, Transposition and Entry into Force

*(i) Entry into force*

Article 20 provides that the Directive enters into force on the day after its publication in the Official Journal, namely 12 June 2005.

*(ii) Transposition*

Article 19 requires that the Directive be transposed into national law by 12 June 2007, that is, a two-year implementation period. However, these measures only need to be applied from 12 December 2007.

This Directive will pose major implementation problems for those countries whose tradition is not to have general clauses. This is a particular problem for the United Kingdom's Department of Trade and Industry and explains why they undertook extensive research into the Directive and its impact on national law even before the Directive was formally adopted.[103] Even so the two-year implementation period will be tight. For the United Kingdom there will be some important policy questions as to whether it gives up its tradition of detailed specific regulation in favour of reliance on general clauses[104] or whether alongside a copy out of the Directive the traditional forms of regulation could survive with modification. The extent to which national laws can survive and how far they will have to be modified will be the subject of intensive debate and also raise difficulties in monitoring for non-compliance by the Commission. This will be an issue not only for the common law countries. Even states that have a general clause will also have a number of detailed rules that impinge on consumer protection. Indeed the scope of the Directive is so broad that it could be interpreted as including many laws of general application (such as harassment) and considering how to deal with these overlap issues will be problematic.

Moreover, states with a general clause will have to resist the easy assumption that they need do nothing to implement the Directive. Early indications suggest that several states with general clauses feel they have to do little or nothing to implement this Directive. This would underestimate the import of the new regime which

---

103   C. Twigg-Flesner, D. Parry, G. Howells, A. Nordhausen, *An Analysis of the Application and Scope of the UCP Directive* (DTI, 2005) available at: http://www.dti.gov.uk/ccp/consultpdf/final_report180505.pdf.

104   A policy that was mooted in the DTI paper *Extending Competitive Markets: Empowered Consumers, Successful Business* (July 2004).

Europe seeks to put in place. These states will have to check that their general clause reflects that contained in the Directive and modify it if necessary. As we shall see the Directive reflects a particular approach to consumer protection and this level of protection must be found in all European states, but no more!

The tendency is for the Commission, supported by the European Court of Justice,[105] to look to see that all the elements of the Directive are transparently introduced into national law. This means that not only the general clause in Articles 5–9, but also the matters listed in Annex I as always being unfair, must be found in national laws. There may be debates as to the extent to which Member States can amplify the rather brief and sometimes cryptic statements of prohibitions specified in Annex I. All this illustrates that the implementation process will not be easy. Creating a legal regime for unfair commercial practices is difficult in itself; aligning it with national traditions is even more complex.

### (iii) Informing consumers

Consumers will need to be informed of the new rules. This is provided for in Article 17, which requires Member States to inform consumers of the national law transposing the Directive. It goes on also to require them where appropriate to encourage traders and code owners to inform consumers of their codes of conduct. It is difficult to know the extent to which these are meaningful obligations and whether the Commission will monitor the diligence with which this obligation is carried out.

### (iv) Revision

One of the consequences of maximum harmonisation is that it fixes the legal ground rules. There is the obvious risk that businesses might find ways to circumvent those rules. We have already noted that there is no safeguard clause. There is also no easy mechanism for revising the Directive. Even the list of practices in Annex I considered unfair in all circumstances can only be added to by formal amendment of the Directive. There is a review mechanism built into the Directive in Article 18. This will be comprehensive, but will focus in particular on the internal market clause (Article 4) and the exemption from that principle for financial services and immovable property (Article 3(9)), as well as the list in Annex 1. It will comment on the scope for further harmonisation and simplification of Community consumer protection law as well as any measures that need to be taken at Community level to ensure appropriate levels of consumer protection are maintained. As regards the last matter, reference is made to the need to have regard to Article 3(5) which allows Member States to retain measures based on minimum harmonisation clauses in EC Directives. It is not clear what lies behind this reference. It is unlikely that the

---

105 See case law on unfair contract terms, Case C–144/99 *Commission v Netherlands*, [2001] ECR I–3541, Case C–478/99 *Commission v Sweden*, [2002] ECR I–4147, and Case C–70/03 *Commission v Spain*, not yet reported.

Commission would want to extend this exemption, but rather it may be alluding to the need to revise those Directives to take account of best practice in the Member States. The consumer *acquis* is currently being reviewed by a group of scholars headed by Professor Hans Schulte-Nölke. When the Commission reflects upon that review it should take account of the fact that if some measures are not included in the specific Directives then national rules may fall foul of the maximum harmonisation rules in the Directive. Although some contract rules are outside the scope of the Unfair Commercial Practices Directive, it is certainly possible to argue that rules on matters such as the availability or length of the cancellation period or the information that has to be provided might be subject to maximum unfair commercial practices harmonisation.

# Chapter 2

# Minimum/Maximum Harmonisation and the Internal Market Clause

Hans-W. Micklitz

## a. Introduction to the Debate

The Unfair Commercial Practices Directive provides for maximum harmonisation by Article 4 – the internal market clause. It reads 'Internal Market – Member States shall neither restrict the freedom to provide services nor restrict the free movement of goods for reasons falling within the field approximated by this Directive'.

Both principles – maximum harmonisation and the internal market clause – have raised much concern in the political debate preceding the adoption of the Directive. The *first* reflects a policy shift in the law making at the European level. It has long been taken for granted that the European Community will normally only set minimum standards when it acts to harmonise rules protecting the economic interests of consumers, leaving room for Member States to maintain or to introduce stronger standards of protection if they so wish. The only device available has then been to use the proportionality test to test whether a Member State has gone beyond what was 'effectively needed' to guarantee the envisaged level of protection. The *second* principle, the so-called internal market clause – as enshrined in Article 4 – is certainly amongst the most complicated rules in the Directive. The European Commission originally had in mind to introduce a fully-fledged version of the country of origin principle into the Directive. The latter was seen as the sole means to eliminate divergent standards of interpretation in the Community. Due to the resistance of some Member States, the adopted version of the Directive does not contain a fully-fledged version of the country of origin principle any more. However, the European Commission sticks to the argument that it is implicitly contemplated by the Directive and its removal was simply because the existing *acquis communautaire* no longer requires its reiteration in a piece of secondary Community law. The European Court of Justice, in its *Tobacco Advertising* judgment,[1] is said to back an understanding of Article 4 which allows a reading of the country of origin principle into the internal market clause.

These two principles, maximum harmonisation and the internal market clause (the country of origin principle), when considered separately already yield a

---

1   Case C–376/98 *Germany v European Parliament and Council* [2000] ECR I–8419.

number of difficulties in the interpretation of the Directive. The combination of the two – maximum harmonisation and country of origin principle – becomes highly explosive. It would mean that Member States' courts are mutually bound to each others' interpretation of the Unfair Commercial Practices Directive. The worst case scenario – or perhaps, depending on one's viewpoint, the best case scenario – would mean that the Member State with the lowest standards of protection could determine the level of protection for the European Community as a whole, provided it complies with the Directive as approved by the European Court of Justice under the preliminary reference procedure. This is why the interplay between the two principles deserves to be analysed separately.

## b. The Legal Background to Maximum Harmonisation and the Internal Market Clause

The meaning of maximum harmonisation, the internal market clause (country of origin principle), and maximum harmonisation and country of origin principle combined will have to be clarified before it is possible to analyse these principles in the context of the Unfair Commercial Practices Directive. Only through this approach can one highlight the overall importance of the policy shift intended by the European Commission and as realised in the final version of the Directive.

### (i) Background of the minimum–maximum debate

There is a broader background to the maximum/minimum debate. It has been a long-established policy of the European Commission to strive for minimum harmonisation in the field of consumer law. This is particularly true in the area of consumer contract law. Minimum harmonisation seemed to be the political consensus between Member States and the European Commission. It allowed for the establishment of a common platform within the European Community for all Member States, but it enabled Member States to maintain or introduce stricter standards. In *Buet*[2] the European Court of Justice had recognised the competence of Member States to set tighter standards on doorstep selling under the Doorstep Selling Directive within the limits of the proportionality principle. In *Doc Morris*[3] the European Court of Justice has most recently confirmed its case law with regard to the Distance Selling Directive. This is the reason why quite a number of consumer law Directives which affect the regulation of unfair commercial practices, but provide for minimum harmonisation in particularly sensitive fields such as direct selling (doorstep selling) and distance selling methods (cold calling), are exempted from the scope of application of this Directive.[4]

---

2    Case 382/87 *Buet v Ministère Public*, [1989] ECR 1235.
3    Case 322/01 [2003] ECR I–4887, at 63.
4    See Chapter 3(f)(vi).

However, the European Commission's policy is changing. Looking back into the regulation of commercial practices, the policy of the European Commission had seemed rather ambiguous. One of the first Directives focusing on consumer protection, the Misleading Advertising Directive, established minimum standards. In this respect it is in line with current mainstream policy. The Misleading Advertising Directive allows divergent standards to apply to the concept of misleading advertising, thereby granting Member States the power to maintain a stricter concept of misleading advertising if they favoured more stringent protection of consumers. However, the European Court of Justice has gradually narrowed down the margin of Member States and advocates one unique concept which reaches beyond the scope of the Misleading Advertising Directive to cover trademark law as well as the specific provisions on advertising of foodstuffs. The European Court of Justice is moving towards taking the notion of misleading advertising as fully harmonised.[5] The Comparative Advertising Directive fits quite well with such thinking as it provides for maximum harmonisation. The justification may be found in Recital 2:

> Whereas the completion of the internal market will mean an ever wider range of choice, whereas given that consumers can and must make the best possible use of the internal market; and that advertising is a very important means of creating genuine outlets for all goods and services throughout the European Community, the basic provisions governing the form and the content of comparative advertising should be uniform and the conditions of the use of comparative advertising in the Member States should be harmonised ... .

This relatively sparse reasoning sufficed for the European Court of Justice to conclude in *Pippig*[6] that the Comparative Advertising Directive has fully harmonised the rules on comparative advertising.

Outside of the Directives on misleading and comparative advertising (the only two so far focusing exclusively on advertising matters, in areas where the Commission initiated EC regulation which, inter alia, deal with commercial practices) no common policy seems recognisable.[7] However, a second glance reveals that the Commission conceded minimum harmonisation only in areas where no agreement could be reached on maximum standards. The above mentioned Doorstep Selling Directive on contracts negotiated away from business premises and Distance Selling Directive are striking examples. However, the Commission has never given up its idea to come to uniform standards at least in the field of commercial practices.

There were early announcements indicating the policy shift which culminated in the Unfair Commercial Practices Directive. However, the Commission took

---

5    See, for a full account of the analysis of the European Court of Justice, H.-W. Micklitz, EG F 'Irreführende Werbung', in *Münchener Kommentar zum UWG*, (Munich: C.H. Beck, forthcoming) No. 26 *et seq.*

6    Case C–44/01 [2003] ECR I–3095.

7    See H.-W. Micklitz, 'A General Framework Directive on Fair Trading', in H. Collins (ed.), *The Forthcoming EC Directive on Unfair Commercial Practices – Contract, Consumer and Competition Law* (The Hague: Kluwer Law International, 2004), 43.

the decisive step in its recent consumer policy programme from 2002–2006. Here it resolutely establishes full harmonisation as the new objective of its politics on commercial practices and on consumer contract law.[8] It is clear that the Commission intends to stop Member States tending their own 'consumer gardens'. The more the Community plans to regulate the internal market, the less it can tolerate solo efforts. The Commission took a first step in this direction with the Distance Selling of Financial Services Directive, concerning distance marketing of consumer financial services. It was largely successful in its efforts, although Member States retained some control of matters such as what information should be provided. In its last communication on European contract law,[9] the Commission announced its intention to review eight consumer law Directives under the perspective of maximum harmonisation. This fits well with the Consumer Policy Strategy 2002–2006. The Commission's proposal on the reform of the EC Directive on consumer credit is striving for maximum harmonisation.[10] The decisive breakthrough, however, came with the Unfair Commercial Practices Directive.

*(ii) Background of the country of origin principle*

For quite a long time little attention has been devoted to the concept of mutual recognition of Member States' national laws. The Commission had always put great weight on completing the internal market on the *Cassis de Dijon* principle, but this is only a concept of conditional mutual recognition, that is, Member States may maintain rules if shown to be justified under Article 30 EC Treaty. However, two important exceptions had been made. In the 'Television without Frontiers' Directive and the Electronic Commerce Directive, the Community introduced the country of origin principle. Both of the Directives concern so-called 'multi-state acts of advertising', that is, where the single advertising act emanating from one country has an effect on the markets of several other countries simultaneously, as is generally the case in cross-border media (as in all kinds of commercial communications media) and in Europe-wide marketing concepts. If the principle of country of determination were to apply, advertisers would be obliged to know the advertising and competition law rules in every country where their advertising may have any perceivable effects. The larger the number of legal systems, the less feasible it becomes to assess the lawfulness of advertising for each place of business separately. The use of the principle of the country of destination raises particular difficulties in cases where the accessibility of the advertisement may no longer be controlled (for example, advertising on the Internet, where advertisers cannot prevent users from a specific

---

8   Consumer Policy Strategy (2002–2006), OJ 8.6.2002 C137/2.

9   COM(2003) 68 final, 12 February 2003.

10  Proposal for a Directive on the Harmonisation of Consumer Credit, COM(2002) 443 final, 11 September 2002, although it is not yet clear at the time of writing whether the Directive will ever be adopted. It even seems possible that the Commission might withdraw its proposal. Now revised draft, 7 October 2005, KOM (2005) 483 endg.

country from accessing their websites).[11] On the other hand, one has to consider the risk for consumers of a socalled 'race to the bottom'. As Directives predominantly provide for minimum harmonisation, companies might try to launch their advertising from those Member States whose legislation meets only minimum standards. Given that Member States have a strong interest in commercial activity in their countries, they might, in addition, be encouraged to lower their legal requirements (to the limit of the minimum). One may wonder whether this would ultimately be detrimental to consumers.[12] The concept of the country of origin principle is likely to foster minimum harmonisation. It does not do very much to encourage full harmonisation, unless it is assumed everyone will uniformly adopt the minimum standard.[13] The effects of the country of origin principle are even more far reaching in those areas where there is no harmonisation at all. Here there is not even a minimum level of rules available and the race to the bottom might become an avalanche.

The country of origin principle was first introduced in the 'Television without Frontiers' Directive and was known as the 'transmission-state principle'. The key provision of the transmission-state principle is Article 2(a)(1), according to which 'Member States shall ensure freedom of reception and shall not restrict re-transmissions on their territory of television broadcasts from other Member States for reasons which fall within the fields coordinated by this Directive'. Its impact becomes clear in combination with the minimum standard principle (Article 3(1)).[14] The Directive regulates how much, when, under which circumstances and what kind of television advertising (including sponsoring and tele-shopping) is allowed. Member States have to implement these minimum standards into their national law. They may, however, adopt stricter rules.[15] It is the possible divergence of rules which gives the transmission-state principle its specific importance: on the one hand, the transmission-state principle intends to ensure free movement of broadcasts without secondary control on the same grounds in the receiving Member States;[16] on the other hand, the different Member States' regulations represent incentives for secondary control over the receiving Member States. In *De Agostini and TV–Shop*[17] the European Court of Justice held that the Directive did not, in principle, preclude the

---

11  N. Dethloff, *Commercial Communications* (Issue 22 December 1999), 2, at 4.

12  P. Mankowski, 'Internet und Internationales Wettbewerbsrecht' (1999), *Gewerblicher Rechtsschutz und Urheberrecht Internationaler Teil* 909, at 914.

13  G. Bender and C. Sommer, 'E–Commerce-Richtlinie: Auswirkungen auf den elektronischen Geschäftsverkehr in Deutschland' (2000), *Recht der internationalen Wirtschaft* 260, at 262.

14  T. Bodewig, 'Elektronischer Geschäftsverkehr und unlauterer Wettbewerb' (2000), *Gewerblicher Rechtsschutz und Urheberrecht Internationaler Teil* 475, at 478.

15  Cf. N. Reich and A. Rosenboom, 'Partial Harmonisation and Pre-emption: The Case of TV Advertising According to Directive 89/522/EEC of 3 October 1989', Opinion submitted to the Swedish Konsumentenverket – KO, October 1994.

16  Cf. Recital 15 of Directive 89/522/EEC.

17  Joint Cases C–34/95, C–35/95 and C–36/95 *Konsumentenombudsmannen v Agostini Förlag and TV–Shop i Sverige* [1997] ECR I–3843.

application of national rules with the general aim of consumer protection, provided that they did not involve secondary control of television broadcasts in addition to the control which the broadcasting Member State must carry out.[18]

The Electronic Commerce Directive applies to all information society services within the meaning of Article 1(2), which means basically all online services, such as the sale of goods and services, electronic newspapers, search engines, discussion groups and so on. In order to remove the obstacles hampering the free exchange of information services, the Directive provides for a country of origin principle in the coordinated field.[19] The country of origin principle not only concerns the Member State legislation as harmonised through the Electronic Commerce Directive, but also all other Member State legislation applicable to information society service providers in general, such as price regulations, especially rebates, gifts, premiums and so on. Due to the fact that a secondary control should be excluded in the 'coordinated field', States other than that in which the service provider is established are basically no longer allowed to take any actions against the information society service or the commercial communication. The implantation of the country of origin principle has initiated a liberalisation process in sales promotion even beyond the scope of the Electronic Commerce Directive. Although Member States are legally allowed to maintain stricter rules on sales promotion measures outside those transmitted via information services, they have felt strong pressure from the business environment to extend such liberalisation independently of the means of communication.

*(iii) Background for combining maximum harmonisation and the country of origin principle*

Whilst both Directives strengthened the legitimacy of the country of origin principle in regulating marketing practices, the principle alone was not agreed as an appropriate means to substitute for the broader harmonisation policy. In its constant effort to achieve the completion of the Internal Market, the European Commission received support from the European Court of Justice in its famous *Tobacco Advertising* judgment.[20] It is in this context that the idea arose within the legal department of the European Commission to combine maximum harmonisation and the country of origin principle.

The facts in *Tobacco Advertising* are well established. It might suffice to recall that under Article 5 of the (annulled) Directive 98/43, Member States retained the right to lay down, in accordance with the Treaty, such stricter requirements concerning the advertising or sponsorship of tobacco products as they deem necessary to guarantee the health protection of individuals. The European Court of Justice takes a critical stance towards minimum harmonisation of this nature. The

---

18  Joint Cases C–34/95, C–35/95 and C–36/95 *Konsumentenombudsmannen v Agostini Förlag and TV–Shop i Sverige* [1997] ECR I–3843 at [32–4].

19  Article 2(g).

20  Case C–376/98 *Germany v European Parliament and Council* [2000] ECR I–8419.

following reasoning taken from the *Tobacco Advertising* judgment has been read by the European Commission as enabling it to compel Member States to allow access of 'substandard' imported products to their markets so that they might compete with the 'better standard' domestic products:

101. Moreover, the Directive does not ensure free movement of products which are in conformity with its provisions.

102. Contrary to the contentions of the Parliament and Council, Article 3(2) of the Directive, relating to diversification products, cannot be construed as meaning that, where the conditions laid down in the Directive are fulfilled, products of that kind in which trade is allowed in one Member State may move freely in the other Member States, including those where such products are prohibited.

104. Furthermore, the Directive contains no provision ensuring the free movement of products which conform to its provisions, in contrast to other Directives allowing Member States to adopt stricter measures for the protection of a general interest.[21]

There is a tendency in legal doctrine to play down the possible effects of *Tobacco Advertising*. In essence, these arguments are based on the particularities of the much-criticised Directive in the field of health policy affairs where Article 152(4)(c) excludes harmonisation. The Tobacco Advertising Directive was said not to improve the circulation and marketing of tobacco products, but to severely restrict it, in particular by the minimum harmonisation clauses.[22] In addition, it is said not to help the functioning of the internal market by promoting competition, because the prohibition on advertising practically prevented the appearances of newcomers.[23] The European Court of Justice had no direct opportunity to give further shape to its constitutional assessment of the notion of minimum harmonisation. Indirectly, it seems as if the European Court of Justice has softened its rather radical approach, namely by recognising that measures for the establishment and functioning of the internal market may also serve to protect consumers' health and that they can be taken to avoid future distortions of competition which are not unlikely to happen.[24] However, the case law concerns the relationship between market freedoms and health

---

21  The Court then goes on to refer in particular to Article 7(1) of Council Directive 90/239 of 17 May 1990 on the approximation of the laws, regulations and administrative provisions of Member States concerning the maximum tar yield of cigarettes (OJ 1990 L137/36) and to Article 8(1) of Council Directive 89/622 of 13 November 1989 on the approximation of the laws, regulations and administrative provisions of Member States concerning the labelling of tobacco products (OJ 1989 L359/1).

22  G. Howells and S. Weatherill, *Consumer Protection Law* 2nd edn (Aldershot: Ashgate, 2005) 134.

23  N. Reich, 'A European Contract Law, or an EU Contract Law Regulation for Consumers?', 28 *Journal of Consumer Policy*, 2005, 383.

24  Case C–491/01 *R v Secretary of State for Health ex parte British American Tobacco (Investment) Ltd., et al.*, [2002] ECR I–11453, in this sense Reich, *op.cit.*

and safety, which is not at issue in the Unfair Commercial Practices Directive.[25] Whilst it might be wrong to overstate the importance of *Tobacco Advertising*, it is equally correct to start from the premise that its effects on European fair trading law and even on European contract law are 'uncertain'. It is striking to recognise that the European Court of Justice combines harmonisation measures to market freedoms. If *Tobacco Advertising* were to become the new and dominant line of argument, two possible conclusions might be drawn with regard to minimum harmonisation and maximum harmonisation:

(1) With regard to minimum harmonisation: *Buet*[26] – and all the other contract or marketing practice-related Directives which refer to minimum harmonisation – would have to be re-read. *Tobacco Advertising* would put pressure on Member States to lower their stronger standards to the minimum European level. The European minimum level might end up becoming the maximum level of harmonisation.

(2) With regard to maximum harmonisation, the legal service of the European Commission understands *Tobacco Advertising*: that there can be no maximum harmonisation without guaranteeing the free movement of products and services.[27] Such a reading seems to be based on the hidden effect of the judgment against the much-criticised Tobacco Advertising Directive, which purported to establish minimum harmonisation but was condemned for failure to establish maximum harmonisation.

The European Commission extensively used the *Tobacco Advertising* doctrine to realise a twofold objective in the preparatory work on the Unfair Commercial Practices Directive: first to argue that Article 95 EC allows for maximum harmonisation only, and secondly that maximum harmonisation combined with the country of origin principle complies with the substance of the *Tobacco Advertising* ruling. The full meaning of the Unfair Commercial Practices Directive, providing for maximum harmonisation in combination with the internal market clause of Article 4, can only be understood against that legal and political background.

---

25  See Case C–210/03 *Swedish Match* [2004] ECR I–11893 and Cases C–154/04 and C–155/04 *Alliance for Natural Health* [2005] ECR 2005 (ECR I-6451). On how public health concerns may properly play a role in the choice of harmonised standards, see Chapter 3(f)(iv).

26  Case 382/87 *Buet v Ministère Public* [1989] ECR 1235.

27  Oral information of Mr. Abbamonte, Head of Unit, DG SANCO given to the European Consumer Law Group at its meeting on 1 October 2004 in Brussels.

## c. Maximum Harmonisation in the Directive

### *(i) The principle and its justification*

During the legislative process there was extensive discussion on whether the Directive should strive for minimum or maximum harmonisation. In its Explanatory Memorandum the European Commission attempted to explain why maximum harmonisation alone would contribute to the achievement of the internal market and strengthen consumer confidence.[28] It is the *Tobacco Advertising* judgment which compels the Commission to demonstrate that there is a relationship between market practices and barriers to trade in the internal market. The Commission relies heavily on an Impact Assessment Study and on the work of the European Advertising Standards Alliance (EASA) in order to demonstrate the relevance of these barriers and distortions. The Commission then states in paragraph 19:

> The impact of these barriers is exacerbated by the differences in the regulation of unfair commercial practices by Member States. The minimum clauses in existing consumer protection legislation, such as the Misleading Advertising Directive, perpetuate this problem by allowing Member States to add divergent requirements and provide differing degrees and types of regulation.

These differences in legislation are said to increase the cost and complexity of enforcement, whether by public authorities or self-regulatory bodies. Setting aside the validity of the figures and estimations quoted in the Explanatory Memorandum, differing regulatory standards might indeed lead to barriers to trade. However, this finding is in no way related to legal rules on marketing practices alone. It is the potential transborder effect of marketing practices which brings the legislative difference to the fore. However, accepting this effect, the question remains whether the general clause, as laid down in Article 5, is or might become an appropriate tool to strive for maximum harmonisation. The concept of 'fairness' affects national cultures and traditions to quite a different degree.[29] Little imagination is needed to predict that differences in the application of the general clause by the Member States' control authorities will develop. Therefore maximum harmonisation is indeed more a political than a legal necessity.[30]

A second strand of reasoning is much more delicate. The Commission argues with reference to the Ex Ante Impact Assessment Study that leaving the existing minimum approach would fail to address the 'lack of consumer confidence' about cross-border consumer protection.[31] This is a rather bold statement, referring as it

---

28  COM(2003) 356 final, 17 June 2003 para. 12 *et seq.*

29  See Chapter 2, in its relation to the scope of the Directive, (d)(ii) and (iii), as well as, in its relation to the concept of fairness, Chapter 4(i)–(v).

30  See G. Howells, 'The Rise of European Consumer Law – Whither National Consumer Law?', *Sydney Law Review*, 2006 (28), 63–88

31  Explanatory Memorandum, COM(2003) 356 final, at para. 28.

does to actual consumer expectations. One may first of all wonder whether consumers really care about the difference between maximum and minimum harmonisation in market practice legislation. Second, it can be taken for granted that consumers in the vast majority of Member States believe in the quality of their own national legal system.[32] National legal systems, however, still differ in their tradition and culture. These differences cannot be 'harmonised' by European regulatory measures. At the very best, it might be that national legal systems approach each other under a common European frame, but such a learning process takes time and it is much more likely that a new European legal culture[33] emerges besides the already existing national legal cultures. Consumer expectations on market practices regulation – if they can be discovered and determined – might indeed focus on 'easy access to the counterparty' in the case of conflict.[34] The consumer confidence argument is based on shaky ground. It is used – and maybe even abused – as a policy argument to legitimate the Commission's preference for maximum harmonisation.

The majority of Member States did not really object to maximum harmonisation as provided for in the first proposal, with the exception of Denmark and Sweden. That is why it was relatively easy for the European Commission to maintain its arguments and to introduce them into the finally adopted version of the Directive. The two strands – barriers to trade resulting from different national legislations and consumer confidence – reappear in Recitals 4 and 5 of the actual Directive.

*(ii) The transition period, Articles 3(5) and (6)*

The European Commission, however, failed to establish that the maximum harmonisation principle would have full effect at the same time as the Directive is meant to enter into force. Article 19 distinguishes between two transition periods; the first – ending on 12 June 2007 – relates to the adoption of the necessary laws and regulations in order to comply with the Directive, the second – ending on 12 December 2007 – to their application. A large majority of Member States sought a transition period which would allow them more smoothly to adapt their rules to the new policy of the European Commission.

In addition, the transition period might serve to shape more clearly the borderline between the harmonised area of the Directive and those fields where Member States are legally allowed to defend their national cultures and traditions. Article 3(5) provides as follows:

---

32  T. Wilhelmsson, 'The Abuse of the "Confident Consumer" as a Justification for EC Consumer Law' (2004) *Journal of Consumer Policy* 317, at 326, although the author shows that this is not always true with regard to some southern European countries.

33  See P. Legrand, 'European legal systems are not converging' (1996) 45 *International and Comparative Law Quarterly* 52; V. Gessner, A. Höland and C. Varga, *European legal cultures* (Aldershot: Dartmouth, 1996); P. Häberle *Europäische Rechtskultur* (Baden-Baden: Nomos-Verlag, 1994).

34  Wilhelmsson, *op.cit.*, 317 at 329.

For a period of six years from 12 June 2007, Member States shall be able to continue to apply national provisions within the field approximated by this Directive which are more restrictive or prescriptive than this Directive and which implement directives containing minimum harmonisation clauses. These measures must be essential to ensure that consumers are adequately protected against unfair commercial practices and must be proportionate to the attainment of this objective. The review referred to in Article 18 may, if considered appropriate, include a proposal to prolong this derogation for a further limited period.

Therefore Member States shall be able to continue to apply national provisions based on minimum clauses which are more restrictive or prescriptive for a period of six years – starting from 12 June 2007 until 12 June 2013. Its application is based on three prerequisites; first, the respective national rules must come under the 'field approximated by this Directive'; second, they must be 'more restrictive or prescriptive'; third, they must be intended to implement Directives containing minimum harmonisation clauses. Only if these requirements are met may Member States escape the maximum harmonisation approach, provided that the national measures are 'essential' to ensure that consumers are 'adequately protected against unfair commercial practices' and are 'proportionate' to the attainment of this objective.

It is the definition of the scope of the 'escape clause' which raises difficulties, rather than its restrictions. The latter formula – 'essential', 'ensure adequate protection' and 'proportionate' – reiterate the *acquis communautaire* with respect to the leeway Member States may have whenever they take regulatory measures that might affect the rules of the Treaty. From the wording it is clear that Member States shall not have competences to introduce new provisions, but only to maintain ('continue to apply') national provisions. The English version of Article 3(5) makes it clear that national provisions are those which implement Directives containing minimum harmonisation clauses. The ruling is bound to national rules implementing previous Directives now within the field of the Unfair Commercial Practices Directive. Then, however, the relationship between Article 3(4), which provides for specific rules in other Community rules to prevail,[35] and the escape clause under Article 3(5), needs to be clarified. Article 3(4) deals only with specific Community rules and implementation in accordance with them; Article 3(5) deals with implementation that in some respect gives better protection via national rules relying on the minimum clause.

The importance of Article 3(5), however, reaches far beyond the maintenance of the existing system of power sharing between the European Community and its Member States. One might read Article 3(5) as an indirect mandate given to the European Commission to check the feasibility of minimum harmonisation Directives. This would mean that all Directives with the exception of the Distance Selling of Financial Services Directive, purporting already to establish maximum harmonisation, would become possible targets of the Commission's policy

---

35  See Chapter 3(f)(v).

shift from minimum to maximum harmonisation as long as they contain unfair commercial practices law provisions which grant Member States powers to maintain or to introduce tighter standards. Article 3(5) of the Unfair Commercial Practices Directive therefore constitutes a review provision, the scope of which remains unclear insofar as the Commission is not directly addressed as an authority. At the same time, however, the provision enables Member States to retain their margin of appreciation as established in the minimum Directives. Recital 14 expressly says that the Directive should be without prejudice to existing Community law which expressly affords Member States the choice between several regulatory options for the protection of consumers in the field of commercial practices.

To the extent that Member States make use of the escape clause they must notify the European Commission without delay of national provisions applied on the basis of Article 3(6), which provides that 'Member States shall notify the Commission without delay of any national provisions applied on the basis of paragraph 5'. According to this unambiguous wording the subject of concern is not the notification of new national special provisions but the notification of 'applied' national provisions which interpret EC law. Taken seriously, the ruling covers two sorts of obligations. First of all, Member States have to notify to the Commission all those national legislations or regulations that are taken in the harmonised field of the Directive, as explained above. However, at the same time, Member States have to notify the Commission of measures taken by the competent national court or the competent control authority applying any of these national provisions. It will have to be shown that such a broad reading is in line with the intention of the Commission to use the internal market clause as a means to overcome the application of diverging standards between Member States. At Community level such a reading would result in the notification of hundreds of cases. If the Commission is really willing to go down this route, it will have a sound reason to argue that the possibility of special national approaches should be removed after the expiration of the six years. These efforts can only be successful if the Commission develops a databank according to the CLAB model.[36]

Theoretically, the exception can be prolonged for a further limited period, provided that the Commission considers this appropriate as a result of a review referred to in Article 18. The prerogative to take action is with the Commission. To recapture this prerogative in the Council, Member States would have to make tremendous efforts.

---

36  H.-W. Micklitz and M. Radeideh, 'CLAB-Europe – The European database on unfair terms in consumer contracts' (2005) 28 *Journal of Consumer Policy* 325.

### (iii) Uncertainties in minimum–maximum harmonisation

Whilst the Directive focuses on maximum harmonisation, its scope of application is limited by all those Directives which according to Article 3(4) contain more specific rules.[37] This area of partially harmonised EC law will certainly become the battlefield in the announced revision of the *acquis communautaire*. However, there is a less obvious rule enshrined in Article 7(5) which in Annex II lists both fully and partly harmonised Directives.[38]

According to Article 7(5) information requirements established by Community law in relation to commercial communication shall be regarded as material in terms of Article 7(1). As most of the Directives only set minimum standards, it could be argued that information requirements would become de facto maximum standards through Article 7(5). Such a view is compatible with the objective of the Directive to establish a standard unfair commercial practice regime at Community level.[39] It is, however, plainly wrong.[40] The history of the Directive does not support such a view, since neither the Member States nor the Commission purported to deal with the difficult conflict hidden in minimum Directives such as for example the legal treatment of cold calling. This understanding is clearly expressed in Article 3(4) which defers the shifting from minimum to full harmonisation, if at all, to a later point in time. Any other understanding does not reflect the interplay of Article 3(4) and the debate on maximum harmonisation. Article 7(5) was never meant to transform minimum Directives into maximum Directives. Such a reading would pre-empt a complicated political bargaining process. Article 7(5) is not a *coup de main* by which the European Commission intended to circumvent and even hollow out Article 3(4).

### d. The Relationship between the Directive and the Proposed Regulation on Sales Promotions

The relationship of the Unfair Commercial Practices Directive to the envisaged Regulation on Sales Promotion is problematic. It would be necessary to clarify that the Regulation takes priority over the Directive as *lex specialis*. The prohibition of commercial practices which are qualified as unfair contains several overlaps with the intended Regulation on Sales Promotion. Without going into much detail it can be seen that the provisions in the intended Regulation are much more specific than those which have been included in the Unfair Commercial Practices Directive.

---

37 See Chapter 3(f)(v).

38 See Chapter 5 (b)(v).

39 See H. Apostolopoulos, 'Neuere Entwicklungen im europäischen Lauterkeitsrecht: Problematische Aspekte und Vorschläge' (2004) *Wettbewerb in Recht und Praxis* 841, at 843.

40 See also H. Schulte-Nölke and C. Busch, 'Der Vorschlag der Kommission für eine Richtlinie über unlautere Geschäftspraktiken KOM (2003) 356 endg.' (2004) 12 *Zeitschrift für Europäisches Privatrecht* 99, at 109.

These conceptual ambiguities could be acceptable so long as there is no European Regulation on Sales Promotion. According to a recent announcement, the European Commission even envisages withdrawing the proposal.[41] If, however, the Regulation is adopted, then it would be urgently required to clarify the relationship of the two instruments. This can only be done by providing that the more specific Regulation would prevail over the Unfair Commercial Practices Directive.

### e. Maximum Harmonisation and the Internal Market Clause in the Directive

*(i) The internal market clause in the legislative process*

The Unfair Commercial Practices Directive pursues in Article 4 a policy which the Commission has started with the adoption of the 'Television without Frontiers' and Electronic Commerce Directives. The Unfair Commercial Practices Directive supersedes both projects since the Commission in its preparatory works purported to combine maximum harmonisation with the principle of country of origin.

Article 4(1) taken with Article 4(2) of the Proposal from June 2003 aimed towards a relatively radical realisation of the principle of country of origin.[42] Before looking at the final version of the Directive it is worthwhile contemplating what the result would have been had the original wording been maintained. The original proposal of the Commission from 20 March 2003[43] provided in Article 4:

Internal Market:

(1) Each Member State shall ensure that traders established on its territory comply with its national provisions on unfair commercial practices harming consumer's economic interests.

(2) Member States shall neither restrict the freedom to provide services nor restrict the free movement of goods in the field approximated by this Directive under Article 3(1) above.

Recital 8 gave the following justification:

---

41 Outcome of the screening of legislative proposals pending before the Legislator COM(2005) 462 final (27 September 2005).

42 There is a comprehensive description and analysis of the situation based on the Proposal in W. Veelken, 'Kundenfang gegenüber dem Verbraucher – Bemerkungen zum EG-Richtlinienentwurf über unlautere Geschäftspraktiken' (2004) *Wettbewerb in Recht und Praxis* 1, at 11 *et seq.*; H. Gamerith, 'Der Richtlinienvorschlag über unlautere Geschäftspraktiken – Möglichkeiten einer harmonischen Umsetzung' (2005) 51 *Wettbewerb in Recht und Praxis* 395, at 407 *et seq.*

43 Brussels, 18 June 2003 COM(2003) 356 final.

The high level of convergence and consumer protection achieved by this Directive create the conditions to make the principle of mutual recognition applicable in the field coordinated by the Directive. The combination of harmonisation and the principle of mutual recognition will eliminate the barriers to trade stemming from the fragmentation of the rules on unfair commercial practices harming consumer economic interests and enable the achievement of the internal market in this area.

Further explanation was provided in the Explanatory Memorandum.[44]

In this context [the general prohibition], the internal market clause plays a vital role: if a practice is judged to be unfair in one Member State it will be able to prevent traders established on its territory from selling to consumers. But unlike now, it will not be able to prevent traders established elsewhere in the EU from selling to its consumers. This means that there will be a high degree of legal certainty because only one set of rules will apply, and the tests in legislation will be more precise than those which are used.

The model proposed by the Commission is of utmost importance in the case of different meanings given to the notion of fairness. At first sight the two paragraphs of the proposed Article 4 sound familiar; only in conjunction with maximum harmonisation do they develop their own dynamic. According to paragraph 30 of the Explanatory Memorandum this conjunction is needed to address the internal market barriers caused by divergent national provisions and to provide the necessary support to consumer confidence to make a mutual recognition approach workable. Member States should not refer to the minimum harmonisation clauses in other Directives to impose additional requirements in the field covered by the Directive.

The official rhetoric of the Commission during the entire legislative process is notable for the constantly repeated argument that the Directive contains sufficiently precise fully harmonised prohibitions which could apply to all Member States equally. The Commission not only bore in mind Annex I and the special provisions on misleading and aggressive advertising, but also the general clause itself. In the Commission's defence it must be said though that the Regulation No. 2006/2004 on consumer protection cooperation was intended to function as an important buffer.[45] Potential disagreement over the opinions on how to interpret or apply individual provisions of the Directive was intended to be clarified by way of exchange of information and consultation. It must be made clear that the entire system of the Unfair Commercial Practices Directive was – and is – not meant to resolve diverging legal opinions in the courts, nor to discuss the intricacies of the dogmas of unfair commercial practices law. The Regulation on Consumer Protection Cooperation must be seen in this light. It is not conflicting court decisions but rather smooth cooperation between Member States' enforcement authorities which seems to be the issue of the moment.

---

44  At para. 49.
45  See Chapter 8(f).

*(ii) The possible scenario of conflict*

The true reason for combining the country of origin principle with maximum harmonisation, however, has never been made explicit. This may be seen in the above mentioned *Tobacco Advertising* judgment which forms the background to the Commission's reasoning. The Commission starts from the premise that Member States might interpret the general clause of Article 5 differently through their authorities so that the protection standards in Member States would continue to vary after the adoption of the Directive. However, the Commission aimed to overcome possible differences between Member States with the help of the internal market clause. This approach is based on the consideration that by way of the general clause a common platform can be established which forms the operative basis for enforcement in Member States. The crux of such thinking is that this platform, for example Article 5, is identical for all Member States and that it conclusively defines the interpretation requirements within the harmonised field of the Unfair Commercial Practices Directive. Differences between modes of interpretation should be accepted in the light of the principle of country of origin, so long as they can be based on the Unfair Commercial Practices Directive.

The consequences of the European Commission's understanding of the internal market clause simultaneously confirmed the worst expectations of all those who criticise the country of origin principle and bring hope to its supporters.[46] The following scenario might describe the potential for conflict: the competent court of one of the 25 Member States – no names are mentioned for obvious reasons – decides on the compliance of a commercial practice with the general clause in Article 5(2). No Member State court could change that decision as long as it complies with a correct interpretation of the general clause.[47] Each Member State's court would formally be bound to the interpretation given to the general clause by another Member State's court. If the latter wanted to rule on an identical commercial practice, then, in order to review the interpretation of the general clause of the former, it would have to address the European Court of Justice under Article 234 EC which then would need to examine whether Community law was interpreted correctly. The *de Agostini* case law could no longer be upheld within the scope of application of the Unfair Commercial Practices Directive.[48] 'Sweden' would have to live with the 'lower standards' of the 'sending country'; it could only invoke resident

---

46 Described in Gamerith, *op.cit.*, 395, at 410.

47 Supportive with regard to the scope of the initial Proposal: J. Glöckner, *Introduction B. No. 182*, in H. Harte-Bavendamm and F. Henning-Bodewig, *Gesetz gegen den unlauteren Wettbewerb* (München: C.H. Beck, 2004); less explicit: Apostolopoulos, *op.cit.*, 841, at 842; explicit: Veelken, *op.cit.*, 1, at 12 who emphasises that ideally there is no regulatory difference between country of origin and marketplace; very briefly: H. Köhler and T. Lettl, 'Das geltende europäische Lauterkeitsrecht, der Vorschlag für eine EG–Richtlinie über unlautere Geschäftspraktiken und die UWG–Reform' (2003) *Wettbewerb in Recht und Praxis* 1019, at 1035 (69).

48 See also Apostolopoulos, *op.cit.*, 841, at 842.

discrimination if it wanted to keep its own protection standards. Such a scenario is no longer simply a theoretical problem. For instance, within the European Community legal assessments of 'low price guarantees' vary extensively. A comparatively liberal approach in Germany contrasts with strict Finnish practice.[49] If the Commission were to manage to enforce its understanding of the internal market clause, this would lead to a situation where the courts of the Member States are bound by their interpretation of the general clause. Depending on which court decides first, more liberal or stricter standards could prevail in Europe – provided the judgment can be based on a correct interpretation of the Directive as approved by the European Court of Justice.

One might argue that such a far reaching consequence would have required precautionary measures to be taken in order to enhance cooperation between the courts of the Member States or between national courts and the European Court of Justice. However, Article 4 in the draft proposal has been drafted for that particular purpose, that is, diverging interpretations should be clarified by way of submission for a preliminary ruling under Article 234.[50] This approach was and is still possible. However, the European Court of Justice cannot decide the case; it can only offer guidance on the interpretation of the general clause. To this extent, reference should be made to the parallel discussion on the interpretation of the principle of good faith in Directive 93/13/EEC.[51] If the Commission's reading of the draft proposal is correct, Member States would be deprived of home country control and could not have argued that the country of origin had not properly implemented or interpreted the provisions of the Unfair Commercial Practices Directive. Such a conflict scenario would invite traders to address Member States which treat advertising restrictions liberally, which would in turn amount to the often-feared 'race to the bottom'.

### (iii) The correct interpretation of the internal market clause in the Directive

Bearing this scenario in mind, it is not surprising that the internal market clause lay at the centre of highly controversial debates during the legislative process. Possible options to reduce the conflicts would have been to shift to minimum harmonisation, possibly in connection with the principle of country of origin,[52] or the inclusion of a safeguard clause allowing the receiving countries to apply a home country control within certain restrictions. This has not been the case. The majority of Member States

---

49  Thereto D. Kocher, 'Ungenügende Harmonisierung im Bereich der irreführenden Werbung am Beispiel der finnischen Rechtsprechung über Tiefstpreisgarantien' (2002) *Gewerblicher Rechtsschutz und Urheberrecht Internationaler Teil* 707.

50  See Veelken, *op.cit.*, 1, at 12; Apostolopoulos, *op.cit.*, 841, at 842; Gamerith, *op.cit.*, 395, at 411.

51  Cf. on the concept of fairness and its links to moral values, Chapter 4c(iii); on the scope of the Directive, Chapter 3(d)(ii)–(iii).

52  As suggested at an early stage by F. Henning-Bodewig, 'E-Commerce und irreführende Werbung' (2001) *Wettbewerb in Recht und Praxis* 771; similarly N. Reich, 'Rechtsprobleme grenzüberschreitender irreführender Werbung' (1992) 56 *Rabels Zeitschrift* 442 and Veelken, *op.cit.*, 11.

– the United Kingdom, Luxembourg and Latvia remained explicit supporters of the Commission's proposal – put pressure on the European Commission to omit Article 4(1) of the draft proposal. Only the wording of Article 4(2) of the draft proposal was kept in the finally adopted version of Article 4 with its position slightly changed. The credo of the provision is written down in Recital 12, which provides that:

> Harmonisation will considerably increase legal certainty for both consumers and businesses. Both consumers and businesses will be able to rely on a single regulatory framework based on clearly defined legal concepts regulating all aspects of unfair commercial practices across the EU. The effect will be to eliminate the barriers stemming from the fragmentation of the rules on unfair commercial practices harming consumer economic interests and to enable the internal market to be achieved in this area.

Further statements on the significance and function of the old Article 4(2) in relation to the new Article 4 do not exist.

Article 4 states in its present form that Member States shall neither restrict the freedom to provide services nor restrict the free movement of goods for reasons falling within the harmonised field of the Directive. Two groups of Member State provisions which are affected by Article 4 can be distinguished: (1) those which fall within the scope of application of the Directive as regards the subject matter – these provisions are subject to maximum harmonisation; and (2) those which do not fall within the scope of application and to which the basic freedoms of the Treaty would apply. The policy of the Commission primarily relates to the first group, as the Directive will be fully effective within the harmonised field. The second group relates to matters of taste and decency and societal interests which are outside the scope.[53]

### (iii) Article 4 in the harmonised field of the Directive

The opinions on the significance of the abandonment of Article 4(1) in relation to the first group, that is, the fully Europeanised area, vary widely.[54] On the one side there is the opinion of Member States, but also of the prevailing legal doctrine, that with the abandonment of Article 4(1) the above illustrated scenario of conflict becomes irrelevant.[55] In other words Member States, their authorities and courts, retain their freedom to interpret and apply the Directive. Glöckner[56] and Gamerith,[57]

---

53  This is the reading defended in Chapter 3(d)(ii).

54  Despite the fact that there is no experience. First examples: F. Henning-Bodewig, 'Herkunftslandprinzip im Wettbewerbsrecht: Erste Erfahrungen – Anm. zu OLG Hamburg Active Two' (2004) *Gewerblicher Rechtsschutz und Urheberrecht* 822.

55  T. Lettl, 'Gemeinschaftsrecht und neues UWG' (2004) *Wettbewerb in Recht und Praxis* 1079, at 1081.

56  J. Glöckner, 'Richtlinienvorschlag über unlautere Geschäftspraktiken, deutsches UWG oder die schwierige Umsetzung von europarechtlichen Generalklauseln' (2004) *Wettbewerb in Recht und Praxis* 936, at 939.

57  *Op.cit.*, 411 (without going into detail regarding the consequences).

however, argue that the discussion on the scope of Article 4 did not come to an end with the compromise found in the Common Position, which was finally adopted. German scholarship and government proceed from the assumption that Article 4 merely mirrors the Cassis de Dijon doctrine, while the Commission thinks that the provision excludes the possibility of justifying restrictions to commercial practices by way of mandatory requirements.[58]

The view taken by Germany suggests that it is possible, by way of relying on the *Cassis de Dijon* doctrine, to maintain stricter advertising restrictions even in the harmonised field, provided they are necessary to protect the interests of the consumers. It is common ground that maximum harmonisation as provided for by the Directive replaces Article 30 EC in the sense given to it by the European Court of Justice. Once the European Community has fully and completely harmonised an area of law in the name of consumer protection, then there is no further scope to use Article 30 EC as a defence for justifying divergent standards. After the adoption of the Unfair Commercial Practices Directive, no Member State may rely any more on Article 30 EC. The only way to object to the effects of maximum harmonisation results from the safeguard clause as enshrined in Article 95(4) EC Treaty. Arguments such as those brought forward by Germany might not be upheld in litigation, in particular as there is no or little precedence in the case law.[59]

These sorts of arguments mislead the participants in the discussion. The legal dispute on the scope of Article 4 does not concern the relationship of Article 28 EC to Article 30 EC, but the question of whether Member States have to live with the consequences of the *Tobacco Advertising* judgment in the meaning given to it by the European Commission, that is that Article 4 in the final version still combines maximum harmonisation with the country of origin principle – that the scenario of conflict is still alive and requires a clear-cut answer.

It is necessary, therefore, to look closely at the decisive merits of *Tobacco Advertising* which could be particularly relevant in a possible dispute over the scope of Article 4.[60] The arguments put forward by the European Court of Justice in paragraphs 101–104 of the judgment, cited above, could be understood as entailing that Member States are forced to open their markets if the standards of control as exercised in the country of origin have been fully 'Europeanised'.[61] The main sentence

---

58  Draft minutes, IP/04/658 18 May 2004, p. 34: 'The Commission can only agree to the deletion of Article 4.1 of its proposal on the understanding that the present directive provides for a full harmonisation of the domain covered by the directive and that for this reason Article 4.1 is not legally required to ensure the proper functioning of the internal market in this field. The practical implication of this directive will be actively monitored by the Commission so as to achieve a uniform application.'

59  Thereto H.-W. Micklitz, N. Reich and S. Weatherill, 'EU Treaty Revision and Consumer Protection' (2004) 27 *Journal of Consumer Policy* 367.

60  See section b(iii) of this chapter.

61  See, on the interpretation of the judgment, S. Weatherill, 'Minimum Harmonisation as Oxymoron? The Case of Consumer Law' in H.-W. Micklitz (ed.), *Perspektiven des Verbraucherrechts* (Baden-Baden: Nomos-Verlag, 2005), p. 15.

here of relevance in paragraph 101 ('the Directive does not ensure free movement of products which are in conformity with its provisions') aims at answering the question of which measures Member States must take so that the harmonised standards grant the undertakings free access to the internal market. Paragraph 104 illustrates the European Court of Justice's possible solution: 'Furthermore, the Directive contains no provision ensuring the free movement of products which conform to its provisions, in contrast to other Directives allowing Member States to adopt stricter measures for the protection of a general interest (...).' At the most one might consider the European Court of Justice believes that Article 95 aims at maximum harmonisation at least in matters that concern the internal market only and do not affect public health matters.[62] Even this interpretation goes far as the European Court of Justice has not yet had a second chance to give shape to its reasoning in paragraph 104 of *Tobacco Advertising*. In *Doc Morris* the European Court of Justice accepted without hesitation the Distance Selling Directive to be based on Article 95 EC although it provided for minimum harmonisation.[63] However, the referring court had not raised the question of whether the Distance Selling Directive on distance selling could be based on Article 95 despite its minimum character. The statement in *Doc Morris* has been made in passing and without further discussion.

The major weakness of the European Commission's argument lies in the missing link between the European Court of Justice's suggested plea for maximum harmonisation under Article 95 and the country of origin principle. The European Court of Justice did not embark on any examination of the country of origin principle. It had no reason to do so, as it did not form part of the much-criticised Tobacco Advertising Directive. So far, the traditional understanding of the interrelationship between the two principles starts from the idea that they are mutually exclusive. If the European Commission decides to harmonise commercial practices or any other field of law, there is no scope any more for the application of the country of origin principle and vice versa. The anchoring of the country of origin principle in the 'Television without Frontiers' and Electronic Commerce Directives confirms such an understanding. The country of origin principle applies only *outside* the harmonised field of law. Legal doctrine discusses the feasibility of combining minimum harmonisation with the country of origin principle, but not the combination of maximum harmonisation and the country of origin principle. All in all, the European Commission's understanding of the *Tobacco Advertising* judgment must be rejected. It cannot be really grounded in the European Court of Justice case law; quite to the contrary, there are good grounds to retain the position of host Member States as supervising authority.[64]

---

62  See section b(iii) of this chapter with reference to the ECJ's case law in footnote 25.

63  Case 322/01 [2003] ECR I–4887 at 63.

64  See Howells, *op.cit.*

*(iv) Article 4 in the non-harmonised area of the Directive*

The significance of Article 4 regarding the second group is disputed. One author[65] is of the opinion that Article 4 also applies to areas which are not completely harmonised. In such a case the trader would have to comply only with the national provisions of the country of origin even in the non-harmonised area without having to fear the control of the receiving state.[66] This cannot be correct. The Unfair Commercial Practices Directive exempts matters of taste and decency as well as societal interests from the scope of the Directive.[67] That is why the European Community will have to live with different standards on commercial practices. This implies that the country of origin and the receiving state may apply different standards. In the non-harmonised area of the Directive there is no room for the country of origin principle. However, each and very Member State that justifies deviating standards under reference to matters of taste and decency as well as societal interests will have to respect the proportionality rule.

*(v) Article 4 and the deferring effect of full harmonisation*

Member States are entitled to defer full harmonisation for six years. This period may be extended. During the period of the first six years after the coming into effect of the Directive, that is, until 12 June 2013, the effects of maximum harmonisation may not be felt. The receiving state retains the possibility of having a secondary control. Until 2013 the European Community will have to accept widely diverging standards in its Member States.

---

65  Veelken, *op.cit.*, 13 *et seq.*

66  Gamerith, *op.cit.*, 411 in the appropriate place it is referred to the country of origin. However, according to the effet utile the reference must be related to the receiving state which is prohibited from a second review.

67  This is the reading defended in Chapter 3(d)(ii) and (iii).

# Chapter 3

# Scope of the Directive

Thomas Wilhelmsson

## a. Introduction

As described in the previous chapter, the Directive according to Article 1 aims at approximating Member State legislation on 'unfair commercial practices harming consumers' economic interests'. These words are repeated in the basic provision on scope in Article 3(1): 'This Directive shall apply to unfair business-to-consumer commercial practices, as laid down in Article 5, before, during and after a commercial transaction in relation to a product.'

These few words already indicate a very broad scope. The concept 'commercial practices' covers a wide variety of business behaviour. In a general classification of EU consumer protection Directives divided between those that are generally applicable and those related to specific sectors or selling methods,[1] this Directive clearly belongs in the former category.

Even though the wording of the above-mentioned provision appears to indicate a broad (in some senses almost unlimited) scope of the Directive, its purpose and function in the context of the internal market must be assumed to affect its application. The regulation of unfair business practices in the EU is closely connected with an idea of creating workable competition with the consumer as a central actor within the internal market. This brings certain forms of market behaviour of traders, related to market transparency and oppressive activities, into the focus of the provisions. However, such general formulations of purpose are very vague, and in practice they must always be met with different traditions concerning both basic approaches and nuances within the Member States. Therefore the message is rather one of caution: when dealing with national regulations that are not within the remit of the Directive, one should be careful not to carry the effects of the Directive further than it clearly intends. As will be noted several times below, this is important in particular with regard to the maximum harmonisation functions of the Directive. The limitations in this respect are highlighted perhaps in the most striking way by the retention of national competencies regarding issues of taste and decency as well as protection of other societal interests.[2]

---

1   COM(2001) 531 final 4.
2   See below, section d.

The definition of the scope of this Directive is particularly important, even more so than for many other consumer protection Directives. There are two reasons for this exceptional importance. First, the main provision of the Directive is a broad general clause according to which unfair commercial practices shall be prohibited. The only formal limitation of the applicability of this broad fairness test concerning commercial practices lies in the scope of the Directive. These limitations of scope must be taken very seriously as tools for preventing too broad an application of the general clause.

Secondly, the limitation of scope is crucial as the Directive, unlike most other consumer protection Directives, is a maximum harmonisation Directive. Therefore the scope does not merely determine the area in which the Member States are obliged to implement the Directive and create sufficient consumer protection with the help of positive national legislation. It also designates the field in which the Member States are not allowed to improve consumer protection by national provisions that would go further than the Directive. As will be shown in the next section of this paper, the Directive may, by its wording, affect a very broad range of national legislative measures and even a number of different fields of law.[3]

Like other harmonisation Directives, the Directive does not make any distinction between these two functions of the provisions concerning scope. Therefore, the obligations of the Member States – both positively to introduce or to continue a protection of consumers that conforms to the Directive, and negatively to refrain from measures that would give consumers a better protection than the Directive – are bound to the same definition of scope. These two functions will, therefore, not be separately addressed below. However, one cannot rule out that, in details, the application of the provisions on scope could be different, depending on what type of case one is confronted with. The reasons for defending a restrictive application of the scope of the Directive are stronger in relation to its negative function of outlawing provisions of national law than for its positive function of creating sufficient and comprehensive consumer protection in the area. One should not, as mentioned above, be too eager to outlaw specific national consumer protection provisions on the borders of the scope of the Directive with the help of its – after all – very broad and vague general clause. As the potential impact of the Directive, according to its wording, may be very broad, a wide application of its harmonisation effects may create results that were probably not intended when the Directive was adopted.

These comments relate to the perceived broadness of the scope of the Directive. In cases where Member States find the scope too narrow, the fact that the Directive is a harmonisation Directive does not seem to preclude them from enlarging the application of those rules at a national basis. Such rules would be outside the scope

---

3   H. Schulte-Nölke and C.W. Busch, 'Der Vorschlag der Kommission für eine Richtlinie über unlautere Geschäftspraktiken KOM(2003) 356 endg.' (2004) 12 *Zeitschrift für Europäisches Privatrecht* 99, 116. A. Beater, 'Europäisches Recht gegen unlauteren Wettbewerb – Ansatzpunkte, Grundlagen, Entwicklung, Erforderlichkeit' (2003) 11 *Zeitschrift für Europäisches Privatrecht* 11, 40 speaks in this respect about '*das Komplexitätsproblem*'.

of the Directive and so also not bound by the maximum harmonisation rule. For example, if some Member State want to extend the protection offered to consumers in the Directive to protect (small) traders as well, this does not conflict with the Directive. As the Directive does not aim at harmonising the protection of traders,[4] it falls to the Member States to decide how they want to arrange this protection, by specific legislation or by enlarging the scope of the consumer protection legislation.

## b. Collective Protection

Given that the Directive, according to its statement of purpose in Article 1, aims at 'approximating the laws, regulations and administrative provisions of the Member States on unfair commercial practices harming consumers' economic interests', it appears to be geared towards harmonising all kinds of legislation regarding unfair commercial practices, with the exception of those kinds of rules that have expressly been left outside its scope according to Article 3. A closer look at the Directive shows, however, that this cannot be the case.

Some limitations appear to be presumed as a background to the provisions on enforcement and penalties in Article 11 and 13 of the Directive, commented upon later in Chapter 8. The enforcement provision in Article 11 deals with court actions and administrative measures to force a business to cease an unfair commercial practice or to prohibit such practices in the first place, and the penalties referred to in Article 13 are obviously of a criminal or administrative law nature. The Directive therefore primarily appears to cover national provisions with remedies of these and similar kinds.

Obviously the focus of the Directive is on what one could call the collective protection of consumers against unfair commercial practices. This covers consumer protection rules in areas such as unfair competition law, with German law as the typical example of such an approach, and 'market law', as this area is often called in the Nordic countries.[5] In some countries, again, the bulk of the provisions in question are located in administrative law. Penal sanctions against unfair commercial practices[6] can obviously also be classified as criminal law.

Nonetheless, even within areas of law that focus on the collective protection of consumers, the scope of the Directive is not fully clear. For example, some Member States may for some types of commercial activity allow only licensed traders to operate. In such cases, withdrawal of a licence may be used as a means to sanction unfair business behaviour. Are rules and practices related to this sanction within the

---

4   See below, section e.

5   Very influential in establishing this concept was U. Bernitz, *Marknadsrätt* (Stockholm: Jurist– och samhällsvetareförbundets förlag, 1969).

6   The existence of such sanctions in the Member States is documented in R. Schulze and H. Schulte-Nölke, *Analysis of National Fairness Laws Aimed at Protecting Consumers in Relation to Commercial Practices* (June 2003), http://europa.eu.int/comm/consumers/cons_int/safe_shop/fair_bus_pract/green_pap_comm/studies/unfair_practices_en.pdf, 88–9.

scope of the Directive? One may assume this to be the case, even though this type of sanction is not expressly mentioned in the Directive. After all, the Directive does not attempt to thoroughly set out remedies, since the Member States are required, in Article 13, to take 'all the necessary measures' to ensure that the provisions of the Directive are enforced.

Rules on collective protection of consumers against unfair business practices can probably be presumed to fall within the scope of the Directive, even when the remedies are not expressly mentioned in the Directive. However, the picture changes when one looks at possible private law remedies for individual cases, in particular damages claims put forward by individual consumers that have suffered as a result of an unfair business practice.[7] These kinds of remedies are not mentioned at all in the Directive. As it cannot obviously be the purpose of the Directive to eliminate the right of individuals to take such actions, one might assume that the Directive is not meant directly to cover such private law rules on individual protection.

Indeed, this is confirmed in the Preamble to the Directive. The Directive 'is without prejudice to individual actions brought by those who have been harmed by an unfair commercial practice'.[8] This comes after the vague statement in the *Follow-up Communication to the Green Paper on EU Consumer Protection* that '[t]he primary focus should be on unfair practices that cause detriment to the interests of consumers as a whole, rather than individual cases'.[9] The rules concerning individual claims are outside the scope of the Directive.[10]

This limitation of the scope of the Directive, admittedly indirect and hidden, nonetheless means that its harmonising obligations on the Member States do not reach rules that only relate to individual claims. If the Directive is to be 'without prejudice' to such actions, it must mean that Member States are free to adopt – and their courts free to develop – both more and less strict rules on unfair commercial practices, as long as the only sanctions available are related to individual actions, such as damages. As for the particular cases of individual claims based on contract, this follows directly from the specific limitation of scope in Article 3(2), which is commented upon below.

Even though this basic approach appears clear, it introduces various kinds of legal difficulties. For example, if the availability and use of class actions spreads in the EU, should the material rules on which such actions are brought be tied to this Directive, if they deal with commercial practices? On the one hand, if a class action appears as a collection of what in principle could be individual claims for damages, it would follow from what has been said above on individual claims that the action

---

7    On the existence of such rules in the Member States, see Schulze and Schulte-Nölke, *op.cit.*, 88.

8    Recital 9.

9    COM(2002) 289 final 9.

10  H. Gamerith, 'Der Richtlinienvorschlag über unlautere Geschäftspraktiken – Möglichkeiten einer harmonischen Umsetzung' (2005) 51 *Wettbewerb in Recht und Praxis* 391, 402.

would be outside the scope of the Directive. On the other hand, a class action for injunction would obviously fall under the Directive because, according to Article 11, it deals with situations in which persons and organisations may take legal action leading to cessation or prohibition. This obvious anomaly is just one example of the delimitation problems that, by necessity, are attached to broad maximum Directives of the type at hand.

Of course, there are no watertight divisions between collective supervision and individual redress. The fact that the Directive is silent on individual claims, and therefore does not impose any obligations on the Member States to harmonise this area, does not mean that the content of the Directive cannot be used in deciding individual issues. Even though the Directive does not give any answer to the question put at an earlier stage of the preparation – 'whether the most blatant and serious breaches of specific provisions of the framework … directive could give rise to liability for damages proven by individual consumers'[11] – it is obvious that the Directive may have an impact upon the assessment of liability for damages, both in serious and less serious cases. This may be, for example, through influencing the construction of the relevant standards of negligence. However, the extent of this impact, and the conceptual inroads it makes into the rules on private law liability – for example through concepts like negligence, breach of duty, breach of law or breach of *bonos mores* – have to be decided on the basis of national private law. There might also be crossovers between the Directive and contractual liabilities, through contractual concepts like undue influence, which vary in their nature and extent.[12] In other words, within national law nothing prevents using the Directive and its implementing legislation to justify individual claims as well.

## c. Commercial Practices

### (i) Content of the definition

The most important concept delimiting the scope of the Directive is 'commercial practices', mentioned both in Article 1 and Article 3(1). This very vague notion does indicate the fact that non-commercial practices, for example information campaigns concerning political or societal matters, as well as 'pure' charity,[13] fall outside its scope, but it is not particularly informative otherwise.

There is an attempt to clarify the notion by a definition of 'business-to-consumer commercial practices' in Article 2(d), according to which this expression 'means any act, omission, course of conduct or representation, commercial communication

---

11 COM(2002) 289 final 15.

12 The relationship between the Directive and contract law is analysed below, in section f(iii).

13 The very common practice of combining charity with commercial activity, such as selling certain products, may very well fall within the scope of the Directive.

including advertising and marketing, by a trader, directly connected with the promotion, sale or supply of a product[14] to consumers'.

This broad definition does not reduce the vagueness of the scope of the Directive to any considerable extent. It attempts to make clear that advertising and marketing and other commercial communications are core objects in the application of the Directive.[15] However, this was already apparent from the context of what is usually regulated in national laws on issues like this. The Directive obviously focuses on advertising and marketing. Indeed, most of the examples given in Annex I belong to the area of commercial communications.

In addition, however, the Directive applies to 'any act, omission, course of conduct or representation' that has sufficient connection with the promotion, sale or supply by a trader. This leaves the door wide open for various interpretations of the scope of the Directive. This openness, that taken literally allows a very broad application, is particularly hazardous because of the maximum character of the Directive. In principle it gives the European Court of Justice the opportunity to outlaw, on the basis of the general clause, almost any national legislation to which it objects on the basis that it relates to promotion, sale or supply to consumers.[16] As it was probably not the purpose of the Directive to give the Court such a very broad mandate, it seems easy to argue for a restrictive interpretation of the words 'any act, omission, course of conduct or representation … directly connected with the promotion, sale or supply of a product to consumers', at least in cases concerning the continuing validity of specific national provisions at the boundaries of the scope of the Directive. As mentioned in the introduction to this chapter, one should be cautious of pushing the negative harmonising effects of the Directive too far.

Given that the Directive focuses on advertising and marketing, one should probably accept a relatively broad understanding of its scope in relation to these activities. For example, even though the wording of the Directive speaks about advertising 'directly' connected with promotion, sale and supply, one may assume that marketing that attempts to build a positive image of the trader, rather than of any specific product, is within the scope of the Directive, even though a strict interpretation of the wording of Article 2(d) alone might lead to another result.[17]

---

14  On the wide definition of product, see below, section e(ii).

15  The drafters of the Directive have wanted to spell this out explicitly 'to make clear the connection with the regulation on sales promotion and provisions incorporated from the misleading advertising Directive', COM(2003) 356 final 9.

16  Compare, for example, the indicative list related to the potential impact of the Directive on a large variety of pieces of domestic UK law, in the report for the English Department of Trade and Industry by C. Twigg-Flesner, D. Parry, G. Howells and A. Nordhausen, *An Analysis Of The Application And Scope Of The Unfair Commercial Practices Directive* (18 May 2005), http://www.dti.gov.uk/ccp/consultpdf/final_report180505.pdf, 78–87.

17  H. Köhler and T. Lettl, 'Das geltende europäische Lauterkeitsrecht, der Vorschlag für eine EG–Richtlinie über unlautere Geschäftspraktiken und die UWG–Reform' (2003) 49 *Wettbewerb in Recht und Praxis* 1019, 1035.

Other provisions of the Directive indicate its broader scope fairly clearly.[18] After all, the final purpose of image advertising is to promote the products offered by the trader. Image advertising that attempts to picture the trader favourably is a form of market communication in the same way as advertising which recommends his product. If a business, for example, promotes itself as an exceptionally consumer-friendly enterprise, and this is considered misleading, the remedies based on the Directive should be available. Admittedly, in some cases it might be difficult to draw the line between image advertising that falls within the scope of the Directive and communication relating to taste and decency that is left outside.[19]

Another difficulty related to the definition of the Directive is that it places the trader on the supply side, without noting any exceptions. A strict understanding would then leave situations when the trader advertises as a buyer, for example of second-hand goods or antiques, outside the scope of the Directive.[20] But since this would conflict with the purpose of the Directive, and as the definition of 'consumer' indicates a larger scope,[21] such a strict reading is hard to defend.

Another difficult case that one should mention concerns marketing communications that formally appear as media content. Such communications, if they are unfair to consumers, may be the object of remedies based on the Directive.[22] In the *Green Paper on European Union Consumer Protection* the variations in the treatment of important emerging hybrids of this nature – 'advertising practices which challenge traditional print media distinctions between media content and advertising (eg website sponsorship, affiliation, remunerated search tools, use of meta-data and links, referrals and reviews)' – are mentioned as one of the problems requiring a European solution.[23] When applying the Directive to communications in the grey area between media content and marketing, one should of course also bear in mind the limitations that may follow from the human and fundamental rights principles concerning freedom of speech and freedom of the press.

When leaving commercial communications and looking at other acts, omissions, courses of conduct or representations that can amount to unfair commercial practices in the sense of the Directive, one encounters many more difficulties in describing the scope of the Directive. As mentioned above, one should be wary of a too wide application of the Directive. However, even with this in mind, the variety of situations in which the Directive may be applied is broad. As the scope includes acts, omissions and courses of conduct it can comprise almost anything that affects promotion, sale or supply. Examples in Annex I concerning personal behaviour,[24]

---

18  See Article 6(1)(f), and comments below in Chapter 5(b)(v).

19  See below, section d(ii).

20  Köhler and Lettl, *op.cit.*, 1035.

21  See below, section e(ii).

22  See also the provision on advertorials in Annex I (11).

23  COM(2001) 531 final 8.

24  See Annex I (24) on a certain form of aggressive behaviour.

means of contacting consumers[25] and sales organisation[26] are at the more obvious end of the scale. The *Green Paper on European Union Consumer Protection* mentions '[n]ew marketing methods, such as cookies, 'spidering', co-shopping and power shopping'[27] as possible objects of the European rules. Many other examples could be given. Only future case law can, in the end, show what kind of activities the Directive will be applied to.

Against this background it is at first difficult to understand the claim in the Preamble to the Directive that the Directive 'does not affect accepted advertising and marketing practices, such as legitimate product placement, brand differentiation or the offering of incentives'.[28] However, even though this statement appears in a context related to the scope of the Directive, it should not be read as such.[29] It simply means, as indicated in the Preamble, that such practices are acceptable as long as they are not seen to impair the consumer's ability to make an informed decision. If, however, they adversely affect the consumer's decision-making, nothing prevents the courts or supervisory agencies from intervening.[30] Product placement, brand differentiation and the offering of incentives are clearly commercial practices which are covered by the definition of the scope of the Directive.

*(ii) Before and after the transaction*

In the *Green Paper on European Union Consumer Protection* the following divergences between the national rules on business-to-consumer commercial practices are cited as reasons in favour of a European approach to the area: 'Commercial practices related to payment, the subject matter of the contract, price estimates, execution, performance, delivery, complaint-handling and after-sales service (eg premium rate help-lines, commercial guarantees, substitution, repair) also differ.'[31]

Even though some of the practices related to these issues have later been removed from the scope of the Directive, for example by the inclusion of the exception concerning contract law, this extract shows how wide a range of commercial

---

25  See Annex I (25) on personal visits and (26) on solicitations by telephone and other remote media.

26  See Annex I (14) on pyramid promotional schemes.

27  COM(2001) 531 final 8.

28  Recital 6.

29  In the Explanatory Memorandum the drafters of the Directive attempt to 'save' brand recognition and product placement by stating that they are 'normal business practices which are in conformity with custom and usage' and therefore in accordance with professional diligence, COM(2003) 356 final 12. In other words, they are in principle within the scope of the Directive.

30  In fact, product placement in television broadcasts is largely forbidden, which makes the comment in the Preamble still more strange: F. Henning-Bodewig, 'Richtlinienvorschlag über unlautere Geschäftspraktiken und UWG–Reform' (2004) 53 *GRUR* Int. 183, 190.

31  COM(2001) 531 final 7.

practices the drafters of the Directive attempted to address. The Directive should focus not only on pre-contractual commercial practices, that is, practices that appear as relevant with regard to the consumer's decision to acquire the product, but also on practices affecting the later stages of contractual relationships.

This is explicitly stated in Article 3(1) of the Directive, which mentions commercial practices 'before, during and after a commercial transaction'. In this sense the scope of 'commercial practices' is here much broader than in such national legislation that only focuses on marketing. The Directive applies 'equally to unfair commercial practices which occur outside any contractual relationship ... or following the conclusion of a contract and during its execution'.[32]

Given that the assessment of whether a commercial practice is misleading or aggressive is related to whether it is likely to affect the transactional decisions of consumers, the wide temporal scope of the Directive has required a similarly wide definition of 'transactional decision'. According to Article 2(k) of the Directive:

> 'transactional decision' means any decision taken by a consumer concerning whether, how and on what terms to purchase, make payment in whole or in part for, retain or dispose of a product or to exercise a contractual right in relation to the product, whether the consumer decides to act or to refrain from acting.

In other words, the Directive 'applies the same fairness principles to commercial practices before and after the point of sale'.[33] This means that practices related to delivery of the product as well as to the payment of the price are included in the scope of the Directive. The same goes for practices related to complaint-handling[34] and after-sales service.[35] Even the commercial practices that a trader employs when it attempts to enforce its claims can be caught by the fairness standard of the Directive. However, the requirement of the Directive that a practice, in order to be unfair, shall materially distort the economic behaviour of consumers or affect their transactional decisions, makes it uncertain whether such commercial practices that are perceived to be unacceptable, but do not require any decision-making or other behaviour of the consumers, are within the scope of the Directive. Harsh debt enforcement, unfair delaying of complaints and unreasonable disconnecting of utility services can be cited as examples of such practices.

---

32 Recital 13.

33 COM(2003) 356 final 8.

34 In COM(2002) 289 final 18, the drafters foresaw a possibility to create rather far-reaching 'fair' obligations in this respect based on the Directive: 'traders should ensure that they respond quickly and effectively to any complaint and make full redress when justified'. However, later this view seems to have given way to a more modest one, focusing only on unfair practices in this context; see, generally, COM(2003) 356 final 8.

35 Again this is rather related to unfair practices. The issue of whether the trader should be obliged to provide after-sales service is probably not meant to be addressed; see COM(2003) 356 final 8 compared to COM(2002) 289 final 18.

The problem of the proper delimitation of the scope of the Directive is even more acute in relation to the post-contractual than to the pre-contractual stage. The exception in Article 3(2), according to which the Directive is without prejudice to contract law,[36] attempts to solve some of the difficulties. However, as will be shown below, this solution is very vague, and in addition there are plenty of very porous boundaries left elsewhere. For example, the relationship between the application of the Directive on complaint-handling and on enforcement and national rules on procedural law is not analysed at all. This is an area in which one obviously has to employ different approaches to the scope depending on whether the Directive is used 'positively' or 'negatively', as mentioned in the introduction to this chapter. Even though one can 'positively' use the general clause of the Directive against a trader who does not fulfil acceptable commercial standards in complaint-handling or debt recovery, it is unlikely to be acceptable that the Directive – a Directive on unfair commercial practices – could be used 'negatively' as a tool to harmonise national procedural provisions on these subjects.

## d. Harming Consumers' Economic Interests

*(i) Economic interests*

According to Article 1, the Directive aims at approximating the rules on unfair commercial practices 'harming consumers' economic interests'. Even though these words do not appear in Article 3 on scope, they have also been considered relevant in determining the sphere of application of the Directive.

The importance of the phrase at hand relates more to the word 'interests' rather than 'economic', since the latter has to be understood very broadly anyway. The Directive is a device that seeks not only to prevent important individual losses of consumers, but also to prohibit those unfair commercial practices that may only slightly affect each individual consumer, but create considerable gains for the trader. In fact, one of the purposes of collective protection of consumers is to create a remedy when the actual losses of individual consumers are so small that individual mechanisms for redress are not worthwhile to use. 'Harming the consumer economically' should therefore not be understood literally. There has to be some 'economic loss', but its extent can be minor in relation to each individual consumer.

The focus on *consumer* 'interests' means that the Directive is concerned only with measures dealing with those commercial practices that affect consumers in a negative way, in other words with measures that in some sense relate to consumer protection. Negatively, this implies that rules on commercial practices that are issued to protect other societal or individual interests are outside the scope of the Directive.[37] The Directive does not require such rules to be introduced or abolished.

---

36  See more closely below, section f(iii).

37  This is the case even when rules on protection on such other interests are included in the same marketing legislation as the consumer protection provisions, as for example in the

## *(ii) Taste and decency*

The main consequence for the sphere of application of the Directive of the reference to consumers' economic interests in Article 1 is that, as a main rule, 'matters of taste, decency and social responsibility will be outside [its] scope'.[38] According to the Preamble the Directive 'does not address legal requirements related to taste and decency which vary widely among the Member States' and the Member States are therefore able to continue to ban commercial practices on these grounds, regardless of the Directive.[39] The Directive's basic purpose, to address issues of market transparency and oppressive practices, naturally leaves issues of taste and decency, as well as social responsibility, outside its scope. As long as there does not exist a common European understanding of moral questions concerning taste, decency and social responsibility, there is also no basis for harmonisation of this area. The basic idea of a Europe 'united in its diversity' speaks for the continuance of a decentralised approach to this area, even though this approach may be at odds with the demands of the internal market.

Of course, if a practice relating to taste and decency also harms the consumers' economic interest, it can be assessed on the basis of the Directive. The response based on the Directive would, however, relate to the consumers' economic interests, even though '[f]ull account should be taken of the context of the individual case concerned in applying this Directive, in particular the general clauses thereof'.[40] In any event, the fact that consumers' economic interests are also involved in the case does not make it possible to outlaw such national legislation that deals with other matters.

This exception for taste and decency relates to the content of national rules, and not to their legal classification. EU law is usually not concerned with the structure of national laws, and it therefore does not require that its distinction between consumer protection and protection of taste and decency is reflected in the national systems. National consumer protection or unfair competition laws that also cover taste and decency issues do not have to be separated from such issues. Questions of taste and decency dealt with on the basis of national consumer protection or unfair competition law fall outside the scope of the Directive in the same way as specific national rules on such issues.

The line between rules to defend taste and decency and rules issued to protect consumers is not always easy to draw. Sometimes a rule might even fulfil both purposes. On the one hand some may argue that the acceptance of differences

---

Danish Marketing Practices Act that covers ethnic and sexual discrimination issues, and the Finnish Consumer Protection Act that in practice has been extended to cover such issues; see, on gender discrimination, Market Court 1994:7.

38  COM(2003) 356 final 10. The fact that issues of this kind are outside the scope of the Directive may also be read as an indication of how to understand the substantive provisions of the Directive, in particular its general clause; see below, Chapter 4(c).

39  Recital 7.

40  Recital 7.

related to taste and decency should be kept relatively narrow, as it otherwise creates opportunities for Member States to circumvent obligations based on the Directive. On the other hand, one may equally well defend a broader reading of 'legal requirements related to taste and decency', as issues of this kind should be at the core of the cultural autonomy of the Member States. From the point of view of legitimacy the latter approach is preferable. European attempts to harmonise issues that are considered nationally to be matters of taste and decency are seldom well-received. In any event, one may expect that the European Court of Justice will receive difficult cases in which it has to decide whether or not a certain national rule is legitimately connected with a national moral conviction on taste and decency.

Some types of rules self-evidently fall outside the scope of the Directive as being indisputably related to taste and decency. Commercial practices that violate national rules on pornography, on the protection of religious beliefs or on combating racism could be cited as such examples. Pornographic or racist advertisements should not be assessed based on these rules, unless they also harm the consumers' economic interests.

Issues related to gender equality and sexism also belong to this sphere. Although, as mentioned above, in some countries rules on gender equality and sexism in marketing have been included in general marketing legislation, and cases may have been decided on the basis of consumer protection legislation, the issue at stake is not the protection of consumers. Therefore it falls outside the scope of the Directive. Advertisers who want to use half-naked women (or men) in their advertisements, or in other ways use messages that are problematic from a gender equality point of view, may continue to face considerable variation in the rules to be applied in different Member States.[41] Examples of such rules can be found in several Member States.[42]

Other issues that appear to be outside the scope of the Directive are, for example, the assessment of whether and to what extent violent scenes are allowed in advertising.[43] The approach to some of the famous Benetton advertisements, containing pictures, for example, of HIV patients and of dead soldiers, is also basically related to how one understands taste and decency. The variations in the assessments of these advertisements in different parts of Europe[44] would therefore not have been affected by the present Directive.

---

41  The Sex Discrimination Directive does not apply to advertising either (Article 3(3)).

42  See above, section d(i), as well as H.-W. Micklitz and J. Kessler (eds), *Marketing Practices Regulation and Consumer Protection in the EC Member States and the US* (Baden-Baden: Nomos, 2002) 57 (Denmark), 71 (Finland), 196 (Ireland), 260 (the Netherlands), 271 (Portugal), 353 (Spain) and 409 (United Kingdom).

43  Compare, on the acceptance of games that involve 'playing at killing' as being regarded as a public policy issue, Case C–36/02 *Omega Spielhallen– und Automatenaufstellungs– GmBH v Oberbürgermeisterin der Bundesstadt Bonn* [2004] ECR I–9609.

44  The Finnish decision is reported in (1996) 45 *GRUR* Int. 251 and comparative comments with references are given by A. Kur, 'Anmerkung' (1996) 45 *GRUR* Int. 255.

Various specific rules on marketing to children are difficult to classify in this context. Many national rules relate to the credulity of minors in the marketplace and offer legal means to prohibit traders from taking advantage of this. If this is the case, the issue is one of consumer protection and such rules fall under the scope of the Directive (which also explicitly recognises the specific protection needs of children and other vulnerable groups, for example in Article 5(3)). On the other hand there are rules that aim explicitly at protecting the moral and physical wellbeing of children.[45] These appear to belong to the sphere of taste, decency and social responsibility. Rules that, for example, prohibit or restrict the use of advertisements that encourage children towards immoral or dangerous behaviour are therefore probably outside the scope of the Directive.[46]

This is again an area in which the maximum character of the Directive will certainly cause many problems of interpretation, as it is not always easy to distinguish provisions that are aimed at protecting the moral and physical wellbeing of children from those protecting them as small consumers in the marketplace. This is shown already by the 'Television without Frontiers' Directive, in which Article 16 asserts that '[t]elevision advertising shall not cause moral and physical detriment to minors and shall therefore comply will the following criteria', but then starts to enumerate examples of typical market-related protection.[47] Because of such uncertainties it is not quite clear, for example, how the Unfair Commercial Practices Directive relates to general and specific bans on marketing to children.[48] On the one hand one could say that this is a matter of taste and decency and therefore should not be affected by the Directive. On the other hand, the Preamble of the Directive indicates otherwise, as in passing it includes the words 'without imposing an outright ban on advertising directed at children'.[49]

It is not only the content of commercial communications that can offend taste and decency. Some sales methods may also be banned on such grounds. As a comment to this limitation of the scope of the Directive, the Preamble notes that '[c]ommercial practices such as, for example, commercial solicitation in the streets, may be undesirable in Member States for cultural reasons'.[50] This important example shows

---

45  See also the proposed Amendment 28 at the Parliament's first reading (Doc. 8492/04) on this issue. Mentioned positively in the Statement of the Council's reasons (Doc. 11630/2/04 REV 2 ADD 1, at 6).

46  As to physical safety and health, this conclusion is supported also by the delimitation of scope mentioned in Article 3(3) and commented upon in the Preamble, Recital 9.

47  At least Article 16(a) and (b).

48  On the Swedish ban under the 'Television without Frontiers' Directive, see Joined Cases C–34/95, 35 and 36/95 *Konsumentombudsmannen v de Agostini & TV Shop* [1997] ECR I–3843. As the European Court of Justice left it to the Swedish court to make the concrete decision whether this ban was conflicting with the Treaty, the Swedish Market Court upheld the ban (Market Court 2000:4).

49  Recital 18.

50  Recital 7. Countries that may want to uphold such a prohibition are, for example, Germany and Denmark.

that the limitation of the scope of the Directive to rules and cases that relate to the economic interests of consumers may also in the future allow relatively wide variation of the national rules on commercial practices.[51] A large variety of taste and decency issues are still kept firmly in the hands of national rule makers.

### (iii) Protection of other societal interests

Even though mostly only issues of taste and decency (often understood very broadly) have been commented upon in relation to the delimitation of scope at hand, some other kinds of issues appear to fall outside the scope of 'consumers' economic interests' as well. The reference in the Preamble to 'cultural reasons' appears to be a far wider concept than 'taste and decency'. Regulations concerning advertising and other commercial practices that aim to protect features of the national culture beyond the requirements of taste and decency are also left outside the scope of the Directive. Already, at an early stage of the preparation of the Directive, the Commission signalled that issues related to 'pluralism' and to 'the protection of culture' should be excluded from its scope.[52]

This means that Member States' rules on language in commercial communications that primarily aim at safeguarding the position of the national language or of a recognised minority language cannot be set aside using the Directive.[53] On the other hand, if language requirements are issued as a means to improve transparency in relation to consumers, they obviously fall within the ambit of the Directive.[54] As the purpose of language rules is not always clearly expressed, and as such rules sometimes even may be adopted for both of the reasons mentioned, this may result in difficult legal problems in drawing the borderline between the acceptable and the forbidden.[55] Again, these difficulties are connected with the decision to make the Directive a maximum harmonisation Directive.

As yet another example of a type of rule, the purpose of which is to cater for other societal interests than consumer protection, one could mention rules related to the protection of the environment. National provisions against commercial

---

51　Advertising in schools may, for example, be deemed culturally unacceptable; a Portuguese limitation of such advertising is mentioned by Micklitz and Kessler, *op.cit.*, 271.

52　COM(2001) 531 final 13.

53　But may of course be in conflict with the basic freedoms of the Treaty; see the Piageme doctrine elaborated first in Case C–369/89 *Piageme and others v BVBA Peeters* [1991] ECR I–2971, according to which '[t]he obligation exclusively to use the language of the linguistic region constitutes a measure having equivalent effect to a quantitative restriction on imports, prohibited by Article 30 of the Treaty' (at 16). See also the concretisation in Piageme II, Case C–85/94 *Groupement des Producteurs, Importateurs et Agents Généraux d'Eaux Minérales Etrangères, VZW (Piageme) and others v Peeters NV* [1995] ECR I–2955.

54　See more in detail below, Chapter 5(b)(iii) and 5(c)(ii).

55　Illuminating is the analysis of the relationship between the French language law (*Loi Toubon*) and European law in H.-W. Micklitz, 'Zum Recht des Verbrauchers auf die eigene Sprache' (2003) 11 *Zeitschrift für Europäisches Privatrecht* 635.

communications that encourage behaviour harming the environment[56] fall outside the scope of the Directive. The treatment of misleading statements on the 'environmental friendliness' of products is more difficult to judge. On the one hand, if consumers' economic interests are understood sufficiently broadly, it should be possible to condemn such statements with the help of the Directive, as they most certainly may affect the transactional decisions of some consumers. On the other hand, if the main purpose of a strict national provision concerning such statements is to care for the environment rather than for the consumers, it would be against the delimitation of the scope of the Directive to outlaw such a provision with the help of the Directive. The maximum character of the Directive, in other words, leads to difficult problems of interpretation in this context as well.

### e. Business-to-Consumer Practices

*(i) Introduction*

According to Article 3(1) of the Directive, it applies only to 'business-to-consumer commercial practices', that is, in the words of Article 2(d), activities of a trader that are 'directly connected with the promotion, sale or supply of a product to consumers'. Business-to-business commercial practices – as well as practices between private persons, which can barely be called commercial at all – are left outside the scope of the Directive.

In other words, the Directive does not attempt to harmonise national rules on unfair commercial practices insofar as they only relate to unfairness between traders. The Directive 'neither covers nor affects the national laws on unfair commercial practices which harm only competitors' economic interests or which relate to a transaction between traders'.[57] This division between rules on consumer protection on the one hand, and rules on the protection of business customers and competitors on the other reflects the situation in some Member States, but is alien to others.[58] This distinction has received much criticism, particularly in German legal literature.[59] It reflects the division of competencies between different Directorates General within the Commission, but also on a deeper level differing views on the character of unfair business practices regulation and whether it forms part of consumer protection law or unfair competition law. It may be a temporary solution, as the Commission has the task of examining the need for EU legislation on unfair competition beyond the

---

56  For an example from the Netherlands, see Micklitz and Kessler, *op.cit.*, 261.

57  Recital 6.

58  The variations in this respect are described as a barrier to trade in the Green Paper, COM(2001) 531 final 6. On the national variations, see more closely, for example, Schulze and Schulte-Nölke, *op.cit.*, 11.

59  Schulte-Nölke and Busch, *op.cit.*, 101; C.W. Busch, 'Ein europäischer Rechtsrahmen für das Lauterkeitsrecht?' (2004) 4 *The European Legal Forum* 91, 93, both with further references.

sphere of the present Directive.[60] In fact the Directive already notes that commercial practices 'which directly harm consumers' economic interests ... indirectly harm the economic interests of legitimate competitors'.[61]

The delimitation of the sphere of application of the Directive to business-to-consumer practices is different from the approach used in its predecessor, the Misleading Advertising Directive. The latter covered misleading advertising and (after a later amendment of the Directive) comparative advertising that harmed both consumers' and traders' interests. Therefore the Misleading Advertising Directive has not been repealed with the adoption of the Unfair Commercial Practices Directive. It has been left in force with regard to advertising which misleads traders, but not consumers.[62] For comparative advertising a more 'complete' form of regulation still remains in the Misleading Advertising Directive. This has been achieved, however, by including in it a reference to the Unfair Commercial Practices Directive in cases where comparative advertising is misleading to consumers.[63] It is therefore also the case that the assessment of whether a piece of comparative advertising harms the interests of consumers has to be done on the basis of the Unfair Commercial Practices Directive.

Undoubtedly these solutions have left EU law with a somewhat complicated and confusing structure that is not very easily accessible to the outsider. There are three pieces of legislation with different scopes:

- The broad Unfair Commercial Practices Directive, covering only business-to-consumer relationships;
- The narrower provisions on misleading advertising in the Misleading Advertising Directive, covering only business-to-business relationships; and
- The specific provisions on comparative advertising in the Misleading Advertising Directive covering both business-to-business and business-to-consumer relationships (but with a cross-reference to the Unfair Commercial Practices Directive with regard to the latter).

*(ii) Definition of consumer*

For the purposes of determining the scope of the Unfair Commercial Practices Directive it contains, in Article 2(a), a definition of the consumer concept: '"consumer" means any natural person who, in commercial practices covered by this Directive, is acting for purposes which are outside his trade, business, craft or profession'.

---

60 Recital 8. In the first consultation round only two Member States wanted the Directive to cover also business-to-business relationships, COM(2002) 289 final 9.

61 Recital 6.

62 The Unfair Commercial Practices Directive Article 14(1), containing an amendment to Article 1 of the Misleading Advertising Directive. See also the Unfair Commercial Practices Directive, Recital 6.

63 The Unfair Commercial Practices Directive Article 14(3), containing an amendment to Article 3a of the Misleading Advertising Directive.

This definition was intended to reproduce the standard definition found in many other consumer protection Directives.[64] These are not, however, completely identical. Whilst the first Directives, such as the Doorstep Selling Directive and the first Consumer Credit Directive, used the phrase 'trade or profession' when enumerating activities that were outside the scope of protection, in the Unfair Contract Terms Directive this was extended to cover 'trade, business or profession'. In the Unfair Commercial Practices Directive yet another word has been added to the list, namely 'craft'. Just as the first extension was not understood to reflect any difference in content,[65] the same can be said concerning the addition of 'craft'. In any event it simply spells out what was already implicit in the definition. The basic message is the same: when a person acts in a professional capacity[66] for an economic purpose, that person is not covered by the consumer protection rules.

The definition is basically a negative one. The only positively worded requirement is that the consumer has to be a natural person. In principle, all practices directed towards legal persons, even if they consist of consumer-like persons (such as associations of consumers), are outside the scope of the Directive,[67] as are also businesses acquiring goods for the use of their staff only.[68] In the context of a collective measure such as the Unfair Commercial Practices Directive, this delimitation causes few problems, as it is difficult to imagine very many situations in which a certain practice only relates to such a consumer-like legal person without at the same time affecting 'real' consumers, and therefore already falling within the scope of the Directive. If problems do arise, as the scope of the Directive cannot be the object of maximum harmonisation,[69] nothing prevents Member States from expanding the scope of protection to cover such 'consumer-like' legal persons as well.

As a negative definition, the definition of 'consumer' does not describe when a person is acting as a consumer, but rather only when the person is not acting as such. It does not expressly tie the application of the Directive to activities related to 'consumption' in any limited sense. The range of activities that fall under the consumer concept is therefore broad – necessarily so. A person is acting as a

---

64  COM(2003) 356 final 9.

65  G. Howells and T. Wilhelmsson, *EC Consumer Law* (Aldershot: Ashgate, 1997) 3.

66  This can even be so when a concrete transaction within this capacity is not commonly performed by him and therefore not covered by his professional experience; see, on the Doorstep Selling Directive, Case C–361/89 *Patrice di Pinto* [1991] ECR I–1189. If a person concludes a contract with a view to pursuing a trade or profession in the future, he is also not deemed to be a consumer; see Case C–269/95 *Francesco Benincasa v Dentalkit Srl* [1997] ECR I–3767. However, as the example concerning pyramid selling in the Annex I (14) shows, one should in the present context obviously understand this delimitation in a narrow way.

67  However, the definitions of natural and legal persons may vary. For example, whilst in the United Kingdom a partnership would be seen as a natural person, on the Continent it would rather be classified as a legal person.

68  See, on automatic drink dispensers, Joined Cases C–541/99 and C–542/99 *Cape Snc v Idealservice Srl* and *Idealservice MN RE Sas v OMAI Srl* [2001] ECR I–9049.

69  See above, section a.

consumer both when that person acquires products for himself or herself and when the products are acquired for the family or to be given as gifts, regardless of the reason for the acquisition, as long as it is not connected with professional economic activity.

Consumer activities are also not restricted to 'products' in the literal sense only. Article 2(c) of the Directive explicitly states that the word 'product' in the Directive means 'any goods or service including immovable property, rights and obligations'.

Given that the word 'product' is defined so broadly, and since the definition does not contain any reference to 'consumption', it appears that also, for example, investment activities are included, as long as they are not related to business activity.[70] The marketing of investment opportunities to individual persons would therefore be within the scope of the Directive.[71] When the Preamble notes that the Directive does not cover 'commercial communication aimed at investors, such as annual reports and corporate promotional literature',[72] this statement is obviously based on an assumption that the material mentioned is directed mainly at professional investors. As far as communication on investment focuses on individual non-professionals, there is nothing in the Directive that would preclude its application to relationships between traders and private investors. It should be noted, however, that Member States, according to Article 3(9), have the right to impose stricter rules than the Directive in the area of 'financial services'.[73]

The definition of 'consumer' in the Directive is not restricted to situations in which the consumer acquires something. Even though the definition of 'business-to-consumer commercial practices' might indicate otherwise,[74] one may assume that 'consumer' in this context includes a non-professional person that sells something to a trader. For example, an advertisement from a trader wanting to buy second-hand

---

70  See also on the Brussels Convention (the Judgments Convention), the English High Court decision *Standard Bank London v D. and S. Apostolakis* [2000] International Litigation Procedure 766, according to which private investors who enter into foreign exchange contracts can be regarded as consumers if they are not engaged in trade. Compare, however, the Greek court decision *Standard Bank of London v Apostolakis* [2003] International Litigation Procedure 29.

71  This area is partially covered also by the provisions relating to investment services in Directive 2004/39/EC on markets in financial instruments amending Council Directives 85/611/EEC and 93/6/EEC and Directive 2000/12/EC of the European Parliament and of the Council and repealing Council Directive 93/22/EEC, OJ 2004 L145/1 that applies both to consumer and professional clients (Article 4(1)(10)). In particular the provisions on conduct of business, including the providing of information and the issuing of marketing communications, in Article 19 of the Directive directly relate to practices covered by the Unfair Commercial Practices Directive as well. As explained later in section f(v) of this chapter, specific EU provisions like the Directive mentioned here prevail over the Unfair Commercial Practices Directive with regard to the specific aspects regulated in those provisions.

72  Recital 7.

73  See below, section f(ix).

74  See above, section c(i).

goods from individuals is within the scope of the Directive. Even a natural person concluding a contract of guarantee may be defined as a consumer in this context.[75]

There has been much discussion on the issue of the extent to which consumer protection Directives are applicable when a person acquires products both for individual and professional use, and at least in situations where the person is acting 'primarily outside his trade or profession', application of EU consumer protection law has been recommended.[76] However, a somewhat more restrictive view of the application of the consumer provisions has been recently adopted by the European Court of Justice in a case concerning purchase of materials for a building partially used for business by a farmer.[77] Yet in relation to a collective measure like the Unfair Commercial Practices Directive, this discussion is not as acute as when applying rules that require the individual contractual relationship to be properly classified. In most cases practices that relate to products to be used both professionally and by consumers also have a sufficiently strong connection with 'pure' consumer interests to be included in the scope of the Directive. The decisive issue here is usually not the purpose of the individual contract, but rather the composition of the group towards which the practice is directed or which it affects. This issue will be analysed in more detail below at the end of this section.

### *(iii) Definition of trader*

The party in a business-to-consumer commercial practice whose activity is to be scrutinised on the basis of the Directive is described as a trader. This concept is defined in Article 2(b) of the Directive: '"trader" means any natural or legal person who, in commercial practices covered by this Directive, is acting for purposes relating to his trade, business, craft or profession and anyone acting in the name of or on behalf of a trader'.

This definition mirrors the definition of 'consumer' above. Persons who act in a professional capacity for an economic purpose and are therefore not consumers appear to be traders if one takes the wording of the Directive literally. Obviously this cannot have been the intended meaning, however, despite the identical wordings. There are large areas of activities – even outside the private sphere – that are neither consumer not trader activities. The best example is of course a person acting as an employee, as he does not act within 'his' trade. In his capacity as employee a person is neither 'consumer' nor 'trader'.

---

75 However, as the European Court of Justice has noted with regard to the Doorstep Selling Directive, 'a contract of guarantee concluded by a natural person who is not acting in the course of his trade or profession does not come within the scope of the directive where it guarantees repayment of a debt contracted by another person who, for his part, is acting within the course of his trade or profession', Case C–45/96 *Bayerische Hypotheken– und Wechselbank AG v Edgar Dietzinger* [1998] ECR I–1199.

76 See, for example, Howells and Wilhelmsson, *op.cit.*, 3.

77 Case C–464/01 *Gruber v BayWA AG* [2005] ECR I–439.

The definition of 'trader' includes both natural and legal persons. In addition, the activities of an individual person can be 'professional' and 'commercial' in the sense of the Directive. How to define the minimum requirements of commercial activity is an open question. A 'one-shot' seller, who is not otherwise commercially active, does not act as a trader, but it is not clear how ongoing the activity must be in order legally to make that person a trader in the sense of the Directive.

In practice, the most difficult and important issue in this context is probably how to apply the Directive to activities of public bodies. As long as they work in the marketplace in similar ways to private traders, it is clear that the Directive applies. The most problematic issues seem to arise when public bodies perform activities that might also be offered by private traders – such as educational and healthcare services – but do it based on public service rather than on market logic. In such situations one might see the 'commercial' nature of the activity as the key criterion. If the activity is not 'commercial', the practices of those performing the activity cannot be called 'commercial'. Of course the content of such a rather conceptual delimitation must be highly dependent on the various traditions of public services in various Member States. In the European setting one may, however, expect a relatively broad construction of the concept of 'trader' in this context.[78]

As it is self-evident that the activity of a 'trader' covers activities conducted on behalf of the trader of all individuals within the organisation, such as employees and directors, one may assume that the end of the definition, 'and anyone acting in the name of or on behalf of a trader', is intended to extend the responsibility of traders beyond the acts of these individuals. In other words, even activities of individual persons who are not themselves traders, nor employed by traders, are within the scope of the Directive, if those activities are performed in the name of or on behalf of a trader. This makes it clear, for example, that arrangements related to home-party selling are within the scope of the Directive.

The last part of the definition may also refer to agents of various kinds, as well as to providers of advertising services. However, from the point of view of the scope of the Directive, agents such as these do not need to have been mentioned, since they are traders themselves and therefore within the ambit of the Directive. The purpose of the last part of the definition may therefore rather be connected with responsibility than scope. It may have been added simply to indicate that the trader in whose interest a certain advertising or other activity is performed bears the primary responsibility for the activity, even where it is performed by an independent agent.

---

78 See, on the wide application of the Product Liability Directive, in the context of public medical service, Case C–203/99 *Henning Veedfald v Århus Amtskommune* [2001] ECR I–3569. Here the European Court of Justice explicitly concluded that 'Article 7(c) of the Directive is to be interpreted as meaning that the exemption from liability where an activity has no economic or business purpose does not extend to the case of a defective product which has been manufactured and used in the course of a specific medical service which is financed entirely from public funds and for which the patient is not required to pay any consideration' (at 22).

## (iv) Business-to-consumer practice

In the context of collective regulation the problems of scope relate less to the definitions of consumers and traders as such, but more to the required relationship between the practice and (a group of) consumers. What should the relationship be between a business practice and consumers in order to be classified as a business-to-consumer practice?

As mentioned above, the Directive, in its Preamble, mentions two groups of practices that fall outside its scope insofar as they affect business-to-business relationships: practices that relate to transactions between traders and practices that harm only competitors' interests,[79] such as the revealing of trade secrets and certain cases of slavish imitation.[80] In these instances the practices, whilst unfair, do not harm the interests of consumers in the manner required by Article 1 of the Directive.

In many cases, however, a practice may harm both other traders – be they potential customers or competitors – and consumers. If this is the case, the practice falls under the scope of the Directive as far as consumers are concerned. If practices such as misleading advertising 'affect both consumer and competitors' interests'[81] the Directive is applicable with regard to the consumer interest.

As the purpose of the Directive relates to the protection of consumers, 'consumer interest' is a natural starting point when discussing the delimitation of its scope. The words 'affect consumer interests' cited above reflect succinctly the basic idea of this delimitation. As long as a practice affects consumer interests to a sufficient degree, it is within the scope of the Directive, even though it may affect the interests of business customers or competitors as well.

In this assessment the focus appears to be on the issue of whether consumers in reality can be assumed to be affected by the practice, rather than on which groups the trader aims to target through the practice. There is no indication in the Directive of a subjective approach that would emphasise the trader's intended purpose as a decisive criterion.

In determining more concretely whether the practice affects consumers, issues such as the nature of the product, as well as the nature of the communication channel, can be decisive. The former is obviously in many cases the most important criterion in this context. If the product, for example, is a lorry, and rarely used by consumers, practices relating to the selling of this product are not business-to-consumer practices. However, if more than a few consumers[82] use or start to use a certain type of product

---

79 Preamble, Recital 6.

80 COM(2002) 289 final 9.

81 COM(2002) 289 final 9.

82 It seems self-evident that one should not focus here on the proportion of consumer customers, but rather on absolute figures. This can easily be demonstrated by a few examples. Even though the overwhelming amount of some food products – for example, wheat-flour – is used by the food industry, nobody would doubt that it is (also) a consumer product. And even though almost all concrete is used by the building industry, marketing of smaller bags of concrete may very well be a business-to-consumer practice (the example is taken from A.

the situation becomes different. A practice that reaches this group of consumers – for example, marketing in a medium that reaches the general public – would affect consumer interests and fall within the scope of the Directive.

As to the communication channel, the marketing of a product used by consumers through a medium that reaches the general public normally indicates that the measure affects consumers, whilst marketing through, for example, a professional or trade journal usually falls outside the scope of the Directive. It is easy, however, to imagine exceptions from such a starting point: the marketing of private cars in a professional journal could probably be caught by the Directive, as at least some of the readers would be affected by these adverts in their capacity as 'consumers'.

The practice should affect the consumer interest in some direct way in order to be covered by the Directive. It is not sufficient that it affects consumers only indirectly, through the impact on the interests of another trader. Competition law is said to have as its purpose – indirectly – to improve the position of consumers, but the Unfair Commercial Practices Directive 'does not deal with antitrust matters'.[83] Anti-competitive agreements, abuse of a dominant position, mergers and acquisitions, boycotts and refusals to supply that may all, even strongly, affect consumer interests in a negative way, fall outside the scope of this Directive.[84]

### f. Some Explicit Additional Delimitations

*(i) Introduction*

The Directive, in Article 3, contains an extensive enumeration of issues that are not covered by the Directive. The logic of this list is not very easy to grasp; it has grown through additions made during different stages of the Directive's preparation. As will be noted below, some of the exceptions are fairly self-evident in the light of what has been said already, whilst other exceptions mentioned in the background documents are not explicitly set out in the Article.[85]

Some additional delimitations are mentioned only in the Preamble, and their effects are therefore far from clear. This is the case in particular with the delimitation concerning intellectual property rights that will be discussed first below, before turning to the enumeration of exceptions in Article 3.

---

Kivivuori, C.G. af Schultén, L. Sevón and J. Tala, *Kuluttajansuoja* (Helsinki: Tammi, 1978) 28 on Finnish consumer protection law).

83   COM(2003) 356 final 10. See also the Preamble of the Directive, Recital 9.

84   COM(2003) 356 final 10.

85   In this context one must mention also the rather mysterious reference to *international private law* in the Explanatory Memorandum. According to this '[t]he Directive is without prejudice to the application of rules governing international private law provisions in the fields which it does not approximate', COM(2003) 356 final 11. Yet is it not self-evident that the Directive is without prejudice to any rules that fall outside its scope?

Less problematic in this respect is the statement in the Preamble of the Directive that *competition rules* and the national rules implementing them are among those rules to which the Directive is 'without prejudice'.[86] As mentioned above, this appears to follow from the fact that only those measures that directly affect consumers are within the ambit of the Directive.[87]

### (ii) Intellectual property rights

The most prominent example of cases that are not mentioned in Article 3 concerns intellectual property rights. In the Preamble, amongst other examples that are then enumerated in Article 3, it is expressly stated that the Directive is without prejudice to rules on intellectual property rights; this goes both for Community and national rules.[88]

Even though this exception might be obvious, its extent is far from clear. As in most Member States national law has considered at least some forms of violation of intellectual property rights to the detriment of competitors, such as slavish imitation, as being within the ambit of unfair practices law,[89] the misuse of such rights to the detriment of consumers may be affected by this branch of the law as well. The Unfair Commercial Practices Directive is unlikely to be intended to have a more restricted sphere of application in this context than previous national laws. This has been confirmed in the final version of the Directive. In Annex I on commercial practices which are under all circumstances considered unfair was added an explicit provision on imitation used to mislead the consumer.[90]

Also, such intellectual property rights as trademarks and registered names can be used to mislead consumers. If a trader acts in this manner, a reference in passing concerning the exclusion of intellectual property rights from the scope of the Directive that is only made in the Preamble should not prevent the application of the Directive.[91]

### (iii) Contract law

The first delimitation mentioned expressly in the Article on scope is the exception concerning contract law in Article 3(2), according to which the Directive 'is without prejudice to contract law and, in particular, to the rules on the validity, formation

---

86  Recital 9.

87  See above, section e(iv).

88  Recital 9.

89  Schulze and Schulte-Nölke, *op.cit.*, 92.

90  Annex I (13).

91  In Finnish practice the Market Court has forbidden a firm to use its misleading registered name (in translation Bankruptcy Liquidation Sales Ltd) in marketing to consumers, Market Court 1980:3. On using marketing legislation against misleading trademarks in Swedish law, see L. Pehrson, *Varumärken från konsumentsynpunkt* (Stockholm: LiberFörlag, 1981) 408.

or effect of a contract'. The need for this provision is not completely clear. The provision seems partially self-evident, and also partially misleading.

As mentioned above in this chapter[92] the Directive is not concerned with individual claims. Already for this reason contract law, insofar as it regulates individual disputes between traders and consumers, is outside the scope of the Directive. The Directive does not directly affect such disputes. In this sense the explicit exception concerning contract law is self-evident, but at the same time too narrow, because it should cover non-contractual damages as well.

However, collective supervision of contract terms is another matter, and indeed the use of unfair contract terms could, in principle, be deemed an unfair commercial practice under the Directive. The rules and remedies to be used in such cases are primarily related to the Unfair Contract Terms Directive. As that is a minimum Directive, it might be caught by the deferred harmonisation provision in Article 3(5) of the Unfair Commercial Practices Directive, if there were not a contract law exception. In this sense, the provision in Article 3(2) has a practical role to play, in stating that the new Directive does not affect the Unfair Contract Terms Directive and national rules within the scope of the latter.

How far the impact of the provision can be extended is, however, far from clear. Collective supervision of contract terms in the sense of the Unfair Contract Terms Directive can easily be classified as 'contract law', at least if this term is understood in a broad sense. However, when, for example, certain rights related to a contract are sanctioned by criminal law rather than private law remedies, one may rightfully ask whether this is still 'contract law' and outside the scope of the Unfair Commercial Practices Directive. The cautious approach towards extending the maximum effects of the Directive too far, advocated in the introduction to this chapter, would speak in favour of a positive answer.

In addition to being partially self-evident, the delimitation concerning contract is misleading, if it is understood literally, as in the Explanatory Memorandum, where it states the Directive 'has no bearing' on the formation, validity and effects of contracts.[93] Indirectly, through contract law principles, it may very well have a bearing on contractual claims, irrespective of the delimitation in the Directive. There may very well be crossover effects from the content of the Directive to contract law.[94] For example, the use of contractual principles concerning illegal or immoral contracts may be affected by the content of the Directive. If certain behaviour on the part of the trader leading to a contract is deemed to be illegal according to the Directive, this may be relevant in a contract law dispute, as it may trigger the use

---

92  Section b.

93  COM(2003) 356 final 10.

94  The difficulties of drawing a strict borderline between contract law and unfair business practices law is clearly demonstrated by the *Compilation of national laws* made in preparing the Directive, published on http://europa.eu.int/comm/consumers/cons_int/safe_shop/fair_bus_pract/index_en.htm; see question VII B: How does your legal system delimit between contract law and unfair commercial practices generally?

of an applicable national rule concerning the invalidity of illegal contracts. Other possible crossovers between the Directive and contract law related to contract law concepts such as undue influence could be mentioned as well. Contract law rules on the liability for marketing statements are also relevant in this context. The extent of possible contract law effects of this nature is of course today a matter of national contract law.[95]

The possibility of such effects is strongly enhanced by the wide temporal sphere of application of the Directive. Given that it also covers commercial practices which take place 'after a commercial transaction' it directly affects the understanding of what is proper behaviour of a trader within a contractual relationship with a consumer. It is impossible to assume that this understanding could have no crossover effect whatsoever on the interpretation of what the contract requires.

The Directive offers a very telling example of this. Annex I mentions as a commercial practice which in all circumstances is considered unfair, '[r]equiring a consumer who wishes to claim on an insurance policy to produce documents which could not reasonably be considered relevant as to whether the claim was valid ... in order to dissuade a consumer from exercising his contractual rights'.[96] Obviously, if an insurance company were to include in the insurance terms a clause demanding the consumer to produce certain documents that the company could not ask for according to this provision of the Directive, it would be rather natural to consider this clause to be invalid. The provision in the Annex would be rather inefficient, if it were simply to have collective consequences which could nonetheless be abrogated in individual cases by a valid contract clause. In principle, of course, the effects of the provision could be limited to remedies such as injunctions, but in many Member States it would most likely affect the private law validity of the clause as well.

Also, other concrete decisions on unfair commercial practices in the post-transactional stage may affect the validity of contract terms in similar ways. If some post-contractual behaviour is considered to be forbidden according to the Unfair Commercial Practices Directive, a contract term that allows or prescribes such behaviour would in many Member States be considered invalid. These crossover effects of the Directive can be related to various national law provisions on illegality, fairness and the like.

In other words, the Directive, and in particular its application on post-transactional issues, may very well affect contract law, despite intentions to the contrary. As the post-transactional scope and relevance of the Directive in general is very vague and unclear, it is at this stage impossible to foresee more concretely the effects that the Directive will have in this respect.

---

95 However, as to liability for marketing, see the Consumer Sales Directive, Article 2(4).

96 Annex I (27).

*(iv) Health and safety*

According to Article 3(3) the Directive is without prejudice to Community or national rules relating to the health and safety aspects of products. The offering of unhealthy or unsafe goods and services is not an unfair commercial practice within the scope of the Directive, but can be remedied with the help of product safety legislation, such as the General Product Safety Directive, and other similar measures. Important European legislation with an impact on health and safety issues can also be found in the areas of foodstuffs and cosmetics regulation.[97]

In addition, issues relating to public health, such as the combating of epidemics and other diseases, as well as public security issues,[98] are outside the scope of the Directive, even when the measures affect commercial practices. The Preamble to the Directive explicitly states that the Member States may, in the future and within their territory, 'retain or introduce restrictions and prohibitions ... for example in relation to alcohol, tobacco or pharmaceuticals' and that this is possible 'wherever the trader is based'.[99] The highly topical issue of combating obesity and the over-consumption of junk food, in particular among children, might also be viewed as an issue of health policy which would fall under the health and safety exception; this would widen the scope for national measures regulating the advertising of such food.

This exception does not mean that health and safety issues are altogether outside the scope of the Directive. Misleading health claims, for example in advertising and other marketing, can be termed, under the provisions of the Directive, as misleading commercial practices.[100] In Annex I, '[f]alsely claiming that a product is able to cure illnesses, dysfunction or malformations' is mentioned as one of the commercial practices which are under all circumstances considered unfair according to the Directive.[101]

This means that the Unfair Commercial Practices Directive covers an area that might be covered by product safety legislation as well, because such legislation often also addresses misleading claims and misleading omission of information.[102] As far as the product safety legislation is Community legislation, formally there is

---

97  In the context of commercial communication one should mention in particular here the Directive 2000/13/EC on the approximation of the laws of the Member States relating to the labelling, presentation and advertising of foodstuffs, OJ 2000 L109/29, as well as Directive 76/768/EEC on the approximation of the laws of the Member States relating to cosmetic products, OJ 1976 L262/169.

98  See also the proposed Amendment 28 at the Parliament's first reading (Doc. 8492/04) on this issue, as well as the reference to it in the Statement of the Council's reasons (Doc. 11630/2/04 REV 2 ADD 1, at 6).

99  Recital 9.

100  COM(2003) 356 final 10, mentioning as an example 'a product which claims to cause hair to grow back on bald heads but does not do so'.

101  Annex I (17).

102  See, for example, the General Product Safety Directive, Article 5(1) and 8(1)(b) as well as in particular Directive 87/357/EEC on the approximation of the laws of the Member

no problem as the situation may be solved with the help of the *lex specialis* provision in Article 3(4), analysed below. However, in relation to national legislation of the same kind, the maximum character of the Directive may cause problems that cannot be solved in an acceptable way without accepting that the 'positive' scope of the Directive is wider than its 'negative' scope, as suggested in the introduction to this chapter. 'Positively' it is clear that the Directive, and the legislation based on it, ought to be applied to misleading health claims in the marketing of products that may have an impact on health and safety. On the other hand, however, if there are stricter rules than the Directive in national product safety or health legislation concerning such marketing, they should not 'negatively' be struck down with reference to the maximum character of the Unfair Commercial Practices Directive, because they may be needed to support health policies that are intended to be outside the scope of the Directive.

And what if there are stricter general national rules on health claims than the provisions concerning misleading claims of the Directive? There may, for example, exist in national law a general rule – perhaps even based on the application of the national general clause – according to which claims that a product may cure diseases should always be considered unfair, if they cannot be very clearly substantiated.[103] Should such a claim not be outside the scope of the Unfair Commercial Practices Directive in its negative sense, as it is 'relating to the health and safety aspects of products', and should the national rule therefore avoid assessment of its compatibility with Article 12 of the Directive that only would allow the courts to require the trader to furnish evidence concerning the health claim, if such a requirement appears appropriate?[104] Or should one rather – in line with the behaviour of the European Court of Justice in matters related to foodstuffs and cosmetics[105] – apply a relatively narrow determination of what is a health policy-related issue, and therefore include provisions on health claims of this nature within the maximum harmonisation scope of the Unfair Commercial Practices Directive? Partial maximum harmonisation is a difficult game.

---

States concerning products which, appearing to be other than they are, endanger the health or safety of consumers, OJ 1987 L192/49.

103   In Finland marketing to the sick should, according to both legislative documents and case law, be assessed very strictly; see T. Wilhelmsson, *Konsumentskyddet i Finland* (Helsingfors: Juristförbundets förlag, 1989) 126.

104   See more closely on the issue of burden of proof below, Chapter 5(b)(ii).

105   Stated very clearly in Case 99/01 *Criminal proceedings against Gottfried Linhart and Hans Biffl* [2002] ECR I–9375 by the Advocate General Geelhoed (at 34): 'As in Clinique, Unilever and Estée Lauder, the health of persons is not an actual issue in this case either. The cases concern descriptions which may, either rightly or wrongly, create the impression on the part of consumers that they possess a certain medicinal function. Measures to prevent buyers from being potentially misled or confused are not, so it would appear to me, bound up with the protection of public health, but rather with the protection of consumers and the fairness of trade.'

*(v) Other Community rules*

Aspects of unfair commercial practices have previously been regulated by EU law through sector-specific Directives that may apply, for example, to certain sectors of trade or industry; to certain specific commercial practices; or to certain marketing media. Such particular rules for particular areas or practices will certainly be adopted in the future as well.[106] The Directive therefore contains, in Article 3(4), an explicit provision on the relationship between the Directive and other Community rules on unfair commercial practices. This provision applies the principle of *lex specialis*. In case of conflict between the more general Unfair Commercial Practices Directive and Community rules that regulate specific aspects of unfair commercial practices – for example, requirements concerning information and its presentation to the consumer[107] – the latter shall prevail with regard to those specific aspects.

Examples of this type include the rules on sponsorship in the 'Television without Frontiers' Directive[108] and the information requirements of the Consumer Credit Directive and the Electronic Commerce Directive.[109] These are to be applied regardless of the Unfair Commercial Practices Directive. Additional examples can be found in Annex II to the Directive, in which there is an extensive list of Community law provisions that sets out rules for advertising and commercial communications. Of course, there are sector-specific Directives that relate to other business practices than commercial communication as well; they should prevail over the Unfair Commercial Practices Directive in a similar manner.

The fact that some aspects of commercial practices are regulated in sector-specific legislation does not preclude the application of the Unfair Commercial Practices Directive to other aspects of those practices. In many cases the application of the specific rules and the Directive will be quite closely related. If, for a certain type of activity, there are particular rules on information requirements, these may apply to the question of what information should be given, but they do not hinder the application of the Unfair Commercial Practices Directive to the question of whether information that actually is given should be deemed misleading.[110]

---

106 A very important example of pending legislation in this area is the proposed regulation on sales promotion. See Proposal for a regulation concerning sales promotions in the Internal Market, COM(2001) 546 final and Amended proposal for a Regulation concerning sales promotions in the Internal Market, COM(2002) 585 final. This legislation will, as mentioned before, probably be dropped; see above Chapter 2(d).

107 Recital 10.

108 The example is mentioned in COM(2002) 289 final 15. The *lex specialis* rule obviously only applies to conflicts between the two Directives. A 'soft' instrument such as the Commission's interpretative communication on certain aspects of the provisions on televised advertising in the 'Television without Frontiers' Directive, OJ C102, 28 April 2004 p. 2, cannot override the Unfair Commercial Practices Directive (as the Communication is also without prejudice to the interpretations given by the European Court of Justice, see at 70).

109 These examples are mentioned in COM(2003) 356 final 11.

110 COM(2003) 356 final 11.

In the Explanatory Memorandum it is stated that the *lex specialis* provision of Article 3(4) does not apply to references in sectoral Directives to broad principles such as the 'general good' or 'fair trade'.[111] This appears quite natural in the sense that such a broad principle in a sector-specific Directive, with perhaps little concrete content given to it in practice, should not have the effect of preventing the application of the Unfair Commercial Practices Directive to the whole area covered by the broad principle. However, this statement is probably not without exceptions. If, for example, on the basis of a broad sector-specific principle, there has evolved a clear case law that adequately protects consumers in some situations, that case law might very well prevail over the general Unfair Commercial Practices Directive.

Article 3(4) covers only sectoral Community rules, including national legislation that correctly implements those rules. It does not extend the exception to national sector-specific legislation. For national legislation, the most important delimitation relates to regulated professions, which is commented upon below.

## (vi) National rules based on minimum clause

The exception concerning sector-specific Community rules in Article 3(4) does not even cover national implementing legislation that makes use of the minimum clause of a sectoral Directive and thereby offers consumers better protection than the Directive. For this specific situation the Unfair Commercial Practices Directive, in Article 3(5)–(6), sets out a temporary limitation of the scope of the Directive. For a certain period, at present six years, Member States shall be able to apply, within certain limits, provisions which implement Directives that contain minimum harmonisation clauses and which are more restrictive or prescriptive than the Unfair Commercial Practices Directive.

This provision of the Directive has been more closely analysed in relation to the general issue of the choice between maximum and minimum harmonisation in the Directive.[112]

## (vii) Jurisdiction

In Article 3(7) there is a curious delimitation of the scope of the Directive, according to which the Directive is 'without prejudice to the rules determining the jurisdiction of the courts'. The Explanatory Memorandum does not explain what kind of situations this provision is intended to cover. Perhaps it is intended to make clear that the obligation of Member States, according to the enforcement provision in Article 11, to provide 'adequate and effective means to combat unfair commercial practices', does not relate to jurisdiction issues. However, this already appears to be relatively self-evident.

---

111  COM(2003) 356 final 10–11.
112  See above, Chapter 2(c)(ii).

## *(viii) Regulated professions*

A very important limitation of the scope of the Directive is the provision on regulated professions in Article 3(8):

> This Directive is without prejudice to any conditions of establishment or of authorisation regimes, or to the deontological codes of conduct or other specific rules governing regulated professions in order to uphold high standards of integrity on the part of the professional, which Member States may, in conformity with Community law, impose on professionals.

As this exception only relates to 'regulated professions', a definition of this concept has been deemed necessary. It is given in Article 2(l):

> 'regulated profession' means a professional activity or a group of professional activities, access to which or the pursuit of which, or one of the modes of pursuing which, is conditional, directly or indirectly, upon possession of specific professional qualifications, pursuant to laws, regulations or administrative provisions.

It is clear from this definition that the exception does not cover all kinds of regulated business activity, but only what can be termed 'professions'. For example, national rules on specific business sectors like banking, insurance, energy or telecommunications, do not fall under this exception. Typical examples of regulated professions are those of being a practising lawyer[113] and various medical professions.

Again, however, the extent of this exception is unclear. Given that the provision speaks of activities both directly and indirectly conditional on possession of specific professional qualifications, and as it does not mention any hurdle for the required qualifications to become relevant, it is in principle broad enough to cover a wide variety of possible professions. Real estate agency, for example, is a regulated profession in many Member States, requiring certain professional qualifications for the persons engaged in such an activity. Formally even the regulation of less specialised professions, such as taxi driving, could fall under the exception. As national law may require a taxi driver to take certain courses before obtaining a licence, this could be understood as the 'specific professional qualifications' mentioned in the Directive. However, admittedly the word 'professional' can also be read as excluding such less specialised activities, and limiting the exception for regulated professions rather to cases of more extensive professional qualifications such as lawyers and doctors.

In the Preamble yet another type of regulated activity is mentioned: the Directive is without prejudice to rules relating to gambling activities.[114] It is not clear, however, on what Article of the Directive this exception is based. It does not appear to fit well into the definition of regulated professions.

---

113    The comparative overview on rules on advertising by members of liberal professions in Schulze and Schulte-Nölke, *op.cit.*, 77, almost exclusively reports on rules concerning lawyers.

114    Recital 9.

As the number of regulated professions and the definitions of their scope obviously varies between different Member States, the scope of the Unfair Commercial Practices Directive will vary accordingly, depending on the content of national law. What in one Member State may be a regulated profession, and therefore at least in some respects outside the scope of the Directive, may in some other Member State be an unregulated activity completely within its sphere of application. In this sense the scope of the Directive is partially determined by national law.

The Directive is 'without prejudice' to national rules on regulated professions. The focus of the delimitation must be on the 'negative' effect of the Directive. A national rule related to a regulated profession, aiming at upholding high standards of professional integrity, that goes further in protecting the consumers than the Directive, cannot be struck down with reference to the Directive, as long as the national regulation is otherwise in conformity with Community law (in particular, with the Treaty). However, the Directive may very well be applied 'positively', even to nationally regulated professions, so far as there are *lacunae* in the national regulation. For example, if there is a national regime for the authorisation of certain professionals, and perhaps even rules on conduct covering some parts of the activity of such professionals, but these rules contain no provisions on advertising the services of the professionals, the Directive should clearly apply to such advertising.

If a certain issue is not covered at all by the national rules applicable to a regulated profession, it is easy to apply the Directive. Difficult issues may arise, however, where the national rules regulate this issue in a way that appears incomplete from the perspective of the Directive. Especially in cases where the national rules, if they were understood as a closed system, would lead to poorer consumer protection than that provided by the Directive, it would seem natural to apply the Directive-based rules together with the national particular rules. After all, the basic idea of the exception is to allow national legislatures to uphold high standards of integrity and an accordingly high level of consumer protection in the area, rather than to allow Member States to lower the consumer protection standard from that prescribed by the Directive.[115]

The exception concerning regulated professions covers all kinds of norms. Not only specific legislative rules concerning the practice of such professions are covered; also norms presented as conditions of establishment or of authorisation regimes are outside the scope of the Directive. Even 'deontological codes of conduct' may be used to introduce stricter requirements on the practices of the professionals than the Directive would otherwise foresee. The philosophical term 'deontological' – a French term of art – probably refers to such codes of conduct that contain normative prescriptions concerning the behaviour of those bound by the code.

---

115 See also the proposed Amendment 27 at the Parliament's first reading (Doc. 8492/04) on this issue, ending with the words: 'provided the aforesaid requirements secure a level of consumer protection at least as high as that secured by this Directive'. According to the Statement of the Council's reasons (Doc. 11630/2/04 REV 2 ADD 1, at 6) the purpose of this Amendment has been taken over, inter alia, in Article 3(8).

*(ix) Financial services and immovable property*

Article 3(9) contains a particular minimum clause related to financial services and immovable property. In this area the Member States are allowed to impose more restrictive or prescriptive requirements than those flowing from the Unfair Commercial Practices Directive. The reason cited for this exception is the 'complexity and inherent serious risks' of this area that makes it necessary to set out detailed requirements and positive obligations on traders.[116] So far this task is entrusted to the Member States, except in some areas where Community rules already exist, and their provisions on the minimum/maximum harmonisation issue are to be applied.[117]

'Financial services' is in this context defined with reference to the Distance Selling of Financial Services Directive. According to Article 2(b) of that Directive: '"financial service" means any service of a banking, credit, insurance, personal pension, investment or payment nature'.

Unlike financial services, 'immovable property' is not defined in the Directive. Acknowledging that the concept of immovable property varies greatly within the EU, one should not give it a traditional national legal interpretation, but rather understand it functionally. For example, the rules on marketing of homes, including apartments, should be within the exception, regardless of whether these are classified as movables in some situations in some Member States.[118] Information requirements related to the selling of houses and apartments are typically within the sphere of this exception. Obviously, some of the rules related to the practices of real estate agents belong to this area as well.[119]

Given that the provision on financial services and immovable property is a minimum harmonisation clause directed towards the Member States, it does not prevent the application of the Directive to these areas in case there is no national legislation. Equally, as it is does require minimum harmonisation it does not allow the Member States to adopt less consumer-friendly rules than the Directive.

*(x) Precious metal*

Finally, according to Article 3(10), the Directive does not apply to rules of Member States that relate to the certification and indication of the standard of fineness of articles of precious metal. Again this delimitation does not rule out the application

---

116   Recital 9.

117   Like the Insurance Directives and the Consumer Credit Directive.

118   For example, in Finland, most apartment houses are constructed as limited companies, and ownership of a flat as ownership of shares, which are classified as movable property.

119   As has been noted above, national rules concerning real estate agents might also be accepted on the basis of the exception concerning regulated professions.

of the Directive to issues that are not directly dealt with in the national certification and indication rules. If, for example, the standard of fineness of a metal is presented in a misleading way in marketing to consumers – for example, where low carat gold is advertised simply as 'gold' or even 'pure gold' – this marketing is within the reach of the Directive.

# Chapter 4

# The General Clause on Unfair Practices

Hans-W. Micklitz

## a. Fair Trading *de lege lata* – References in Secondary Law

The Unfair Commercial Practices Directive introduces, in Article 5, a general clause outlawing unfair commercial practices. This seems to confirm what can be derived from existing EU law, where the formula appears in different forms – mostly as 'fair trading'.

The term 'fair trading' can be found in various shapes and forms in the relevant secondary law, regulations and Directives. On closer inspection,[1] the term is mentioned more than 30 times without the Community legislator providing a definition of 'fair trading' or 'fair commercial practices'. Both terms are used synonymously. References to fair trading with regard to competition or trade are not only found in the fringe areas of European secondary law such as product- or media-related provisions which, inter alia, deal with fair standards of advertising practices, but also in core areas such as the Misleading Advertising Directive, the Trade Mark Directive, the 'Television without Frontiers' Directive, the Distance Selling Directive, the Comparative Advertising Directive, the Electronic Commerce Directive and the Distance Selling of Financial Services Directive. The fact that the reference depends on the context is characteristic of the regulatory technique of the Community. Therefore it is not fair advertising as such that is of concern, but fair competition, fair trading or fair practice generally. Sometimes references contain value judgments on those marketing practices which are said to be illegal[2] or must be ethically acceptable.[3]

More precise statements on the specific context are shown in the Misleading Advertising Directive. Article 1 states that (until the coming into force of the Unfair Commercial Practices Directive) it is the purpose of the Directive to protect consumers, persons carrying on a trade or business or practising a craft or

---

1 The assessment is based on an analysis of all appropriate Directives and regulations which deal with unfair trading law. The author has built up a databank including the relevant court decisions.

2 Regulation No. 213/1999 which lays down measures to prohibit the release for free circulation, export, re-export or entry for a suspension procedure of counterfeit and pirated goods.

3 Regulation No. 178/2002 establishing the European Food Safety Authority.

profession, and the interests of the public in general, against misleading advertising and the 'unfair consequences thereof'. At first glance this reference can be read not as if every misleading advertisement is necessarily unfair, but only if its 'unfair consequences' are taken into account. The objective of the Directive relating to Trade Marks is even more precise. Article 1 states that the Directive should apply to every trademark in respect of goods or services which is the subject of legal provisions of other Member States, such as provisions against unfair competition, civil liability or consumer protection. Repeatedly it refers to the task of unfair trading law with regard to trademarks; it is intended to prevent the unjustified use or impairment of a trademark by a competitor.

This heterogeneous and incoherent picture is reiterated in the various conclusions of the Advocates General (in which the term 'fair trading' is mentioned more than 32 times) and the relevant decisions of the European Court of Justice (in which the same term is mentioned more than 25 times). The reference frequently relates to the repetition of the relevant European or national provision. It would appear that no attempt has been made to give shape to the term 'fair trading' and define its content. The Advocates General and the European Court of Justice have been more specific when it comes down to determining whether an advertisement violates the rights of the trademark owner in an unfair manner.

Secondary law presents a similar picture; there seems to be a broad consensus between Member States and the organs of the Community that fair trading is to be considered as forming part of the European legal system. This thesis allows the consideration of whether there has been a European principle of fairness in existing EC law which not only applies to advertising law but also to restrictive practices and trademark law.[4] However, considering the context-specific use of the reference to 'fairness' in numerous Directives and regulations, it is difficult to arrive at general conclusions on the role and function of the fairness doctrine in assessing advertising practices. The adoption of the Unfair Commercial Practices Directive represents a decisive step. From the point of view of legal policy it can be said that the European Commission had contributed to paving the way for the elaboration of the Unfair Commercial Practices Directive by its repeated use of the term fairness in the past.

## b. The Structure of the General Clause in the Unfair Commercial Practices Directive

The structure of the general clause in the Unfair Commercial Practices Directive is threefold;[5] on the first level there is the 'big' general clause – the prohibition of

---

4    M. Radeideh, in *Fair Trading in EC Law* (Groningen: Europa Law Publishing, 2005) starts from the premise that a European concept of fairness already exists. However, it does not apply to advertising which does not communicate any information.

5    C. Busch, 'Ein europäischer Rechtsrahmen für das Lauterkeitsrecht? – Der Vorschlag der Europäischen Kommission für eine Richtlinie über unlautere Geschäftspraktiken' (2004) 4 *The European Legal Forum* 94; Radeideh, *op.cit.*, 260.

unfair commercial practices in Article 5; on the second level there are the 'small' general clauses – prohibition of misleading advertising (Articles 6 and 7) and the prohibition of aggressive advertising (Articles 8 and 9); and the third level consists of a list of trade practices in Annex I which are unfair *per se*.

## (i) Threefold structure

The general clause, Article 5, defines the general legal framework. The Commission has decided – in conformity with the principal concept of the (continental) European Member States[6] – in favour of a general clause banning 'unfair commercial practices'. It purported to include the different general clauses and principles of Member States in a harmonised European framework, simplifying the normative orientation of the market users, be they traders or consumers.[7] Pursuant to Article 5(1), unfair commercial practices are prohibited *per se*; this corresponds with most continental legislation. Pursuant to Article 5(2), a commercial practice shall be deemed unfair if it is contrary to the requirements of professional diligence, and if it materially distorts, or is likely to materially distort, the economic behaviour towards the product of the average consumer whom it reaches or to whom it is addressed, or of the average member of the group, when a commercial practice is directed to a particular group of consumers. The requirements set out in Article 5(2) must be satisfied cumulatively in order to justify unfairness.

On the second level the Directive deals with those advertising practices which are particularly unfair. According to Article 5(3), those commercial practices in particular which are unfair are misleading in terms of Article 6 (misleading actions) and Article 7 (misleading omissions) or aggressive in terms of Article 8 (aggressive commercial practices) and Article 9 (harassment, coercion and undue influence). For the majority of Member States, the Unfair Commercial Practices Directive contains a number of new provisions which were not previously familiar or which were not regulated so clearly. The latter is particularly true for the newly-inserted element of misleading omissions. This demonstrates extremely clearly the information paradigm of European unfair trading law.[8] More or less unfamiliar to the legal systems of Member States is the concept of a separate general clause which prohibits aggressive trading practices, even if the advertising measures hiding behind them are sanctioned under different terminology.[9]

The third level is represented by Annex I to the Directive, according to which 31 individually listed misleading and aggressive commercial practices are *per se* unfair. This illustrates that there are commercial practices which do not need to be

---

6   H.-W. Micklitz and J. Keßler, *Marketing Practices Regulation and Consumer Protection in the EC Member States and the US* (Baden-Baden: Nomos-Verlag, 2002).

7   See Explanatory Memorandum, COM(2003) 356 final, para. 30.

8   See Chapter 5(c)(i).

9   See Chapter 6(a)(i)–(iii).

individually assessed. Listing such prohibited market practices is also a model which is new to some Member States.

### (ii) Consequences and questions arising from the threefold structure

The Community legislator has not provided any guidance on the possible consequences which will result from the threefold structure – in particular of the role and function of Article 5 – the so-called 'big' general clause. That is why there is considerable uncertainty at all levels. The first set of questions relates to Article 5, which could be understood as a safety net applying to all of those practices which are neither covered by Annex I nor able to be subsumed under the 'small' general clauses. Article 5 would then be an interpretation aid, bridging the gaps resulting from the reading of the 'small' general clauses on misleading and aggressive commercial practices – or Annex I. This reading would provide Member States with significant leeway in the way they apply the Directive. However, another reading is also possible, which starts from the premise that the threefold approach of the Directive must be turned upside down. Any application would have to start with the test of whether the practice is prohibited under Annex I and, if not, whether it is misleading or aggressive. Only if these tests fail would the unfairness test come to be applied. Under this reading, Article 5 is a remedy of last resort which only applies to particularly unusual circumstances.

A second set of questions concerns the internal consistency of the different prohibitions. Since the requirements of the 'big' (unfair) and the 'small' (misleading and aggressive) general clauses are not entirely congruent, the question is whether or not the requirements of the 'big' general clause would have to be satisfied when assessing misleading and aggressive commercial practices. Last, but not least, a third set of questions deals with the function of Annex I. There is some dispute over how to read the wording of the Directive, that the practices listed in Annex I are unfair *per se*. The main question is whether it is permissible to assess individual cases and, if so, whether the requirements of the 'big' general clause can be or must be taken into consideration. All these questions will have to be answered. However, this must be done in the light of the concept of fairness which stands behind the Directive.

### c. The Concept of Fairness

### (i) The challenge – fairness, national morals, taste and decency, national cultures – how are they interrelated?

The true challenge of the Directive is to put the term 'fairness' into concrete form within a European context. This requires the establishment of an autonomous concept of fairness. Only an autonomous understanding complies with the well-settled approach of the European Court of Justice of not relying on how a legal term or concept is defined in a particular national legal order. The term must be shaped in the context of the European legal order, or more precisely in the context of the Unfair Commercial Practices Directive. Whilst this might ideally provide a European understanding free from national concepts, in practice there is a linkage between that European concept and national concepts. The Unfair Commercial Practices Directive cannot and should not 'reinvent the wheel'; that is why national concepts on fairness still matter. It is at this point that matters become complicated. National legal orders have been using different methods for controlling 'unfair' commercial practices; some are more market-based, others are more value-based. This is made explicit in the difference between banning *unfair* marketing practices on the one side, and striking down marketing practices which are not in compliance with *bonos mores* on the other.[10] Through *bonos mores* a *moral* dimension is inserted in the control of commercial practices. This is very much highlighted in the fight over how to assess the famous 'Benetton' advertising. In order to avoid misunderstanding, it must be clearly understood that each concept controlling commercial practices starts from a particular moral premise. The only question is whether the background morals relate to values that govern the market, such as 'market freedoms' or whether non-market-related values are equally taken into account. The Directive does not provide much guidance in finding out whether its notion of fairness is morally bound or not. However, there are two references in the recitals which might help to clarify the notion of fairness: one on 'taste and decency', the other on 'social, cultural and linguistic factors'.

Recital 7 refers to matters of 'taste and decency' which are not addressed by the Directive and are to remain in the hands of the Member States. In this respect one might easily read the Directive as relying on a distinction between a European concept of fairness and national matters of taste and decency. This distinction has a twofold purpose; on the one hand, it serves to define the scope of the Directive and on the other it affects the concept of fairness as such.[11] It will be argued that a European concept of fairness cannot be developed without considering the relationship between 'fairness' and 'taste and decency'.

There are two references to cultural factors in the recitals. The first, Recital 7, refers to commercial practices which are undesirable in Member States 'for cultural reasons', as for example, commercial solicitation in the streets. From the context, it seems as if the Directive uses both 'taste and decency' and 'culture' as synonyms. However, there is a second reference in Recital 18. Here the Directive refers to the well-established case law of the European Court of Justice under which the average consumer might be used as a yardstick to assess the 'fairness' of the commercial practice, but where also 'social, cultural and linguistic factors' have to be taken into account. In this context it seems as if the Directive differentiates between 'taste and decency' and 'national cultures'. The latter concept is far wider and it includes

---

10  See the reference in Chapter 1(b)(i)–(ii) on the differences between Member States, which shall – in theory – be eliminated by the Directive on Unfair Commercial Practices.

11  See, on the scope, Chapter 3(d)(i)–(ii).

societal interests[12] which are not affected by 'taste and decency', such as equality and sex discrimination.

So, in a rather bewildering fashion, the Directive brings together the notion of 'fairness', 'national morals', 'taste and decency', and 'national cultures'. Without really clarifying the interrelationship between these terms, the Directive seems to indicate that it is possible to distinguish between matters of taste, decency and culture which are said to remain outside the scope of the Directive, and matters of fairness, which are inside its scope. The difficulties which are enshrined in such a piece of EC regulation are obvious. One issue alone might help to underline the need to arrive, if possible, at a clearer idea of what might lie behind the notion of 'fairness'. The general clause provides for the particular protection of vulnerable groups, such as children and the elderly, against unfair commercial practices. Does the Directive here overstep its own boundaries, insofar as matters of morals, taste, decency and culture are integrated into the concept of fairness? One might reject the idea of construing protection of children and the elderly as a matter of taste and decency. However, is such a policy concept not linked to a particular understanding of morals which should govern society, or is it even an expression of a particular 'state' national culture? According to this view, the idea of fairness would be affected by non-market-related factors. However, one might argue the opposite. Today's market economy gains influence over ever broader fields of society and affects various persons (children and the elderly as economic actors in the market) or fields of interest (social policies, such as the protection of children and the elderly as far as they are related to economic policies) which have long been regarded as being outside the market economy.

It will be argued that a European concept of fairness will have to grasp the interrelationship of market-related values and non-market-related morals, such as matters of taste, decency and culture, since it seems easy to predict that conflicts between Member States and/or with the European Commission and the European Court of Justice will emerge. These will concern the correct definition of a European concept, which allows for the establishment of the internal market, whilst leaving room in the European Community for differing opinions on the reach and importance of non-market-related morals, taste, decency and culture to suppress 'unwanted' commercial practices.

*(ii) European fairness as an autonomous concept*

At an early stage in legal doctrine the question was raised whether it could be concluded from the character of the Directive as a 'framework Directive' that the term 'fairness' could be given shape through the respective national concepts.[13] If

---

12 See Chapter 3(d)(iii).

13 See H. Köhler and T. Lettl, 'Das geltende europäische Lauterkeitsrecht, der Vorschlag für eine EG–Richtlinie über unlautere Geschäftspraktiken und die UWG–Reform' (2003) *Wettbewerb in Recht und Praxis* 1019, at 1038; objecting, J. Glöckner, *Introduction B. No.*

this were true, then the Community legislator would have given up the idea that it could be the purpose and objective of the Directive to create a standard measure under Community law. However, every statement given by the Commission shows that it intended regulating unfair commercial practices law uniformly so as to break down remaining barriers to intra-Community trade. This is the link to the Commission's favoured concept of full harmonisation.[14] Another interpretation would leave it to the discretion of Member States to interpret the general clause in the light of their traditions, non-market-related morals and cultures, since they could – under the framework of the Directive – maintain already existing concepts, be they morally and/or culturally loaded or not. It ignores the fact that the European Court of Justice, through established practice, interprets EU law autonomously, especially in areas where there are legal principles in the form of general clauses. The decision in *Freiburger Kommunalbauten*[15] cannot be used as a counter-argument, since the German Supreme Court wanted the European Court of Justice to decide on the legality of a particular standard term, and not on the question of how to read the concept of good faith in the Unfair Contract Terms Directive. If the German Supreme Court had asked the European Court of Justice to clarify whether the concept of good faith allows for the control of procedural good faith only, or whether it equally requires the control of substantive good faith, the European Court of Justice would have been obliged to accept its responsibility and provide guidance on the criteria according to which Member States are allowed to control unfair contract terms.[16] In adopting the Unfair Commercial Practices Directive the term 'fairness' found its way into European unfair commercial practices law. It is the task of the European Court of Justice to provide guidelines for giving shape to the term within a European context so that it can be applied properly. This task cannot be left to Member States.

Closely connected with the question of whether the concept of fairness is a European one, is the question of whether the wording of Article 5 (unfair, *bonos mores*, good faith and so forth) is of significance in the development of a European concept of unfair commercial practices law. As early as 1965, Ulmer referred to the relativity of terms and instead highlighted the objective of the regulation as the crucial criterion for judging commercial practices.[17] Henning-Bodewig and Schricker start

---

195–198 in H. Harte-Bavendamm and F. Henning-Bodewig, *Gesetz gegen den unlauteren Wettbewerb* (München: Verlag C.H. Beck, 2004); J. Glöckner, 'Richtlinienvorschlag über unlautere Geschäftspraktiken, deutsches UWG oder die schwierige Umsetzung von europarechtlichen Generalklauseln' (2004) *Wettbewerb in Recht und Praxis* 936, at 942; with regard to the necessity of a European concept, A. Bakardjieva, *Fair trading law in flux?* (Stockholm University: dissertation, 2003).

14  See, on full harmonisation, Chapter 2(c).

15  Case C–237/02 *Freiburger Kommunalbauten v Hofstetter* [2004] ECR I–3403.

16  See, on these differences, *Director General of Fair Trading v First National Bank plc* [2002] 1 AC 481; [2001] 3 WLR 1297; [2002] 1 All ER 97 294.

17  E. Ulmer, *Das Recht des unlauteren Wettbewerbs in den Mitgliedstaaten der Europäischen Wirtschaftsgemeinschaft: Gutachten erstattet im Auftrag der Kommission der Europäischen Wirtschaftsgemeinschaft vom Institut für Ausländisches und Internationales*

from the same premise.[18] Schulze and Janssen also proceed from the assumption that the general idea which forms the basis of already existing general clauses in Member States (fairness, *bonos mores* and good faith) was identical. All of these general clauses purported to prevent market conduct which was considered not to be in compliance with what should be acceptable in a market-based society. All national provisions are said to have in common the requirement that the conduct in question was detrimental to the person protected, or at least could be detrimental.[19] This understanding of the relativity of concepts cannot be followed. It is necessary to find a conceptual basis for the general clause in the Directive which allows for achieving the internal market whilst respecting Member States' sovereignty in non-market-related matters. An attempt will be made to show that ethical and moral terms in a European concept of fairness, such as good morals and *bonos mores*, jeopardise the achievement of this objective since they introduce socio-political disputes – non-market-related moral issues, matters of taste and decency or cultural differences – into the European law on unfair commercial practices.

This, however, is not to say that all 25 Member States necessarily need to use the same terminology. A survey of the translation of Article 5 into the languages of the different Member States illustrates the difficulties which arise in practice. The language used in drafting the Directive was English and refers continuously to 'unfair commercial practices'. To the extent that German-speaking lawyers were involved in the discussion, the term 'unfair' was equated with the term '*unlauter*'; otherwise they would have stuck to the terminology of '*gute Sitten*'. Taking the same approach, French-speaking lawyers translate 'unfair commercial practices' as '*pratiques commerciales déloyales*'. It is remarkable how, in these three different legal systems, the element of 'unfairness' is reformulated for the national context. Again, this may be suitable so long as the terminology will assist in the understanding of European unfair marketing practices law as a means of achieving the internal market and not as reintroducing the concept of national morals. This would, however, be the case if the term '*bonos mores*' had continued to be used, for example, in countries where the legislation is based on the (now outdated) German approach which relied on '*bonos mores*'. To this extent the Unfair Commercial Practices Directive places restrictions on Member States as regards its implementation.[20]

---

*Patent–, Urheber– und Markenrecht der Universität München, Band 1: Vergleichende Darstellung* (München: C.H. Beck Verlag, 1965) at 259, 260.

18  F. Henning-Bodewig and G. Schricker, 'Stellungnahme des Max–Planck–Instituts für ausländisches und internationales Patent–, Urheber– und Wettbewerbsrecht zum Grünbuch zum Verbraucherschutz in der EU KOM (2002) 531 endg.' (2002) *Gewerblicher Rechtsschutz und Urheberrecht Internationaler Teil* 319, at 322; also Glöckner, *Introduction B No. 182*, in Harte-Bavendamm and Henning-Bodewig, *op.cit.*

19  R. Schulze, 'Das Recht des unlauteren Wettbewerbs in den EU-Mitgliedsstaaten' (2004) 4 *The European Legal Forum* 77, at 80.

20  H. Gamerith, 'Der Richtlinienvorschlag über unlautere Geschäftspraktiken – Möglichkeiten einer harmonischen Umsetzung' (2005) 51 *Wettbewerb in Recht und Praxis* 391, at 395, 419, 431.

## (iii) European fairness and national morals

The development of an autonomous terminology requires that it be possible for 25 Member States to agree on a standard measure of how to define the term 'fairness' in a positive way. A possible and necessary demarcation between fairness on the one hand and non-market-related morals[21] on the other shall be illustrated with the help of three examples which were and still are discussed extensively in the legal systems of Member States. The examples of *Benetton*, *Männeken Pis* and *Zagorka* help to put the European concept of 'fairness' in concrete terms.[22] These three examples equally demonstrate that 'non-market-related moral issues' are not a matter of the scope of the Directive alone. They can only be given shape in its inherent relation to a European concept of 'fairness'. In this respect these examples are meant to demonstrate the types of conflict which already exist and which will probably grow once the Directive has come into effect.

It can be assumed that Benetton advertisements are known to the reader. Their admissibility has been considered twice by the German Federal Constitutional Court and twice by the German Federal Supreme Court (BGH).[23] In essence, the question was whether or not the advertisements were contrary to public policy. A dispute arose between the two federal courts regarding the construction of German unfair commercial practices law. In an exaggerated fashion it could be said that the Constitutional Court understands unfair commercial practice as market communication where the addressees are required to make their own value judgments, whereas the Supreme Court condemned the advertisements as being morally offensive.

On Sunday 13 February 2005, Männeken Pis produced a piece of news in a German daily newspaper which said that following heavy protests in Greece, the Belgian mobile services provider Proximus had terminated an advertising campaign which showed the well-known 'Männeken Pis' as the pillar of a temple on the Acropolis. On Wednesday of that week, Athens had officially protested against the 'unacceptable' illustration on an advertising billboard exposed at the airports of Brussels and Charleroi. The Greek chargé d'affaires in Belgium complained that the picture of the Erechtheion Temple was used in the advertisement without prior permission, and also that it insulted the archaeological inheritance of Greece, given that the monument is of religious significance. She asked Proximus to withdraw the billboard. This shows that the behaviour of the Belgian mobile service provider was permitted under the freedom of market communication and yet considered morally offensive by the Greek government.

---

21  See again Chapter 3(d)(iii) on societal interests.

22  E. Millan and R. Elliott, 'Offensive Advertising, Public Policy, and the Law: The Rulings on the Zagorka Case' (2004) 27 *Journal of Consumer Policy* 477, at 480.

23  The intricacies of the discussion have resulted in a number of publications. See, for a full account of the conflict between the German Supreme Court and the German Constitutional Court, I. Scherer, § 4–2 No. 165 et seq in K.-H. Fezer, *Gesetz gegen den unlauteren Wettbewerb* (München: Verlag C.H. Beck, 2005).

The final example concerns a particularly sensitive area of advertising: discrimination against women. In the spring of 2001 Zagorka (a brewery) launched a new television advertisement for its prime brand. The content of the advertisement could be summarised as follows: a young man is repairing an old Volkswagen Beetle. As the man lies beneath the car, two delicate female legs appear and elegantly kick the man's spanner away. The man searches for his tool, but instead of the spanner he finds a bottle of beer. The scene is followed by another one in which the man and the woman are embracing, each with a bottle of beer in hand, and enjoying the drink. A male voiceover brings the message of the advertisement to the viewer: 'What does a human being need? A new car, a nice woman and a good beer'; the message is repeated and also displayed as a written text. The problems which arose from this advertisement can best be described through the jokes which went through the Bulgarian media in the aftermath of this advertisement:[24] 'They sent into space first a dog, then a woman, and finally a human being'; or 'A shepherd was asked: "Have you seen a couple passing by?" He replied: "No. A while ago a human being and a woman passed by, but I have not seen a couple"'. The legal focus of the discussions – which are not yet concluded – is whether the advertisement suggests to differentiate between a 'human being' and a 'woman' by objectifying the woman. Similarly, in Germany in the 1950s there was the advertising pitch: 'May I introduce to you my car, my home and my wife'. Only as little as one law suit around 'Zagorka', which was led by a woman, resulted in a decision against the claimant. Legal actions were brought by individual women, and one association of women, seeking damages. The then competent commission for consumer protection objected to initiating legal proceedings since there was no discrimination. The vice-director (female) stated: 'As a consumer I would not be offended by an advertisement of the kind of Zagorka'. Advertising agencies relied on the freedom of communication and the autonomy of the addressees; critics want to rely on unfair commercial practices law as a means to pursuing socio-political objectives.[25]

In a *sociological* context it seems that there is a universal freedom of communication (freedom of speech) which is invoked as a constitutional and human right by those benefiting from it, whereas critics rely on diverging morals in the respective legal systems. The universal freedom of communication influences the term 'fairness' as an element of integrity. Fairness can then be taken to mean universal economic clarity, unambiguousness and transparency in the sense of functioning competition. The degrees of freedom which can be or must be granted to Member States which fall below – or above – such a doctrine of fairness are culture-specific variations of a western common ground based on codified customs, that is, tradition in each aspect. From a *legal* perspective, universal freedom of communication in terms of internal market logic and national traditions (morals) would come into conflict if the

---

24 Millan and Elliott, *op.cit.*, 477, at 484.

25 See the detailed illustration of the issue, including a number of examples which resulted in the intervention of the German Werberat, in A. Steinbeck, *§ 4–1, No. 221*, in particular the conclusion, *No. 231* in K.-H. Fezer, *op.cit.*

European Court of Justice were to comment on *Benetton*, *Männeken Pis* or *Zagorka* and if it were to qualify the validity of fairness in relation to national traditions. Yet what exactly is at stake here? Is it different understandings over morals (*Benetton*), is it simply a matter of taste and decency (*Männeken Pis*), or does the conflict affect even the national culture (*Zagorka*)? One might easily disagree on the classification undertaken here. However, one might more readily agree that all three issues affect non-market values (not even morals). One could even take an easier example, such as the use of the Bible in advertising, to show that some advertising gives rise to moral issues.[26]

The potential conflicts between the economically established universal validity of the concept of fairness and non-market-related national morals can only be resolved by establishing a European concept of 'fairness'. The term 'fairness' as applied in the Unfair Commercial Practices Directive should not be given a moral dimension which reaches beyond the market. Rather it is a reflection of the concept of workable competition.[27] To this end, it is suggested that one must distinguish between the market-related term 'fairness' at Community level and the regulation of morals reaching beyond market values under national concepts. The reference system for determining fairness can be derived from the economic constitution of the EC,[28] and the reference system for non-market-related morals from its national context.

It seems as if the EC – through the Unfair Commercial Practices Directive – has found a 'solution' for a conflict which has been apparent ever since the beginning of marketing practices law, that is, the relationship between competition and morals. This would explain why the European Commission has been keen to exclude the protection of non-economic interests of consumers (such as health and safety) from the scope of application. In that respect the social dimension of the economic constitution of the European Community is abandoned. The Commission backs the internal market, for the realisation of which the consumer is used as an instrument. The distinction between 'competition' and 'morals' is also persuasive, given that the EC cannot rely on morals beyond the market; this is illustrated by the difficulties to integrate non-economic values into the European legal system. The Unfair Commercial Practices Directive purports to avoid anticipated differences on ethical values by separating 'morals' and 'competition'. However, it might be reiterated that this distinction only works on a superficial level. Referring to competition theories

---

26 Cf. P. Moritz, 'Kultur und Moral im Wandel der Gesellschaft' (2002) 42 *Medienimpulse* 13 *et seq.*; and G. Buschmann, 'Die Bibel in der Cannes bzw. Kann-Rolle der Werbung, Ein ungewöhnlicher Zugang zum Thema Bibel im Religionsunterricht' (2002) *Medienimpulse* 45.

27 Cf. W.B. Schünemann, '"Unlauterkeit" in den Generalklauseln und Interessenabwägung nach neuem UWG' (2004) 8 *Wettbewerb in Recht und Praxis* 925.

28 W. Veelken, 'Kundenfang gegenüber dem Verbraucher – Bemerkungen zum EG– Richtlinienentwurf über unlautere Geschäftspraktiken' (2004) *Wettbewerb in Recht und Praxis* 1, at 16; H. Apostolopoulos, 'Neuere Entwicklungen im europäischen Lauterkeitsrecht: Problematische Aspekte und Vorschläge' (2004) *Wettbewerb in Recht und Praxis* 841, at 846; Schünemann, *op.cit.*, *Wettbewerb in Recht und Praxis* 925, at 931.

is impossible without reflecting on moral issues. In competition theory the ethic of freedom and responsibility takes priority.[29] That is why one might distinguish between market-related morals and non-market-related morals.

Having these differences in mind, it is argued that any direct 'moralisation' of commercial transactions *sub specie* burdens the efficiency of a competition-driven market economy which forms the basis of the individual and collective benefits for all participants in the market. If that were to be ignored, then the participants in the market would have to satisfy requirements which they do not need and, which – as *Benetton* has shown – can obviously not be satisfied. Unfair Commercial Practices law is said to be inapt to solve moral issues. From this perspective it might be comprehensible why the Unfair Commercial Practices Directive leaves all those pieces of secondary Community law unaffected, where the European Community has adopted Directives and regulations which touch upon moral issues; for example, the much-criticised Directive on banning tobacco advertising or restricting health-related advertisements. These rulings affect national morals. These Directives and regulations must be understood as an attempt by the European Community to develop a European moral which reaches beyond a mere internal market logic.

The Unfair Commercial Practices Directive does not touch on non-market-related national morals since it focuses entirely on the protection of the economic interests of the consumer. It is thus compatible with the concept of workable competition which sustains the internal market. This is the *effet utile* of the Directive which needs to be considered as a guiding maxim for the huge number of possible conflicts. European unfair commercial practices law is likely to lead to a demoralisation of potential conflicts concerning advertising measures. The question remains whether the distinction is valid and whether the demarcation of fairness and non-market-related national morals can be maintained. In any case, the distinction seems to be more coherent than any methodical attempt to pursue the existing contradictions and the conceptual inconsistencies, in order to moralise European unfair commercial practices law. The 'big' general clause in Article 5 would become the pivotal point of the legal application – the legal policy battlefield between European fairness and national morals. This would play down the significance of the two 'small' general clauses on misleading and aggressive marketing practices. The big general clause in Article 5 would be declared the major reference point for assessing commercial practices and the importance of the 'small' general clauses and Annex I would be played down. Such a reading might be comprehensible taking into account the fragile political integration process of the European Union outside and beyond market integration. However, it seems more convincing to leave a margin of appreciation to Member States where it is integrated in the Directive, specifically in terms of the protection of non-market-related national morals against the function-related and

---

29 W.B. Schünemann, *§ 3 No. 165, 166, 167*, in Harte-Bavendamm and Henning-Bodewig, *op.cit.*; G. Schricker/F. Henning-Bodewig, 'Elemente einer Harmonisierung des Rechts des unlauteren Wettbewerbs in der Europäischen Union' (2001) *Wettbewerb in Recht und Praxis* 1379, at 1380; Veelken, *op.cit.*, at 15.

competition-orientated European concept of 'fairness'. Such a twofold distinction appears sensible; Member States only need to justify their reliance on non-market-related national morals in order to escape the tight grip of the Unfair Commercial Practices Directive.

### *(iv) Taste and decency*

The difference between a Europeanised concept of 'fairness' and national morals is to some extent mirrored in the Unfair Commercial Practices Directive. Pursuant to the second sentence of Recital 7 it does not address commercial practices which relate to legal requirements related to taste and decency which vary widely among Member States. 'Taste and decency' sounds very much like *Sitte* (*bonos mores*) and *Anstand* (decency). Such a reading would link taste and decency to national morals. Taste and decency would then be some sort of a subcategory of national morals, less but still to some extent value loaded. Such a reading derived from German thinking might overstate the argument. Taking into account the history of the Directive it becomes apparent that all parties involved in the proceedings were aware of the fact that the Unfair Commercial Practices Directive was intended to interfere with national customs and habits, but not national morals. In this respect it can be quite rightly assumed that 'taste and decency' are used as synonyms for 'customs and habits'. However, customs and habits might affect the concept of 'fairness' at least as far as customs and habits reflect market-related values. That is why it might be helpful to use again the distinction between market and non-market values in order to sharpen the line between the reach of the European concept of 'fairness' and the competencies of Member States. It suffices to reiterate the well-established case law of the European Court of Justice that consumer 'habits' and 'customs', as long as they are market–related, do not merit protection *per se*. This is the background for the European Court of Justice decisions on English UHT milk[30] and German beer.[31]

The Directive does not seem to carry this line of argument on with respect to taste and decency. By virtue of Recital 7 Member States are authorised 'to continue to ban commercial practices in their territory, in conformity with the Treaty, for reasons of taste and decency even where such practices do not limit consumers' freedom of choice'. The Directive proceeds from the assumption that taste and decency do not – or do not necessarily – have an impact on the consumer's (economic) freedom of choice.[32] This would explain why Member States can be granted a margin of appreciation with regard to taste and decency. The recital states 'even where such practices do not limit consumers' freedom of choice'; note, it does not state 'only' where there is no such limitation. Obviously the competence of Member States is to apply both arrangements where taste and decency do and do not limit the consumer's

---

30  Case 124/81 *Commission v UK* [1983] ECR 203.

31  Case 178/84 *Commission v Germany* [1987] ECR 1227 at 32.

32  In this direction, T. Lettl, *Der lauterkeitsrechtliche Schutz vor irreführender Werbung in Europa* (München: Verlag C.H. Beck, Habilitation, 2004) 25.

freedom of choice. Given that the Directive purports to protect the economic interests of the consumer, it is the primary objective to guarantee the economic freedom of choice of the consumer. If taste and decency do not limit the freedom of choice, then potential prohibitions ensuring the functioning of the internal market become pointless. Such idealistic impairments (*ideelle Beeinträchtigungen*) of the consumer's autonomy caused by taste and decency can remain within the margin of appreciation of Member States since they do not impact on the economic freedom of choice of the consumer. Idealistic limitations therefore can be put on an equal footing with national non-market-related morals. These are the easy cases.

However, taste and decency is not restricted to forms of idealistic limitation. Member States can 'also', probably should 'especially', prohibit advertising measures for reasons of taste and decency which limit the consumer's economic freedom of choice. To this extent, not only idealistic limitations are of concern, but also possible severe limitations of the consumer's economic freedom of choice where the advertiser exploits taste and decency as a means of advertising, for example, commercial soliciting in the streets. The competence which is granted to Member States increases the risk – or, depending on the perspective, safeguards the possibility – of an ethically and morally motivated application of the competition-based fairness doctrine by Member States. Arguments aiming at defending the national sovereignty are now embedded in the different interpretations of taste and decency. In light of the distinction drawn here between fairness and national non-market-related morals, a broad reading of taste and decency, which considerably enlarges Member States' competence, seems to challenge the *effet utile* of the Directive. The competition-orientated concept of 'fairness' strives for the freedom of market communication. National restrictions can only be maintained if they enshrine national non-market-related morals.

Depending on how Member States and the reviewing authorities behave, the European Court of Justice will have to carry out much demarcation work. So far the European Court of Justice seems to take a relatively generous standing. In *Omega*[33] the European Court of Justice held that Community law does not contravene the national prohibition of commercial practices which are considered a violation of human dignity. The blacklisted practices concerned the organisation of commercial gaming events which entailed the simulated killing of other human beings.

### (v) National cultures

The general phasing out of social and cultural aspects which, from a historical point of view, appears correct, has been part of the EC approach so far and has been put in a concrete formula by the European Court of Justice in its *Lifting* decision.[34] Social, cultural and linguistic factors constitute the starting point for shaping a

---

    33  ECJ Case C–36/02 *Omega v Oberbürgermeisterin der Stadt Bonn* [2004] ECR I–9609.

    34  Case C–220/98 *Lifting–Crème* [2000] ECR I–117.

European concept of 'fairness' under the Unfair Commercial Practices Directive. The European Court of Justice, and with it the European Commission, suggests that national cultures have to be kept separate from any concept of European fairness. A closer look, however, shows that difficulties might easily arise if specific issues have to be discussed.

At the outer end of possible conflicts rank different understandings over the relationship between religions and commercial practices. The European Community is not a homogenous society; and a possible admission of Turkey to the EC might enhance the role of religious values in a market economy.[35] It does not seem far-fetched that the notion of 'fairness' could become the battlefield of differing ideas and even ideologies of what might be regarded as fair commercial practices in an ever broader European Community. For those who might reject that scenario, attention should be drawn to the 'cultural' dimension in the above mentioned *Männeken Pis* story. The use of the Erechtheion Temple was said to offend not only the archaeological but also the *cultural* inheritance of Greece. However, some years ago, when Atlanta – instead of Athens – was chosen to hold the Olympic Games, Greek newspapers published on the front page a picture of the Erechtheion Temple where the pillars had been replaced by Coca Cola bottles. Greece saw no difficulty in forcefully rejecting any parallel between the different uses of the cultural heritage. She simply claimed the power to make use of the national cultural heritage for her own national objectives. But what would have happened if a non-Greek newspaper had done the same after the election of Atlanta? There is no clear-cut answer to such conflicts. In one way or another the European Court of Justice will have to face the challenge of defining whether and to what extent Member States might prohibit commercial practices interfering with national cultures.

## d. Requirements of Professional Diligence

The general clause in Article 5 consists of three parts. Article 5(2)(a) refers to the requirements of professional diligence and 5(2)(b) to the material distortion of economic behaviour of the consumer. Article 5(3) recognises a special need of protection for a certain group of consumers. The terminology used in 5(2), professional diligence and economic behaviour of the consumer are further defined in Articles 2(h) and (e), respectively. There is, however, no definition for the group of consumers who are in particular need of protection.

Article 2(h) defines professional diligence as a standard of special skill and care which a trader may reasonably be expected to exercise towards consumers, commensurate with honest market practice and/or the general principle of good faith in the trader's field of activity. The first draft proposal referred to 'normal market

---

35  See, on the role of Christian values in the European Constitution, J.H.H. Weiler, *Ein christliches Europa Erkundungsgänge* (Salzburg: Pustet Verlag, 2004); cf. also Schünemann, *§ 3 No. 66*, in Harte-Bavendamm and Henning-Bodewig, *op.cit.*, with references to the older discussion.

practice'. In its reasoning the Commission used the analogy of the widely known term as used in business accounting, namely good business conduct or due diligence as derived from Italian law.[36] This did not correspond entirely with the concept of 'the perception of decency of the reasonable average seller' as applied in German case law.[37] Not least because of this, the standard had been extensively criticised as it was said to bear the risk of setting in stone the status quo of what happens to be customary in a particular area. This would have resulted in commercial customs becoming the benchmark. Such an approach would actually have reduced the criterion of professional diligence to its factual aspect.[38] The finally adopted version clarifies this to the extent that the reference to customary market practice has been abandoned. Honest market practice combines both facts and norms. The normative reference system is crucial. The Directive purports to seek the realisation of the internal market, which can only be guaranteed in a competitive environment. The competitive background of unfair commercial practices law clearly restricts any attempt to start from subjective standards. The Directive embeds an objective review standard. Objectivity can only be guaranteed if it is not the competitors' interests which are decisive, but also the taking into account of all circumstances, including the interests of the consumers.[39]

*(i) Criticism of the conceptual approach*

In the light of its legislative history, criticisms that professional diligence in the Unfair Commercial Practices Directive only protects individuals and competitors in the meaning of Article 10(2) of the Paris Convention is far-fetched.[40] The latter was designed in the nineteenth century to set up standards on intellectual property rights. Article 10 *bis* contains an obligation of the signatory States to take appropriate measures to ensure effective protection against unfair competition which means any act of competition contrary to honest practices in industrial or commercial matters. Honest practices are often understood as synonyms for professional diligence

---

36 Article 2598 of the Italian *codice civile* refers to *correttezza professionale*, F. Henning-Bodewig, 'Stellungnahme des Max-Planck-Instituts zum Vorschlag einer Richtlinie über unlautere Geschäftspraktiken vom 18 June 2003 und einer Verordnung über die Zusammenarbeit im Verbraucherschutz vom 18 July 2003' (2003) *Gewerblicher Rechtsschutz und Urheberrecht Internationaler Teil* 926, at 928; Busch, *op.cit.*, at 94; Glöckner, *op.cit.*, at 939. Such a conclusion must be taken with care as Italian unfair trading law is not considered being a pioneer in Europe.

37 BGH (1960) *Gewerblicher Rechtsschutz und Urheberrecht* 558, at 560 – 'Eintritt in Kundenbestellung'; BGHZ 54, 188, at 190 – 'Fernsprechwerbung'; BGHZ 81, 291, at 296 – 'Bäcker-Fachzeitschrift'.

38 Glöckner, *op.cit.*, 939; Schünemann, *op.cit.*, 929.

39 This has been convincingly established by J. Keßler, 'UWG und Verbraucherschutz – Wege und Umwege zum Recht der Marktkommunikation' (2005) *Wettbewerb in Recht und Praxis* 264, at 270 for § 1(2) of the German Unfair Competition Act.

40 But Glöckner, *op.cit.*, 940.

aiming at the protection of individual interests and not of the competition as such. In such a reading of the Paris Convention, that is, of professional diligence, morality, rather than distortion of competition, would be the decisive criterion. It was the EC legislator's intention, however, to free unfair trading law from tortious traditions which are still alive in Germanic and Romance law tradition and to set up a regulatory framework which understands unfair commercial practices law as a means of regulating communication in the market. This is why the professional diligence has nothing to do with liability measures.[41]

The argument, however, that professional diligence is incompatible with the objective of consumer protection carries more weight. Consumers are not in a position to establish honest market practices. Their interests only count indirectly as a normative corrective of factual standards set by the traders, if at all. This idea is reflected in the reference to good faith which was inserted in the definition on the European Parliament's insistence. However, such arguments do not take the upgrading of consumer protection into account. The Unfair Commercial Practices Directive has made it abundantly clear that consumer protection may no longer be regarded as a means to correct business practice, but equally as an important protective objective.

The recitals of the Directive do not help in clarifying the significance of professional diligence with regard to the integration of consumer protection. The Commission was guilty of circularity when it stated in paragraph 53 of the Explanatory Memorandum to its first proposal that professional diligence, in order to be sensible and in compliance with primary Community law, could only relate to measures of care and skill exercised by a good businessmen in the majority of Member States. The uncertainty of the legal term was said to be decisive and needed to be clarified irrespective of whether it concerned 'fair market practice' or 'professional diligence'.[42] The question remains what is meant *in concreto* by equal protection of the consumer in relation to professional diligence.

The Commission has failed so far to give consumer associations a formal role in the elaboration of codes of conduct or soft law rules. The participation of consumer associations in the drafting of such rules, which would almost certainly be considered as the yardstick in case of conflict,[43] would put such rules in a different perspective. This is particularly so if participation and the opportunity for providing input are not merely to be of a symbolic character. Such regulation would come close to the concept of co-regulation in terms of the terminology introduced by the Commission, given that the interests of consumer organisations would be procedurally guaranteed. So long as this is not the case, any attempt to treat honest market practice equally to customary market practice should be treated with caution. In the light of the explicit setting of the objectives of the Directive it might be presumed that marketing

---

41 Schünemann, *op.cit.*, 931 and also Gamerith, *op.cit.*, 395, at 417.

42 Cf. the criticism of the terminology by Glöckner, *op.cit.*, 936, at 939; Schünemann, *§ 3 No. 82* in Harte-Bavendamm and Henning-Bodewig, *op.cit.*

43 See Chapter 7(k).

practices standards which have been set up by the business sector, to the extent that they are invoked, are fully considering the consumer interests. This would shift the burden of 'proof' to the trader, who would then be required to establish that the rules are a reflection of honest business practices.

At the same time, it must be clarified whether Article 5(2) constitutes an obligation to act, that is, making information on the appropriate rules on professional diligence available.[44] Given the significance of information duties in marketing practices regulation,[45] and the special position codes of conduct are given in Article 6(2), such an obligation to inform would be a first step to understand consumer protection not only as a means of correction but as an integral part of a European concept of 'fairness'.

*(ii) National, European and international professional diligence*

Theoretically, national, European and international requirements can be considered as a point of reference to give shape to professional diligence. It is necessary to interpret professional diligence autonomously. This is the established practice of the European Court of Justice:[46]

> The need for a uniform application of community law and the principle of equality require that the terms of a provision of community law which makes no express reference to the law of Member States for the purpose of determining its meaning and scope must normally be given an independent and uniform interpretation throughout the community; that interpretation must take into account the context of the provision and the purpose of the relevant regulations.

In this light it is even more difficult to define the term 'professional diligence' genuinely within a European context. The European Court of Justice has used honest market practices in *Gillette*[47] in putting Article 6(1)(c) of the Directive 89/104/EEC on trademarks into more specific terms which are, however, of no direct help for defining professional diligence. Attempts by the European Court of Justice to put honest market practices in the respective national regulatory context must be rejected. The European Commission has in mind to make use of professional diligence in order to develop European business standards through codes of conduct.

Here the conceptual shortcoming of the Directive which – very weakly[48] – favours codes of conduct, but which fails to provide regulatory provisions, becomes evident. There are no European codes of conduct which are included in the regulatory concept of the Directive. The Directive does not give shape to the idea of co-regulation which

---

44   Objecting: Veelken, *op.cit.*, at 15.

45   See Chapter 5(c)(i).

46   ECJ Case 327/82 *BV Vee e Vleeshandel v Produktschap voor Vee en Vlees Ekro* [1984] ECR 107 at 11; cf. Radeideh, *op.cit.*, at 266.

47   Case 228/03 *Gillette* [2005] ECR I–2337 at 49.

48   See Chapter 7(e).

is politically favoured but neglected in practice. There might be codes of conduct, but they have been elaborated by the market participants themselves without the participation of consumer organisations. They determine the 'customary', the actual features of professional diligence. Their applicability within a European context is limited. At best Article 5(2) might be read as giving the European Commission the opportunity to develop its preferred model of co-regulation, at least à la longue.

The remaining gap can be bridged – to a certain extent – by applying the advertising rules of the International Chamber of Commerce.[49] These non-binding rules are highly appreciated, at least in some Member States. The real issue, however, is whether national rules can be used as a reference point to put professional diligence into specific terms. The Unfair Commercial Practices Directive purports to Europeanise fairness. A reference to national customs would result in a re-nationalisation of fairness. If national courts were to consider national customs which are set out by codes of conduct and professional rules, they would run the risk of being confronted with the argument of market segregation. This is particularly so with regard to codes restricting the advertising of liberal professions. The suggestion in Article 5(2) leads into a dead end. As long as co-regulation has not been put in specific terms, and as long as there are no codes of conduct which can function as a normative basis for defining professional diligence, the first constitutive element of the general clause in Article 5(2) remains legally meaningless.

### (iii) The significance of professional diligence for misleading and aggressive commercial practices

The term 'professional diligence' is of no relevance for misleading actions, misleading omissions and aggressive commercial practices. Misleading and aggressive practices are to be regarded as *per se* violations of professional diligence. This consequence was clearly stated in paragraph 57 of the Explanatory Memorandum to the first draft proposal. Similar wording is no longer contained in the final version of the Directive. The contrary cannot be concluded by virtue of Article 7(4)(d) either, according to which traders are required, in the case of an invitation to purchase, to provide information about the arrangements for payment, delivery, performance and the complaint handling policy, if they depart from the requirements of professional diligence. This negative exception is unlikely to be suitable as an argument to make professional diligence a decisive criterion when examining misleading advertising.[50]

---

49 W.L. Craig, W.W. Park and J. Paulsson, *International Chamber of Commerce Arbitration* (New York: Oceana Public., 3rd edn, 2000).

50 M. Röttinger, '"Unfair commercial practices" – Ein Beispiel europarechtlicher Rechtssetzung mit vielen offenen Fragen' (2003) 4 *Medien und Recht* 246, at 251.

*(iv) Consequences arising from the lack of Europeanised professional diligence*

The consequence which results from the deficient configuration of the concept of professional diligence is striking. A European concept of 'fairness' has to rely on the second pillar provided for in Article 5(2). The 'material distortion of the economic behaviour of the consumer' functions *de facto* and *de jure* as the decisive yardstick by which to assess unfair commercial practices. This conclusion unites all critics of a fairness formula linked to professional diligence.[51]

### e. Material Distortion of the Economic Behaviour of the Consumer

Article 5(2) refers to the material distortion of the economic behaviour of the consumer which is defined in Article 2(e) as using a 'commercial practice to appreciably impair the consumer's ability to make an informed decision, thereby causing the consumer to take a transactional decision that he would not have taken otherwise'.

The two provisions, Article 5(2) and Article 2(e) are not entirely compatible. Article 5(2) refers to a commercial practice which materially distorts, or is likely to materially distort, economic behaviour. Article 2(e) used 'appreciable' rather than 'material' to describe the measure of impairment. Further inconsistencies result from the economic 'behaviour' of the consumer and his ability to make an informed 'decision'. It seems obvious that the distortion of 'economic behaviour' as stated in Article 5(2) is not identical to the ability to take a 'transactional decision' in terms of Article 6(1) and Article 7(1) as defined in Article 2(k). Article 2(e) refers to an 'informed decision' which is intended to be different from a 'transactional decision'. Vice versa, the notion of informed decision seems narrower than economic behaviour.

The interplay between economic behaviour, informed decision and transactional decision must be clarified first, before it is possible to have a deeper look at what is hidden behind this relatively unspecified threefold terminology. It is the consumer's autonomy which must be impaired. But what does autonomy mean and if it is impaired, does the trader have to have tried to influence the consumer's autonomy intentionally? Is fault required? Last but not least, not each and every commercial practice will impair the consumer's autonomy, but only those which materially distort his autonomy. So there seems to be a threshold which must be met in order to label a commercial practice as unfair. This seems to suggest that the advertising at stake must have in fact impaired the consumer's autonomy. However, this is not the case: a *potential* effect on his behaviour seems to suffice. That is why the Directive does not establish a causal link between the commercial action and the consumer's behaviour. The Directive goes very much into detail here and requires a explanation of the terms used in order to show which requirements have to be met before the

---

51  This consequence confirms Radeideh's view, *op.cit.*, that a principle under the same name already exists *praeter legem*.

'economic behaviour of the consumer has been materially distorted' by commercial transactions.

*(i) Economic behaviour, informed and transactional decisions*

The threefold terminology, as introduced by the Community legislator – economic behaviour (Article 5(2)), informed decision (Article 2(e)), transactional decision (Article 2(k)) – should not be overestimated in their significance and function. On a scale, economic behaviour seems to be the most significant and transactional decision the narrowest of the three, informed decision ranking in the middle. All three terms have in common the intention to ensure the consumer's autonomy during pre-contractual negotiations.[52] One might feel tempted to speculate over the difference between 'behaviour' and 'decision'. However, it is not the consumer's behaviour *per se* which is of concern to the objective of the Directive, but his behaviour in the market. This can only be affected if the consumer does not merely 'behave', that is, examines advertising or otherwise or is affected by commercial practices, but also is willing to take decisions. Therefore he needs information to do so. Only informed decisions of consumers contribute to workable competition on the market. The reference to the market shines through in the manner of the informed decisions which the consumer takes; the market is the focus. Here the consumer's economic interests are affected. That is why his decisions must be regarded as transactional decisions. At this point the Community legislator steps in and provides a definition. According to Article 2(k) a 'transactional decision' means:

> any decision taken by a consumer concerning whether, how and on what terms to purchase, make payment in whole or in part for, retain or dispose of a product or to exercise a contractual right in relation to the product, whether the consumer decides to act or to refrain from acting.

The last half sentence expressly shows that the transactional decision in Article 2(k) is not to be treated in the same way as the decision to conclude a contract even if this might often be the case in practice.[53] This means that the Directive also applies to decisions to use a certain supplier or to continue or end a professional relationship.[54] The definition is not really helpful either.

It seems more sensible to understand the three terms as one and not to become entangled in their different wording. If at all, it seems appropriate to proceed from

---

52 The definition is problematic with regards to the evaluation of after-sales practices which do not distort the pre-contractual process of taking a decision. See C. Twigg-Flesner, D. Parry, G. Howells and A. Nordhausen, *An Analysis of the Application and Scope of the Unfair Commercial Practices Directive*, (Report for the Department of Trade and Industry, 18 May 2005), 2.39, 14 at: http://www.dti.gov.uk/ccp/consultpdf/final_report180505.pdf.

53 But R. Sack, 'Die relevante Irreführung im Wettbewerbsrecht' (2004) *Wettbewerb in Recht und Praxis* 521, at 522.

54 Röttinger, *op.cit.*, 251.

the consumer's 'behaviour' as this requirement is mirrored in Article 5(2) and it encompasses both informed and transactional decisions. Such a pragmatic reading facilitates the use of the terms which have an impact on the entire Directive. It must be interpreted in the light of the objective of the Directive. Therefore it is necessary to reduce the terminology to its most basic function, which is to keep and maintain the consumer's autonomy. Therefore the context in which the three different terms are used in the Directive is irrelevant. No distinction is to be drawn between the economic behaviour of the consumer in Article 5(2) and the transactional decision in Article 6(1) and Article 7(1). The true challenge is to give shape to the consumer's autonomy, which lies at the heart of the Directive.

*(ii) The objective side of the distortion: the autonomy of the consumer*

On its own, the concept of autonomy in the Unfair Commercial Practices Directive, even in the entire European unfair trading law, seems largely incomprehensible. In essence it is a legal term; however, it needs a reference point outside the legal system. This is usually seen in the competition law order as designed and understood by the different competition theories and concepts (*Wettbewerbstheorien und Wettbewerbskonzepte*). Some writers consider the reference to the competition order to be a circular argument, as it enshrines a given understanding on 'good' and 'fair' competition.[55] They search for a connection to the real world translated into the control question of whether a consumer can, subsequent to the immediate motivating effect provoked by the advertisement, still approve his or her transaction in the form it has been taken. Such an understanding relates the concept of autonomy to behavioural science, that is, to behavioural economics. That is why the findings of behavioural economics could and should be used to define the autonomy of the consumer. These findings, however, question the premise of Community law *ex ante*, namely to take an informed decision, as they do not consider actual behaviour to be a sufficient guide. The term 'informed consumer', which forms the basis of Community law, bears a normative character. It is only from this perspective that the consumer can fulfil his role and function as a guarantor for the realisation of the internal market. It is therefore decisive whether the commercial practices distort the 'outward freedom' of action (*äußere Handlungsfreiheit*).[56]

In order to define whether the outward freedom of action of the consumer is distorted, the modalities and the circumstances which relate to the conclusion of the contract, the contents and the conditions of the contract as well as after-sales service need to be taken into account. Possible factors therefore include all practices, be it information and non-information marketing methods which touch upon the outward

---

55  Glöckner, *Introduction B No. 137, 138* in Harte-Bavendamm and Henning-Bodewig, *op.cit.*

56  The outward freedom has to be kept distinct from the inward freedom. The former is an objective category related to the market behaviour, the latter covers the subjective side of autonomy, that is, intent and fault, see section e(iii).

freedom of action. To this extent, there is a link between the concept of autonomy, which unifies economic behaviour, the informed and transactional decision, and the term 'commercial practices' which accompanies the commercial transaction from the cradle to the grave, including advertising, pre-contractual negotiations and after-sales service. The necessary taking into consideration of all factors which impact on the taking of the decision is restricted by the exclusion of elements which do not materially distort the decision of a consumer. As a matter of fact there is a connection between the materiality threshold and the autonomy concept. Depending on how the requirements on transactional decisions are defined, the materiality threshold varies in its content and scope.[57]

The touchstone for the autonomy concept of the consumer is the assessment of emotional advertising. It is sufficient to distort the free making of a decision and thus the economic behaviour of the consumer. Pursuant to the concept developed herein, Community law may only control emotional advertising to a limited extent. The situation is different, though, where the advertiser's strategies used are so serious and burdensome that the consumer finds himself unduly influenced or thinks himself to be unduly influenced. An adequate assessment of emotional advertising under Community law requires an overall view of the legal and economic concept of 'fairness' as enshrined in the Directive. The Unfair Commercial Practices Directive purports only to limit the margin of appreciation at the extreme ends of the distortion of the freedom to take decisions leaving a broad spectrum available to the creativity of market communication. At one end there is the economic – but not only the economic – freedom to take a decision. It requires the consumer to question his emotions critically and to reduce them to a rational core. At the other end there is the protection of the consumer against aggressive advertising, harassment, coercion and undue influence. In this respect it could be alleged that European unfair commercial practice law legitimately economises emotions – as has already happened in the area of health-related advertising.[58] As a result, the economic autonomy of the consumer should normally not be distorted by emotional advertising. If the emotions are appealed to in a tasteless and indecent manner, then the question arises whether more stringent measures are justified by reference to deviating national morals.

*(iii) The subjective side of the distortion – intent and fault*

The word distortion already pushes for the question whether, in addition to the 'objective' distortion of the autonomy by unfair commercial practices, there is or even must be a requirement of a respective 'subjective' intention of the trader. Article 2(e) defines 'to materially distort the economic behaviour of consumers' as using a commercial practice to appreciably impair the consumer's ability to make an informed decision. The word 'to' might suggest such a subjective requirement

---

57  See section e(v).

58  See, for example, Case C–465/98 *Verein gegen Unwesen in Handel und Gewerbe Köln eV gegen Adolf Darbo AG.* [2000] ECR I–02297.

of commercial practice.[59] By such a reading an element of fault would be indirectly inserted into European unfair commercial practices law. It might be possible to adhere to this wording and to conclude that it must be the objective and purpose of the actions to distort the consumer but this need not be their intention.[60] However, it is also possible to conclude from a systematic reading of the definitions and the limited significance of the term 'transactional decision' that the wording of Article 2(e) alone cannot justify the existence of a subjective element. Other interpretations seem less credible, taking into account the rather unconvincing system of the Directive. Therefore in answering the question of whether European secondary law contains an element of fault, it must be looked at against the background of the competition theory concepts against which the Directive and the entire European unfair commercial practices law must be seen.

The concept of workable competition favoured here demoralises unfair trading law. For this reason there cannot be an element of intention, or any other subjective objective, in Community law when determining whether the rules of the Directive are violated. Despite the fact that formulations are unfortunate and allow for different interpretations, giving the term 'fairness' a subjective dimension would be contrary to the concept of workable competition enshrined in the Directive.[61] Only this reading will be compatible with a modern concept of unfair marketing practices law which establishes objective standards of conduct in the market and which presses for compliance with these standards irrespective of whether the advertiser 'intended' to mislead the consumer with his unfair commercial practices or not. This does not mean that there may be no direct link between the commercial practice, the behaviour and the decision; a connection must be objectively established.

*(iv) The relevance of the materiality criterion*

Article 5(2) refers to 'to materially distort', the German version to '*wesentliche Beeinflussung*' and the French version to '*manière substantielle*'. Irrespective of any difference in the meaning, the methodological relevance of the materiality criterion needs to be assessed. The views in legal literature vary widely. Overall, there are three different approaches. The first refers to the question of whether by inserting the materiality criterion the threshold should be lowered.[62] Accordingly, the kind of violation, the degree of fault or the significance of the legal object affected could be considered in defining the threshold. The second variant consists in understanding the materially criterion as a procedural rule governing the burden of proof, thereby

---

59 Cf. Köhler and Lettl, *op.cit.*, 1019, at 1035; critical: Veelken, *op.cit.*, at 8; Gamerith, *op.cit.*, 395, at 417 speaks of an element of intention.

60 Köhler and Lettl, *op.cit.*, 1037; Veelken, *op.cit.*, 9 n. 119; Apostolopoulos, *op.cit.*, 846.

61 For the entire German law, Schünemann, *§ 3 No. 229* in Harte-Bavendamm and Henning-Bodewig, *op.cit.*

62 P. Heermann, 'Die Erheblichkeitsschwelle i.S.d. § 3 UWG–E' (2004) *Gewerblicher Rechtsschutz und Urheberrecht* 94, at 96.

freeing the claimant from having to prove the materiality of the unfair competition practice which is prone to distort competition.[63] From this perspective[64] only the market strength of the unfairly conducting market participant or an empirically provable risk of imitating the unfair conduct could be taken into account. This dispute needs to be resolved against the background of the concept of workable competition defended here. The exclusion of non-material distortion from the scope of unfair trading law corresponds with the vision of 'competition' whose functioning is not distorted by minor interruptions. The advantage of this model is that it does not proceed from an ideal situation, but takes into account the real functional conditions of competition. In this respect 'material distortion' must be understood as objectively lowering the threshold of relevance. That is why all efforts to declare the criterion as being irrelevant or tautological need to be rejected.[65] A non-material distortion is said to constitute no distortion by definition since it will have no impact on the consumer's making of a decision.

According to the third variant,[66] the introduction of a threshold of relevance brings about a definition of the scope of application as regards subject matter. Commercial practices which concern the relationship between the trader and the final consumer, but do not distort the economic freedom of the consumer to take a decision as they do not reach the threshold of relevance, would fall outside the scope of application of the Directive. Full harmonisation would not be a regulatory bar in terms of Article 4. As a final consequence, this would grant Member States a significant margin of appreciation to prohibit advertising practices even if they are non-material in a sense that they distort the economic freedom of consumers to take a decision. Consequently, this line of argument draws a distinction between economic distortions and idealistic distortions, the former coming under the scope of the Directive and the latter falling outside its scope. Here Member States remain competent and are able to refer to different national morals in order to deal with idealistic behaviour.

*(v) The practical significance of the materiality threshold*

In compliance with the argument pursued herein, the reasoning to the first Proposal contained situations in which the threshold was said not to be reached, for example, incentives such as the offering of free coffee or the free transportation to the place of business.[67] These examples are no longer contained in the final version. Instead Recital 6 speaks of a 'negligible' impact, which is likely to be the same as 'immaterial'. The final sentence in Recital 6 counts as being non-material 'accepted advertising and marketing practices, such as legitimate product placement, brand differentiation or the offering of incentives which may legitimately affect consumers' perceptions

---

63  Schünemann, *§ 3 No. 241* in Harte-Bavendamm and Henning-Bodewig, *op.cit.*
64  Schünemann, *§ 3 No. 278* in Harte-Bavendamm and Henning-Bodewig, *op.cit.*
65  Cf. Radeideh, *op.cit.*, at 263.
66  Veelken, *op.cit.*, at 7.
67  Explanatory Memorandum, *op.cit.*, paras 54 and 55.

of products and influence their behaviour without impairing the consumer's ability to make an informed decision'. The wording presents a circular reasoning as only 'legitimate' product placement and so forth shall be non-material. This is only the case if the measure does not reach the materiality threshold. Even if this is taken for granted the restriction remains that the decision of the consumer must not be unlawfully distorted. Such clarification is superfluous, at least in this form.

The restriction of the prohibition of unfair advertising to 'material' distortion purports to free transactions from the eventuality that even minor distortions will be judged unfair. As shown by the rules on misleading and aggressive marketing practices in Article 6(1), Article 7(1) and Article 8, only (significant) distortion will come into play, where it is apt to cause the consumer to take a decision that he would not have taken otherwise. In other words, the commercial practice must be likely to distort the consumer's ability to take an informed decision.[68] Contrary to the occasional presumption in German case law, the unfair verdict does not apply to the free transportation to the place of business,[69] as this usually does not prevent an informed decision being taken. The situation becomes more complicated if the incentive is relatively valuable, such as a free flight.[70] The limitation cannot be set in stone. To the extent that free gifts are of concern and that they are intended to persuade the consumer to enter into a contract, then reference must be made to the (at least until recently) envisaged Regulation on Sales Promotion which proceeds from the assumption that a sufficiently informed consumer cannot be distorted in his decision-making, although Member States are trying to defend residual competences to prohibit certain abuses. It remains to be seen whether the Commission manages to adopt the still pending project. According to a recent announcement, the European Commission even envisages withdrawing the proposal.[71] Beyond mere policy considerations, hard legal arguments can be found in *Pall/Dahlhausen*, where the European Court of Justice held that statements about the origin of the trademark which are misleading are not likely to trigger a misconception which would be relevant to taking a transactional decision.[72] The case *in concreto* concerned the evaluation of the existence of the danger of confusion under trademark law. However, the ruling expresses a more general legal thought. Not every omitted or even false piece of information is material in terms of the threshold of relevance.

The threshold of materiality is inseparably linked to the model of the informed consumer.[73] However, this link is being torn into pieces where particularly vulnerable groups of consumers are addressed by the commercial practices. In this respect the

---

68  Explanatory Memorandum, *op.cit.*, para. 54.

69  Explanatory Memorandum, *op.cit.*, para. 54.

70  Henning-Bodewig, *op.cit.*, 926, at 927; similarly Busch, *op.cit.*, 94, at 96.

71  Outcome of the screening of legislative proposals pending before the legislator COM(2005) 462 final (27 September 2005).

72  Case 238/89 [1990] ECR I–4827.

73  See Chapter 5(b)(iii)–(iv).

differentiation between the average consumer and particularly vulnerable groups in Article 5(3) impacts on the threshold of materiality.

### (vi) Actual or potential distortion

According to Article 5(2) in the German version of the first Proposal, unfair commercial practices not only needed to be material but also actually distorting, that is, '*im konkreten Falle unter Würdigung aller tatsächlichen Umstände*' (in the specific case taking account of all factual circumstances). The English version merely stated that the unfair commercial practice is to be regarded as unfair 'if it materially distorts or is likely to materially distort the economic behaviour with regard to the product of the average consumer whom it reaches or to whom it is addressed'. There was no such reference to the specific case and its facts at issue. However, the differences between the English and the German versions can be set aside, as the reference to actual and factual circumstances has been abandoned in the German final version. During the second reading, the European Parliament suggested the amendment of Recital 7 so that where the Directive, and in particular the general clause, applied, the merits of each case would be considered extensively. The Commission accepted the amendment. That is why Recital 7 contains a final sentence saying: 'Full account should be taken of the context of the individual case concerned in applying this Directive, in particular the general clauses thereof'. This wording serves as a guideline for interpretation of the Unfair Commercial Practices Directive and impacts on Article 5.

If one looks into the system of the Directive, it becomes apparent that there is an almost identical reference to the 'factual context', as seen in the initial Proposal, in Article 6(2) (misleading actions) and Article 7(1) (misleading omissions), both in the German and the English versions. However, this reference is put into perspective when one remembers that likely distortion suffices. The different wording in Article 5 (no reference to the factual context), Article 6 (with reference), and Article 7 (with reference) should not be overestimated. It is more likely that the differences result from a lack of attention to details which is all too characteristic in today's legislation. It can be taken for granted that the Unfair Commercial Practices Directive proceeds from an interaction of normative requirements on the consumer and his actual behaviour. This does not mean that the actual behaviour – even if it was only potential – needs to be determined empirically.[74] The EC legislator has put the significance of the intervention threshold into perspective. It is therefore irrelevant whether commercial practices have distorted the consumer materially 'in fact'. It suffices that commercial practices are likely to distort rational decision-making. Community law requires the national control authorities to take a prognostic decision on the possibility of a material distortion.

The difference between 'norms' and 'facts', between the normative concept of the circumspect consumer and the factual circumstances at issue, is of utmost importance

---

74  Also Köhler and Lettl, *op.cit.*, 1019, at 1037 (79).

for the interplay between European law and the European Court of Justice providing guidance on how to read and interpret commercial practices and the national law and national courts to apply the transposed European law to the circumstances of the given case. Nearly 50 years of experience demonstrate the clash between broad and demanding European principles and the process of their application and transformation within national legal systems. The European Court of Justice adheres to the limits of its jurisdiction and provides guidelines on how to read and understand the relevant provisions of EC unfair commercial practices law. Sometimes, however, it has overstepped the boundaries and decided the case at issue directly. This is not the place to deal with the effects of norms and facts *in extenso*. However, common standards in Europe can only be developed if the distinction between norms and facts is not (mis)used by national courts to circumvent the prerequisites of European unfair commercial practices law. One might wonder to what extent it is possible to merge the concepts instead of insisting on their differences. European unfair commercial practices law is certainly rather hostile against overemphasising the role of 'facts', as is clearly indicated in Recital 18. That is why the assessment of facts lies in the hands of judges. They have to define the factual circumstances. This is already a rather normative position, as the consumers' specific expectations and actions are of limited relevance. They are filtered through the normative perspectives of the judges sitting in the court. That is why it might be worth considering to what extent it is possible to 'standardise' the factual circumstances, that means to fully evaluate the circumstances at stake but in a typified or generalised form.

### (vii) Causality between the distortion and the process of taking the decision

It seems that Article 2(e) establishes a causal link, requiring the commercial practice to be such that it causes the consumer to take a transactional decision that he would not have taken otherwise.[75] This wording does not mean causality *strictu sensu*. Causality would require submitting evidence that the commercial practices are generally likely to distort the consumer in taking his decision. So far research efforts have widely failed to provide full evidence that there is such an empirical link. Legal disputes turn around the question of which methods are suitable in defining the causal link. That is why the relationship between distortion and decision-making is normative – fictitious – just as the benchmark consumer is nothing but a legal fiction. From a legal point of view it is crucial whether the measure, or more precisely the chosen method, is likely to distort the consumer. To this extent 'causality' is contained already in the decision whether the autonomy of the consumer is distorted or is likely to be distorted by a commercial practice.[76]

---

75  Glöckner, *Introduction B No. 137, 138*, in Harte-Bavendamm and Henning-Bodewig, *op.cit.*

76  Similarly Radeideh, *op.cit.*, at 263, 277, 278.

## f. The 'Average Consumer' and Particularly Vulnerable Groups

Almost no other topic of European unfair marketing practices law has been dealt with in legal literature to such an extent as the consumer image, the *Verbraucherleitbild*. Depending on the viewpoint, the normative orientation of EC law and its focus on the average consumer – the consumer who is informed and reasonably circumspect – is favoured or rejected.[77] For a long time it looked as though the normative consumer image concerned Germany alone. German consumers were said to be so stupid that they were unable to discover the hidden messages behind each and every advertisement. However, during the preparatory work of the Directive it became apparent that the Commission's efforts to codify in a Directive the image of the average consumer as created by the European Court of Justice met strong opposition. The Scandinavian countries in particular argued against the normative concept of the informed and circumspect consumer, insofar as it would be a general yardstick which would endanger the protection of particularly vulnerable consumer groups such as children and the elderly. With the support of the European Parliament, the Unfair Commercial Practices Directive provides two ways in which the general fairness clause is varied for such vulnerable consumers. One applies where the practice is targeted at all consumers and the other where, among the consumers, socalled 'vulnerable groups' of consumers are identified. Only in the latter context is the concept of vulnerability used expressly; the former simply refers to average members of particular groups of consumers, who may or may not be vulnerable. However, it is clearly intended to help groups such as the young and the elderly.

The protection of particularly vulnerable groups introduces into the concept of 'fairness' an element of social policy. This element clearly forms part of the European concept of 'fairness'; it is not outside the scope of the Directive. It is not like non-market values, taste, decency and cultures.[78] In this respect a common denominator all over Europe must be found. In theory, the protection of particularly vulnerable groups under Article 5(3) should be kept separate from matters of taste, decency and culture. If, however, commercial practices affect the vulnerable consumer in a way which brings to bear matters of taste, decency and even culture, the starting point should always be to solve the conflict under the basis of Article 5(3). Otherwise the *effet utile* of the Directive would be undermined.

### (i) The average consumer as a standard model

Unfairness is generally measured against the model of the 'average consumer', that is, the 'average consumer, who is reasonably well-informed and reasonably observant and circumspect' in terms of the established case law of the European Court

---

77  See Chapter 3(d)(ii) and Chapter 5(b)(iii).
78  See, on the reach and importance of Article 5(3), Chapter 3(d)(ii).

of Justice. The average consumer is the measure of all things.[79] He appears in the Directive in Article 5(2) without being defined further. The clause containing such a definition in the Proposal was deleted, not least on the insistence of the Scandinavian Member States. Recital 18 refers to the European Court of Justice's construction of an average consumer. It states that the European Court of Justice has found it necessary, in adjudicating the effect of misleading advertising – oddly enough it only refers to the Misleading Advertising Directive – to examine the effect on a 'notional, typical consumer'. The case law of the European Court of Justice on the average consumer seems firmly established so far. It reaches beyond unfair marketing practices law and forms part of the *effet utile*, irrespective of the fact that the European Court of Justice has developed its conception of the consumer from primary law and that it has transferred it from there to all relevant areas of law such as administrative law, food, cosmetics and trademark law. The question has been raised to what extent the deletion of the 'average consumer' reference in the text of the Directive should and must be understood as a paradigm change. This could mean that the Directive is meant to challenge the well-established case law of the European Court of Justice. One might, however, also argue that the Directive tries to find a compromise in establishing a two-tier approach.[80] Such an understanding would explain why both notions appear in Article 5, the 'average consumer' and the 'vulnerable consumer'. In the context of the analysis of Article 5 it might suffice to say that commercial practices may generally not be assessed against the understanding of particularly vulnerable or untypical consumers. The average consumer is the rule, whereas the particularly vulnerable consumer is the exception.

### (ii) Particularly vulnerable consumer groups as a special provision

Ever since the passing of the Unfair Commercial Practices Directive the 'average consumer' is only appropriate as a reference model where the commercial practices appeal to or at least reach the 'consumer in general'. To the extent that commercial practices are addressed to a special group of consumers, the understanding of the average member of the respective group is the measure in question. Article 5(3) refers to consumers who, because of their mental or physical infirmity, age or credulity are particularly vulnerable to certain commercial practices or underlying products. The wording has a normative component as it purports to evaluate the advertising measure from the perspective of the average member of this group. In order to preserve the harmonious relation with the consumer image developed under primary law, the European Court of Justice's formula on 'social, cultural and linguistic factors' to be

---

79  Case C–470/93 *Mars* [1995] ECR I–1923; Case C–210/96 *Gut Springenheide* [1998] ECR I–4657; Case C–303/97 *Sektkellerei Kessler* [1999] ECR I–513; Case C–220/98 *Lifting–Crème* [2000] ECR I–117.

80  See, for a full account of the concept and the importance of the legislative history of the Directive, and where the envisaged reference to the average consumer has been abandoned, Chapter 5(b)(iii).

taken into account must be recalled. In this respect the European Court of Justice has already anticipated an opening up of its concept, although it does not deal with particularly vulnerable groups of consumers in terms of the Directive, but simply refers to 'social factors'.[81]

However, Recitals 18 and 19 provide some insight into the objectives of Article 5(3). The Community obviously thinks of 'children' and 'the elderly' as groups who should be protected not to a greater extent *per se*, but only against those commercial practices or products whose advertising is particularly appealing to them. Such an understanding is supported by Article 16 of the consolidated 'Television without Frontiers' Directive which states that television advertising must not cause 'minors' physical or psychological damage. There is no definition in the Directive of what 'mental or physical infirmity' or 'credulity' could mean. However, it is not only necessary to define the different groups listed, but also to determine the average intellectual capacity of children, the elderly, mentally or physically disabled as well as credulous persons. In this respect the objection is not entirely unjustified that Article 5(3) seems to establish a completely different consumer image. This is a model which has made its career in post-war German case law and which has repeatedly been the subject of ironic and even cynical comments.[82]

The Directive purports to prevent the status quo being reintroduced by means of differentiated degrees of protection *de facto* and *de jure*.[83] The 'average consumer' is generally the measure of all things. Article 5(3) is the exception to the rule. This objective is achieved through the second sentence of Article 5(3), which highlights that the common and legitimate advertising practice of making exaggerated statements or statements which are not meant to be taken literally shall be maintained. Exaggeration forms part of the core of advertising, irrespective of its addressees. In this respect advertising is even protected under the European Convention on Human Rights. This means that children must learn to put into perspective the message conveyed by advertising and the elderly must not take the message in the advertising for granted if the exaggeration is self-explanatory.

### (iii) Children, the elderly, disabled and credulous people

It will be necessary to differentiate between the different groups mentioned. There is no disagreement that children and the elderly are particularly vulnerable and require protection. The question then is up to what stage does a child remain a child and from what stage does an elderly person become so. Advertising addresses the respective target groups in a really distinct manner. Very small children are addressed through their parents, adolescents can become addressees themselves. There is no definition

---

81  See Chapter 1(c)(iv).

82  Cf. with regard to the German legal situation, I. Scherer, 'Schutz "leichtgläubiger" und "geschäftlich unerfahrener" Verbraucher in *§ 4 Nr. 2 UWG* n.F. – Wiederkehr des alten Verbraucherleitbildes "durch die Hintertür"?' (2004) *Wettbewerb in Recht und Praxis* 1355.

83  Radeideh, *op.cit.*, at 264, 279, fears that this might be the unintended result.

under Community law defining minors or the elderly. Minors and the elderly appear in secondary law; however, it remains within the discretion of the Member States to define those terms. This could change if the Commission still manages to push through its proposal for a Regulation on Sales Promotion measures, according to which children up to the age of 16 are to be regarded as children.[84] The situation as regards the elderly is just as heterogeneous. On the one hand, dynamic and wealthy retired people will always remain a target group for advertising. The picture is different as regards the elderly who are bedridden and require external help. In this case nursing staff may be considered the addressees of the advertisements.

People suffering from physical (hardness of hearing, limited eyesight) or psychological (schizophrenia, depressions, neurosis) impairments are particularly vulnerable and in need of protection. There are evident problems of demarcation. But compared to children and the elderly, it seems less relevant as they do not represent a target group to the advertising business. To the extent that advertising is addressed to nursing staff, different measures apply, as for advertising addressing small children.

The biggest challenge arises from the definition of credulity. One tends to reason from a semantic point of view and to interpret, as a result of putting age and credulity on an equal footing, that they are similar categories and that credulity refers to a similar group of people. This, however, seems not to be the intention of the EC legislator – at least not according to the recitals. Distinct from, for example, the German legislator, the Directive refrains from putting commercial inexperience alongside credulity. A certain degree of help in putting credulity into a specific context is provided by the European Court of Justice in *Océano*,[85] *Heininger*[86] and *Cofidis*.[87] Within limits, the European Court of Justice is prepared to protect the legally ignorant consumer. This means that there are three terms which need to be delineated: credulity, commercial inexperience and ignorance of the law. In Germany the use of the average consumer as the standard model is strongly rejected in order to prevent '*Kaffeefahrtenteilnehmer*' (especially older people participating in organised tours including sales promotions) from becoming the general yardstick against which the fairness of advertising measures should be assessed. Scherer[88] writes: 'The credulity and commercial inexperience of the consumer (provided he actually is) as alleged by German case law is based on the fact that these consumers are too lethargic, too inattentive, too apathetic, too passive and too indolent to obtain information'. If this wording were taken as the appropriate yardstick, then only sales in hostels for asylum seekers and disabled would ever qualify as being unfair.

---

84  Article 2(j) of the last version, dated from 19 September 2004, Interinstitutional File 2001/0227 (COD) CONSOM 68 MI 250 CODEC 1014.

85  Joint Cases C–240/98 and C–244/98 *Océano Grupo Editorial and Salvat Editores v Sánchez Alcón Prades* [2000] ECR I–4941.

86  Case C–481/99 *Heininger v Bayerische Hypo- und Vereinsbank* [2001] ECR I–9945.

87  Case C–473/00 *Cofidis v Fredout* [2002] ECR I–10875.

88  Scherer, *op.cit.*, 1355, at 1357.

This harsh wording should not hide the fact that the Directive legitimately addresses a central problem concerning European and national unfair commercial practices law. Member States will retain a margin of appreciation in determining the need for protection of weaker parts of the population as the Community is far from agreeing and wanting to agree on such subtle, and at the same time fundamental, social policy questions. Article 5(3) also takes into account that the Community consists of 25 different traditions and cultures. Member States which take measures protecting certain consumer groups against unfair advertising under Article 5(3) must be aware that these might be challenged under the Directive and under the Treaty. Under both the Directive and Treaty the European Court of Justice might have to clarify the concept of vulnerable groups, if Member States refer to 'social and cultural factors', in order to defend a particular social policy. They would then be required to justify why the measures in question are necessary and whether they are appropriate and proportionate to achieve the level of protection envisaged.

*(iv) The purpose of the commercial practices*

The decision whether an advertisement is addressed to particularly vulnerable consumer groups may not be particularly easy; and the evaluation of spill-over effects is equally problematic. Advertisements which are addressed to adults can reach children. Depending on the way in which the advertising measure is interpreted, the potential addressee might differ.[89] However, it is right here where the different attitudes in Member States towards advertising to children gains importance. The Scandinavian countries have much more experience in dealing with advertising to children. In this respect these countries have fewer difficulties in applying the Directive than Member States which do not have such a tradition.

According to Article 5(3) it must be differentiated whether the trader could reasonably be expected to foresee that the commercial practices can materially distort the economic behaviour, not of the entireness of all consumers, but only of a clearly identifiable group of consumers who are particularly vulnerable. The indication in Article 5(3) and the recitals that the practices distort or are likely to distort this group seems to suggest that there is a subjective element in the design and choice of the advertising measure and that it pursues a particular objective. However, Article 5(3) does not require the existence of a subjective element.

The phrase to be 'reasonably expected to foresee' is also found in the EC Product Safety Directive and the Consumer Sales Directive. First it concerns the balancing of the interests of different perspectives; the producer purports to put on the market his products and the consumer expects to buy safe products. Secondly 'reasonably expected to foresee' is translated to intent and negligence, a view which had already not been in compliance with the requirements in the Consumer Sales Directive. As a matter of fact it concerns the establishment of a certain amount of self responsibility which is imposed on the consumer when investigating the products. 'Reasonably

---

89 Röttinger, *op.cit.*, at 251.

expected to foresee' requires the balancing of the opposing interests of the advertiser and the addressee. Neither the advertiser nor the addressee decides whether a commercial practice is addressed to a certain group of consumers. By inserting the requirement 'reasonably expected to foresee' Community law puts the determination into an objective perspective. Empirical evidence that a commercial practice pursues a certain objective or that certain groups are affected by the practice is irrelevant. It is the courts which will decide the issue. This shows that the Community legislator has found a means of dealing with and judging these types of conflicts sensibly.

*(v) The abolition of statistical evidence?*

Incidentally, and almost unnoticed, the Unfair Commercial Practices Directive generally questions the necessity of statistical evidence.[90] Recital 18 states: 'The average consumer test is not a statistical test. National courts and authorities will have to exercise their own faculty of judgement, having regard to the case law of the Court of Justice, to determine the typical reaction of the average consumer in a given case'. This statement is unequivocal. The context is obvious. Recital 18 exclusively deals with the consumer image, the average consumer and particularly vulnerable groups. It makes it clear first of all that no statistical evidence is needed to show that the consumer's autonomy is impaired. One might, however, go one step further and understand Recital 18 as abolishing statistical evidence. This would mean that the wording in Recital 18 'is not a statistical test' no longer leaves room for statistical relevance if actually produced. In the light of the conflict between German courts and the European Court of Justice one may expect Recital 18 to put an end to the still existing practice of using statistical evidence as a means for proof in Germany and Austria. It would then halt what is a never-ending discussion. Most of all, it would facilitate making the normative requirements under Community law compatible with the factual circumstances to be taken into consideration by the national courts.

It must be recalled that the European Court of Justice has developed a standard formula in its case law[91] which not only holds together inconsistent secondary law, but also refers to primary law. To this extent there is an interaction between primary and secondary law. The recognition of statistical evidence is not limited to the respective merits of the case. The Unfair Commercial Practices Directive purports to catch the remaining differences by the wording 'having regard to the case law of the Court of Justice'. This could mean that the European Court of Justice is required to amend its case law before Germany and Austria can be forced to abolish empirical evidence. The competence that Member States extracted from the European Court of Justice in numerous references to maintain empirical evidence as an appropriate means to assess facts could now be overcome by the Directive. In this respect Member States,

---

    90  This corresponds with the reading of Glöckner, *op.cit.*, at 941 n. 56; thereto T. Lettl, 'Gemeinschaftsrecht und neues UWG' (2004) *Wettbewerb in Recht und Praxis* 1079, at 1100.

    91  Case C–210/96 *Gut Springenheide* [1998] ECR I–4657 and Chapter 5(b)(ii).

in particular Austria and Germany, could lose by the Directive what they have gained from the European Court of Justice.

## g. Language and Fairness

The Directive remains silent on the significance of the language in advertising. However, it should not therefore be concluded that language is irrelevant in evaluating fairness. The Community legislator has rather put aside the question – in compliance with the established policy on language – of whether the use of a particular language, or of linguistically alienated messages, is likely to distort commercial transactions. As a matter of fact the problem arises with advertising measures which provide information. Therefore it is intended to explain the significance of language in the context of Articles 6 and 7, misleading actions and omissions. The formula of the European Court of Justice, according to which Member States are authorised to take into account cultural and linguistic factors, must be considered.[92]

## h. Relationship of the General Clause and the Special Provisions

*(i) Concept and practical significance*

As far as the relationship between the general clause in Article 5 and the special provisions in Articles 6 and 7 on misleading actions or omissions as well as the prohibition of 'aggressive commercial practices' as contained in Articles 8 and 9 are concerned, all these particular rules represent market behaviour-related forms of the prohibition of unfair commercial practices, according to Article 5(4). In other words: 'misleading' or 'aggressive' marketing strategies in terms of Articles 6 to 9 are always regarded as unfair.[93] This is also true by virtue of Article 5(5) for commercial practices listed in Annex I, which are not 'particularly' unfair but which 'shall in all circumstances be regarded as unfair'. It is therefore irrelevant whether these practices contradict the 'requirements of professional diligence' or whether they are likely to 'materially distort' the economic behaviour with regard to the product of the average consumer. If the probability of misleading advertising, the (likely) harassment, coercion and undue influence of the consumer exists, a violation of the trader's professional diligence and a distortion of the consumer's behaviour is irrebuttably presumed. Paragraph 56 of the Explanatory Memorandum to the first

---

92  See Chapter 3(d)(iii).

93  Röttinger, *op.cit.*, 251; Veelken, *op.cit.*, at 15; Explanatory Memorandum, *op.cit.*, para. 56. Different view: Gamerith, *op.cit.*, 395, at 415, who considers it to be possible that a general clause which is put into specific terms by case law affects the question of what to regard as misleading or aggressive. He states that a particular practice is either 'just' to be subsumed under misleading or aggressive or as 'another violation' against professional diligence under the general clause.

draft contained this clarification; the wording in the adopted version as laid down in Recitals 13 and 17 appears less outspoken. Recital 13 states that the general clause is 'elaborated' by rules on the two types of commercial practices, namely misleading commercial practices and aggressive commercial practices; this indication is not particularly helpful.

Particular countries which are experienced in dealing with a general clause have raised concerns about the idea that it could be possible without taking into account the specific circumstances to label commercial practices as misleading or aggressive *per se*. The reference to the general clause will help overcome potential conceptual deficiencies resulting from the application of Articles 6 to 9. Such an understanding does not comply with the concept of the Directive, under which reference to Article 5 may only be tolerated as a means of last resort.[94]

The criticism becomes harsher when the legal qualification of the list of proscribed practices is discussed. Some authors[95] believe that the Commission tried to standardise individual cases which could be interpreted in different ways. This regulatory technique is said to violate primary EC law and so the transposition of the list should therefore be rejected, for 'principled reasons'. Most of the practices listed are said to be already integrated in Articles 6 to 9 and Annex I. It is objected that the Annex does not allow the taking into account of concrete individual circumstances. However, Recital 17 states the complete opposite. Annex I is said to contain the full list of the 'only commercial practices' which 'can be deemed to be unfair without a case-by-case assessment against the provisions of Articles 5 to 9'. This is the reason why Article 5 differentiates between misleading and aggressive practices, which are 'in particular unfair' (Article 5(4)) and the commercial practices contained in Annex I, which are unfair 'in all circumstances' (Article 5(5)). Within Articles 5 to 9, the Directive allows the taking into account of the merits of the case, but not as regards commercial practices contained in Annex I. The Commission has defended its approach right from the beginning.[96] The list of blacklisted practices which are presumed to be unfair *per se* has been extended over the legislative process. The European Parliament alone has suggested 21 amendments, some of which were taken on board.[97] The final version contains 31 prescribed advertising practices. So there is much pressure from the legal-political side on the role and function of the practices listed.

The legal classification of Annex I will largely influence the significance of the Directive. If it emerged that as a matter of fact the list concerned matters more appropriately dealt with as individual cases, then the Commission would have failed to clear up the market by blacklisting certain market practices. The consequence

---

94  See section h(ii).

95  Gamerith, *op.cit.*, 395, at 425 *et seq.*, with detailed analysis, as well as a conclusion at 432.

96  This clarification was contained in the Proposal, see Explanatory Memorandum, *op.cit.*, para. 56.

97  Opinion of the 'Ausschuss für Verbraucherpolitik' from 21 January 2004, at 39 *et seq.*

would be that Member States would be given the opportunity of taking the individual circumstances of each case into consideration in their implementing legislation, whereas the Annex seems to exclude such an individualisation as it declares the enlisted practices to be unfair 'in all circumstances'. The result of this could only be diverging national standards. The Commission purports to avoid such a drifting apart. If the objective of the Directive is taken seriously, then it is of the utmost importance to establish the normative core of the individual prohibitions. Again here it is necessary to overcome the boundaries between European norms and national factual circumstances.[98]

If 'unfair' market behaviour, as it actually appears, is taken into account in the light of the current legal practice in Member States, then the overwhelming number of 'unfair commercial practices' would fall within the special provisions in Articles 6 to 9 (misleading and aggressive commercial practices) or within the list in Annex I to the Directive. If this reading is correct – and this is at least the intention of the EC legislator and even the *effet utile* of the Directive – the general clause in Article 5 is of conceptually limited significance. Accordingly, the number of cases requiring the application of the general clause should be limited.[99] Quite the opposite is argued by those who consider the Unfair Commercial Practices Directive to be deficient. They argue that if the general clause were not broadly applicable, then there would be a significant lack in protection.[100] Four examples are given: first, setting significant incentives in order to make consumers buy a product – this problem is deferred by the EC legislator into the Regulation on Sales Promotion, although it might remain in the ambit of the Unfair Commercial Practices Directive now; second, the denigration of a competitor's reputation; third, the unfair imitation of another product by false indication of origin which is said to be covered by Article 6(2)(a); and finally, the legal assessment of doorstep advertising which exceeds the degree of harassment by way of an unsolicited phone call by far.[101] This is not to say that the Directive is flawed. The question needs to be answered to what extent EC law has merely accepted these gaps, considering the existing measures irrelevant under unfair commercial practices law, or whether it was concerned with measures which are so severe that the general clause functions as a residual category.

*(ii) The general clause as safety net*

The special prohibitions contained in Articles 6 to 9, read together with the corresponding number in the list, delineate fairness in business practice. At the same

---

98  See under section e(vi).

99  Explanatory Memorandum, *op.cit.*, para. 52; see also Apostolopoulos, *op.cit.*, 847; Röttinger, *op.cit.*, 251.

100  Gamerith, *op.cit.*, 395, at 418, 419.

101  The ECJ has confirmed the minimum character of Directive 85/577/EEC. That is why Member States may restrict direct selling methods, see Case-20/03 *Staatsanwaltschaft* v *Burmanjer* (2005) ECR I-4133.

time these rules limit the residual function of the general clause. Cases of misleading or aggressive advertising which are not regulated cannot become the subject matter of a review of fairness through the backdoor by referring to the general clause.[102] The general clause only applies in extreme and evident circumstances to bridge gaps. The Unfair Commercial Practices Directive represents a conceptual unity, the rigidity of which forces Member States to adjust their legal systems. The *status quo ante* cannot be retained under the regime of the Directive.[103] Commercial practices which have no connection to the competitive order but which are morally questionable cannot be pursued by reference to the general clause of the Directive.[104]

Defining the general clause as a safety net allowed the Commission to make harmonisation of unfair marketing practices law palatable to Member States. It can be easily ignored therefore that there is a fundamental difference between already existing general clauses in Member States and the new general clause under EC law. Member States cannot rely on Article 5(2) to 'rescue' those advertising restrictions which do not or only partly fall within the scope of the special provisions of Articles 6 to 9. Nonetheless, this is a line of argument which can be found in German legal doctrine which discusses in depth the impact of the Directive on German law, and in particular the role and function of the general clause. In referring to possible divergences between the special provisions and the German Unfair Competition Act, Glöckner[105] argues that possible gaps (for example, with regard to misleading advertising) may be bridged by reference to the general clause. If the special provisions under German law reach further than Articles 6 and 7 of the Directive, no clash of principles is said to occur, as the concept of misleading advertising is said not to be finally and exhaustively regulated by Articles 6 and 7 of the Directive. Pursuant to such argument Member States are given a large margin of appreciation which runs counter to the concept of the Directive. The general clause as laid down in Article 5 cannot be used as a residual category with the help of which unsolved issues in the EC legislative process can be brought back into the concept of 'fairness'. The general clause does not authorise Member States to defend the *status quo ante*. The exact opposite is true and in conformity with EC law.[106]

---

102   This is convincingly illustrated by the German Unfair Trading Act, Schünemann, *op.cit.*, 925, at 927.

103   Schünemann, *op.cit.*, 925, at 929 with references in n. 41 to the intention of the German legislator to maintain the status quo; however, see for somewhat different understanding, Chapter 5(a) under reference to the Explanatory Memorandum, *op.cit.*

104   Cf. 'Busengrapscher' and 'Schlüpferstürmer', BGH (1995) *Gewerblicher Rechtsschutz und Urheberrecht* 592; thereto Schünemann, *op.cit.*, 925, at 934.

105   Glöckner, *Introduction B No. 192* in Harte-Bavendamm and Henning-Bodewig, *op.cit.*, Glöckner, *op.cit.*, 942.

106   It is precisely in this direction, according to the new German Unfair Trading Act, because of its entirely different structure; Schünemann, *§ 3 No. 45 'Prinzip der axiologischen Subsidiarität', No. 46, a material taking back of the extensive general clause which is increased by the Unfair Commercial Practices Directive*, in Harte-Bavendamm and Henning-Bodewig, *op.cit.*

A Member State which imposes a prohibition on the basis of Article 5(2), which goes beyond Articles 6 to 9 and Annex I is under enormous pressure to justify the national prohibition under existing EC law. The very open wording in paragraph 50 of the Explanatory Memorandum which would have granted Member States a wide margin of appreciation is no longer contained in the final version.[107] The example given therein (the Commission refers to the legal treatment of so-called tied sales) is conceptually unsuitable. If anything it comes under the category of taste and decency such as the treatment of commercial solicitation in the streets.[108] In setting aside the approach found in paragraph 50 the Commission sharpened the focus of the Directive. Member States can use the general clause in two ways: when referring to taste and decency they might argue that stricter prohibitions are needed to protect national morals or they might argue that the case at issue is one which falls within the scope of the general clause in its function as a safety net. In this respect paragraph 50 rightly referred to changing technologies and market developments. Member States are prevented from resubmitting unsolved conflicts on the admissibility of certain forms of advertising to the general clause. The general clause is a means of last resort which allows the suppression of newly emerging commercial practices which may be judged unfair, because no European standard yet exists which allows for a value judgment. However, there is one important exception to that rule. The Unfair Commercial Practices Directive is applicable without prejudice to secondary law, which sets minimum standards only in Article 3(4), thereby explicitly granting Member States the power to define stricter standards, such as is the case for telephone marketing (cold calling).[109]

*(iii) The system of Annex I*

Even a cursory reading of Annex I makes evident that it only distinguishes between misleading and aggressive practices. This gives the impression that only those practices which are either misleading or aggressive are regarded as unfair *per se*. The Directive does not list any examples which fall within the scope of the general clause. Different interpretations are possible. Practices which are qualified as being misleading or aggressive encompass those which are unfair. This would constitute an extremely wide interpretation which can be illustrated with the help of examples of misleading practices. Some Member States might consider pyramid and snowball systems unfair *per se* without referring to their misleading character at all.[110] A different interpretation is given by the Community legislator, who deliberately refrained from giving examples illustrating the general clause in specific terms in order to underline the exceptional character of the provisions. Such an interpretation

---

107   This corresponds exactly with the arguments raised by Köhler and Lettl, *op.cit.*, 1019, at 1039 (82) based on the first Proposal.
108   See Chapter 3(d)(ii).
109   See Chapter 3(f)(vi).
110   Gamerith, *op.cit.*, 395, at 426.

would be in line with the conceptual structure of the Directive. However, it waters down the terms 'misleading' and 'aggressive'. As a matter of fact, clarity is only obtained by allocating the 31 prohibited practices under each of the individual prohibitions: Article 5 (the general clause), Article 6 (misleading actions), Article 7 (misleading omissions), Article 8 (aggressive commercial practices) and Article 9 (use of harassment, coercion and undue influence). It is therefore crucial to establish generalised principles, as this is the only way in which a common standard can be enforced throughout the Community. This is done below.[111]

---

111   See Chapters 5(d)(i)–(ii) and 6(g).

# Chapter 5

# Misleading Practices

Thomas Wilhelmsson

## a. Introduction

It has often been stated that the main focus of EU consumer protection law is on consumer information.[1] This has certainly been the case in the regulation of commercial practices. EU legislation in this area has been geared towards creating well-informed and confident consumers to such an extent that a commentator has claimed it to be possible to distil from this material in the *acquis communautaire* a general principle of fair trading that: 'consumers must be enabled to make their choice in full knowledge of the facts'.[2] Whether such a far-reaching conclusion can really be substantiated need not be discussed here. It is sufficient to note that the most important venture into the heartland of unfair commercial practices regulation so far, the Misleading Advertising Directive, is focused on the information content of commercial practice.

In the context of the Unfair Commercial Practices Directive information plays an important role as well. Insofar as one sees the purpose of the Directive as being the creation of workable competition within the internal market, the exchange of information between businesses and consumers is a key issue. It is therefore not surprising that the regulation of misleading practices is one of the pillars on which the concretisation of the fairness principle of the Directive rests. This is also in line with the legal situation in the Member States before their adoption of the Directive. Even in those countries in which there already existed a general clause concerning unfair business practices, a particular provision on misleading practices or misleading advertising had usually already been adopted.[3]

Misleading commercial practices are defined in Chapter 2, Section 1 of the Directive. The Section contains two Articles: Article 6 on misleading actions and

---

1    See, for example, S. Grundmann, W. Kerber and S. Weatherill (eds), *Party Autonomy and the Role of Information in the Internal Market* (Berlin: Walter de Gruyter, 2001) and G. Howells, A. Janssen and R. Schulze, *Information Rights and Obligations* (Aldershot: Ashgate, 2005).

2    M. Radeideh, *Fair Trading in EC Law* (Groningen: Europa Law Publishing, 2005) 184.

3    R. Schulze and H. Schulte-Nölke, *Analysis of National Fairness Laws Aimed at Protecting Consumers in Relation to Commercial Practices* (June 2003), http://europa.eu.int/comm/consumers/cons_int/safe_shop/fair_bus_pract/green_pap_comm/studies/unfair_practices_en.pdf, 24.

Article 7 on misleading omissions. In Annex I of the Directive, which lists those commercial practices always considered unfair, 23 concrete examples of misleading practices are given.

The section on misleading commercial practices, as well as that on aggressive commercial practices, is intended to concretise the general clause in Article 5 of the Directive. These two types of unfair commercial practices have received specific attention, because they are seen as being 'by far the most common'.[4] This implies that, in the application of the general clause, there can be other types of unfair practices than misleading and aggressive practices. This has been analysed in more detail in Chapter 4. In other respects, the relationship between the general clause and the specific provisions is not, however, completely clear. It is not very well spelt out whether, and in what way, the general clause may have a role to play in the areas that are covered by the particular provisions on misleading and aggressive practices.

Two questions arise from this. On the one hand, one may ask whether, for example, Articles 6 and 7 are to be understood as exhaustive in their areas, or whether a practice that fulfils some of the conditions, but not all, still may be outlawed as unfair according to the general clause. This issue (analysed more closely in Chapter 4) of course, to some extent, determines the legal weight or legal exclusivity of the conditions to be described later. An approach that allows for the use of the general clause, if necessary, even within the area covered by the particular provisions, corresponds to the practice in at least some Member States[5] and seems to be in line with the Explanatory Memorandum to the Directive proposal, according to which the 'specific categories do not prejudice the autonomous function of the general prohibition'.[6] Admittedly, the contrary opinion may also be defended with good arguments.[7]

The other question concerns the relevance of the general clause in the interpretation of the particular provisions. Given the wording of the Directive, expressed in Article 5(4), which hints that the regulation of misleading commercial practices in Articles 6 and 7 shall be understood as a particular example of unfairness according to the general clause, it would seem to imply that the principles expressed in Article 5 would be relevant when discussing the proper understanding of Articles 6 and 7. On the other hand, the Explanatory Memorandum to the Directive proposal states very clearly that the specific provisions concerning misleading and aggressive practices are meant to function 'independently' of the general clause,[8] which means that if a commercial practice is found misleading 'it will automatically be unfair, without any further reference to the conditions contained in Article 5'.[9] Despite this statement,

---

4   Unfair Commercial Practices Directive, Recital 13.

5   For example the Nordic countries; so, for example, already in the 1980s Finnish Market Court Decisions 1980:19, 1982:10–12 and 1982:16.

6   COM(2003) 356 final 13.

7   See Chapter 4(h)(ii).

8   COM(2003) 356 final 8.

9   COM(2003) 356 final 13.

which is useful as a general rule or premise, the general clause may in some situations add elements to the understanding of the specific provisions. As will be seen later, the notions related to professional diligence and the definition of the target consumer group in the general clause – particularly the provision concerning vulnerable consumers – are helpful in the context of misleading commercial practices as well.

The Directive makes a distinction between misleading actions and misleading omissions. These practices are regulated in different articles. There is no clear line, however, to be drawn between these two cases. Many such practices that are not positively untruthful, but are likely to deceive consumers, are built on combinations of information that is given, but is insufficient, and relevant information which is omitted. In such cases it is often a matter of choice whether one connects the deception to the act or to the omission. The wording of the Directive seems to indicate that practices that involve an active misleading component, an active use of a half-truth to create the misleading effect, should be judged according to Article 6, whilst Article 7 would be primarily related to situations in which the omission to give certain information could be regarded as unfair as such, without any positive action having created the need for (additional) information. Even with this understanding, however, the borderline is vague. This vagueness is illustrated by the fact that the examples on misleading commercial practices in the Annex are not – and at least in some cases cannot easily be – divided between the articles on actions and omissions. Acknowledging this vagueness as to the respective scope of both articles, Article 6 should be interpreted with due regard to Article 7 and vice versa, in particular in the areas in which the scope of the articles may overlap.

The provisions on misleading practices are meant to include the rules previously contained in the Misleading Advertising Directive,[10] the scope of which has now been narrowed to cover only business-to-business relationships. Materials relating to the Misleading Advertising Directive therefore may still have some weight when discussing the content of the new Directive. For example, the notion of the 'average consumer' in this context draws to some extent on the practice of the European Court of Justice concerning the Misleading Advertising Directive.[11]

## b. Misleading Actions

### (i) Definition

According to Article 6(1) of the Directive:

> A commercial practice shall be regarded as misleading if it contains false information and is therefore untruthful or in any way, including overall presentation, deceives or is likely to deceive the average consumer, even if the information is factually correct, in relation to

---

10   COM(2003) 356 final 14.

11   Unfair Commercial Practices Directive, Recital 18. See also Extended Impact Assessment, SEC(2003) 724, 24.

one or more of the following elements, and in either case causes or is likely to cause him to take a transactional decision that he would not have taken otherwise.

This provision defines the basic features of practices that may be deemed misleading actions according to the Directive. Some basic conditions are mentioned in the provision. The first and foremost of them of course relates to the 'untruthfulness' or 'deceptiveness' of the information and practice. The assessment of deceptiveness should be judged in accordance with what can be expected from the 'average consumer'.[12] Secondly, the Directive requires the deception to be relevant or 'material':[13] it should be likely to influence transactional decisions in order to be understood as being unfair. Finally, the article contains an enumeration of elements to which the information or deceptiveness should relate, that might (but probably should not) be understood as a condition for applying the article. These prerequisites are analysed more closely below, before proceeding to the specific cases concerning the confusing use of competitor's goodwill and non-compliance with codes of conduct expressly regulated in Article 6(2).

In the above enumeration of conditions there is no reference to the subjective assessment of the behaviour of the trader. 'Negligence', 'recklessness' or 'intention to deceive' on the part of the trader is not mentioned as a prerequisite for employing the remedies of the Directive.[14] Therefore, according to the Directive, it is also possible to issue injunctions and make use of other remedies against traders that have provided misleading information without any fault on their part. As will be shown later, however, the Member States have relative room for manoeuvre concerning the precise provisions on the remedies for infringement of the Directive.[15] Nonetheless, one may note that some of the provisions on misleading commercial practices which are in all circumstances considered unfair do contain prerequisites of a subjective nature.[16]

The definition of misleading actions in Article 6 is obviously intended to be understood rather broadly. It not only covers cases where false or misleading information is actually given concerning a product or service, or concerning some other elements of a consumer transaction, but also extends to 'practices' that are likely to deceive the consumer. For example, in the Annex, marketing methods

---

12 This is mentioned as one of the three conditions for application in COM(2003) 356 final 13. However, rather than a condition, the average consumer test is an instrument for applying some of the other conditions.

13 The term 'materiality condition' is used in the Explanatory Memorandum to the Commission proposal, COM(2003) 356 final 13.

14 The lack of relevance of subjective criteria is also noted in the report for the English Department of Trade and Industry by C. Twigg-Flesner, D. Parry, G. Howells and A. Nordhausen, *An Analysis Of The Application And Scope Of The Unfair Commercial Practices Directive* (18 May 2005), http://www.dti.gov.uk/ccp/consultpdf/final_report180505.pdf, iv and 51.

15 See Chapter 8.

16 At least Annex I (6) ('intention'), (13) ('deliberately') and (18) ('intention').

such as bait advertising, bait and switch advertising, advertorials and pyramid promotional schemes are mentioned as misleading commercial practices.[17] Examples such as these would at least in some jurisdictions rather have been dealt with on the basis of the general clause than as an instance of a misleading action. The broader notion of 'misleading actions' in the Directive makes it understandable that the list of commercial practices which are considered unfair in all circumstances simply contains cases of misleading and aggressive practice, with no examples based directly on the general clause in Article 5. In fact, the Commission believes that the general clause 'is likely to be used infrequently because the two categories of misleading and aggressive commercial practices capture the vast majority of cases'.[18] The broad understanding of misleading actions has to be borne in mind when analysing the basic requirements for applying Article 6.

The breadth of the notion of misleading actions is relevant with regard to use of national materials to illuminate both the possible interpretations of the Directive and the margins it offers for national reasoning. Materials that in some jurisdictions are related to, for example, a general clause on unfair business practice rather than to a more specific regulation of misleading activities, may nonetheless be highly relevant when discussing Article 6 of the Directive – and to some extent Article 7 as well, although this latter article seems more specifically geared towards informational issues in a more limited sense.

### (ii) The untruthfulness/deceptiveness condition

According to the Directive a commercial practice shall be regarded as misleading, if it either contains false information and is therefore untruthful, *or* if it deceives or is likely to deceive.[19] Of course, these should not be seen as two distinct categories, but rather as points on a scale starting from clearly untruthful statements and ending in practices that appear deceptive in very subtle ways. The untruthfulness condition clearly raises less legal complications than deception, but some remarks can even usefully be made on that condition.

Both the truthfulness and non-deceptiveness requirements concern all information included in the commercial practice. Article 6 of the Directive expressly uses the phrase 'if it contains false information' instead of speaking, for example, about information given by the trader. This means that the trader cannot escape responsibility for information that is used in his practice even when an external source of the information is mentioned. For example, citations from product tests

---

17  Annex I (5), (6), (11) and (14).

18  COM(2003) 356 final 12.

19  The deceptiveness requirement also relates to the materiality condition, analysed in more detail below. It means, among other things, that minor errors may be accepted.

or references to letters from 'satisfied customers' are prohibited if such documents contain false information.[20]

It also seems fairly clear that an untruthful practice continues to 'contain false information', even if the material includes a general term according to which, for example, statements in advertising or oral statements are not meant to be binding. Here one may refer to what will be mentioned below on the relevance of the 'overall presentation', when assessing whether a practice is to be considered misleading.

'Information' clearly means statements concerning facts that can be empirically proven or at least can be understood as such. Aesthetic and emotional assessments do not typically convey information that can be deemed either correct or false. An advertisement concerning 'the most beautiful dress' or 'a very funny movie' cannot be considered false, even where most consumers would dislike the dress or leave the movie theatre without having laughed a great deal. However, even such assessments may in a deceiving way convey impressions of facts that can be deceptive and are hence prohibited. It depends on the consumer and the context to what extent such aesthetic and emotional assessments are regarded as implied and deceptive statements of facts. In drawing the line between the accepted and the prohibited one therefore has to fall back on the 'average consumer' assessment analysed below. One can easily expect that the issue is in many cases linked to cultural and linguistic preconceptions, as the understanding of aesthetics, humour and similar phenomena are strongly culturally determined. What in one culture appears to be a purely subjective and emotional assessment may in another seem much more objective and dependent on facts. Therefore obviously there has to be sufficient national leeway in applying the European rules in this context. The possibility of taking into account national 'social, cultural or linguistic factors', mentioned below in the context of the 'average consumer test', may be of use in this context.

The acceptance of assessments of the kind mentioned above is reinforced by the attitude towards commercial exaggeration expressed at the end of Article 5(3) of the Directive. According to this provision the protection of the particularly vulnerable 'is without prejudice to the common and legitimate advertising practice of making exaggerated statements or statements which are not meant to be taken literally'. This provision reflects the idea that not only general commercial exaggeration of the more imprecise type – 'our product is the best!' – but also more concrete false statements may be acceptable, if they are not intended to be taken literally, so long as this intention was discernible for the average consumer. However, as the criteria mentioned in Article 5 are not meant directly to affect the application of Article 6, one probably should not in the context of Article 6 define such obviously false statements as falling outside the falseness

---

20  Good examples from Finnish practice on banning of misleading use of product tests in marketing: Market Court 1982:1, 1989:13, 1991:6 and 1997:3; and on letters from satisfied consumers: Market Court 1982:14. Similar cases can be mentioned from some other Member States as well; see *Compilations of National Laws* made in preparing the Directive, published on   http://europa.eu.int/comm/consumers/cons_int/safe_shop/fair_bus_pract/index_en.htm, First Part, 62–64.

category.[21] Rather the same result may be achieved, if required, by the application of the materiality condition, to be analysed below. If the consumer understands a certain piece of information is obviously false it is not likely to cause him to take a transactional decision. Again, it is clear that the concrete assessment of whether a certain piece of information is so self-evidently false that it should not be taken literally is linked with cultural and linguistic features that vary between the Member States. The use of irony, understatements and overstatements is more dangerous in some countries, because of a tendency to construe such statements literally.[22]

When speaking about the prohibition of the use of false information in commercial practices the most difficult issue often relates to the *burden of proof* concerning the untruthfulness of the information. As is rightly noted in the Explanatory Memorandum to the Commission proposal, consumers are generally not in a position to prove that a factual claim made by the trader is untrue. Because the trader is in a far better position in this respect, he should not make factual claims the accuracy of which he cannot prove.[23] This was reflected directly in the proposed Article 6, which contained a provision on 'claims about the product which the trader cannot substantiate'.[24] This would have introduced a relatively clear-cut rule, presuming marketing information to be false if it cannot be substantiated by the trader.[25] Corresponding to similar rules in at least some of the Member States[26] the use of statements that cannot be substantiated would have breached a substantive provision of the Directive and would have been treated as an unfair business practice. However, in the adopted version of the Directive this rule was left out from the substantive part and turned into a primarily procedural rule. According to Article 12 of the Directive courts or administrative bodies should be enabled to require the trader to furnish evidence as to the accuracy of factual claims if such a requirement appears appropriate on the basis of the circumstances of the particular case. To this procedural rule is then added a substantive remedy: that courts and administrative authorities should have powers that enable them to consider factual claims as inaccurate if the evidence demanded is not furnished or is deemed insufficient. This procedural turn leaves the Directive more flexible, but also much more unclear on this point. It leaves it to the

---

21  M. Radeideh, *Fair Trading in EC Law* (Groningen: Europa Law Publishing, 2005) 265 rightly points out that '[i]t is absolutely contrary to the general purpose of the Directive, not to allow commercial practices which impair the consumer's ability to make an informed decision on the one hand, but to allow "exaggerated statements or statements that are not meant to be taken literally" and to consider them "legitimate" on the other hand'.

22  Such a habit is very typical of Finnish culture.

23  COM(2003) 356 final 15.

24  COM(2003) 356 final, proposed Directive Article 6(1)(f).

25  As reflected in the proposed Amendment 37 at the Parliament's first reading (Doc. 8492/04) the express mentioning of the trader is not necessary in this context. If the statement is otherwise substantiated the trader does not need to do so.

26  As in the Nordic countries; see *Compilations of National Laws, op.cit.*, First Part, 44–5. According to this Compilation the burden of proof also rests with the defendant, for example, in Austria, Ireland and Spain.

courts to decide *in casu* whether they wish to press the trader for substantiation of the statements and whether on the basis of missing or insufficient evidence they will consider the information as 'inaccurate' (obviously meaning 'false' in the context of Article 6). Given that 'it is for national law to determine the burden of proof',[27] this will likely entail that courts in such Member States where it is accepted practice to consider the use of factual claims that cannot be substantiated as unfair or misleading can continue more or less along the same lines without breaching the Directive.

Proceeding now to the specific problems at the more difficult end of the scale, namely in relation to the 'deceptiveness' condition, there is a need for various kinds of more or less vague legal assessments to be made. These inevitably provide the courts with a great deal of freedom when making evaluations *in casu*.

Obviously deceptiveness does not require untruthfulness. As expressly stated in Article 6, a practice may deceive the consumer even if the information is factually correct. Half-truths, or combinations of given facts with information being omitted, may result in a picture that is misleading, even though one cannot point at any single concrete piece of information that would actually be false.

As expressly stated in the article, the 'overall presentation' is relevant in the assessment of deceptiveness. It directs the assessment towards the commercial practice as a whole. It is an 'important principle ... that the effect of the commercial practice in its entirety, including the presentation, must be considered'.[28] For example, the layout of an advertisement and the size and location of the pieces of information have to be taken into account. A heading or a picture may create a false impression even though the correct facts are given in the text of an advertisement. Information given in small print cannot necessarily be used to correct the false impressions created by the headings and the pictures.

Consumers may be deceived not only by statements and other linguistic information. Other practices that are likely to deceive consumers are equally targeted by Article 6. A typical example is the use of boxes for products that are much larger than the amount of the product they contain. Such packaging – representing the 'overall presentation' of the offer – may be deceptive, even if the correct quantity of the product is printed on the box.[29] Another common example of misleading by conduct rather than by a statement is the attempt by a trader to appropriate the reputation of a competitor, by copying a product or a marketing measure. Insofar as consumers are misled, such activity is now clearly within the scope of the Directive after the last minute addition of such a case to the list in the Annex on commercial practices which are in all circumstances considered unfair.[30]

---

27  Unfair Commercial Practices Directive, Recital 21.

28  COM(2003) 356 final 14. The vague line between Article 6 and Article 7 is well illustrated by the fact that the cited sentence is followed by the sentence: 'If the presentation is obscure, Article 7 makes clear that this is tantamount to an omission.'

29  The Swedish Marketing Act of 1995 contains an explicit prohibition on the marketing of misleading packaging sizes (Sec. 7).

30  See Annex I (13) on promoting a product similar to a product made by a particular manufacturer in such a manner as deliberately to mislead the consumer into believing that the

It is a common feature of all of these examples concerning deceptiveness that it is impossible to draw a clear general line between the acceptable and the prohibited. The deceptive effect of half-truths, headings and pictures and non-linguistic practices is related to how these are understood or, rather, are likely to be understood by the consumers under specific circumstances. This brings the average consumer, a person relevant for many of the assessments according to the Directive, to the centre stage. A commercial practice is deemed to be misleading if it deceives, or is likely to deceive, the average consumer. The 'average consumer test' is the instrument by which the assessment of deceptiveness is to be made in a specific case.

This test may also be helpful given that many of the assessments to be made, in particular concerning the deceptiveness of commercial practices, are culturally bound. What in one culture is read as a deceptive half-truth may be perfectly clear in another culture. Interpretations of headings, pictures and non-linguistic practices relate to how such messages and practices are read within a particular cultural setting. Insofar as the national, and local, cultures vary in such respects within the EU, then variations as to the assessment of deceptiveness have to be accepted as well.

### (iii) The average consumer test

The concept of the average consumer is discussed in detail in Chapter 4. The drafters of the Directive obviously intended that this concept should be understood more or less similarly in the context of Articles 6 and 7 as in Article 5. In this context it should therefore basically be sufficient to refer to what has been said on this issue in that chapter. However, some additional comments related to the regulation of misleading practices should be made.

In particular, when speaking of potentially deceptive practices, such as half-truths, misleading headings and pictures as well as other misleading practices, the fact that the Council in its Common Position removed the definition of 'average consumer' previously included in the proposal[31] may be relevant. The Directive no longer expressly defines, in its articles, the average consumer as one 'who is reasonably well informed and reasonably observant and circumspect'.[32] Even though this formula is derived from the practice of the European Court of Justice,[33] which is meant to continue to have some relevance in this context and therefore still is

---

product is made by that same manufacturer.

31  Statement of the Council's reasons, 11630/2/04 REV 2 ADD 1, 11.

32  COM(2003) 356 final, proposed Directive Article 2(b).

33  See, for example, Case C–470/93 *Verein gegen Unwesen in Handel und Gewerbe Köln e.V. v Mars GmbH* [1995] ECR I–1923 at [24], Case C–210/96 *Gut Springenheide GmbH and Rudolf Tusky v Oberkreisdirektor des Kreises Steinfurt – Amt für Lebensmittelüberwachung* [1998] ECR I–4657 at [31, 37], Case C–303/97 *Verbraucherschutzverein e V v Sektkellerei G.C. Kessler GmbH und Co.* [1999] ECR I–513 at [36], Case C–220/98 *Estée Lauder Cosmetics GmbH & Co. OHG v Lancaster Group GmbH* [2000] ECR I–117 at [27], Case C–465/98 *Verein gegen Unwesen in Handel und Gewerbe Köln e V v Adolf Darbo AG* [2000] ECR I–2297 at [20], Case C–112/99 *Toshiba Europe GmbH v Katun Germany GmbH* [2001]

expressly mentioned in the Preamble of the Directive,[34] the deletion of the vague and not very consistently applied formula[35] from the definitions of the Directive may leave more room for national courts actually to make a realistic overall assessment of the commercial practice as required by Article 6. This might mean taking into account the fact that most consumers do not read advertisements and other commercial communications carefully, in an observant and circumspect way, but rather hastily look at the headings and pictures. Even though the choice of an 'average consumer' as the benchmark, rather than a credulous one, was an express trade-off in order to reach agreement,[36] this does not necessarily mean that one must have high expectations of the behaviour of consumers according to the Directive. In the empirical sense the average consumer is in many contexts not very observant or circumspect. The 'average consumer' might in some situations act rather as a 'casual observer' and one may therefore very well include elements of hasty observation in the concept of average consumer.[37] In fact, the Directive acknowledges this, when noting the importance of the 'overall presentation' when assessing an advertising measure, as mentioned above.

In any event, the courts have to decide what is expected of the average consumer, as 'average consumer' is not meant to be understood as a concept with a precise empirical or mathematical content.[38] This leeway for the courts is underlined by the words 'likely to deceive'. Empirical proof concerning the typical reaction of consumers is not required in order to deem a practice misleading. The court's impression of likelihood is sufficient. In addition, given that the burden of proof also in this context follows national law, one cannot avoid the influence of the national cultural background and traditions and of national and local consumer expectations on what is to be expected of an average consumer in a concrete case.

---

ECR I–7945 at [52], and Case 44/01 *Pippig Augenoptik GmbH & Co. KG v Hartlauer Handelsgesellschaft* [2003] ECR I–3095 at [55].

34  Unfair Commercial Practices Directive, Recital 18.

35  On the incoherence of the decisions of the European Court of Justice in this respect, see, for example, A. Beater, *Verbraucherschutz und Schutzzweckdenken im Wettbewerbsrecht* (Tübingen: Mohr Siebeck, 2000) 95.

36  Extended Impact Assessment, SEC(2003) 724, 26. Examples from Belgium and Germany on diverging consumer concepts are given in the Extended Impact Assessment, SEC(2003) 724, 8.

37  See the reference to the German Scanner advertising case (BGH 20 December 2001) in the Extended Impact Assessment, SEC(2003) 724, 8. See also the interesting analysis of various consumer images (*Verbraucherleitbilder*) in the Member States by T. Lettl, *Der lauterkeitsrechtliche Schutz vor irreführender Werbung in Europa* (München: Verlag C.H. Beck, 2004) 306, who distinguishes five such images and thereby uses the focus on 'average' and on 'hasty observation' as different parameters. In his analysis the consumer image of some Member States (Denmark, Finland, the Netherlands and Greece) is then based on *both* the conception of an 'average consumer' and the idea of hasty observation.

38  See more closely Chapter 4(f)(v).

The description of the yardstick to be used in the average consumer test in Article 6 is not identical to the corresponding description in Article 5. The most obvious difference between Article 5 and Article 6 lies in the fact that the Article 5 general clause not only mentions the 'average consumer' as the yardstick to be used in assessing unfairness, but also, in Article 5(2)(b), notes as an alternative 'the average member of the group when a commercial practice is directed to a particular group of consumers'. In addition, in Article 5(3) there is the specific provision on the protection of vulnerable consumers, allowing the assessment even of those practices that reach the generality of consumers from the perspective of the average member of the vulnerable group. No such alternatives and additions to the average consumer concept can be found in Article 6. This raises the question of how this difference should be understood. Does the independent nature of the specific provisions in Article 6 prevent the use of specified consumer groups as a yardstick when applying these Articles?

It would indeed be possible to make such a separation between the two Articles. The division of labour between Article 5 and Article 6[39] would then be the following: Article 6 would, in a rather broad fashion, focus on how the average consumer would understand a certain commercial practice and whether such a person would be likely to be deceived by it or not. Only cases of deception that could be broadly generalised in this way would fall under Article 6, whilst those cases where the commercial practice would only mislead a specific target group or a vulnerable group would have to be dealt with under the general clause. The more wide-ranging formal assessments concerning the misleading nature of a particular action should then be made on the basis of Article 6, whilst Article 5 would be more directed towards assessments *in casu*.

However, this solution would imply giving a rather broad role to the general clause of the Directive, as in practice many commercial practices target certain groups and the assessment of misleading effects has to be made also in relation to such groups. Putting such emphasis on the general clause does not correspond to the belief of the Commission, mentioned above, that the general clause will play a minor role, given that 'misleading and aggressive commercial practices capture the vast majority of cases'.[40] In any event, it would be impossible in practice to relate the assessment of deceptiveness purely to an abstract average consumer and refrain from taking into account the understandings of consumers within the group that is targeted by the practice, in cases where such a target group can be identified. Therefore 'the average consumer' in Article 6 should probably be read as also comprising, in accordance with Article 5(2)(b), 'the average member of the group when a commercial practice is directed to a particular group of consumers'. This seems to be in conformity with the stated purpose of the average consumer test in the Directive. In the Preamble to the Directive it is underlined that a commercial practice that is 'specifically aimed at a particular group of consumers, such as children',

---

39  The same would then of course be applied to Articles 7–9 as well.
40  COM(2003) 356 final 12.

should be 'assessed from the perspective of the average member of that group'.[41] In the Explanatory Memorandum to the proposed Directive the Commission expressly states, without limiting the statement to Article 5, that the 'average consumer test' related to the specific provisions on misleading and aggressive practices should be understood 'in line with the conditions of the general prohibition', which means that the commercial practice also in this context should be assessed from the perspective of the average member of the target group.[42] In other words, the notions and behaviour of the consumers of the target group should be the decisive criterion when assessing whether a practice is to be considered misleading.

Such a use of Article 5(2)(b) in the context of Article 6 seems relatively easy to defend when speaking about a misleading practice that has a particular vulnerable target group. However, the specific rule concerning the possibility taking into account the needs of particularly vulnerable consumers in Article 5(3), when the practice is addressed towards the generality of consumers, seems somewhat more difficult to fit into the wording of Article 6. This particular protection of the vulnerable might therefore have to be related rather to Article 5 than to Article 6. However, the overall coherence of the approach might recommend the inclusion of Article 5(3) in the application of Article 6 as well. In any event, one should note that this difficulty regards only the protection of vulnerable consumers against practices that 'reach' – which probably should be read as 'target' – the generality of consumers. If the practice is even impliedly directed in particular to a vulnerable group, Article 5(2)(b) applies, and the notions and behaviour of the consumers of this group should, with more certainty, be taken into account also in the context of Article 6.

The focus on the target group facilitates the taking into account of national and local cultural habits in the assessment, the need of which has been mentioned in several contexts above. The 'average consumer' does not necessarily have to be understood as the 'average EU consumer' only; for many situations one may even seriously doubt the possibility of constructing such an 'average' that would not be purely fictitious. The 'average consumer' may refer to the average on a certain national or local market as well. In case the business practice in question targets a certain national market or a certain area, this 'relativisation' of the average consumer is easy to relate to the above analysis of at least a possible understanding of the Directive. The average consumer test provides 'a means to take into account relevant social, cultural or linguistic characteristics of targeted groups'.[43] The situation becomes more difficult when a practice targeting the whole or large part of the EU is assessed, and various cultural backgrounds make it seem more deceptive in some countries than in others. Here the need for efficient consumer protection and respect for national cultures is most clearly clashing with the internal market function of the Directive. One cannot, however, rule out the possibility of diverging national assessments in such situations. When there is a need for a different assessment

41  Recital 18.
42  COM(2003) 356 final 13.
43  COM(2003) 356 final 8.

the courts should, as the European Court of Justice has stated, make use of their understanding of the relevant national 'social, cultural or linguistic factors'[44] in their own environment. This practice of the Court is endorsed in the Directive.[45]

In this context it is interesting to note that this Directive also passes over the very difficult issue of the relevance of *language*. Are 'average consumers' supposed to know only their mother tongue, or should they have command of other languages as well?[46] What level of command should they have in such a case? It is well known that there are huge differences in the learning and understanding of foreign languages between the consumers of the Member States. Even though the Directive is silent on this point – which has caused much discussion and led to various solutions within EU legislation thus far[47] – the issue cannot be ignored. In the context of misleading information the language in which the information is given is clearly relevant. It is of course particularly important in the context of misleading omissions, and it will be mentioned again later in that context. However, the issue of language may also arise in the context of misleading actions. For example, how would one deal with a commercial in the English language that is broadcast all over the EU and is easily understood by the average Englishman, but may be misleading for a person who has only a limited command of the language? There is also the issue of half-truths and misleading headings, pictures, packages or other practices: can they be corrected in a language other than that of the consumer? As long as different solutions are not enacted, or introduced by the European Court of Justice, one would have to assume that not only the 'relativised' but also the general average consumer test, because of the variations in language skills, allow national assessments that underline the role of the national languages in this context. Naturally, if a national court considers that consumers of its country, for example, within some particular market,[48] usually

---

44 Case C–220/98 *Estée Lauder Cosmetics v Lancaster Group ('Lifting')* [2000] ECR I–117 at [29]. See also Case C–313/94 *Fratelli Graffione SNC v Ditta Fransa* [1996] ECR I–6039 at [22].

45 See Recital 18. In the Statement of the Council's reasons (11630/2/04 REV 2 ADD 1) 5 it is expressly said that an amendment proposed by the Parliament (amendment 107, Doc. 8492/04) to include the words 'taking account of social, cultural and linguistic circumstances' in the Directive, was taken into consideration in the new wording of Recital 18.

46 There was a belief that this problem was diminishing among those preparing the Unfair Commercial Practices Directive within the Commission. In the Extended Impact Assessment, SEC(2003) 724, 5 it is noted: 'Language barriers are falling. 53 per cent of EU consumers say they can speak at le[a]st one European language in addition to their own and 26 per cent two other languages, while 71 per cent think that everyone in the EU should be able to speak another European language in addition to their mother tongue.'

47 See H.-W. Micklitz, 'Zum Recht des Verbrauchers auf die eigene Sprache' (2003) 11 *Zeitschrift für Europäisches Privatrecht* 635.

48 For example, e-commerce may be assessed somewhat differently than physically localised trading. Compare C. Coteanu, *Cyber Consumer Law and Unfair Trading Practices* (Aldershot: Ashgate, 2005) 183, who more generally raises, but does not resolve, the question: 'In online consumer transactions, consumers should be experienced in using and

possess sufficient language skills to understand communications in a foreign language, it can take this into account in its assessment.

Not only foreign languages may be difficult to master for the consumer. The consumer's ability to understand his own language, at least in written form, may be quite limited as well. How far should one take into account that, at least in some Member States, there are perhaps millions of practically illiterate persons who do not have the ability to read commercials in a reasonably observant and circumspect way?

### (iv) The materiality condition

Not all false or deceptive information is prohibited by Article 6 of the Directive. Only if the practice that contains false information or is deceptive causes or is likely to cause the consumer to take a transactional decision that he would not have taken otherwise, shall it be regarded as misleading. The falseness or deceptiveness of the information or practice should be relevant and material to the decision-making of the consumers.[49] If it has no effect whatsoever on the decision-making obviously it does not need to be prohibited.[50]

The materiality condition may take various types of false information outside the scope of the prohibition of misleading actions in Article 6. Information that has no relation whatsoever to the product or service to be acquired, such as a background fairytale or other story in a commercial, should not be judged according to this provision. More generally, as mentioned above, statements which are not meant to be taken literally and are understood as such by average consumers may be hit by the materiality condition. Cultural and linguistic features of the various Member States may of course affect the ways in which messages are understood in this respect and may therefore require locally sensitive assessments.

'Minor' errors may also be assessed under this condition. Some inaccuracy of detail may be so insignificant that it is judged not to affect the transactional decisions of consumers. However, one should be cautious not to go too far in this direction. The definitions and the provisions on proof of the Directive indicate that the requirements for the materiality condition to be fulfilled are easily satisfied. As it is very difficult

---

sorting the information. Would consumers have the right to be ignorant in this fast-moving environment?'

49    See also the Nissan judgment, Case C–373/90 *Criminal proceedings against X (Nissan)* [1992] ECR 131. The threshold for intervention, however, seems to be put rather high in this case; A. Bakardjieva Engelbrekt, *EU and Marketing Practices Law in the Nordic Countries – Consequences of a Directive on Unfair Business-to-Consumer Commercial Practices* (Report for the Nordic Council of Ministers Committee on Consumer Affairs, 2005), http://www.norden.org/konsum/sk/rappdownload.asp, 35; and it should not necessarily determine the approach to the Unfair Commercial Practices Directive.

50    This rule is obviously directed against the practice of some Member States (such as Germany) to outlaw any inaccuracy in advertising, 'even if the inaccuracy had no bearing on consumers' decisions'; see Explanatory Memorandum, COM(2003) 356 final 5.

to ascertain what factors affect consumer behaviour and in what way, it is sufficient for a practice to be assessed as misleading that it is likely to affect the transactional behaviour of average consumers in some way. Even small details of information can indeed have this effect.

The low hurdle of the materiality condition is, first, clearly reflected in the definition of 'transactional decision' in Article 2(k) of the Directive.[51] According to this provision:

> 'transactional decision' means any decision taken by a consumer concerning whether, how and on what terms to purchase, make payment in whole or in part for, retain or dispose of a product or to exercise a contractual right in relation to the product, whether the consumer decides to act or to refrain from acting.

This provision expressly states that in the phase before the contract is concluded, information is material where it not only affects the decision of the consumer whether to buy or not, but also where it in any way affects his decisions concerning the modalities and terms of the purchase. In other words, information relative both to the conclusion of the contract as such and to the content of the contract is relevant. In addition, both information that induces some kind of action on the part of the consumer and information that makes him refrain from action, for example from demanding better terms, is said to affect his transactional decision. So broadly speaking, information that in any way affects the involvement of the consumer in the transaction is deemed to be material.

In addition, as analysed in more detail in Chapter 3, Article 2(k) reflects the broad scope of the Directive, covering also transactional decisions after the conclusion of the contract. Decisions concerning payment, concerning retention and disposal of products and concerning exercise of contractual rights are transactional decisions in the meaning of the Directive and false or deceptive information or practices that affect such decisions are therefore considered to be material in the application of Article 6 on misleading actions. Such misleading information can of course be given both before and after the conclusion of the contract. Misleading activity before conclusion of the contract that is likely to affect the consumer's decisions at later stages, concerning payment, disposal or exercise of rights, is prohibited, as well as similar misleading activity during the contractual relationship. Even after the contractual relationship has ended, the trader may resort to actions that seem to be prohibited according to Article 6, for example, if the trader publicly gives false information concerning the environmental qualities of his product and thereby causes consumers to make decisions concerning its disposal that they would not have done otherwise.

The low hurdle related to the materiality condition is lowered further by the relaxed attitude towards the proving of materiality. No empirical proof concerning the influence of certain information on the actual transactional decisions of

---

51   See also on the concept 'materially distorting the economic behaviour of consumers' used in Article 5 of the Directive, above Chapter 4(e).

consumers is required, although such information can be used self-evidently as an argument to strengthen a difficult case. According to the Directive it is sufficient that a certain untruthful or deceptive practice 'is likely' to cause the consumer to take the transactional decision. In addition, as issues concerning the burden of proof are left to the national courts and authorities, this of course leaves them with a broad level of discretion. This is probably a good solution, since the question of how the decision-making of consumers is affected by various kinds of information and practices is most certainly to some extent determined by national social, cultural and linguistic factors.

The yardstick of the Directive for these assessments is the well-known figure of the 'average consumer'. The word 'him'[52] in the phrase 'causes or is likely to cause him to take a transactional decision' clearly refers to 'the average consumer' in the preceding part of the sentence. What has been said above about the average consumer test – that it provides the necessary means to take into account also social, cultural and linguistic characteristics of the relevant consumer groups – is also applicable in this context.

### (v) What information?

The provision on misleading actions does not end with the materiality condition. It goes on to enumerate the types of issues to which misleading actions according to the Article can relate. The nature of this enumeration is unclear; it is not evident whether one should regard it as an additional condition related to the object of the information or whether it rather has merely a clarifying and pedagogic function.

As the list of enumerated elements is very broad, this question at first glance seems to be relatively theoretical in the sense that most types of relevant information are included in any event. However, one important item that seems to be lacking from the enumeration is information concerning competitors.[53] In the area of comparative advertising this should not pose a problem, because here the consumers have retained their remedies under the Misleading Advertising Directive, and there has been added to that Directive a cross-reference to the Unfair Commercial Practices Directive, according to which comparative advertising should not be misleading.[54] As the definition of comparative advertising is very broad, meaning 'any advertising which explicitly or by implication identifies a competitor or goods or services offered by a competitor',[55] misleading statements concerning other traders can usually be expected to be dealt with under the Misleading Advertising Directive.

---

52 The Commission does not seem to be preoccupied with gender-neutrality when drafting Directives.

53 H. Köhler and T. Lettl, 'Das geltende europäische Lauterkeitsrecht, der Vorschlag für eine EG–Richtlinie über unlautere Geschäftspraktiken und die UWG–Reform' (2003) 49 *Wettbewerb in Recht und Praxis* 1019, 1039.

54 Misleading Advertising Directive Article 3a(1)(a). See above Chapter 3(e)(i).

55 Misleading Advertising Directive Article 2(2a).

However, one can also find examples concerning the shortcomings of the enumeration that cannot be dealt with under other Directives. Such examples are likely to occur in relation to information that is given at the post-contractual stage. As most of the items in the list relate to pre-contractual practices, it is not obvious whether the list will prove to be sufficiently comprehensive in covering practices relating to later stages of the contractual relationship.

In such cases, where the question of the nature of the enumeration has practical consequences, arguments for both understandings – an additional condition or just a pedagogic tool – can be put forward. For the reasons mentioned below the broader, pedagogic understanding is defended here. Adding another condition to the application of Article 6 does not seem necessary.

The wording of Article 6 as such rather indicates the opposite. It states rather bluntly that a commercial practice shall be regarded as misleading if it is untruthful or deceptive 'in relation to one or more of the following elements'. As it is nowhere said that the enumeration of the elements should be regarded as non-exhaustive or as examples only, this could indeed easily be read as 'the following and no other' elements. In the light of the wording alone one would rather think that this enumeration would amount to an exhaustive condition for applying Article 6 and that false information falling outside the list would be irrelevant in the application of the Article. For example, for a British lawyer this would probably be the most natural way of reading the Article.[56]

However, Annex I of the Directive shows that such an exhaustive understanding of the list of elements in Article 6 is probably not well-founded. At least some of the examples concerning misleading commercial practices in the list of 'worst' commercial practices, which are in all circumstances considered unfair in Annex I of the Directive, relate to information that is difficult to place naturally under any of the 'elements' enumerated in Article 6. Examples are the operating of pyramid promotional schemes, making claims concerning possibilities of winning in games of chance and passing on inaccurate information on market conditions.[57] If so many of these examples relate to other information, it is difficult to understand why other practices that are perhaps not in all circumstances considered unfair could not be judged according to Article 6 just because the information is not contained in the enumeration of elements in that Article.

In addition, there is no real practical need for having the enumeration of the elements function as a condition for applying the Article. A strict adherence to the enumeration does not seem to add much to legal certainty, both because the enumeration is long and vague, and because a misleading use of information not included in the list could in any event potentially be held to violate the general clause in Article 5 of the Directive. As far as there is a need to move some kinds of false

---

56 Taking into account the way in which the enumeration of the Trade Description Act 1968, Section 2(1) has been understood, see, for example, G. Howells and S. Weatherill, *Consumer Protection Law* (Aldershot: Ashgate, 2005) 404.

57 Annex I (14), (16) and (18).

information outside the ambit of the prohibition, the application of the materiality condition can fulfil this need. Information that is not material to the decision-making of the consumer is not relevant according to that condition. An additional condition related to the content of the information is not required. If a piece of information is relevant to the transactional decision of the consumer, should it be deemed irrelevant just because it is not expressly included in the enumeration?

For reasons such as this it might be better to understand the enumeration of elements in Article 6 as a pedagogic overview of the different kinds of information that may be relevant, an overview that is needed because the Directive is to be applied within very different legal cultures with different preconceptions, rather than as an exhaustive list that would have the role of an additional condition for the application of Article 6.[58] This understanding also seems to accord with the ideas of the drafters of the Directive: the Explanatory Memorandum mentions three conditions, namely deceptiveness, materiality and 'average consumer', for the application of the provision.[59]

The first example of relevant information, in Article 6(1)(a), does not require any comments. It is self-evident that false or deceptive information concerning *the existence or nature of the product* can be misleading in a relevant way.

The second example, concerning the *main characteristics of the product*, in Article 6(1)(b), is probably the largest category, showing in itself that the enumeration of elements is intended to be very broad. Indeed, when looking at the concrete examples concerning main characteristics in the same paragraph (where they are presented in an order seemingly not based on any logic) the qualification 'main' loses almost all content. This paragraph covers, first, what one obviously would regard as characteristics of the product, namely product-specific information such as fitness for purpose, usage, quantity, specification, results to be expected from its use[60] and material features of tests or checks carried out on the product[61] as well as composition and accessories. An important characteristic that is not expressly mentioned, but that obviously falls within this list, is the environmental quality and effects of the product; misleading statements concerning such matters in many

---

58 Such an interpretation is also recommended by W. Veelken, 'Kundenfang gegenüber dem Verbraucher. Bemerkungen zum EG–Richtlinienentwurf über unlautere Geschäftspraktiken' (2004) 50 *Wettbewerb in Recht und Praxis* 1, 19. Also H. Gamerith, 'Der Richtlinienvorschlag über unlautere Geschäftspraktiken – Möglichkeiten einer harmonischen Umsetzung' (2005) 51 *Wettbewerb in Recht und Praxis* 391, 422 strongly criticises the idea of an exhaustive list.

59 COM(2003) 356 final 13.

60 The Explanatory Memorandum mentions the examples 'weight loss, hair re-growth or enhanced performance', COM(2003) 356 final 14. Falsely claiming that a product is able to cure illnesses, dysfunction or malformations is in all circumstances considered unfair; see Annex I (17).

61 In this context one could also refer to the specific prohibitions on using trust and quality marks without authorisation as well as wrongly claiming approval by public or private bodies, in the Annex I (2) and (4).

Member States are dealt with under legislation of this kind.[62] In addition to the actual characteristics of the product, however, the paragraph mentions elements that relate to the process of production, such as the method and date of manufacture or provision and geographical or commercial origin. As parts of the main characteristics of the product are further mentioned, perhaps somewhat surprisingly, elements related rather to the contractual situation and performance, such as availability,[63] execution and delivery. Some surrounding issues such as benefits[64] and risks are also expressly noted in this context, and, finally, even after-sales customer assistance[65] and complaint handling are defined as belonging to the main characteristics of the product. As clearly stated in the Explanatory Memorandum, the absence of after-sales services is not as such considered unfair – as was suggested during the drafting of the Directive – but the shaping of false impressions concerning it is; if 'the trader's conduct would lead the average consumer to have materially different expectations about the after-sale service available',[66] Article 6 is applicable.

In Article 6(1)(c) the third group of elements somewhat overlap with the examples in the preceding group. These are various *issues related to the contract and the business practice* rather than to the product as such. Under this heading is gathered, first, information concerning the extent of the trader's commitments. Information concerning benefits as well as after-sales customer assistance and complaint handling mentioned above could be repeated also in this context. Other commitments as well should of course not be described in a deceptive way. Secondly, issues such as the motives for the commercial practice and the nature of the sales process belong to this group of elements. Attempts to disguise the commercial nature of the trader's activity fall under this heading.[67] Product placement as disguised marketing is another possible example.[68] Commercial practices that appear as attempting to sell

---

62  See, for example H.-W. Micklitz and J. Kessler (eds), *Marketing Practices Regulation and Consumer Protection in the EC Member States and the US* (Baden-Baden, Nomos, 2002) 57, 72, 93, 115, 198, 261, 299 and 410. On the Misleading Advertising Directive having covered such issues, see D. Krimphove, *Europäisches Werberecht* (München: Verlag Franz Vahlen, 2002) 305.

63  See also the specific prohibitions on bait advertising and bait and switch advertising in the Annex I (5) and (6).

64  Here one could perhaps also refer to the Annex I (19) on offers of competitions or prize promotions without awarding the prizes.

65  See in this context also the very specific prohibition in the Annex I (8) on undertakings to provide after-sales service in another language than the consumer could expect, in certain situations. See also below on Article 6(1)(e).

66  COM(2003) 356 final 13–14. As example is mentioned a claim of a computer supplier that a dedicated technical support hotline is available. See also Annex I (23) on the creation of false impressions concerning after-sales service in another Member State.

67  See also Annex I (22) on some false claims indicating that the activity is non-commercial.

68  The line between illegitimate product placement and legitimate use of products in a programme is of course very difficult to draw. In the Commission interpretative communication on certain aspects of the provisions on televised advertising in the 'Television

one product, but in fact aim at inducing consumers to enter other transactions also belong to this category.[69] Marketing of something which is a one-off purchase, even though it creates more enduring liabilities for the consumer, is a typical example. The inducement of false beliefs in the consumer concerning the need for quick decisions also seems to be covered.[70] The blurring of the line between marketing measures and other types of information, so that marketing is not easily identifiable as such by the consumers, is yet another example.[71] This is closely related to the third example in the group, dealing with sponsorship. The false and deceptive use of any statement or symbol in relation to direct or indirect sponsorship can constitute misleading practice according to Article 6. This may mean both indicating a sponsorship that does not exist as well as denying an existing sponsor. Finally, deceptive information concerning the approval of the trader or the product is mentioned. In most cases such information is in all circumstances considered unfair according to the Annex of the Directive,[72] but as the approval is also particularly mentioned in the Article it indicates that there may be cases falling outside the specific wordings of the Annex that should be prohibited on the basis of an assessment according to Article 6.

A very obvious category of relevant elements is mentioned in Article 6(1)(d), namely elements related to *price*. Deceptive information concerning the price, the manner in which the price is calculated, or the existence of a specific price advantage is of course relevant in this context. This is an important group of misleading actions in practice. Various kinds of marketing practices may be used to create the impression of an advantageous offer. Catchwords such as 'gratis', 'free' and 'without charge'[73] may be used in a deceptive way to attract customers. Deceptive use of sales, rebates, closing offers,[74] making the offer seem more advantageous than it is in reality, is

---

without Frontiers' Directive, OJ 28 April 2004 C102/2–11, the Commission recommends the use of 'the criterion of the "undue influence" of the good, service, brand or company name', following, for example, from recurring presence not warranted on editorial grounds; see at [33] and [34].

69  Here as well one could mention the prohibition of bait and bait and switch advertising in the Annex I (5) and (6). See also *The Unfair Commercial Practices Directive. Report of DTI workshop on the evidence for a 'general duty to trade fairly'* (July 2003), www.dti.gov.uk/ccp/consultpdf/unfaircon.pdf, according to which the bait advertising prohibition 'could cover traders who offer a low call-out rate followed by substantial charges for extra work'.

70  See more concretely the prohibition of false statements about the timely availability of a product, Annex I (7).

71  In the Green Paper, COM(2001) 531 final 8, one problem particularly mentioned to be addressed was '[n]ew advertising practices which challenge traditional print media distinctions between media content and advertising (e.g., website sponsorship, affiliation, remunerated search tools, use of meta-data and links, referrals and reviews)'. See also the provision on advertorials in the Annex I (11). The same issue is dealt with also in Article 7, see below, section c, with the commentary to Article 7(2).

72  See Annex I (4) and also (2).

73  Specific restrictions on the use of these terms are set in the Annex I (20).

74  See also Annex I (15), concerning false claims that the trader is about to cease trading or move premises.

common and national legislation in the Member States contains many specific rules on such offers.[75] Even though such national legislation has to be reassessed in the light of the Directive,[76] one cannot overlook the fact that consumers in various countries may understand special offers in different ways, partially because they have grown used to certain ways of regulating special offers in their own country.[77] As long as there is no Community-wide practice in this area, a culturally sensitive application of the Directive appears necessary in this context[78] as well as in many other contexts.[79]

The fifth category of elements in Article 6(1)(e) mentions the *need for a service, part, replacement or repair.* If the trader downplays the need for service and repair or the costs connected therewith, this may constitute a prohibited misleading action. In the after-sales situation information concerning such items may, on the other hand, be misleading in a manner that is prohibited if it leads to false impressions in the other direction. Causing the consumer to believe that he needs costly service, replacement or repair, even though the real need for such measures is not of that size, is misleading. This may also be the case when, for example, the service as such is included in the guarantee, but the consumer has to pay for spare parts that are unnecessarily changed during the service. If consumers are falsely told that repairs are too costly and they thereby are induced to buy expensive replacements, this may also be considered a misleading practice.

Article 6(1)(f) also takes into account the fact that information concerning the nature, attributes and rights of the *trader* is in many cases obviously material for the consumer. The Article mentions as examples 'his identity and assets, his qualifications, status, approval,[80] affiliation or connection[81] and ownership of industrial, commercial or intellectual property rights or his awards and distinctions'. The representation of a seller alleging in a misleading way that he is a wholesaler or manufacturer, and accordingly can sell more cheaply, might be mentioned as an

---

75 See, on the many and varied details, Micklitz and Kessler, *op.cit.*, 9, 32, 52, 67, 85, 108, 138, 181, 212, 227, 252, 277, 293, 333 and 397.

76 The variations in the regulation of price reduction techniques is mentioned in the report by Schulze and Schulte-Nölke, *op.cit.*, 99 as one of the potential barriers to trade resulting from the divergences between Member State laws.

77 As Schulze and Schulte-Nölke, *op.cit.* note, there are 'considerable differences' in this area. The comparative overview concerning special sales events/special offers/liquidation sales (55) and rebates and free gifts (60) in their report is illuminating.

78 See also Köhler and Lettl, *op.cit.*, 1038, who because of this reason recognise the possibility for national legislation to concretise the rules of the Directive in this area.

79 The adoption of a Regulation on Sales Promotions would have lead to a more strict uniformity in this area: see Proposal for a regulation concerning sales promotions in the Internal Market, COM(2001) 546 final and Amended proposal for a Regulation concerning sales promotions in the Internal Market, COM(2002) 585 final. As mentioned earlier this project is probably not continuing; see above Chapter 2(d).

80 See also on the use of trust and quality marks, Annex I (2).

81 See also on false claims that the trader is a signatory to a code of conduct, Annex I (1).

example in this context.[82] All kinds of marketing and business practices related to the image of the trader also fall under this category. Image marketing that is not directly connected with the selling of a certain product can be remedied on the basis of this Article, as long as it is likely to cause consumers to make transactional decisions – and the ultimate goal of most image marketing is indeed to have such effects on consumer's behaviour.

Finally, in Article 6(1)(g) are mentioned the *consumer's rights and risks*. Various kinds of information obviously belong under this fairly broad heading. As to the rights of the consumer, it is obvious that a false description in an advertisement or some other pre-contractual business practice of the rights of the consumer under the contract can constitute a misleading action, even if the correct information can be obtained from the contractual provisions themselves, because of the importance of the 'overall presentation'. In addition, deceptive information about rights that lack practical significance, or cannot be used because of a lack of remedies, or are not in practice followed by the trader seems to belong to this category. Overemphasising the value of certain rights offered by the trader can have similar misleading effects.[83] Another aspect of the consumer's rights that can be mentioned in this context are his rights in relation to the purchased product, both as regards competing rights of third persons and as regards the possibilities lawfully to use the product.[84] Rights and risks also include consumer duties. Information understating the consumers' duties is as misleading as information overstating their rights. Also practices that give the consumer an impression of being under a duty that he does not have in reality can be deemed misleading.[85] Claims concerning risks are also mentioned in this context. Product-related risks are enumerated already in Article 6(1)(b), and the use of the word in this context rather refers to other kinds of risks played on in the contractual situation.[86] Finally, information concerning consumer rights and risks is also obviously of great importance in the after-sales period. A practice that misleads the consumer whether and how to exercise a contractual right in relation to the product, a transactional decision mentioned in Article 2(k), is included in the scope of Article 6. To make this clearer still, Article 6(1)(g) expressly mentions as an example the misleading of consumers concerning their right to replacement or reimbursement under the Consumer Sales Directive.

---

82   See on such a provision in Spanish law, *Compilations of National Laws, op.cit.*, First Part, 27.

83   See also Annex I (10) on presenting legal rights as offered by the trader.

84   This may also be said to relate to the 'main characteristics of the product', see above on Article 6(1)(b). See also Annex I (9) on false statements that the product can be legally sold.

85   See on invoicing without preceding order, Annex I (21).

86   See on claims concerning risks to personal security related to non-purchase, Annex I (12).

*(vi) Imitative marketing*

Article 6(2)(a) includes a particular provision aimed at covering 'marketing of a product by imitating the distinguishing features of another product in a way which causes confusion between the two products'.[87] According to this provision:

> A commercial practice shall also be regarded as misleading if, in its factual context, taking account of all its features and circumstances, it causes or is likely to cause the average consumer to take a transactional decision that he would not have taken otherwise, and it involves … any marketing of a product, including comparative advertising, which creates confusion with any products, trade marks, trade names or other distinguishing marks of a competitor.

The most important message of this provision is probably indirect, namely the message that imitation as such is not prohibited. The intention of the Directive 'is not … to reduce consumer choice by prohibiting the promotion of products which look similar to other products unless this similarity confuses consumers as to the commercial origin of the product and is therefore misleading'.[88] Imitation – not even slavish imitation – as such is not prohibited according to the Directive, as long as it does not cause confusion among consumers.[89] The possible remedies for competing traders offered for example by intellectual property rules of course fall outside the scope of the Directive, as it does not regulate business-to-business relationships.[90]

Misleading confusion can be caused not only by imitation of a product, but also through marketing. A marketing message may expressly or impliedly, in a deceptive way, for example by using the same themes, layouts, melodies and so forth as the competitor uses, cause consumers to confuse the products offered with the products of a competitor.

In addition, comparative advertising may cause similar confusion. In this respect the special provision in Article 6(2)(a) should be read in connection with the provisions on comparative advertising in the amended Misleading Advertising Directive. Although the provisions concerning misleading advertising in that Directive are, after the adoption of the Unfair Commercial Practices Directive, limited to cover only the protection of traders against misleading advertising, the Misleading Advertising Directive continues to lay down 'the conditions under which comparative advertising is permitted'.[91] However, from a consumer point of view one important aspect of comparative advertising is included in Article 6(2)(a) of the Unfair Commercial Practices Directive, namely the risk of confusion.

---

87  COM(2003) 356 final 14.

88  Recital 14.

89  See also Annex I (13) that explicitly forbids the promotion of similar products deliberately to mislead the consumer.

90  See above Chapter 3(e), as well as on intellectual property rights Chapter 3(f)(ii).

91  Misleading Advertising Directive, Article 1, as amended by Article 14(1) of the Unfair Commercial Practices Directive.

Consumer confusion over products, but also, more generally, over trademarks, trade names and other distinguishing marks, are covered by the provision. This would probably be the case even without the express wording of the provision, as confusion regarding such marks ultimately may lead to confusion concerning products.

The provision on imitation contains the same tests as the general provision on misleading actions in Article 6(1). The average consumer test and the materiality condition are worded in the same manner, and the term 'confusion' is parallel to the deceptiveness condition in the general provision. It is therefore difficult to see why a specific provision of this kind was needed, instead of just including matters involving imitation in the lengthy enumeration of elements included in Article 6(1). Perhaps it was just the desire to indicate, albeit indirectly, as mentioned above, that product imitation as such is not to be prohibited.

Comparing Article 6(2) with Article 6(1) more closely, there are differences in wording. Perhaps the most striking one is that the prerequisite 'creates confusion' uses an empirical language, in comparison with 'likely to deceive' that hints at a looser assessment of probability. On the other hand, however, the words at the beginning of Article 6(2), 'in its factual context, taking account of all its features and circumstances', seem even looser than the corresponding words in Article 6(1), 'in any way, including overall presentation'. All in all, therefore, even taking into account the different wordings, it is hard to see real differences between the conditions mentioned in the provisions. In practice, 'creates confusion' has to be read as 'is likely to create confusion'.

### (vii) Non-compliance with codes of conduct

As is analysed in more detail in Chapter 7, the Directive purports to strengthen the role of codes of conduct as a self-regulatory mechanism to enable traders to apply the Directive effectively.[92] Therefore the role of codes of conduct has also been expressly addressed in the provision concerning misleading actions, in Article 6(2)(b).[93] This paragraph is commented upon more in detail in the above-mentioned chapter. Only a few general comments are made in this context.

According to that Article, non-compliance of a trader with commitments contained in codes of conduct by which the trader has undertaken to be bound may constitute a misleading commercial practice. There are two specific conditions for this effect mentioned in the provision. First, the commitment contained in the code should set out a firm duty – and not simply be aspirational[94] – and be capable of being verified and, secondly, the trader should have indicated in a commercial practice that he is

---

92  Recital 20.

93  See also Annex I (1) on a trader claiming to be a signatory of a code of conduct when he is not, and Annex I (3) on falsely claiming that a code has public or other endorsement.

94  Meaning 'best efforts', COM(2002) 289 final 11.

bound by the code. In such a case non-compliance with the code is considered a misleading activity, according to Article 6(2)(b).[95]

The beginning of Article 6(2) provides the same common general provision to both imitative marketing and non-compliance with a code of conduct. What has been said above on the parallel nature of the conditions for applying Article 6(2) with those of applying Article 6(1) could be repeated in this context as well. Every non-compliance with a code of conduct is not relevant. The non-compliance should be material and therefore be likely to cause the average consumer to take a transactional decision he would not otherwise have taken. Matters of taste, decency or social responsibility, often addressed in codes of conduct, are therefore relevant only when they are likely to affect transactional decisions in this way.[96] This is the case if 'the trader establishes a specific connection between its actions in these areas and its product in its marketing material'.[97]

The provision is applicable to both national and EU-wide codes of conduct.[98] This is one of the points in which the Directive indirectly accepts that there may be a need for different standards of conduct in various parts of the internal market. If traders sign up to national codes, their behaviour will be judged according to the national standards. However, a trader from another part of the Union, who has not signed up to the national code, is not automatically judged according to that standard. Only commercial pressure may force him to adopt the national standard, as he may otherwise face difficulties in approaching consumers who set store in the national standards. In this way the Directive accepts and endorses a competition between codes of conduct, meaning, that is, a competition between national understandings of 'fairness'.

## c. Misleading Omissions

### (i) An indirect duty to inform

Not only actions that mislead consumers to take decisions they would not have taken otherwise are outlawed by a specific provision in the Directive. The Directive also acknowledges that the consumer needs information in order to be able to take an informed transactional decision and accordingly, in Article 7, forbids the misleading omission of information. As noted above, Article 7 seems to be preoccupied with 'pure' omission, whilst the combination of action and omission seems to fall under

---

95   The conditions have been rewritten since the 2003 proposal, see COM(2003) 356 final, proposal Article 6(2)(b). The second condition was introduced on the basis of a parliamentary amendment, Amendment 40 at the Parliament's first reading (Doc. 8492/04).

96   See generally on these matters falling outside the scope of the Directive, above Chapter 3(d)(ii).

97   COM(2003) 356 final 15.

98   COM(2003) 356 final 15.

Article 6. However, there cannot and need not be any precise line between misleading actions and misleading omissions.

A provision that deems pure omission to be unfair under certain conditions indirectly contains a duty to disclose. The Commission, however, has preferred not to describe the provision in such language. As mentioned in the Explanatory Memorandum, the regulation of misleading omissions attempts to 'avoid the need for a positive duty to disclose' that in the earlier stages of preparation met criticism for being unduly onerous and costly for traders.[99] However, even though the adopted provision does not contain a far-reaching 'duty to disclose to the consumer all material information which is likely to affect the consumer's decision',[100] it does contain an indirect duty to inform the consumers, under the conditions mentioned in the Article. Therefore, despite the cautious wording of the Commission, one may very well in this context speak of a duty to provide information,[101] which probably goes further than what has been previously accepted in many Member States.[102] The purpose of providing the consumer with relevant information in the pre-contractual stage has indeed been seen as one of the central aspects of the Directive.[103] Such an emphasis on the duty to inform would correspond to the general focus on information of the Directive and of EU consumer law in general.

The cautious description of the Commission, however, is correct in the sense that it is difficult to construct very detailed and costly duties of disclosure with the help of the provision in Article 7(1), given that it is worded as a fairly vague general clause. The duty of the trader according to the Directive 'is not to omit "material" information ... where this information would not be apparent from the context'.[104]

Even though the duty of disclosure of the Directive is indirect, in the sense that the remedies focus on the prohibition of an omission rather than the imposing of a particular duty, this does not necessarily mean that national law would be prevented from framing the rules in the language of more directly imposed duties. As the remedies related to the Directive are in the hands of the Member States, this might indicate that remedies directly attached to breaches of duties to inform could be in

---

99   COM(2003) 356 final 8.

100   COM(2002) 289 final 9.

101   In the report of Twigg-Flesner *et al*, *op.cit.*, 54 the authors note that 'the UCPD effectively imposes a duty of disclosure, whereas existing UK law makes no such demand'. Radeideh, *op.cit.*, 271 also speaks about the Directive 'as a tool to incorporate some basic positive information duties'.

102   See on the various limitations of the information duty so far in force in the Member States, Lettl, *op.cit.*, 307–310. As shown here, the provision of an information duty is as such not new; see also Schulze and Schulte-Nölke, *op.cit.*, 32.

103   H. Schulte-Nölke and C.W. Busch, 'Der Vorschlag der Kommission für eine Richtlinie über unlautere Geschäftspraktiken KOM(2003) 356 endg.' (2004) 12 *Zeitschrift für Europäisches Privatrecht* 99, 104–105.

104   COM(2003) 356 final 14.

conformity with the Directive, as long as the content of the duties do go no further than what is foreseen by the indirect duties of the Directive.[105]

The basic rule concerning misleading omissions can be found in Article 7(1):

> A commercial practice shall be regarded as misleading if, in its factual context, taking account of all its features and circumstances and the limitations of the communication medium, it omits material information that the average consumer needs, according to the context, to take an informed transactional decision and thereby causes or is likely to cause the average consumer to take a transactional decision that he would not have taken otherwise.

The conditions for applying this Article are partially the same as in Article 6 on misleading actions, but naturally they also differ in some respects. The average consumer test and the materiality condition, referring to likely effects of the misleading practice on the consumer's decision-making ('causes or is likely to cause … a transactional decision'), are identical with what can be found in Article 6. It is therefore sufficient to refer here, *mutatis mutandis*, to what has been said above concerning these issues.

The central issue in this context, however, is what information consumers require to be given in various situations. What information does the 'duty to disclose' comprise? The basic starting point is that only omissions concerning 'material information' are covered by Article 7. In the article this is expressed by the words 'material information that the average consumer needs … to take an informed transactional decision'. As these words are additional to the words concerning the 'materiality condition' at the end of the provision, they are probably meant to add something to the prerequisites for its application. The words seem to refer to 'objective' informational needs of consumers rather than to the likely effects of the information or omission on consumers' behaviour, which is covered by the materiality condition. Distinguishing the test expressed in these words of Article 7 from the 'materiality condition' common for both Articles 6 and 7, one could call the additional Article 7 requirement the 'consumers' informational needs test'. This is done here despite the fact that the test does not focus exclusively on the informational needs of consumers, as the Directive recognises that the context and the communication medium must affect the expectations concerning the information to be given.

For the particular cases of invitation to purchase and information requirements established by Community law, Article 7 contains specific provisions. Before proceeding to an analysis of the informational needs test and the specific provisions, something should be said concerning the question of when a specific item of information is to be considered 'omitted' or 'hidden'.

---

105  So Bakardjieva Engelbrekt, *EU and Marketing Practices Law in the Nordic Countries – Consequences of a Directive on Unfair Business-to-Consumer Commercial Practices*, *op.cit.*, 37.

*(ii) Omission and withholding of information*

For most cases the concept of 'omission' does not need any further clarification. Omitted information is information that is not given to the consumer. However, in some cases the line between omission and inclusion is not that obvious. What about information given only on some occasions, or in a foreign language, or hidden in some way? In Article 7(2) it is clarified that there can be a misleading omission even though the information is given, if it is not given in a sufficiently clear manner:

> It shall also be regarded as a misleading omission when, taking account of the matters described in paragraph 1, a trader hides or provides in an unclear, unintelligible, ambiguous or untimely manner such material information as referred to in that paragraph or fails to identify the commercial intent of the commercial practice if not already apparent from the context, and where, in either case, this causes or is likely to cause the average consumer to take a transactional decision that he would not have taken otherwise.

This provision again highlights the vague borderline between misleading actions and omissions. As stated above, false impressions induced by headings, pictures and so forth may constitute misleading actions according to Article 6, even though they are corrected in the small print of the advertisement. When speaking of 'pure' omissions regulated in Article 7, the focus is on information that should have been given in any event, without regard to headings and pictures, but the use of small print may be regarded as similarly insufficient in this context as well. This does not mean that the assessment of the use of small print necessarily should be exactly the same according to Article 6 and Article 7: for some situations one might argue that more eye-catching information is required to correct such misunderstandings that the trader has induced himself, by headings and the like, than when he is giving information demanded by the provision in Article 7.

The cited provision indicates that 'hidden' information can render an omission as misleading as information that is omitted altogether. Information may be hidden in various ways. Providing information in small print in some less eye-catching part of the marketing materials is just one example.

The information should also be understandable. Unclear, unintelligible and ambiguous information may be treated as omitted information. The assessment of when information is so unclear that it cannot be considered as having been provided, in practice necessarily will be highly dependent on what content one gives to the average consumer test. As mentioned above, the test opens the assessment towards including the 'social, cultural or linguistic' factors of the consumer's own environment.[106] One might assume that the issue of how information given is understood is an issue where there is a strong need for diverging national assessments related to variations in national consumer cultures.

It is interesting to note that the *language* question is not explicitly dealt with in this provision, although in the context of a duty of disclosure it cannot be overlooked

---

106   See above, section b(iii).

or dispensed with.[107] The ability to use the same business practices throughout the European Union of course becomes less valuable for the traders if there is an obligation to give information that has to be translated every time an internal border is crossed. However, the silence of the Directive on this matter shows that this problem has not been solved, and that the drafters of the Directive have not wanted openly to admit it. As the Directive now stands, the *in casu* assessment of whether a required piece of information is given in a sufficiently clear way has to take into account the fact that language barriers between consumers have not fallen,[108] and that many consumers are not in sufficient command of foreign languages. It may be that some information can be given in a language that is understandable by most, having some knowledge of 'bad English', or by use of generally understood symbols, but more advanced information can hardly be given in a language other than that of the average national consumer. The large variations between language skills make national assessments that underline the role of the national languages more or less inevitable. Within some particular markets, for example the marketing of highly technical devices used by 'specialised' consumers, national courts may of course find that consumers do have sufficient language skills to understand communications in a foreign language.

The required information should also be given in a timely manner, in order not to be irrelevant. This provision shows that separate pieces of the trader's activity should be judged independently when applying Article 7. Article 2(d) of the Directive provides that a practice means 'any act, omission, course of conduct or representation, commercial communication'. Even though the primary purpose of this provision is not the definition of what pieces of conduct one should understand as different practices,[109] it indicates that one has to view the various activities of the trader also as distinct. So information given to consumers through one channel does not necessarily compensate for the omissions in another channel. The reference to 'untimely manner' in the provision also takes into account the fact that information given during different phases of the process of acquiring consumer products may have different impact on the decision-making of the consumer. For example, it is a well-recognised fact that information given at very late stages of the process, when the consumer has effectively made up his mind, often does not have any impact. Such information may therefore not be sufficient to cure an omission and make the practice as a whole acceptable.

Finally, the provision mentions as a particular example of a misleading omission that the trader 'fails to identify the commercial intent of the commercial practice if not already apparent from the context'. This sentence repeats in a more general form the principle that marketing should always be identifiable as marketing, which was

---

107 Compare on language in the context of misleading actions, above section b(iii).

108 Compare the belief in the falling of language barriers in the Extended Impact Assessment, SEC(2003) 724, 5, referred to in more detail above in section b(iii).

109 This should probably not even be defined in the same way for all cases, as in one case a mere singular act may constitute unfairness, whilst in another case the combination of many acts may have a misleading effect.

mentioned already above.[110] In fact the sentence does not seem to add much to the content of the Directive and rather obscures its structure. Misleading the consumer as to commercial intent is better considered as a misleading action rather than a misleading omission.

### (iii) The consumers' informational needs test

The indirect duty of disclosure based on Article 7 concerns certain important pieces of information. It covers information that is of central relevance to consumer decision-making. The key concept used to delimit the information that has to be given is the 'informed transactional decision'. The legal ideal, in this provision, is a consumer who is equipped with the information to make decisions in the marketplace. Therefore, repeating the whole key sentence, a commercial practice is considered misleading if it 'omits material information that the average consumer needs, according to the context, to take an informed transactional decision'.

A more precise definition of what information a consumer needs in various contexts is difficult to give. Obviously the decision is to some extent dependent on the level of knowledge and skills of the consumers to whom the commercial practice is addressed. What constitutes decisive information for an average consumer in one country may be self-evident for a consumer from another. Therefore, here again one obviously encounters a situation on which there must be some leeway for the courts to take into account social, cultural or linguistic factors of the local environment.

The informational needs of the consumer obviously depend on what phase of the relationship the commercial practice relates to ('according to the context'). When speaking about information duties the central focus is usually on the pre-contractual information requirements, and the Directive gives a more precise provision on what information shall be regarded as material in the case of an invitation to purchase. This provision, Article 7(4), is commented upon below. However, Article 7 has a broader scope, consonant with that of the Directive, and duties of disclosure based on the article may therefore be related both to earlier and later stages of the marketing and contracting process than that covered by Article 7(4). For example, after the contract has been concluded, a complete silence concerning some essential right of the consumer may in some cases constitute a misleading omission.

This provision uses the word 'context' twice. The assessment of what information the consumer may require is contextual also in another sense than that mentioned above. It takes into account what information can reasonably be given and expected in the respective context of the commercial practice, the type of commercial practice, the medium used and so on. The provision uses very vague language in this respect, as it speaks about a commercial practice which, 'in its factual context, taking account of all its features and circumstances and the limitations of the communication medium ... omits material information'. This wording almost gives the court a *carte blanche* to decide what information should be given in which type of commercial practice. It

---

110   Section b(v), in the comment to Article 6(1)(c). See also Annex I (11) and (22).

is very difficult to foresee concretely what information will be required in different contexts, taking into account the rather broad variations in the previous national rules concerning this issue.[111] Information concerning price[112] is an obvious matter for inclusion in this context, but so far as products are concerned the obligation to indicate the selling price, and in some cases the unit price, is already quite comprehensively regulated elsewhere.[113] Information on risks[114] connected with the use of the goods may also be noted as an example of an issue that the trader might be required to address in various contexts. Many other examples could, depending on the context, be mentioned as well.[115]

In the assessment, particular emphasis is to be put on the medium used to communicate the commercial practice. According to Article 7(3), where the medium 'imposes limitations of space or time', these shall be taken into account in the assessment. Obviously, the possibility to convey information through television advertising is more limited than through newspaper ads, and this should be a relevant factor when deciding what information the consumer is considered to need in the respective advertisement. The provision acknowledges, however, that the various activities of the trader also should be scrutinised together. When referring to the limitations imposed by the medium one should also take into account 'any measures taken by the trader to make the information available to consumers by other means'. Thus even though a certain piece of information cannot reasonably be given in a television advertisement, the lack of this information may still constitute an omission, if the information is not sufficiently supplied by other means. The television advertisement could, for example, contain a reference to the homepage of the trader where sufficient information is given. Of course, this is not to say that information on a homepage should be considered sufficient for all kinds of information.[116]

---

111    See, on the various national concepts of 'material information' and so on, *Compilations of National Laws, op.cit.*, First Part, 57–62.

112    See on the national rules in this respect, *Compilations of National Laws, op.cit.*, First Part, 28–34.

113    The Directive 98/6/EC on consumer protection in the indication of the prices of products offered to consumers, Articles 3–6.

114    As analysed in Chapter 3(f)(iv), these issues partially fall outside the scope of the Directive. However, as mentioned there, one might still apply the Directive 'positively' to health and safety issues, in cases where no special rules exist. As far as risks relate to issues other than health and safety, they are of course covered by the Directive.

115    Köhler and Lettl, *op.cit.*, 1041 mention information that an offered model is already taken out of production ('Auslaufmodell').

116    H. Apostolopoulos, 'Neuere Entwicklungen im europäischen Lauterkeitsrecht: Problematische Aspekte und Vorschläge' 50 *Wettbewerb in Recht und Praxis* 841, 848, analysing the proposed Directive, emphasises that the most important information should be actively given to the consumer, and not just made available for him through an Internet address or a telephone number. See also the Swedish case Market Court 2004:16, in which in a television advertisement Vodafone, in a catching way, offered low price mobile phones. The offer was, however, substantially restricted by a number of conditions, which were shown

*(iv) Material information in invitation to purchase*

In Article 7(4) the Directive contains a list enumerating the information that shall be regarded as material in the specific situation of an invitation to purchase. This provision concretises the general rules of the article for probably the most important situation in which a misleading omission can occur.

The term 'invitation to purchase', which delimits scope of Article 7(4), is defined in Article 2(i) of the Directive. According to that provision it 'means a commercial communication which indicates characteristics of the product and the price in a way appropriate to the means of the commercial communication used and thereby enables the consumer to make a purchase'. According to the definition, advertising and other commercial communication that is concrete in its identification of product and price, so that the consumer can be induced to a decision to purchase, is understood as an invitation to purchase. No specific 'invitation' or similar wording is needed. The purpose of the definition is rather to delimit the scope of the provision excluding more general forms of commercial communication, such as general brand and product awareness marketing.[117] What is focused on here are commercial practices that are 'targeted enough … for the fair trading rules to apply'.[118] The assessment whether this is the case is to be based on the purpose of fair trading regulation and not on traditional contract law concepts concerning the *invitatio ad offerendum*.[119]

The relationship between Article 7(4) and the preceding paragraphs of the Article is not spelt out in the Directive. It is not quite clear whether Article 7(4) is thought of as completely replacing the preceding paragraphs within its sphere of application, or whether it just defines material information, but leaves the other tests, the average consumer test, the materiality condition and the rule on hidden information, to be applied also in this context. In principle the provisions at the beginning of the Article might be used both to limit and to enlarge the sphere of relevant misleading omissions in case of an invitation to purchase.

As to the possible limiting functions of the preceding paragraphs, it seems obvious that Article 7(4) is at least aimed at replacing all the parts of the consumers' informational needs test, not only those that relate to the needs of the 'informed consumer', but also the contextual ones, relating to the nature of the medium used. The references to 'context' and 'medium' in Article 7(4) indicate this fairly clearly. As to the related materiality condition and the average consumer test, the solution must be regarded as unsettled. On the one hand, if the trader can show that an omission to provide information that is demanded according to Article 7(4) is not likely to cause the average consumer to take a transactional decision he would not have taken otherwise, there seems to be no need for taking action against the omission. On

---

only for three seconds in small print. The advertisement was forbidden, despite the defendant's objection that more detailed information was offered on the Internet.

117    These are mentioned in COM(2003) 356 final 14.

118    Radeideh, *op.cit.*, 274.

119    Schulte-Nölke and Busch, *op.cit.*, 106; Radeideh, *op.cit.*, 273–4.

the other hand, concerning the efficient functioning of the supervision of the rules, it would be advisable to limit the possibility of using *in casu* defences against the detailed rules. Perhaps, however, the problem is more theoretical than practical. The presumption that the omission to give information required in Article 7(4) is likely to cause transactional decisions may in practice be so strong that defences of that kind will seldom be used in any event.

Regardless of what stance one adopts to the above issue, the enumerated items of information to be given in the case of an invitation to purchase do not have to be provided under all circumstances. Article 7(4) itself contains a limitation. The information mentioned shall be regarded as material, 'if not already apparent from the context'. The purpose of this restriction is to avoid an excess of information both for traders and for consumers.[120]

On the other hand, as to the enlargement of the sphere of misleading omissions in the case of an invitation to purchase, it seems obvious that the specific provision in Article 7(3) on the hiding of information, which above was understood as having relevance also to the language issue, should be applicable also in the context of Article 7(4). Its necessity in this context can hardly be disputed. More difficult is the issue whether even the definition of material information is exclusive in the sense that the list of items is to be considered exhaustive in this context, or whether other items can be asked for on the basis of the general provisions at the beginning of the Article. From the point of view of harmonisation one could argue for exclusiveness of the list in Article 7(4). However, given the need to take into account both particularities related to specific lines of business as well as social, cultural or linguistic factors within the local environment when defining consumer needs of information, one should not rule out the possibility that the court in a particular case could state, on the basis of Article 7(1), that a certain item of information that is not included in the enumeration in Article 7(4) should be given in an invitation to purchase.[121]

It has to be noted in this context that the Preamble even seems to recognise a possibility for the national legislature to expand the list in certain situations. It notes that the full harmonisation approach 'does not preclude the Member States from specifying in national law the main characteristics of particular products such as, for example, collectors' items or electrical goods, the omission of which would be material when an invitation to purchase is made'.[122] The acceptance of the possibility of adding other items in particular cases on the basis of Article 7(1) seems to be in line with the recognition of a certain space for national decision-making.

Five items to be regarded as material are enumerated in the Article.

---

120   Extended Impact Assessment, SEC(2003) 724, 27.

121   See also Schulte-Nölke and Busch, *op.cit.*, who argue that Article 7(4) should not be understood as a maximum standard concerning information requirements.

122   Recital 14. Compare, however, what is said on specific information requirements in Recital 15, related to existing Community law instruments. See below under Established information requirements, section c(v).

First, information should be given concerning the *main characteristics of the product*. However, this is only to the extent appropriate for the medium and product. In many cases, when dealing with well-known products, one may presume this information to be apparent from the context.

Secondly, the consumer is deemed to need some information about the *trader*. Geographical address and identity, such as trading name, as well as the same information for traders on behalf of whom the trader is acting, are deemed relevant. When purchasing from a shop, information concerning address and identity is obviously mostly apparent from the context. However, in various forms of distance selling it is important for the consumer to know a physical address to turn to.[123]

Thirdly, information concerning the *price* is obviously material for the consumer. According to this provision, the total price should be stated, including taxes, additional freight, delivery or postal charges. If, because of the nature of the product, the price cannot reasonably be calculated in advance, the manner of calculation should be given, and if additional charges cannot reasonably be calculated, the consumer should be informed that such charges may be payable. It should be underlined, however, that the latter options are available only if advance calculation is not reasonably possible. If calculation can be done the trader is obliged to do so and give information concerning the final and total price. If a certain price is stated in the heading or in the main part of an advertisement, and information on additional charges is given in small print, this may constitute a misleading action according to Article 6.

Fourthly, the trader is obliged to provide information concerning arrangements for *payment, delivery, performance and complaint handling policy*, if these depart from the requirements of professional diligence. If the behaviour of the trader in these respects is of a normal standard, no disclosure according to Article 7(4) is required. Information has to be given only concerning substandard practices. If, for example, the trader has a policy not to answer, or only to react negatively to complaints, or if he regularly refuses to accept non-binding rulings by authorities such as the Office of Fair Trading or by public or semi-public complaints bodies, he must inform the consumers about this practice.[124] The criteria for assessing the standard of the behaviour of the trader in this respect are 'the requirements of professional diligence'. The definition of 'professional diligence' in Article 2(h) shows the target behaviour to be a departure from 'honest market practice and/or the general principle of good faith'.[125]

Finally, information is required concerning withdrawal or cancellation rights, when such a right exists for the product or transaction in question. This information requirement relates to the cancellation rights (sometimes also termed rights of

---

123   For electronic commerce such information is required by the Electronic Commerce Directive, Article 5.

124   Of course, as traders can hardly be expected to give such information, this rather gives the supervising authorities an additional indirect means of reaction against traders with such policies.

125   See more closely on the 'requirements of professional diligence' above, Chapter 4(d).

withdrawal) based on several consumer protection Directives.[126] However, as the scope of the provision is not limited to these cases, it seems to cover cancellation rights based only on national legislation – both legislation extending the scope of the Directive-based rights and purely domestic legislation – as well.[127] The national legislative environment may therefore lead to differing demands on the information between different countries.

### (v) Established information requirements

Finally, Article 7(5) mentions that information requirements established by Community law in relation to commercial communication, including advertising and marketing, are regarded as material in the application of Article 7. To help those applying the Directive, a list of relevant legislative acts of Community law is included in Annex II of the Directive. These include consumer protection Directives, insurance Directives and investor protection Directives.[128] The list is expressly said to be non-exhaustive. If a Directive is missing from the list it is not necessarily irrelevant from the point of view of the Unfair Commercial Practices Directive, and new Directives containing information requirements that are material in this context may of course also be adopted.

As with Article 7(4), the relationship between Article 7(5) and the preceding paragraphs of the Article is left unclear. In the context of Article 7(5) one might argue that omissions of legally required information should always be subject to legal measures and therefore that one should probably not limit the application of Article 7(5) by applying the other conditions and tests in Article 7. Even in cases where, for example, it is not likely that an average consumer would have been caused by the omission to take a transactional decision, the breach of the legislative requirements could constitute a relevant omission in the sense of the Directive.

The question whether the particular information duties mentioned in other Community law Directives can be supplemented by information duties derived from Article 7 of the Unfair Commercial Practices Directive is also not regulated in Article 7(5) of the Directive. If there is no express or implied indication in the particular Directive that the Unfair Commercial Practices Directive should not

---

126   See the Doorstep Selling Directive Article 5, the Distance Selling Directive Article 6, the Timeshare Directive Article 5 and the Distance Selling of Financial Services Directive Article 6.

127   Compare below on the lack of relevance of national rules in relation to Article 7(5). This is, however, indicated in the text of that provision.

128   Provisions of the Distance Selling Directive, Package Tour Directive, Timeshare Directive, Price Indication Directive, Medicinal Products Directive, Electronic Commerce Directive, Consumer Credit Directive, Distance Selling of Financial Services Directive, Transferable Securities Directive, Insurance Mediation Directive, Life Assurance Directive, Financial Instruments Directive, Third Non-life Insurance Directive and Prospectus Directive are mentioned.

apply, it is difficult to argue that it should not.[129] The presumption therefore seems to be that the Directive may be used to supplement the informational duties of such specific Directives.

Article 7(5) only relates to Community law information requirements. As the Directives mentioned are largely minimum Directives the Member States may have introduced additional information requirements. In the Preamble to the Directive it is clearly stated that the omission to give such information 'will not constitute a misleading omission under this Directive', but should rather be remedied with the help of consumers' individual contractual rights.[130] The same could obviously be said concerning information requirements that do not relate at all to Community legislation. However, it seems that the statement of the Preamble is perhaps worded too broadly. Even though national legislation is not relevant in the context of Article 7(5) it can be a part of the social and cultural factors to be taken into account in the application of the other parts of Article 7.[131]

### d. Practices That Are Always Regarded as Unfair

*(i) Nature of the Annex*

Annex I of the Directive sets out a blacklist of commercial practices which are considered unfair under all circumstances, as referred to in Article 5(5). Most examples on this list (23 out of 31) are presented under the heading of misleading commercial practices. In content they therefore relate closely to the assessment of commercial practices based on Article 6, as described above. They can be read as illustrations of the approach adopted in the Article, and have accordingly been referred to above.

However, the examples of the Annex are not meant primarily to be examples concerning the approach to be followed in the application of the Articles of the Directive. On the contrary, if a case falls under one of the cases mentioned in the Annex, the specific Article need not be applied at all. The blacklist gathers examples of practices that in all circumstances should be considered unfair. It means that no case-by-case assessment against the provisions of Articles 5–9 of the Directive is required.[132] If the practice is mentioned in the list, this is a sufficient prerequisite for using the appropriate remedies against it, and it cannot be made legitimate with any kind of improvement that does not bring it outside the wording of the Annex.

As the provisions enumerate those practices that are particularly reprehensible, one should not apply the wording of the Annex *e contrario*. One cannot assume that

---

129   See also Veelken, *op.cit.* 23, who states that the issue can only be solved in relation to each particular Directive.

130   Recital 15.

131   Observe, however, the warning related to this provision against an overload of information, in the Explanatory Memorandum, COM(2003) 356 final 14.

132   Recital 17.

practices which are similar to those of the Annex, but not prohibited by it, can be regarded as acceptable. As the list only mentions practices that in all circumstances shall be considered unfair, other practices, even close to those mentioned in the list, can be condemned using a case-by-case assessment based, for example, on Articles 6 or 7. As illustrations of the application of the articles on misleading practices they can also only be used to show what kind of practices are considered unlawful, but not to support conclusions on what can be deemed acceptable.

The list of the Annex is intended to be 'the full list of all such practices'.[133] The list is in, other words, meant to be exhaustive. All other practices than those mentioned in the list should be subject to a case-by-case assessment according to the relevant articles of the Directive. To make sure that this understanding will prevail, a sentence was added to Article 5(5) during the final stages of adoption of the Directive, according to which '[t]he same single list shall apply in all Member States and may only be modified by revision of this Directive'.[134]

Formally, one certainly has to adhere to this provision. However, from a practical point of view one may raise real doubts concerning the adequacy of this starting point. Obviously there are, and one can imagine, many other practices than those mentioned in the Annex that are misleading or aggressive in such a repulsive way that it is clear that they cannot be accepted on any kind of assessment. As this is the case, it seems rather misleading to state that the blacklist is exhaustive and that these other cases have to be scrutinised every time case-by-case. One may therefore assume that a court, if confronted with such a repulsive practice and attempting to produce as much legal certainty as possible, could state the practice to be misleading in practically all circumstances, and thereby in practice add examples to the list of commercial practices which are in all circumstances considered unfair – even though they formally cannot be added to the list of the Annex. At least the European Court of Justice could presumably act in this manner.[135] However, one can imagine the probable reluctance of the Court to take firm stands concerning the application of the Directive to particular detailed practices.[136] It might do so only when the

---

133   Recital 17.

134   Repeated also in Recital 17. The Commission already uttered the wish that the list 'can be changed or added to only in the same way as the rest of the Directive' in COM(2003) 356 final 9.

135   Compare the firm approach of the Court in Joined Cases C–240/98 to 244/98 *Océano Grupo Editorial SA v Rocío Murciano Quintero, et al.*, [2000] ECR I–151, concerning the Unfair Contract Terms Directive.

136   The Court seemingly has backtracked from the *Océano Grupo* approach in Case C–237/02 *Freiburger Kommunalbauten GmbH Baugesellschaft & Co. KG v Ludger Hofstetter et Ulrike Hofstetter*; see at [22]: 'It follows, as the Advocate General has observed at point 25 of his Opinion, that in the context of its jurisdiction under Article 234 EC to interpret Community law, the Court may interpret general criteria used by the Community legislature in order to define the concept of unfair terms. However, it should not rule on the application of these general criteria to a particular term, which must be considered in the light of the particular circumstances of the case in question'. However, there is not necessarily a conflict

repulsiveness of the practice is obvious – and such cases might not be brought to the European Court as they are perceived as clear in any event.

*(ii) The cases*

As mentioned above the Annex contains 23 items under the heading misleading commercial practices. These provisions are based on experiences from various Member States. Therefore, it is 'difficult to discern clear logic, coherence or policy priority in the selection and ordering of the examples on the list'.[137] In fact, even the way in which the provisions are located under the two headings – misleading and aggressive practices – can be questioned. For example, statements on the availability of the product for a limited period of time and claims on risks to the personal security of the consumer[138] could just as well be considered examples of pressure selling that belong under the heading aggressive commercial practices. On the other hand the last item in the list of aggressive practices, the creating of a false impression that the consumer has already won, or will win, a prize,[139] could equally be understood as a case of misleading practices.

The lack of systematic structure of the Annex and its roots in details of national laws make it difficult to say anything general about the content of the list. However, as the purpose of the Annex, described above, is clearly to offer a list of *per se* condemned practices that is as similar as possible in the various Member States, the application of the list must be distanced from the particular national roots of each provision. Therefore, and as the published discussions concerning the preparation of the Directive contain very few comments on the content of the Annex, it is difficult at this stage to offer a more detailed description of the content of many of the provisions than can be determined from the language of the provisions themselves. In fact, many of the provisions are phrased in a very concrete language, in order to offer sufficient guidance for the achievement of a relatively uniform application in different national contexts. For this reason, the content of the Annex is cited as such below. Some comments related to the *travaux préparatoires* and to Member State laws are added in the footnotes.

It should be noted, however, that many of the prohibitions of the Annex, despite the intention to render them as concrete and understandable as possible, appear

---

between *Océano Grupo* and *Freiburger Kommunalbauten*, as the former dealt with an issue expressly mentioned in the Annex of the Directive, and in addition it rather focused on a rule of national procedural law that could impede the effectivity of the Directive.

137    Bakardjieva Engelbrekt, *EU and Marketing Practices Law in the Nordic Countries – Consequences of a Directive on Unfair Business-to-Consumer Commercial Practices, op.cit.*, 43. The relationship between the Annex and the proposed Sales Promotion Regulation, mentioned above, is also difficult to grasp, as some of the provisions of the Annex clearly fall under the proposed content of the Regulation. This overlap may not become reality, as the Regulation will probably not be brought forward, see Chapter 2(d).

138    Annex I (7) and (12).

139    Annex I (31).

fairly cryptic and difficult to understand without knowledge of the actual practice (often based on experiences in some Member States) that the provision attempts to eradicate. It is also fairly unclear what discretion this leaves to the Member States – many existing laws concerning pyramid selling, for example, are fairly detailed. It is also not clear whether the list has to be implemented as such or whether the implementing provisions can be scattered over various parts of national legislation or even be left to be mentioned only in the national *travaux préparatoires*.[140]

Of course, the Annex has to be read in the context of the whole Directive. In the analysis of the general rules on misleading practices of the Directive, reference has been made to provisions of the Annex that relate to various aspects of those rules.[141] It might be helpful in the application of the Annex, even though it is formally separated from the *in casu* assessments of the general rules, to look also at the rules of the articles with which they are connected.

Misleading practices that are always regarded as unfair are, in the words of the Directive:

(1) Claiming to be a signatory to a code of conduct[142] when the trader is not.

(2) Displaying a trust mark, quality mark or equivalent without having obtained the necessary authorisation.[143]

(3) Claiming that a code of conduct has an endorsement from a public or other body which it does not have.

(4) Claiming that a trader (including his commercial practices) or a product has been approved, endorsed or authorised by a public or private body when he/it has not[144] or making such a claim without complying with the terms of the approval, endorsement or authorisation.

(5) Making an invitation to purchase products at a specified price without disclosing the existence of any reasonable grounds the trader may have for believing that he will not be able to offer for supply or to procure another trader to supply, those products or equivalent products at that price for a period that is,

---

140 Compare, on the Annex to the Unfair Contract Terms Directive, Case C–478/99 *Commission v Sweden* [2002] ECR I–4147. In this case the Court accepted that the Annex was implemented only through the *travaux préparatoires*, with regard to the traditions in the Nordic legal culture (at [23]). However, as the said Annex was only indicative, and this was noted by the Court (at [20] to [22]), this case is not necessarily decisive with regard to the Annex of the Unfair Commercial Practices Directive.

141 See in particular above, section b(v).

142 On the definition of a code of conduct, see below Chapter 7(f).

143 It is unclear whether 'authorisation' means decisions not only of public but also of private bodies. EU policies in this area rather seem to support a broader reading.

144 This may include the use of professional titles, such as 'advocate' and 'dentist', without having the necessary authorisation, in cases where such authorisation is needed; the provision is obviously understood in this way in the report by Twigg-Flesner *et al*, *op.cit.*, 123.

and in quantities that are, reasonable having regard to the product, the scale of advertising of the product and the price offered (bait advertising).[145]

(6) Making an invitation to purchase products at a specified price and then:

(a) refusing to show the advertised item to consumers; or

(b) refusing to take orders for it or deliver it within a reasonable time; or

(c) demonstrating a defective sample of it, with the intention of promoting a different product (bait and switch).

(7) Falsely stating that the product will only be available for a very limited[146] time, or that it will only be available on particular terms for a very limited time, in order to elicit an immediate decision and deprive consumers of sufficient opportunity or time to make an informed choice.

(8) Undertaking to provide after-sales service to consumers with whom the trader has communicated prior to a transaction in a language which is not an official language of the Member State where the trader is located and then making such service available only in another language without clearly disclosing this to the consumer before the consumer is committed to the transaction.

(9) Stating or otherwise creating the impression that a product can legally be sold when it cannot.

(10) Presenting rights given to consumers in law as a distinctive feature of the trader's offer.[147]

(11) Using editorial content in the media to promote a product where a trader has paid for the promotion without making that clear in the content or by images or sounds clearly identifiable by the consumer (advertorial). This is without prejudice to Council Directive 89/552/EEC.[148]

---

145    This form of misleading advertising is often mentioned under the heading 'enticement'. See under this heading on national provisions forbidding such advertising of a product without having a sufficient stock of the product, Micklitz and Kessler, *op.cit.*, 11, 35, 53, 68, 87, 110, 140, 185, 228, 252, 279, 295, 400. The provision of the Annex seems to be in conformity with the laws of most of the old Member States.

146    This word was introduced instead of 'short' on the basis of a parliamentary amendment, Amendment 71 at the Parliament's first reading (Doc. 8492/04). It reflects better the idea that the problem lies in an emphasis on the fact that the period ends at some not too distant point of time, which forces the consumer to make a decision.

147    This may apply to an express marketing of 'guarantees' that do not contain more rights than those that are granted the consumer according to the law in any event. There is much practice of this kind in Nordic law; see B. Dahl and P. Møgelvang-Hansen, *Garantier* (Copenhagen: Jurist– og Økonomforbundets Forlag, 1985) 117–134. See also the Consumer Sales Directive Article 6(2).

148    The Television Directive, in Chapter IV, contains provisions on television advertising, for example, on advertising having to be recognisable as such (Article 10), sponsorship (Article 17) and teleshopping, both on ordinary channels and on channels exclusively devoted to teleshopping (Article 19). Also the Electronic Commerce Directive, which is not mentioned in the provision, contains a provision according to which promotional offers and promotional competitions shall be clearly recognisable as such (Article 6(c) and (d)). The extent to which

(12) Making a materially inaccurate claim concerning the nature and extent[149] of the risk to the personal security of the consumer or his family if the consumer does not purchase the product.[150]

(13) Promoting a product similar to a product made by a particular manufacturer in such a manner as deliberately to mislead the consumer into believing that the product is made by the same manufacturer when it is not.

(14) Establishing, operating or promoting a pyramid promotional scheme where a consumer gives consideration for the opportunity to receive compensation that is derived primarily from the introduction of other consumers into the scheme rather than from the sale or consumption of products.[151]

(15) Claiming that the trader is about to cease trading or move premises[152] when he is not.[153]

---

information on the Internet can be regarded as information 'in the media' is obviously not quite clear.

149    This phrase was chosen as a response to a parliamentary amendment pointing out that not only misleading about the existence of a risk, but also overstating the risk should be prohibited; Amendment 73 at the Parliament's first reading (Doc. 8492/04).

150    Marketing playing on superstition may fall under this provision; see on the regulation of this issue in national laws *Compilations of National Laws, op.cit.*, Second Part, 17–18.

151    'Multi–Level Marketing', 'Snowball Systems', 'Pyramid Schemes' have been much discussed and have led to interventions in many national laws, and the Commission has looked into the issue; see the survey H.-W. Micklitz, B. Monazzahian and C. Rössler, *Door-to-Door Selling – Pyramid Selling – Multilevel-Marketing. A Study Commissioned by the European Commission* (November 1999), published at http://europa.eu.int/comm/dgs/health_consumer/ library/surveys/sur10_01.html as well as H.-W. Micklitz and B. Monazzahian, 'Multi Level Marketing and Pyramid Systems – Proposal for Action in the European Community' (2000) 8 *ConsumerLaw Journal* 223. See also, for example, Micklitz and Kessler, *op.cit.*, 31, 51, 66, 84, 106, 137, 179, 211, 227, 250, 276, 293, 330, 395, and Schulze and Schulte-Nölke, *op.cit.*, 50–52, both showing the variations of the national solutions. In the Annex the unfairness of such a scheme is related to the compensation being derived largely (but not only) from introducing other consumers than from the sale of the product. Other aspects of such schemes – for example, related to the misuse of the inexperience of the consumer concerning activity of this kind (see Köhler and Lettl, *op.cit.*, 1043) – may in an *in casu* assessment be found to violate the general clause or the other articles of the Directive. It is interesting to note in this context that participants in a pyramid scheme are regarded as consumers, even though they could be defined as small traders as well.

152    The description seems to leave the selling off of seasonal products outside the scope of the provision, and left to be judged on the basis of the articles of the Directive. There are various rules on such seasonal sales in the Member States; see, for example, R. Schulze and A.U. Janssen, 'Das Recht des unlauteren Wettbewerbs in den EU–Mitgliedsstaaten' (2004) 4 *The European Legal Forum* 77, 84.

153    This provision does not take a stand on the question of how long the trader can use the argument that he is about to cease trading or move premises, although Member State laws contain very differing rules on the maximum length of sales of this kind; see, for example, Schulze and Janssen, *op.cit.*, 84, and C.W. Busch, 'Ein europäischer Rechtsraum für das Lauterkeitsrecht?' (2004) 4 *The European Legal Forum* 91, 96. However, applying this rule,

(16) Claiming that products are able to facilitate winning in games of chance.

(17) Falsely claiming that a product is able to cure illnesses, dysfunction or malformations.[154]

(18) Passing on materially inaccurate information on market conditions or on the possibility of finding the product with the intention of inducing the consumer to acquire the product at conditions less favourable than normal market conditions.

(19) Claiming in a commercial practice to offer a competition or prize promotion without awarding the prizes described or a reasonable equivalent.

(20) Describing a product as 'gratis', 'free', 'without charge' or similar if the consumer has to pay anything other than the unavoidable cost of responding to the commercial practice and collecting or paying for delivery of the item.[155]

(21) Including in marketing material an invoice or similar document seeking payment which gives the consumer the impression that he has already ordered the marketed product when he has not.

(22) Falsely claiming or creating the impression that the trader is not acting for purposes relating to his trade, business, craft or profession,[156] or falsely representing oneself as a consumer.

(23) Creating the false impression that after-sales service in relation to a product is available in a Member State other than the one in which the product is sold.

### e. Understanding Misleading Practices

With regard to the central role of information in EU consumer law, it is not surprising that misleading practices are very much in the forefront of the practices that the Unfair Commercial Practices Directive attempts to remove from the European market. It is fair to say that misleading practices are the core object of the Directive. In this sense the Directive carries on the tradition of the Misleading Advertising Directive. The Unfair Commercial Practices Directive, however, goes further than this Directive, in particular concerning the information duties of the traders.

The category of misleading practices in the Unfair Commercial Practices Directive is meant to be broad. It covers both untruthful and deceptive practices and deception by both linguistic and other means. As to the materiality of the deception, according

---

one obviously has to assume some reasonable maximum period before the trader is planning to cease the trade or move premises during which these facts can be referred to in marketing.

154 The Explanatory Memorandum mentions as an example of a misleading health claim a claim that the product causes a bald person's hair to grow back, COM(2003) 356 final 10. Although not specifically stated in the memorandum, this example would obviously fall under the cited provision of the Annex.

155 This seems to imply that a trader cannot use these words, if receiving the 'free' gift requires the purchase of another product (a combined offer); see on some national laws in this respect, Micklitz and Kessler, *op.cit.*, 38, 113.

156 For example, falsely claiming to act solely for charity.

to the Directive practices that are likely to cause a consumer to take a transactional decision he would not have taken otherwise are caught by the provision.

The breadth of the concept of misleading practices is best illustrated by Annex I of the Directive. Most of the items in the Annex are gathered under the heading 'misleading practices', and some of these are not matters that one intuitively would expect to find under this heading.

A disappointment in the context of the regulation of misleading practices is the provision on the burden of proof concerning the untruthfulness of information given by the trader. Instead of a clear-cut rule, as can be found in the laws of some of the Member States, according to which factual claims that the trader cannot substantiate are regarded as false, the Directive only contains a procedural provision, according to which courts or administrative authorities are enabled to require the trader to furnish evidence of the accuracy of the claim when such a requirement appears appropriate. This *in casu* rule is prone to be used differently in different Member States, as their traditions in this respect vary.

The Directive goes further than its predecessor, as it contains an explicit rule on misleading omissions. Notwithstanding the hesitation of the Commission to call it a rule on a duty of disclosure, in practice it creates or affirms such a duty. The Directive can be said to contain a more far-reaching information duty than the law in at least some of the Member States. Admittedly, the duty is described in very vague wording. Only in the particular context of an invitation to purchase is the information duty of the trader described in somewhat more detail.

Both the consumer's need for information as well as his likelihood to be misled by statements and other practices are partially dependent on his cultural background. Therefore, in various contexts, attention has been drawn to the possibility of the courts taking into account 'social, cultural and linguistic factors' in the application of the Directive. The Directive does not require total conformity across the internal market.

# Chapter 6

# Aggressive Commercial Practices

Geraint Howells

## a. Introduction

### (i) Beyond misleading practice

When the Commission started discussion on the possibility of an Unfair Commercial Practices Directive one of the open questions was whether the scope of such a measure should be restricted to misleading and deceptive practices or be extended to cover all unfair practices.[1] The Commission was aware that there were unfair commercial practices (other than misleading and deceptive practices) that could be problematic from an internal market perspective because of the different approaches adopted at the national level.

One of the problems with including 'aggressive practices' is that the term is not a developed concept within most Member States or European law. It potentially covers a wide array of practices and legal instruments, some of them only tangentially related to trade law. Many practices that might potentially be labelled 'aggressive' would fall within the scope of the seemingly ill-fated Sales Promotion Regulation.[2] But beyond this, the Green Paper pointed to rules on lotteries and gambling, mock auctions, pyramid-selling and multi-level marketing and 'bait and switch' tactics.[3] Indeed the Green Paper provided case studies on multi-level distance selling and power shopping (or co-shopping).[4] It talked about a general clause in a framework Directive potentially covering undue influence and said it would draw upon national examples covering, inter alia, undue influence and pressure, vulnerable consumers, equitable bargains and good faith. Thus the ambitions of the Commission from an early stage seemed to extend beyond merely regulating misleading and deceptive practices.

The *Follow-up Communication to the Green Paper* made it clear that the Commission felt the scope should be based on the 'wider concept of "fair commercial practices" and not only the narrower concept of "misleading practices"'.[5] It suggested

---

1   *Green Paper on European Union Consumer Protection*, COM(2001) 531 at 2.
2   COM(2001) 546.
3   COM(2001) 531 at 7. See also Chapter 4, (c) (i)-(iii)
4   *Ibid.*, at 8.
5   *Follow-up Communication to the Green Paper on EU Consumer Protection*, COM(20002) 289 at 8.

one possible category of fairness/unfairness might be a prohibition on physical force, harassment, coercion or undue influence by business.[6] In the Annex setting out possible elements of a framework Directive the use of force, harassment, coercion and undue influence were cited as elements common to most legal systems.[7] It then went on to provide examples of what amounts to aggressive selling and suggested the term covers both practices that (1) exploit characteristics or circumstances of the consumer, or, (2) unduly pressure consumers to agree to the purchase of goods and services.[8] Examples of the former were given as taking advantage of a specific misfortune of the consumer such as a bereavement or serious illness in his family or anxieties about personal security or debt. Examples provided of the latter include making it clear to the consumer that he cannot leave until a contract is signed or prolonged visits by sales representatives who ignore requests to leave. This was the first embryonic attempt to flesh out the concept of aggressive practices. It reveals that some practices can be aggressive by their very nature; others because of the way they relate to a particularly vulnerable individual.

The Explanatory Memorandum to the first proposal for a Directive (hereafter Explanatory Memorandum)[9] actually gave surprisingly few hints of what amounted to aggressive practices. It did offer some examples of undue influence. These turned on whether the practice could have significantly limited the consumer's ability to make an informed decision. Perhaps the best overall rationalisation of what constitutes an aggressive practice is found in Recital 16 to the Directive which states that provisions on aggressive practices should cover practices which significantly impair the consumer's freedom of choice.

*(ii) How far beyond misleading practices?*

Article 8 provides that:

> A commercial practice shall be regarded as aggressive if, in its factual context, taking account of all its features and circumstances, by harassment, coercion, including the use of physical force, or undue influence, it significantly impairs or is likely to significantly impair the average consumer's freedom of choice or conduct with regard to the product and thereby causes him or is likely to cause him to take a transactional decision that he would not have taken otherwise.

Infringement on the consumer's freedom to choose is the central element of the aggressive practices concept. But there is a fine line between legitimate hard selling and aggressive selling. The balance between legitimate persuasion on the one hand and harassment, coercion and undue influence can be hard to fix in many instances and the Directive is not particularly helpful in assisting with drawing those

---

6   *Ibid.*, at 9.
7   *Ibid.*, at 16.
8   *Ibid.*, at 17–18.
9   COM(2003) 356.

boundaries. Certainly as Schulze and Schulte-Nölke note: 'All kinds of advertising are *per definitionem* aimed at influencing the transactional decisions of potential customers.'[10] One might add that all marketing practices, not just advertising, intend to encourage the consumer to buy or behave in the manner the trader desires. The problem is to determine the boundaries for any further intervention once one has greater ambitions than merely regulating misleading practices. To do this the rationale for any extension of control needs to be determined to give guidance on how to apply the concept.

The Directive can be criticised for failing to provide a sufficiently clear rationalisation of its policy in extending to cover aggressive practices. For instance, it only provides a definition of undue influence. Harassment and coercion are not expanded upon. The blacklisted practices in Annex I are sketchy and not wholly consistent with any theories that might be contingently derived from the legislative texts. As we have seen the preparatory texts were also not very enlightening about the core ideas underpinning the 'aggressive practices' concept or how that should be concretised.

The Treaty talks about 'a high level of consumer protection' and extending to aggressive practices might indicate that this injunction is being taken seriously. Yet there are reasons to suspect the Directive should be read in the context of a European legal regime that adopts a liberal view of what marketing practices should be allowed. This liberal orientation is underlined by the fact that it is not every aggressive commercial practice that is condemned. It is clear from the scope of the Directive that it is only concerned with practices harming the consumer's economic interests.[11] Moreover, only those that *significantly* impair the consumer's freedom of choice are caught.

An issue arising from the use of the average consumer standard relates to the extent to which individuals have the freedom to signify their opposition to a practice so as to render its use towards them as aggressive even if it would generally be permitted.[12] It must be assumed that the standard is objective (based on how the trader's practice is normatively evaluated) rather than subjective (based on the consumer's personalised assessment of it). Nevertheless can the individual affect the objective assessment of trader's conduct in the light of their objections to practices? In other words to what extent, in the interest of efficiency, does the Directive require all consumers to accept practices that are acceptable to the average consumer? Does the Directive require consumers to accept practices they perceive as infringing their private sphere, that is, house calls, or mail shots, by virtue of the Directive, even in the face of their objections? The answer might lie in Article 8's emphasis on the

---

10 'An Analysis of National Fairness Laws Aimed at Protecting Consumers in Relation to Commercial Practices', available at: http://europa.eu.int/comm/consumers/cons_int/safe_shop/fair_bus_pract/green_pap_comm/studies/unfair_practices_en.pdf.

11 Article 1.

12 H.-W. Micklitz, 'Grundlagen', in *Münchener Kommentar zum UWG* (Munich: C.H. Beck, forthcoming) No. 136.

assessment of the practice in its factual context. A notice on a letterbox objecting to flyers would be hard to miss and easy to comply with. By contrast a preference for only being called between 6pm and 8pm at night would be harder to ascertain and comply with, and a ban on a practice in a public place, like street solicitations, would be impossible to gear to individual wishes.[13]

As the basis for intervening against aggressive practices is so unclear, there remains much scope for argument as to what practices are caught. The danger for European harmonisation is that these debates will be nationally conditioned. Micklitz has argued that aggressive practices as a concept is culturally influenced.[14] Admittedly, the concept of aggressive practices as a term of art is not well developed at either national or European level. Nevertheless, national laws may reflect certain conceptions of aggressive practices in the various bans or controls they place on commercial practices and this may lead national courts and regulators to interpret the Directive through this lens. This may be particularly true of countries with strict controls such as Germany, Austria and the Nordic states.

### (iii) Aggressive practices – elements of an underdeveloped concept

The concept of aggressive practices is underdeveloped in the Directive. Some steps towards a better understanding of the principle are needed if the principle is to be applied in a coherent and consistent manner. This will have to be developed through the national and European courts, but this chapter will attempt to provide some assistance from what can be distilled from national and European sources.

In the Directive aggressive practice is a generic term that embraces three concepts – harassment, coercion and undue influence. These terms must be explored as the most obvious source for the meaning and scope of aggressive practices. Whether these three concepts reflect distinct conceptions of aggressive practices or overlapping rationales needs to be explored. As part of our search for a core understanding it will also be necessary to study the factors of which the Directive directs account should be taken when making any assessment of the aggressiveness of a commercial practice. These not only have practical relevance, but may also shed some light on the nature of the substantive protection.

The aggressive practices listed in Annex I as being unfair in all circumstances are another important resource when trying to understand the concept of 'aggressive practices'. Ideally, it should be possible to use them to test any theory derived from the general test. Unfortunately that will not be a very fruitful exercise. The items in Annex I tend to include obvious instances of aggressive practices, but provide little guidance for the grey areas where debate about the scope of the concept comes to the fore. They are also rather terse. Moreover, it is not always easy to see how the

---

13 Of course Recital 7 seems to allow Member States to ban street solicitations for cultural reasons.

14 H.-W. Micklitz, 'Aggressive Werbung', in *Münchener Kommentar zum UWG* (Munich: C.H. Beck, forthcoming) No. 2. See also Chapter 4, (c) (i)-(iii).

aggressive practices in Annex I relate to the Directive's meaning of aggressive and some look more like instances of misleading practices.

The practices listed in Annex I in many ways resemble the way aggressive practices have been dealt with in many national legal systems. There have been punctual rules tackling specific unwelcome conduct rather that the development of a general principle. This may be because it is easier to illustrate aggressive practices than express the underlying basis of the principle. To this extent one can see a good deal of scope for the judge at first instance to make a decision on the basis of her appreciation of the factual matrix she is presented with. One might expect that the European Court of Justice will be reluctant to lay down too detailed guidelines and will want to defer to the national court's exercise of discretion.[15] Nevertheless we seek to provide some suggestions as to the meaning that should be given to aggressive commercial practices in European law.

Although relatively undeveloped in the commercial practices context, the terms harassment, coercion and undue influence have often been discussed in contract or tort law contexts. One issue will be the extent to which issues and debates in those fields can be exported into the commercial practices context. For the most part this should probably be avoided. Occasionally the literature and examples provided by private law may be helpful, but often those rules use similar terminology to serve different functions. Equally whilst it has been suggested that over time the Directive's concepts may influence the private law concepts,[16] there may be a fairly strong curtain dividing the law of trading practices and general private law.

## b. Aggressive Practices

Article 8 sets out three conditions that have to be fulfilled before a commercial practice is regarded as aggressive. There must have been (1) harassment, coercion or undue influence; (2) that significantly impairs or is likely to impair the average consumer's freedom of choice or conduct; and (3) which causes or is likely to cause him to take a transactional decision that he would not otherwise have taken. Moreover, the practice has to be assessed in its factual context.

Article 9 lists factors that have to be taken into account in assessing whether there has been harassment, coercion and undue influence. These are:

(a) its timing, location, nature or persistence;

(b) the use of threatening or abusive language or behaviour;

---

15 In the spirit of Case C–237/02 *Freiburger Kommunalbauten v Hofstetter* [2004] 2 *C.M.L.R.* 13.

16 C. Twigg-Flesner, D. Parry, G. Howells, A. Nordhausen, *An Analysis of the Application and Scope of the UCP Directive*, (DTI, 2005) available at http://www.dti.gov. uk/ccp/consultpdf/final_report180505.pdf.

(c) the exploitation by the trader of any specific misfortune or circumstance of such gravity as to impair the consumer's judgement, of which the trader is aware, to influence the consumer's decision with regard to the product;

(d) any onerous or disproportionate non-contractual barriers imposed by the trader where the consumer wishes to exercise rights under the contract, including rights to terminate a contract or switch to another product or another trader;

(e) any threat to take any action that cannot legally be taken.

If harassment, coercion or undue influence is proven there is no need to also establish that there was a breach of professional diligence. The Explanatory Memorandum to the First Proposal makes it clear that such conduct will always violate the requirements of professional diligence.[17] For the same reason the Explanatory Memorandum explains that there is no reference to material distortion of the consumer's economic behaviour. Such practices are conclusively presumed to distort consumer behaviour. It explains that the materiality condition is captured by the requirement that the commercial practice 'thereby causes or is likely to cause the average consumer to take a transactional decision that he would not have taken otherwise'.

We will now look at the three elements needed to establish an aggressive practice.

### (i) Harassment, coercion, or undue influence

First, there must have been harassment, coercion, including the use of physical force, or undue influence. These concepts inform the scope of the Directive's definition of aggressive commercial practices. Unless a practice falls within this triumvirate there is no aggressive practice which is unfair by virtue of Articles 8–9, although it may be possible to find a breach of the Article 5 general clause. However, the Directive only provides a definition of undue influence, leaving the two other terms undefined and needing to be given a European meaning, no doubt based on an analysis of the rules common to the Member States. The specific concepts are looked at below; in this section we look at some general questions relating to them and their relationship to each other.

It may be worth noting how harassment, coercion and undue influence are translated in at least the French and German versions of the Directive. These refer respectively to '*harcèlement, de la contrainte, influence injustifié*' and '*Belästigung, Nötigung, unzulässige Beeinflussung*'. This is mentioned to underline that these are European terms given a distinct meaning in the context of this Directive and not clones of national concepts. In this respect the greatest danger might be to assume that the English contract law concept of undue influence, which is surrounded by a number of detailed rules, had been imported into the Directive.

Schulze and Schulte-Nölke, in their report to the Commission, divide aggressive practices between harassment and coercion (which they describe as the most blatant

---

17 *Op. cit.*, at 13.

forms of aggressive practices that seek to pressurise the consumer to influence their transactional decision); and more subtle ways of unduly influencing the consumer.[18] In the latter they include advertising that plays on emotions or fears and the exploitation of trust in third parties by, for example, using a teacher as promoter within a school. In fact none of these would fall automatically within the Directive's definition of undue influence as it will be seen that this depends upon the trader exploiting their position of power.

If one were trying to assess which of the three concepts was closest to the other, one might rather see the divide between harassment on the one hand and coercion and undue influence on the other. Harassment often relates to techniques or manners of communicating with the consumer that are viewed as anti-social, whereas coercion and undue influence concern the application of pressure on the consumer. Undue influence arises from the exploitation of a position of power, whereas coercion covers other cases.

However, there is no need when litigating to invoke such distinctions, although such conceptualisations may assist in revealing the core meaning of the term 'aggressive'. Article 8 states that a commercial practice shall be regarded as aggressive if by harassment, coercion or undue influence it causes impairment of the consumer's choice. However, the 'or' should not be read disjunctively in the sense of requiring the practice to be allocated to one of the three concepts. Aggressive practices can fall into one, two or all of those concepts and there is no need to allocate it to a particular head. It is the overall impact that counts. Rogue traders will often use a variety of techniques at the same time to persuade consumers to behave in the desired manner. Some of these practices may include physical force, others might not, and may well mix harassment, coercion and undue influence. Disregarding the boundaries between the concepts can be useful in such situations and it should be sufficient to find that enough of the rogue practice falls within those three concepts without having to determine which category each practice falls within. Indeed there is no threshold intensity that has to be reached as regards the harassment, coercion or undue influence. The threshold criteria come in at the next stage of impairment of freedom of choice, which must be significant. This threshold can be established by a combination of harassment, coercion and undue influence. Even if one of them would not be sufficient in itself, their combination might render the aggressive practices unfair. As Köhler and Lettl suggest, a clear distinction between the three kinds of aggressive commercial practice is neither possible nor necessary.[19] It is not necessary because the factors in Article 9 apply equally to all three criteria.

It is unclear from the syntax of Article 8 whether the reference to physical force is meant to be connected to coercion alone or both harassment and coercion. Although

18 *Op.cit.*, at 36–8.

19 'Das geltende europäische Lauterkeitsrecht, der Vorschlag für eine EG–Richtlinie über unlautere Geschäftpraktiken und die UWG–Reform' (2003) *Wettbewerb in Recht und Praxis* 1019.

some writers[20] suggest it only applies to coercion (after which it immediately appears), and this would indeed be a reasonable way to read the provision, such a restricted reading would not be practical. It seems sensible to view it as covering both harassment and coercion, for clearly many instances of harassment will involve the actual or threatened use of physical force. However, it is equally clear that harassment and coercion need not involve the use of physical force or even the threat of physical force. Harassment and coercion can take on forms that have no element of physical threat.

Nevertheless, the placement of the reference to physical force in Article 8 would seem to suggest that undue influence excludes circumstances involving violence. On this reading the Article would distinguish between harassment and coercion that may involve physical force and undue influence derived from non-physical abuse of position. However, this is not entirely consistent with the definition of undue influence which talks about applying pressure 'even without using or threatening to use physical force'. The expression 'even without' implies undue influence could include the use of physical force. However, the better approach might be to leave physical force to be dealt with under the harassment and coercion headings. This would be the only way to give any sensible interpretation to the placing of the reference to physical force in Article 8, but is unsatisfactory given the definition of undue influence. This problem again points to the difficulty of treating the three terms as separate concepts and underlines the advantages of seeing them as an indivisible triumvirate.

### (ii) Impairment of the consumer's freedom of choice or conduct

The aggressive practice must have two causal effects. It must impair the consumer's freedom of choice or conduct and in turn this lack of freedom must cause him to take a transactional decision that he would not otherwise have taken. The requirement that the aggressive practice must significantly impair or be likely to impair the average consumer's freedom of choice or conduct with regard to the product encapsulates the core mischief the rules on aggressive practices are aimed at. The autonomy of the consumer's decision-making process is central to the Directive. Articles 6–7 protect that by preventing consumers from being deceived; Article 8 seeks to stop practices that restrict the consumer's exercise of free choice.

Once again the average consumer is taken as the standard against which practices are judged. The reader should refer to the previous discussion[21] on whether the average consumer in Articles 6–8 should be modified to take account of the vulnerable as provided for under Article 5 or whether Articles 6–8 should take a harder stance and simply judge practices through the lens of the 'reasonably well-informed and reasonably circumspect' consumer, leaving Article 5 to deal with exceptional cases.

---

20 H. Apostolopoulos, 'Neuere Entwicklungen in europäische Lauterkeitsrecht: Problematische Aspekte und Vorschläge' (2004) *Wettbewerb in Recht und Praxis* 841.

21 See Chapter 4(b).

However, this would not be a sensible approach for it would simply mean working through the Article 8 test only to have to then go on and consider the same issues again in the context of Article 5. Although it is not drafted so as to facilitate such a reading, policy suggests that the variation for the vulnerable should apply when applying Article 8. Indeed particularly with respect to Article 8 the characteristics of the consumer that make him vulnerable will be essential elements of many factual contexts and it would be perverse to then apply an abstract average consumer test.

The fact that the average consumer is taken as the standard suggests that the legal standard expects a certain degree of robustness from consumers. Obviously, to the extent that this standard is modified to take account of the interests of vulnerable consumers, there will be greater protection. However, the requirement that the freedom of choice be significantly impaired also underlines the expectation that consumers cannot complain about every practice that makes them feel uncomfortable or pressured. However, this does raise the issue of whether consumers can, by making their objections to practices known, turn them into harassment, for the trader would be going against the consumer's wishes. Some examples will be considered in the harassment section, but it has already been noted that the answer might lie in the need to take account of the factual context. Linking this to the average consumer standard, the test would be whether an average consumer would find this aggressive assuming they had made their objection known.

However, this highlights a more fundamental flaw in a test based on impairment of choice. This may work with many examples concerning coercion and undue influence. Even if a particular individual is able to withstand such pressure in appropriate cases, it will be possible to argue that the average consumer would have their freedom of choice or conduct significantly impaired. Impact on freedom of choice is, however, not the objection to many practices considered to be harassing. Many such practices concern protection of the consumer's private sphere rather than fears that they are forcing consumers into choices or conduct they would not normally make.[22]

For instance, few people actually respond to unsolicited e-mails. It does not affect transactional decision-making for most consumers, but it does irritate many and it is often considered anti-social and should fall for consideration as an aggressive practice. Likewise the making of persistent and unwanted solicitations by telephone is unlikely to impair the freedom of the average consumer.[23] One might even predict it would have a negative effect on the average consumer and put them off trading with that business. But this is a practice that is always regarded as aggressive. It is hard to see a way of resolving this conundrum. One must conclude that either the Article is badly drafted (the most likely answer) or argue that practices that merely irritate or upset are not aggressive/unfair practices. The consequence would be that they fall outside the scope of the Directive, are not subject to the internal market clause and Member States remain competent subject to general internal market rules. They

---

22 Köhler and Lettl, *op.cit.*, at 1045.
23 Item 26, Annex I.

might fall for review under the Article 5 general clause, but again that might be hard to apply because of the requirement that the practice has an impact on the consumer's behaviour. This can hardly have been intended by the drafters of the Directive. It is true that Recital 7 does recognise that there are some practices that can continue to be banned even though they do not limit the consumer's freedom of choice. But this is on the grounds of taste and decency; although the example of controls on street solicitations seems to give taste and decency a broad interpretation.[24] Moreover this refers to the power Member States have to go beyond the Directive and does not argue that these practices should fall within the European concept.

Not every impairment of choice qualifies as the basis for establishing an aggressive practice. Only those that significantly impair the consumer's freedom of choice or conduct are captured. When is an impairment of freedom of choice or conduct significant? The European Court of Justice has had to consider the meaning of significant in other contexts, for example, when assessing whether the impact of activities has had a significant impact on the environment.[25] The Court has in that context rejected setting precise thresholds and commented that the threshold proposed by the Commission, of complete defeat of objectives or destruction of essential components, was very high and noted examples of where it had been more flexible in the past.[26] This suggests that the Court would not be too demanding as regards the significance test. At least it is unlikely to be very prescriptive. It will be a factual question taking into account the extent to which the freedom is impaired and the extent of the infringement.

The difficulty is to find a measure against which to judge how significant an impairment of judgment is. In the environment context the nature of the land concerned can be compared with the nature and scale of the threat to it. The impact of aggressive practices is more difficult to assign a rating to. Certainly it would usually be a matter of great concern if a consumer is physically threatened and any impairment resulting from that is likely to be considered significant. Going beyond physical threats it may be necessary to see what aspects of the decision-making process consumers view as important to protect their freedom. Consumers usually expect to have as much time as they want to make an unhurried decision and to be able to treat their own interests as central and not have to be concerned with the welfare of the seller or take account of threats to treat them unfairly if they do not behave as the trader wants. Obviously the extent to which an aggressive practice invades this autonomous decision-making process will be important, as will the practical options which the consumer has to ignore the practice and remove themselves from the trader's influence.

---

24  See Chapter 3(d)(ii).

25  Case C127/02 *Landelijke Vereniging tot Behoud van de Waddenzee v Staatssecretaris van Landbouw Natuurbeheer en Visserij* [2005] All E.R. (EC) 353, [2005] Env. L.R. 14.

26  Case C–355/90 *Commission v Spain* [1993] ECR I–4221; and see also Case C–96/98 *Commission v France (Poitou)* [1999] ECR I–8531.

The provision refers to the impairment of the consumer's choice or conduct. This is intended to be broad so that there is no need to argue about whether something was a choice or not. Obviously there will always be an element of choice implicit in all conduct of the consumer. There is no need to get into semantics over whether something was a choice or conduct. However, it clearly does not only cover situations where the consumer has to make a choice. The fact that a consumer is forced to conduct himself in a certain way will be enough. This conduct might even be in line with the consumer's legal obligations. For example, to 'persuade' a consumer to make payments due may be aggressive if carried out inappropriately.

### (iii) Taking a transactional decision that he would not otherwise have taken

It is not enough that the consumer's freedom is impaired. This must in turn cause or be likely to cause him to take a transactional decision that he would not have taken otherwise. Where the control on the basis of the aggressive practice is abstract in nature, the fact a particular individual would not have taken a different decision notwithstanding the aggressive practice would not be relevant. The test would be whether the average consumer, if impaired in this way, would be likely to take a different transactional decision.

More difficult causal issues might arise where individual redress is involved. Although the Directive is not primarily concerned with individual redress, some Member States may choose to allow such redress. In such cases it will be relevant that, whereas it may be possible for an aggressive practice to impair the freedom of an average consumer, it might be shown on the facts that the particular consumer would not have made a different decision in any event. There might be evidence that he had already made his mind up before the aggressive practice was exercised or that the aggressive practice did not affect him. Admittedly it might be difficult to conceive of a consumer complaining about a practice and yet the trader being able to show that notwithstanding the practice the consumer would in any event have chosen to go ahead and contract with him, but this possibility must exist. This will of course only arise where the national enforcement procedures foresee individual action.

The meaning of 'transactional decision' has been fully explored elsewhere.[27] It will most likely not usually be a difficult hurdle to satisfy. It should also be applicable even to situations where the aggressive practice does not require any transactional decision to be taken by the consumer, such as where goods are snatched back. This can be achieved by reading the provision as covering situations where the consumer would have made a different transactional decision had he known of the trader's conduct.

---

27  See Chapter 4(e).

*(iv) In its factual context*

The requirement in Article 8 that the factual context be taken into account might suggest that there can be no abstract controls or blanket prohibitions on aggressive practices. Every situation must be assessed individually. This of course would be contrary in spirit to Annex I which specifies aggressive practices that are unfair in all circumstances. It might work for cases based on coercion and undue influence, but would prevent any general rules prohibiting practices because of their harassing potential, such as cold calling. This would be problematic from the internal market point of view. The requirement to take the factual context into account should not prevent general prohibitions. It simply requires that the concrete form of the practice be assessed.

*(v) Legal and illegal means*

Where a trader uses illegal means this will be highly indicative that a practice is aggressive. Article 9(e) for instance talks about taking account of threats 'to take any action that cannot legally be taken'. But the fact that account has only to be taken of this factor suggests that illegal means will not always be a *sine qua non* for a finding of aggressive practices. Some acts may be illegal through carelessness rather than aggressiveness. However, the converse is also true. There is no requirement that a practice be intended to be aggressive or even that the means used are illegal. National law may of course treat practices found to be aggressive as being illegal, but there is no requirement that there be any other independent illegality. Indeed often it will not be what is done but the manner or circumstances in which it is carried out that renders a practice aggressive.

## c. Harassment

*(i) Protection of private sphere*

Harassment is concerned with the invasion of an individual's private space. We have already noted that there are serious problems with reconciling many of the practices that are clearly intended to be caught by this provision, with the requirement that the practice impairs the average consumer's freedom of choice or conduct. Very often harassing practices do not lead to consumers taking a transactional decision as a result of them; they are simply annoyed by the interference. Of course sometimes the harassment is so extreme that it does lead to a consumer being forced into a decision against his or her better judgment; the classic example being the consumer who is forced to sign a contract in the early hours of the morning because the salesman has refused to leave until the deal is made. Such examples are rare. Even these raise the question of whether the average consumer would give in to such pressure, but the courts can probably improvise around that issue. The more fundamental problem is that the harassment provision is intended to prevent objectionable behaviour that does not necessarily affect the consumer's transactional decision. This is difficult to reconcile with the wording of Article 8.

## (ii) Relevant factors

All the factors listed in Article 9 are potentially relevant to an allegation of harassment, but it is worth focusing on a few in particular. The first set in Article 9(a) relating to timing, location, nature or persistence have great relevance in relation to harassment and give an insight into the types of practices typically associated with harassment. Very often a practice is harassing because of where it takes place, especially if it is in the home or on the doorstep or involves being accosted in public. Equally telephone calls, and perhaps to a lesser extent e-mails, because they require consumers to engage with the trader, can be seen to invade their private sphere. Timing may affect the extent to which the practice is deemed harassing; telephone calls late at night or salesmen staying late may be deemed more harassing than calls that respect civilised hours. Equally such practices can become harassing if they are persisted with. Thus one call trying to sell you a product might be acceptable, but 'persistent and unwanted solicitations', as Item 26 in Annex I puts it, will be harassing.

Below certain practices that have traditionally been regulated because of their potential to harass are assessed to see how these rules measure up to the Directive's standard. Practices falling into this category have tended to have been subject to regulation at the national and even EU level more than instances of coercion and undue influence. Where there are Community rules regulating specific aspects these take preference over the provisions in the Directive, even if they are more protective.[28] Likewise in principle national measures based on minimum harmonisation Directives are valid for six years.[29]

Harassment can also have elements of threatening or abusive language or behaviour, which is again mentioned in Article 9(b). We have already addressed the issue of whether the reference to physical force only relates to coercion and suggested that this argument is best avoided by viewing the three concepts as indivisible aspects of the broader test of aggressive practices.

## (iii) Objective or subjective test

There are three approaches that can be taken when assessing whether a practice amounts to harassment. First is the objective way of establishing what conduct is generally understood to be harassment and prohibiting it. This has typically been the approach of consumer protection legislation that has banned or controlled practices that are considered objectionable and is the approach of the Directive.

---

28 Article 3(4), see Chapter 3(f)(v).
29 Article 3(5), see Chapter 3(f)(vi).

Second, some legislation has required that the harassment be intentional with the objective of disturbing the person being harassed. Equally there may be a requirement that conduct amounts to a course of conduct or has a degree of persistence before it is treated as harassment. This approach is usually found in legislation that has a 'truly' criminal element and is perhaps inappropriate in trade practices legislation. The Directive does not explicitly require that the conduct be intentional or negligent, but one might imagine it being taken into account in borderline situations. Certainly the more persistent conduct is, the more likely it is to be found to be harassing.

Third, practices can be deemed harassing if they are perceived as such by the recipient. This overtly subjective test is often found in labour law and especially workplace codes of practice to help engender a safer, more pleasant environment where workers can object to behaviour without having to establish either that it was intended to upset them or would be found harassing by the average worker. This subjective approach is also in its extreme form inappropriate to trade practices law, but again takes us back to the issue of the extent to which individual consumers can demand greater protection because of their particular views of the permissible interference with their private sphere. Whilst the standard of the average consumer precludes pandering to the sensitivities of the individuals, nevertheless where individuals have made clear their objection to a practice this should be accommodated within an objective framework. The question would then be whether it would be harassment to ignore the objections of an individual to a practice that would otherwise be acceptable. For example, it might be considered harassment to call someone back when they had made it clear they did not want any further contact, whereas a second call might in other circumstances not be sufficiently persistent to amount to harassment.

### (iv) General harassment laws

One problem with harassment is deciding how to handle the relationship between trade practices laws regulating harassment and general laws that might also be applied to traders. General torts and crimes linked to assault and threatening behaviour might well be relevant, as might specific statutes dealing with harassment.[30] Obviously, given the maximum harmonisation nature of the Directive, national trade practices law that exceeds the protection offered by the Directive will have to be revised. General laws related to harassment deal with a wide variety of situations beyond the consumer context – tenant disputes, neighbourhood and relationship disputes and general public order, to mention just a few. It would be unrealistic to suggest that these should be reformed because of the demands of the Unfair Commercial Practices Directive, although some have called for their modification when applied to traders.[31] There remains the potential, however, that traders may object to these laws being applied to them if they infringe the Unfair Commercial Practices Directive.

---

30  For example, the United Kingdom's Protection from Harassment Act 1997.

31  Cf. Twigg-Flesner *et al*, *op.cit.*

The answer to such challenges would seem to lie in the fact that those general laws serve other, public order, purposes rather than merely protecting the consumer. The danger nevertheless exists that the mere threat of having to grapple with European law may deter many regulatory authorities from continuing the action once it is raised as an issue.

### (v) Particular practices

*Means of communication* The Directive on Privacy and Electronic Communications[32] prohibits automatic calling machines, faxes or e-mail without prior consent. These may or may not amount to aggressive practices within the Directive, but that is largely academic as the specific Community rule governs. More problematic is the relationship between the other provisions on unsolicited communications in the Privacy and Electronic Communications Directive and the Unfair Commercial Practices Directive. Article 13(3) of the Privacy and Electronic Communications Directive gives Member States the option with respect to other unsolicited forms of direct marketing to either introduce an opt-in system requiring prior consent or an opt-out system allowing subscribers to indicate that they do not want to receive such communications. This would cover unsolicited telephone calls, for instance. An unsolicited telephone call would most likely not be treated *per se* as aggressive under the Directive, for Item 26 in Annex I only prohibits 'persistent and unwanted solicitations by telephone, fax, e-mail or other remote media'. Köhler and Lettl suggest that this causes problems, since because of the internal market clause in the Unfair Commercial Practices Directive a country like Germany that requires prior consent for telephone marketing would have to accept unsolicited calls from a country like the United Kingdom which operates an opt-out system.[33] Obviously German consumers would not think to register as they would assume their consent was required. However, this should not be a problem, for as the specific aspect is governed by another Community rule, Article 13(3) of the Privacy and Electronic Communications Directive should permit Germany to impose prior consent and this would trump the internal market provision.

Item 26 in Annex I includes other remote media. An example would be a mailshot. It has been argued that the requirement in the Annex provision for persistency is not necessary in all circumstances if the general test of aggressive practice is relied upon. Indeed it should be remembered that the Annex only intends to cover cases which are in all circumstances unfair, leaving other instances to be assessed on a case-by-case basis. Thus it has been suggested that a notice on a letter box making it clear that mail or mailbox advertising is not welcome should suffice.[34] But who would be guilty of an aggressive practice in such a situation? Surely it could not be the trader, unless the trader delivered the letters personally. If anyone it must be the mail delivery service.

---

32  Directive 2002/58/EEC: OJ 2002 L201/37.
33  Köhler and Lettl, *op.cit.*, at 1044.
34  *Ibid.*

A trader might be more to blame if a registration with a mailing preference service was ignored, but should this amount to an aggressive practice? It may be annoying to have circulars pushed through the door and endless mail circulars, but it is noticeable that the legislator has not controlled these to the same extent as other media and has left a role for voluntary action. This may be because these are viewed as less of a threat to the consumer's private sphere as the individuals can more easily ignore such solicitations and/or because they are better left to self-regulatory solutions and the market. Traders who choose to ignore consumer preferences are unlikely to endear themselves to potential customers. Equally treating this practice as aggressive may be unfair to small traders who often use practices like leafleting and yet may not have the means to ensure all consumers' preferences are complied with. The extent to which an individual can render a practice aggressive by voicing his opposition has already been discussed; that discussion suggested that there may be limits to the extent to which the general standard can be modified.

*Place*    Practices might be deemed harassing because of the place where they are conducted. Usually suspicion arises whenever a trader operates off trade premises, because these situations have the potential to surprise the consumer or make him feel uncomfortable in having a normal marketplace relationship with the seller. Most obviously the consumer's private sphere is invaded when he is approached at home. This disturbs him and psychologically places him in a potentially vulnerable position, because of the natural desire of most people to be pleasant to strangers in their home. Although the home is the most obvious non-retail place where consumers are approached, similar pressures apply to approaching the consumer at work. Especially when one thinks of debt enforcement, one might appreciate why the consumer would feel harassed when being approached at the workplace. At the other extreme consumers might feel harassed when approached by traders in public places disturbing their daily activities.

As Köhler and Lettl point out, Annex I to the Directive is unhelpful. It provides that it is an aggressive practice to ignore a consumer's request to leave his home or not to return. But as they note, this is no more than stating the obvious. What is more at issue is whether selling off trade premises (in the home, workplace or street) is to be treated as an aggressive practice and if so under which conditions. Some countries, such as Denmark and Luxembourg, do ban doorstep selling whilst most states ban some forms of soliciting on the street.[35] In this context it may be necessary to consider Recital 7 which states:

> Commercial practices such as, for example, commercial solicitation in the streets, may be undesirable in Member States for cultural reasons. Member States should accordingly be able to continue to ban commercial practices in their territory, in conformity with Community law, for reasons of taste and decency even where such practices do not limit consumers' freedom of choice.

---

35  For instance, in relation to money loans in the United Kingdom.

The fact that taste and decency is outside the scope of the Directive is not doubted; what is surprising is that taste and decency stretches to matters such as commercial solicitations on the street. If this is treated as merely an example of other forms of practices that can be continued to be banned on grounds of taste and decency, this has the potential to emasculate the internal market objectives of the Directive. Especially as solicitations in the home will in most cases be viewed as greater infringements than solicitations on the street, there would a risk of the exceptions overwhelming the general principle. For this reason, this clause in the Recital will probably be narrowly interpreted and require proof of specific cultural requirements over and above consumer protection concerns. The United Kingdom government, for instance, is consulting on whether doorstep solicitations of property services should be prohibited or greater restrictions introduced.[36] This can hardly be justified on cultural grounds as it is in fact an attempt to change the culture of those who sell property services in the United Kingdom.

Most solicitations off trade premises will not be aggressive *per se*. Rather the timing, manner and nature of the practice will determine in particular instances whether the practice will be deemed aggressive in the concrete circumstances.

*Practices*    Some specific practices may be prohibited for cultural reasons in certain Member States. For instance, some societies may place controls on the marketing of baby products to new parents on the grounds that this might be distasteful in case the baby has died. The Swedish Market Court has prohibited such marketing during the first six weeks.[37] It would be difficult to characterise this as aggressive to the average consumer. If such national laws are to be maintained reliance will have to be placed on Recital 7, but we have already noted that there probably will be a tendency to interpret that narrowly.

Most commercial practices can be harassing if carried out in an intemperate and disrespectful manner. Many of these may be viewed as examples of coercion as well as harassment. One particular practice that is, however, often characterised as harassment is inertia selling. The demanding of payment for unsolicited goods is deemed aggressive by Item 29 in Annex I. Similarly one might readily find that certain objectionable practices of rogue debt collection agencies amount to harassment.

Harassment covers a broad church for it includes within its scope both trade rules that ban certain practices that relate to the protection of the consumer's private sphere as well as those concerned with impairment of the consumer's freedom of choice or conduct. The reason for prohibiting the former is not because they necessarily cause consumers to make decisions against their free will, but because they infringe societal standards of what is proper conduct and respect for the individual. Such controls sit uneasily within the framework of the Directive, which is premised on controlling practices that affect the consumer's transactional decisions.

---

36  Doorstep Selling and Cold Calling (DTI, July 2004).
37  Schulze and Schulte-Nölke, *op.cit.*, at 37.

## d. Coercion

### (i) Relationship with other concepts

Coercion as a concept has lots of work to do given the Directive's drafting. As undue influence requires the exploitation of a position of power, coercion must encompass all other aggressive practices that are not harassment. This means that the practices that Schulze and Schulte-Nölke characterised as unfair due to their playing on emotions, fears and the exploitation of trust in third parties would fall for consideration under coercion.[38] Although it is clear coercion is not restricted to the use of physical force, it is unclear how far it extends and indeed whether it reaches the Schulze and Schulte-Nölke categories. Here the interplay of cultural conditions are to the fore.[39] It will be a challenge for the Directive to ensure a common European understanding of which sales techniques aimed at manipulating the consumer's will are permitted and which are deemed illegitimate, and to determine the extent to which Member States have leeway to recognise national social, cultural and linguistic factors.

### (ii) Physical and psychological

It is clear from the wording of Article 8 that coercion can include the use of physical force, but is not limited to physical coercion. The use of violence or the threat of violence to force someone to enter into a contract, or the more likely scenario of threatening them to extract a payment, are obvious examples of coercion. Coercion can, however, be of a psychological nature. Where this exploits a position of power it may be possible to characterise it as undue influence, but it many cases it will be easier to treat these as examples of coercion to avoid possible arguments surrounding the meaning of 'position of power'. It may be possible to give 'position of power' a very broad reading which would include most consumer transactions given the natural imbalance of power between consumers and traders, but the concept must be intended to cover a narrower range of situations. The relationship between coercion and undue influence will be clearer, or at least the arguments about the boundaries between the two better appreciated, after the concept of undue influence has been more fully explored. Nevertheless, the fluid nature of this division underlines why it is best not to require the aggressive practice to be tied to one of the three concepts of harassment, coercion or undue influence.

The coercion must significantly impair or be likely to significantly impair the average consumer's freedom of choice or conduct. This does not mean that coercion must overwhelm the consumer. Often the consumer will have a choice to ignore the pressure, but a practice will still be aggressive if there is significant impairment either as a direct reaction to the coercion or because the consumer calculates that it is in his interests to accept the outcome being aggressively forced upon him by the trader.

---

38 *Op.cit.*
39 Micklitz, *op.cit.* See footnote 14.

## (iii) Relevant factors

The relevance of most of the factors in Article 9 can readily be understood in relation to coercion and the reader is referred to the general discussion on them. Some of them do highlight the grey area between coercion and undue influence. For instance, the factors relating to the trader imposing onerous and disproportionate barriers when the consumer wishes to exercise rights under the contract, or the trader threatening to take action that cannot be legally taken, illustrate why it is safer to deal with such issues as coercion rather than undue influence, so as to avoid any argument that undue influence requires a special relationship or debates about whether a position of power exists simply based on the contractual relationship.

## (iv) Borderline with legitimate pressure

Coercion is not defined, but impliedly can be understood to refer to means other than harassment used to impair the consumer's freedom of choice or conduct that do not rely on abuse of a position of power. The difficulty is that in most cases there will in theory be freedom on the consumer's part not to give in to the practice; the problem is that the consumer will in practice feel pressured or 'coerced' to act in the way the trader wants. The task for the Directive is to establish what is legitimate pressure and what is coercion. Marketing is after all about making people feel that they should buy your products.

Annex I provides some useful examples of when the line between legitimate and illegitimate marketing may be overstepped. Thus whilst advertising must be accepted as part of the marketplace, direct exhortations to children to buy products or persuade their parents to buy products are not allowed.[40] Of course parents might be able to resist such pressure, but they can feel coerced. Equally inertia selling can make consumers feel they have to buy the goods or at least be responsible for their safekeeping or return.[41] Similarly informing the consumer that the trader's job or livelihood will be at jeopardy is viewed as coercive.[42]

The Schulze and Schulte-Nölke categories of commercial practices that play on emotions, fears and the exploitation of trust in third parties will have to be reviewed under this standard. Most cases will not be clear-cut and there will have to be a concrete assessment of whether the trader has stepped over the mark of what is illegitimate. The Explanatory Memorandum to the First Proposal suggested that offering incentives such as a free bus to an out-of-town store or refreshments whilst shopping might influence consumers, but not unduly so because their ability to make an informed transactional decision would not be impaired.[43] More generally it is argued that sales promotions could not be considered aggressive practices *per se*.

---

40  Item 28, Annex I.
41  Item 29, Annex I.
42  Item 30, Annex I.
43  COM(2003) 356 at 15.

This discussion illustrates a lack of clarity at the core of the Directive. For a start, discussing these examples in terms of undue influence simply does not make sense. That requires an abuse of a position of power and offering a free bus service or refreshments cannot in any realistic way be equated with a position of power. However, if you substitute pressure/illegitimate pressure for influence/undue influence you do get a flavour for the issues raised by coercion, where the allegation concerns general mårketing practices rather than pressure applied to individuals.

There is a general liberalisation process in Europe towards allowing more freedom to traders in the use of sales promotion. Although Europe looks likely to abandon the Sales Promotion Regulation, it would be unfortunate if the Directive was to be used to restrict the freedom to make such offers, especially given the views expressed in the Explanatory Memorandum. There may be many good arguments against some such promotions, but the line seems to be drawn as treating many such offers as non-aggressive. Critics may be vocal against practices such as giving away a CD with newspapers in Greece, or the first volume of a dictionary in the German *Die Zeit* newspaper,[44] but the fact that these things are happening in countries that were previously very restrictive might be taken as indicative of a change in culture. How great that change in culture is and the extent to which Member States will be able to continue to reflect national traditions is perhaps still to some extent an open question. The Directive is certainly part of a liberalising approach of European law, but there are caveats which Member States might be able to use to continue more protective national policies.

Where the free gift is more expensive than a free bus service or refreshments, there might be more of an argument that it is coercive to the extent of impairing the consumer's freedom of choice or conduct. In the United Kingdom, Hoover made a spectacular mistake when promoting cheap holidays to purchasers of their vacuum cleaner. Undoubtedly many customers bought vacuum cleaners they did not want in order to take advantage of the offer. This may have unfairly slanted the market in vacuum cleaners, but it is hard to describe the consumers as being coerced.

In many promotions, unlike in the Hoover example, the problem is that the offers have onerous conditions that have to be complied with for eligibility, or limited availability of stock or substantial charges that have to be paid. Item 31 of the Annex addresses some of these concerns in relation to prize lotteries. In truth many of these problems are more appropriately dealt with as misleading practices. Even where the trader expressly makes clear that the consumer has to pay money or incur a cost, there will often be some deception as to the total costs involved in obtaining the prize or the value of the prize.

Nevertheless, this illustrates the broader point that even though sales promotions might not be considered aggressive *per se*, the way they are carried out might be coercive. Thus offering free transport or refreshments may be fine, but then to remind the consumers of the free gift when trying to sell the product can be viewed

---

44  Micklitz, *op.cit*. See footnote 14, see also Chapter 4, (c) (i)-(iii).

as impairing their freedom of choice. Equally conduct in the course of offering a promotion might be harassment.

### e. Undue Influence

*(i) The definition*

'Undue influence' is the only one of the three concepts within the 'aggressive practices' definition to be specifically defined in the Directive. Article 2(j) provides that it means 'exploiting a position of power in relation to the consumer so as to apply pressure, even without using or threatening to use physical force, in a way which significantly limits the consumer's ability to make an informed decision'.

*(ii) Physical force*

Although it is inelegantly expressed, it is nevertheless apparent that undue influence can involve force or the threat of force. The wording in Article 2(j) 'even without … physical' suggests that if there were physical force as well there would certainly be undue influence. This of course makes the drafting of Article 8 perplexing, for whilst it specifically states that coercion should include the use of physical force and above it was argued that harassment must also potentially include such violence or potential violence, it seems to suggest that undue influence does not include physical force. Yet here the definition of undue influence leads to the opposite conclusion and physical force seems to be included.

Article 8 seems at fault by suggesting physical force only relates to coercion. Even if our view is wrong that harassment does not include physical force, this would not explain the position with regard to undue influence. Moreover, it seems counter-intuitive to suggest that something could not be harassment because it involved force. It is probably best to assign this to poor draftsmanship and a desire to include physical force somewhere on the face of the Article. It also underlines the desirability of viewing the three concepts – harassment, coercion and undue influence – as interdependent elements of a single overriding test.

*(iii) Position of power*

The fundamental questions about the undue influence concept are what is meant by a position of power and when does conduct amount to exploitation of that position?

It would not be realistic to argue that because of the structural inequalities of the market all traders are always in a position to unduly influence consumers. However, the English common law has a well-developed doctrine of undue influence that shows that some consumer relationships can give rise to positions of power/

influence.[45] Moreover it has been argued that the position of power can relate to both economic or intellectual domination and can derive out of many social ties besides the purely professional.[46] One of the relevant factors in Article 9 with respect to undue influence is the exploitation by the trader of any specific misfortune or circumstances of gravity.[47]

The Directive's definition of undue influence undoubtedly includes situations where traders have some particular suasion over the consumer. Although such situations can arise both pre-contractually and during the performance of the contract, once a consumer has entered into a contractual relationship this can give the trader a certain position of power in relation to the consumer. This would cover situations where the consumer is dependent upon the cooperation of the trader, either to perform the contract or (as several of the examples in Annex I illustrate) admit responsibility under the contract and the trader exploits this need for cooperation. For example, Item 27 of Annex I refers to insurance companies requiring documents that could not reasonably be considered relevant before fulfilling their obligations. This is an example of an insurance company aggressively exploiting the vulnerable position the consumer is in. In similar vein, factors to be taken into account by virtue of Article 9 are any onerous or disproportionate non-contractual barriers imposed by the trader where a customer wishes to exercise rights under the contract.[48]

Sometimes traders use psychological tools, based around the notion of 'fictive friendships', to exhort the consumer to buy in order to maintain the relationship or even assist the trader who is painted as being in need of the consumer's purchase. Item 30 of Annex I covers situations where traders explicitly inform the consumer that their job or livelihood will be in jeopardy if he does not buy the product. This can amount to coercion. It would in common parlance be said to be a means of unduly influencing the consumer, but it may be difficult to say that it is exploiting a position of power unless the relationship can be viewed as one where the consumer has become psychologically dependent on the trader. Once again it shows the fluidity of the concepts and the advantage of not being forced to pigeon-hole practices into particular concepts.

The English common law of undue influence is complicated by rules about when undue influence will be presumed. The Directive does not establish any such

---

45 *Royal Bank of Scotland v Etridge* [2002] 2 AC 773. We have so far and for good reason avoided trying to analyse these concepts in the light of the private law. However, it is instructive to note in this area the presumption of undue influence in 'consumer' relationships such as those of lawyer/client and doctor/patient relationships. There would be no automatic presumption in the case of a banker/customer but this might arise on particular facts. The principle is summed up so that if: 'the complainant placed trust and confidence in the other party in relation to the management of the complainant's financial affairs, coupled with a transaction which calls for explanation, [this] will normally be sufficient, failing satisfactory evidence to the contrary, to discharge the burden of proof.'

46 Köhler and Lettl, *op.cit.*, at 1046.

47 Article 9(c).

48 Article 9(d).

presumption. Instead it provides that it is for national law to determine the burden of proof.[49] One area in which national implementation in practice might differ is with regard to the willingness to draw such presumptions, with the existence of traditions of national law presumptions possibly being a decisive factor.

Another issue raised by the English undue influence cases is the extent to which parties can be affected by the undue influence of another of which they have notice. Similar examples are raised by Schulze and Schulte-Nölke with respect to the exploitation of trust in third parties.[50] The examples they gave were of teachers used as promoters in schools and the Chairman of the workers' council in the workplace. It could be argued that these are not cases of undue influence by the trader, but by the third party. However, where traders know of such influence, or even encourage it, they should surely be tainted by it. Similarly accepting guarantees from people emotionally connected to debtors should raise issues of undue influence. The English common law accepts that such a guarantee might not be tainted by undue influence so long as the guarantor has been fully and probably independently advised. It is to be established what relevance independent advice plays in assessing undue influence under the Directive. The next section suggests that it may be relevant in assessing whether the trader has exploited the position of power.

### (iv) Exploitation of position of power

It is important to remember that it is not enough that the trader is in a position of power. For a practice to be aggressive that position must have been exploited. Some traders inevitably find themselves dealing with consumers in weak and vulnerable situations. The classic example is funeral directors who have to supply services to people who have been recently bereaved.[51] What is important is how the trader handles that vulnerability. In some situations, the trader might be advised to recommend the consumer to seek independent advice in order to remove any suspicion of exploitation.

Often the debate will turn on whether traders have overstepped the mark and gone beyond protecting their interests and begun exploiting the consumer. Thus companies can legitimately require the consumer to substantiate their claims, but if they seek to take advantage of the consumer's difficulties in accessing justice by failing to deal with correspondence in the hope of forcing them to drop the claim, this could be viewed as aggressive.[52]

Equally, Article 9 seems to assume that threats to take legal action will in principle be allowed, but requires account to be taken of threats to take action that cannot

---

49 Recital 21.

50 *Op.cit.*, at 38.

51 There were attempts to make express reference to the position of funeral directors in the European Parliament amendments.

52 Item 27 Annex I provides that it is where the failure is systematic and the correspondence is pertinent.

legally be taken. Even legal threats can be made in an aggressive manner (that is, harassingly) and where there are procedures that have to be followed, such as default notice procedures in consumer credit, then it might be deemed aggressive to take any efforts to enforce the agreement otherwise than through those procedures.

## f. Relevant Factors

The factors that have to be taken into account under Article 9 in determining whether a practice uses harassment, coercion or undue influence have already been considered in so far as they assist in amplification of those concepts. However, in principle all the factors in Article 9 relate to all three concepts. Article 9 is mandatory in tone requiring that 'account shall be taken of these factors'. A decision-maker would thus have erred in law by refusing to hear such evidence (although the exact rules of evidence remain a matter for national procedural law) or failing to take such evidence into account. However, such evidence only has to be taken into account and it is for the decision-maker to determine what weight to give the factors. Article 9 is not an exclusive list of factors that should be taken into account. Indeed it can be viewed as merely developing the general principle, found in Article 8, that the assessment of an aggressive practice should be made 'in its factual context, taking account of all its features and circumstances'.

The first list of factors relate to timing, location, nature or persistence.[53] It is self-evident that timing, location and persistence might affect the assessment of a practice. For example, approaching someone late at night might be viewed as more aggressive than during working hours. Practices that might be acceptable in the shop might be viewed as aggressive on the doorstep. One approach to a consumer might be acceptable, persistent approaches might be considered aggressive, particularly where the consumer has made it clear that such approaches are unwelcome. It is harder to determine what light the call to reflect on the 'nature' of the practice sheds on the assessment. It is after all whether the nature of the practice is aggressive that is being assessed. It may simply mean that the form of the practice may be significant, for example something in a printed advertisement might be acceptable, but not if repeated orally on the phone or in the consumer's home. Nature can mean the tone of the practice, but is a neutral term which adds little to the assessment. This kind of assessment is better captured by the second indent that covers the use of threatening or abusive language or behaviour.[54]

The third indent covers situations where the consumer is particularly vulnerable and the trader exploits the situation. It covers situations both where there is a specific misfortune or circumstances of such gravity as to impair the consumer's judgment in a way that influences the consumer's decision with regard to the product. It would seem to intend to cover both one-off events and state of affairs. An example of the former might be a lawyer offering his professional services at the scene of a car

---

53  Article 9(a).
54  Article 9(b).

crash; the latter might include selling products to someone who is seriously ill. Certainly products can be marketed to the seriously ill, but account must be taken of the circumstances in assessing the practice. However, in assessing the practice account should only be taken of circumstances that the trader was aware of. Thus whilst, for example, bereavement should be taken into account if the trader is aware of it, nevertheless an otherwise generally accepted practice should not be rendered aggressive just because it affects a recently bereaved person where the trader could not have known of those circumstances. There might be some issues concerning the extent to which the trader should have been aware or have taken steps to make himself aware of the circumstances of the intended recipient. Article 9(c) is concerned with actual knowledge, but constructive knowledge which the trader should have had can be part of the general factual context that Article 8 directs the assessment to be made within.

Article 9(d) refers to 'any onerous or disproportionate non-contractual barriers imposed by the trader where a consumer wishes to exercise rights under the contract, including rights to terminate a contract or to switch to another product or another trader'. Lawyers love missing commas and there does seem to be a missing comma after the second 'contract' in this phrase, for it is highly unlikely that a contract would expressly give a consumer the right to switch to another trader. It is more feasible that switches between products of the trader are foreseen in order to allow up or down grades as consumers' needs change. Nevertheless this provision does seem intended to cover both the exercise of rights and also simply attempts to change product or trader. Even where such switches might breach the consumer's contract with the trader, the trader's reaction might amount to an aggressive practice. The provision refers to non-contractual barriers imposed. Contractual terms would fall for assessment under the Unfair Contract Terms Directive. Examples of non-contractual barriers might involve the trader in creating new obligations, such as requiring the production of certain documents or the payment of certain fees before allowing the consumer to exercise his right under the contract, including termination of the contract, or to switch to another product or trader. There may be legitimate requests that traders can make in such circumstances. The provision only attracts attention to onerous or disproportionate measures. For example, a utility supplier might legitimately require that a transfer only be made after it has been able to read the meter.

Onerous or disproportionate are phrased as alternatives. The intention is clearly to have a broad scope, but the use of the word 'or' does mean that in theory any onerous but proportionate, or disproportionate but non-onerous, non-contractual barrier would also call for consideration. But such practices are hardly likely to be viewed as aggressive.

Finally, Article 9(e) requires account to be taken of any threat to take any action that cannot legally be taken. For example, a trader might make up a claim for the use consumers have made of goods, which is not recognised in national law, when a consumer seeks to reject defective goods. Equally it might cover an attempt to bring an action where this is not possible because the agreement is a non-enforceable agreement. It could also be read more broadly and encompass actions that cannot be taken until certain legal conditions have been fulfilled, such as repossessing goods when this is not allowed without a court order under consumer credit laws. It could of course include any action that is illegal under the general law, such as violence.

### g. Practices Considered Aggressive in all Circumstances

We have already made some general comments about the nature of Annex I in relation to those misleading practices that are in all circumstances considered unfair.[55] Those general comments apply equally to the following practices that are in all circumstances considered aggressive. It is worth emphasising that whilst in this section only those practices listed under the aggressive practices heading in Annex I are considered, there are in fact some of the practices labelled 'misleading' in Annex I that could as easily have been placed in the aggressive practices list.[56] Equally some in the aggressive practices list could have been appropriately included under the misleading practices banner.[57]

Annex I provides that the following aggressive practices are considered unfair in all circumstances:

(24) Creating the impression that the consumer cannot leave the premises until a contract is formed.

(25) Conducting personal visits to the consumer's home ignoring the consumer's request to leave or not to return except in circumstances and to the extent justified, under national law, to enforce a contractual obligation.[58]

(26) Making persistent and unwanted solicitations by telephone, fax, e-mail or other remote media except in circumstances and to the extent justified under national law to enforce a contractual obligation. This is without prejudice to Article 10 of Directive 97/7/EC and Directives 95/46/EC[59] and 2002/58/EC.

(27) Requiring a consumer who wishes to claim on an insurance policy to produce documents which could not reasonably be considered relevant as to whether the claim was valid, or failing systematically to respond to pertinent correspondence, in order to dissuade a consumer from exercising his contractual rights.[60]

---

55 See Chapter 5(d).

56 For example, Items 7 and 12.

57 For example, Item 31.

58 This allows legitimate debt enforcement, but only under the conditions laid down by national law.

59 Directive 95/46/EC of the European Parliament and of the Council of 24 October 1995 on the protection of individuals with regard to the processing of personal data and on the free movement of such data: OJ 1995 L281/31. Directive as amended by Regulation (EC) No. 1882/2003: OJ 2003 L284/1.

60 It is unclear whether the second limb of systematically failing to respond to pertinent correspondence applies to all attempts to enforce contractual rights or only in relation to claims

(28) Including in an advertisement a direct exhortation to children to buy advertised products or persuade their parents or other adults to buy advertised products for them. This provision is without prejudice to Article 16 of Directive 89/552/EEC on television broadcasting.

(29) Demanding immediate or deferred payment for or the return or safekeeping of products supplied by the trader, but not solicited by the consumer except where the product is a substitute supplied in conformity with Article 7(3) of Directive 97/7/EC (inertia selling).

(30) Explicitly informing a consumer that if he does not buy the product or service, the trader's job or livelihood will be in jeopardy.

(31) Creating the false impression that the consumer has already won, will win, or will on doing a particular act win, a prize or other equivalent benefit, when in fact either:

    – there is no prize or other equivalent benefit,

or

    – taking any action in relation to claiming the prize or other equivalent benefit is subject to the consumer paying money or incurring a cost.[61]

## h. Towards an Understanding of Aggressive Practices

'Aggressive practices' is in fact a label that catches a variety of objectionable trade practices. Article 8 (by using three terms to explain aggressive practices – harassment, coercion and undue influence) – gives an insight into the scope of the provision, but also reflects the different, if sometimes overlapping, rationales that underpin it. There should be no need to prove that a practice falls within any specific concept. Also all three concepts can involve both physical force and/ or psychological pressure, despite some problems with reading the Directive to conform to this common sense approach.

There are some divisions within the concept of aggressive practices. Undue influence requires the exploitation of a position of power. This must mean something more than the general advantages traders have over consumers. It might be based on abuse of a specific power relationship or it can derive from how circumstances have conspired to give the trader the upper hand in dealings with the consumer. By contrast harassment and coercion are concerned with the way traders behave even if there is no exploitation of a position of power. A major difficulty in those contexts is to distinguish between legitimate and illegitimate pressure. It is likely, for instance, that the Directive is not intended to challenge sales promotions, that may influence consumers but do not overpower their ability to make a free choice. The Directive is

---

on insurance policies. Possibly it is restricted to insurance policies or otherwise one might expect them to be in separate items, but equally the failure to respond is equally objectionable in all circumstances. However, the requirement to demonstrate a 'systematic failure' will be difficult to establish.

61  It has already been noted that this is more akin to a misleading practice.

also likely to require a certain robustness from consumers. Where the trader seeks to take unfair advantage of a consumer's predicament or uses illegal means, then it is more likely that a practice will be found to be aggressive. The concept of harassment, however, clearly seems to have been intended to be broader and to include restrictions on practices that consumers feel invade their personal space, even if this would not lead the average consumer to take a different transactional decision. It is uncertain the extent to which the standard expected of the trader should take account of the objections of the consumer. There must be scope for the interaction between trader and consumer to be taken account of because Article 8 calls on the factual context to be taken into account. Although the factual context will be decisive in many cases, this should not prevent appropriate blanket bans.

Chapter 7

# Codes of Conduct

Geraint Howells

## a. Codes, Soft Law, Self-Regulation and Co-Regulation

Codes of conduct (as they are called in the Unfair Commercial Practices Directive) are also known by various other names such as codes of practice, codes of best practice, codes of good conduct, consumer charters and so on. When used in a general sense the term 'code' can refer to a wide variety of documents, ranging from purely industry statements of practice through to rules that have legal significance and are drawn up by governments. Later consideration will be given to which of these many forms fall within the definition of the term 'code of conduct' in the Unfair Commercial Practices Directive. First, however, we note the broad scope of the development of codes and soft law instruments within European legal culture.

Codes are a form of 'soft law' rule. Soft law rules cover a wide array of instruments whose unifying characteristic is that they are not binding, at least until a party formally agrees to be bound by them. The UK's National Consumer Council has usefully set out the range of instruments that are encompassed by the phrase soft law and suggests they range from unilateral codes of conduct, through customer charters, unilateral sectoral codes, negotiated codes, 'recognised' codes, official codes and guidance to legal codes.[1] The word 'code' is viewed as being synonymous with soft law and soft law is in turn often used interchangeably with the phrase 'self-regulation'. In fact as one moves towards legal codes the softness of the legal instrument decreases as does the degree of 'self' in the 'self-regulation'.

Co-regulation has now become a term of currency whose relationship to self-regulation needs to be explained. The National Consumer Council reserves self-regulation for situations where soft law gives genuine additions to the protection afforded by traditional regulation.[2] Co-regulation in their understanding covers situations where the state has a real interest in the outcome, where soft law replaces or elaborates traditional regulation. A report commissioned by DG SANCO claims that the Commission itself divides instruments into two categories: self-regulation (legal rules drawn up by and for an enterprise) and voluntary regulation (rules encouraged by decision-makers and drawn up in cooperation with the players concerned), but then confusingly also states that the Commission uses three categories of self-

---

1    National Consumer Council, *Soft Law in the European Union* (2001) at 3.

2    *Ibid.*, at 4.

regulation, voluntary agreements and co-regulation.[3] Elsewhere one of the present authors has suggested that co-regulation can be 'co' in two senses.[4] It can be 'co' by combining soft law within a regulatory structure; as typified by new approach technical harmonisation Directives and their modern off-spring the 'framework' Directive. They can also be 'co' in the sense of combining all stakeholders in the process of elaborating the rules. Often of course both elements are present. For instance, in new approach Directives standards amplify essential safety criteria and are developed through open procedures within standardisation bodies.

Codes of conduct in the sense that the term is used in the Unfair Commercial Practices Directive requires that the provisions not be imposed by the Member States. It is perfectly in order for the Member States to assist in their development, they must simply not be backed up by law, regulation or administrative provision. Moreover, traders must agree to be bound by the code. This would have excluded technical standards, for whilst traders comply with them to obtain a safe harbour under safety legislation, they do not normally undertake to comply with them, if they were not in any event outside the scope of the Directive because they concern safety rather than trader behaviour. Standards for trader behaviour, for example, in relation to complaints handling might be caught so long as the trader undertook in advance to comply with them. More typically the Directive seeks to regulate trade association codes which members undertake to comply with as part of their terms of membership of the trade association. The exact requirements are considered below in section f.

### b. A 'Win-Win-Win' Solution

Codes of conduct play an important philosophical role in modern regulatory debates both at the European level and within many national legal systems. Codes are seen as representing a 'win-win' or even a 'win-win-win' solution. Supporters of such soft law rules claim consumers win by obtaining protection sooner, and which is often more relevant to their actual needs than that provided by the law. The protection might even exceed that obtainable by legal regulation or deal with subject matter such as taste and decency that legislators struggle to deal with. Industry wins by being able to ensure the rules introduced are achievable and can be implemented in as user friendly a manner as possible. Regulators win by passing on much of the cost to industry and appearing to promote the freedom of economic partners to exercise their own autonomy.

---

3   Lex Fori, *Study identifying best practice in the use of soft law and analyses how this best practice can be made to work for consumers in the European Union* available at http://europa.eu.int/comm/consumers/cons_int/safe_shop/fair_bus_pract/green_pap_comm/studies/enfo02_en.pdf (hereafter Lex Fori).

4   G. Howells, 'Co-regulation's Role in the Development of European Fair Trading Laws', in *The Forthcoming Directive on Unfair Commercial Practice*, H. Collins (ed.), (Hague: Kluwer, 2004).

Of course others have pointed to the limitations of codes.[5] They only cover traders who sign up to them, are difficult to enforce, are not always open to stakeholder involvement and have sometimes contained few tangible benefits for consumers. Critics note that soft law solutions at the EC level have often been adopted from a point of weakness when it has been obvious that the legislator was unwilling to adopt formal legal rules. These have taken the form of non-binding Recommendations sometimes promoting the adoption of codes.[6] Thus industry has not been obliged to take codes too seriously in the European context.

## c. Varying Attitudes to Codes

There are very different attitudes to codes present within the Community. A comparison between the British and German approaches is instructive. The British favour the use of codes, in the sense of non-binding rules, more than the Germans.[7] Indeed a study for the European Commission suggested that the UK had 'a virtual monopoly on the analysis of, and reflection on, soft law'.[8] The Office of Fair Trading encourages the use of codes of practice that are drafted in practice by trade associations. Although the codes might in appropriate circumstances be found to constitute an implied term of the consumer's contract[9] or false claims to abide by codes might breach trade descriptions legislation,[10] in principle the code provides voluntary obligations for which there is no formal legal sanction. By contrast Germany is characterised as having only conducted a limited experiment in self-regulation in specific areas of advertising. There is a certain irony here for Gunther Teubner[11] has pointed out that trade self-regulation is the dominant characteristic of the German rather than the UK economy. In Germany, business associations negotiate technical standards and standard contract terms with government and also via the cartel office. However, this manifests itself in different ways. Teubner notes that the main outcome of this is standard form contracts, that is, a binding set of legal rules which are also supported by the general contract law regime including the principle of *Treu und Glauben*, which the standard clauses help to inform the content of.

---

5 European Consumer Law Group, 'Non-Legislative Means of Consumer Protection' (1983) 6 *J.C.P.* 209; G. Howells, 'The Function of Soft Law in EC Consumer Law', in *Law-making in the European Union*, P. Craig and C. Harlow (eds), (Hague: Kluwer, 1998) and National Consumer Council, *op.cit.*

6 Commission Recommendation 92/295/EEC on codes of practice for the protection of consumers in respect of contracts negotiated at a distance (distance selling): OJ *L156/21.*

7 G. Teubner, 'Legal Irritants: Good Faith in British Law or How Unifying Law Ends Up in New Divergencies' (1998) 61 Modern Law Review 11.

8 Lex Fori, *op cit.*

9 *Bowerman v ABTA, The Times*, 24 November 1995.

10 *Re VG Vehicles (Telford) Limited* (1981) 89 *ITSA Monthly Review* 91.

11 G. Teubner, op.cit., at 26.

Looking to the North of Europe we see the Consumer Ombudsmen playing an important role in the development of soft law rules in the Nordic countries. The example of Denmark, which is fully set out in the compilation of national laws found on the Commission's website, is illustrative.[12] There are some purely voluntary self-regulatory codes in Denmark, but more distinctive is the use of three forms of co-regulation by the Ombudsmen. The Ombudsmen can negotiate with business and consumers to develop guidelines in particular areas. In practice these guidelines are only ever made where there is unanimity. Breach of the Guidelines can then be made the subject of an order under Section 17 of the Marketing Practices Act, but only against members of organisations that have approved the guidelines and organisations may terminate agreement subject to notice. In other areas such as the marketing of alcoholic beverages codes of conduct/guidelines are drawn up on the initiative of the Ombudsman who takes part in the negotiations but hands enforcement over to a committee or fund. A third form involves guidance drawn up by the Ombudsman where no formal negotiation takes place, although there is consultation with interested parties. This guidance is only the Ombudsman's interpretation of the law and therefore is not as binding as the guidelines drawn up after negotiation.

The Netherlands also has an important role for self-regulation. The Self Regulation Coordination Group of the *Sociall Economishe Raad* develops equitable General Terms and Conditions key to which are the establishment of 'consumer complaints boards' under the auspices of the Foundation for Consumer Complaints Boards.[13]

As a rule of thumb codes are less common the further South and East one goes in the Community,[14] although there are exceptions to this. The Schulze/Schulte-Nölke report, for instance, noted the important role self-regulation plays in Italy in relation to advertising.[15] Indeed if one focuses only on advertising then one gains a different impression of the use of codes as the influence of the International Chamber of Commerce Code of Practice on Advertising has ensured a wide acquaintance with self-regulatory rules. Most European countries have general advertising codes, the notable exception being Germany where there are only a few specific advertising codes. It is only when soft law approaches to marketing practices more generally are considered that the differences between the Member States' use of codes emerges more clearly.

Another area where a distinctive approach to self-regulation can be perceived is in relation to e-commerce. Governments are placing faith in trustmarks to promote standards in business-to-consumer Internet trading. This trend was recognised in the

---

12 See: http://europa.eu.int/comm/consumers/cons_int/safe_shop/fair_bus_pract/national_laws_en.pdf.

13 See: http://www.ser.nl/_upload/en_consumer_field.pdf.

14 The *Green Paper on European Union Consumer Protection* COM(2001) 531 final at 7 refers to self -regulation in Denmark, Sweden, Finland, the United Kingdom, Ireland and the Netherlands, and then states that it is 'less well-known in other Member States'.

15 *An Analysis of National Fairness Laws Aimed at Protecting Consumers in Relation to Commercial Practices*, available at: http://europa.eu.int/comm/consumers/cons_int/safe_shop/fair_bus_pract/green_pap_comm/studies/unfair_practices_en.pdf at 22–3.

*Green Paper on European Union Consumer Protection*.[16] Examples were cited of e-commerce codes of conduct in Denmark, Sweden, Finland, the United Kingdom, the Netherlands and Germany. The differences between them resulting from national rules were also commented upon.

Industry is generally more favourably disposed to codes than consumer groups. Codes are often seen as a weaker form of protection than the law from the consumer's perspective. Of course, to some extent, this depends on the culture surrounding such soft law instruments which varies from state to state. It also depends on the nature of the code. Codes interact with the legal system in very different ways. Some are purely private agreements drawn up by trade associations, others are more like official quasi-governmental statements of good practice, which might involve consultation with industry and/or consumer organisations by governmental bodies.

### d. Support for Codes in EU Policy

The important role envisaged for self-regulatory solutions has been to the forefront for a long time in EU policy statements. Some of the caution towards 'soft law' solutions on the part of the consumer movement is perhaps explained by the history of the EU's engagement with soft law The EU became enthusiastic about 'soft law' as early as the *Second Programme for a Consumer Protection and Information Policy*[17] when it accepted a continued role for legislation, but suggested 'the application of certain principles might also be sought by other means, such as the establishment of specific agreements between the various interests held'.[18] But those were recessionary times and this statement had to be read in the context of the not too hidden warning to the consumer movement to 'take into account the economic and social implications of the decisions on which it might wish to be consulted'.[19] This policy has continued to be at the heart of EU policy and the *Lisbon White Paper on European Governance* called for greater use to be made of alternative forms of different policy tools such as 'framework Directives' and co-regulatory mechanisms.[20] The Commission's Consumer Policy Strategy 2002–2006 stated that: 'In line with the governance initiative it would mean reinforcing business and consumer responsibility through making better use of alternative forms of regulation such as self-regulation and co-regulation, standardisation.'[21] The *Green Paper on European Union Consumer Protection* noted that any proposal for co-regulation would have to comply with the conditions set out in the *Lisbon White Paper*.[22]

---

16 COM(2001) 531 final, *op.cit.*, at 8.

17 OJ 1981 C133/1.

18 *Ibid.*, Item 6.

19 *Ibid.*, Item 4.

20 COM(2001) final 428.

21 OJ 2002 C137/1 at 6.

22 *Op.cit.*, at 15. See *European Governance*, COM(2001) final 428 at 21.

## e. Codes in EU Legal Instruments

Despite all this rhetoric 'soft law' rules have not had an auspicious history at the EU level outside the area of technical harmonisation. Recommendation 90/109/EEC on the transparency of banking conditions relating to cross-border financial transactions[23] was so ineffective that a Directive had to be introduced.[24] A study of the implementation of Commission Recommendation 97/489/EC concerning transactions by electronic payment instruments and in particular the relationship between issuer and holder[25] found the Recommendation was ineffective and widely not followed in many respects.[26] Likewise Commission Recommendation 88/590/EEC concerning payment systems, and in particular the relationship between cardholder and card issuer,[27] was found to have not been fully implemented in practice.[28] Commission Recommendation 92/295/EEC on codes of practice for the protection of consumers in respect of contracts negotiated at a distance (distance selling)[29] had to give way to a Directive.

It has also proven problematic to develop codes at the European level. In the Green Paper on European Union Consumer Protection the lack of effective means of ensuring effective EU-wide self-regulation was noted.[30] In its Follow-up Communication it said the development of EU-wide codes should be encouraged with membership of a code providing an implicit 'presumption of conformity' as standards do under the New Approach. It also promised to consult on whether the Commission should endorse codes to give this presumption of conformity. However, by the time the Directive was published the Commission had retreated from any desire to endorse codes or give them an official presumption of conformity status. It still,

---

23 OJ 1990 L67/39.

24 Directive 97/5/EC of the European Parliament and of the Council of 27 January 1997 on cross-border credit transfers: OJ 1997 L43/25; and see also now Regulation (EC) No. 2560/2001 of the European Parliament and of the Council of 19 December 2001 on cross-border payments in euro OJ 2001 *L344/13.*

25 OJ 1997 L208/52.

26 See 'Study on the implementation of Recommendation 97/489/EC concerning transactions carried out by electronic payment instruments and in particular the relationship between holder and issuer' (May 2001) available at http://europa.eu.int/comm/internal_market/payments/.

27 OJ 1988 L317/55.

28 C. Knobbout-Bethlem, *A survey of the implementation of the EC recommendation concerning payment systems*, (BEUC, 1990); and J. Mitchell and W. Thomas, *Payment card terms and conditions in the European union, A survey of the implementation of European Commission Recommendation 88/590/EEC on payment systems* (International Consumer Policy Bureau, 1995).

29 OJ L156/21.

30 *Op.cit.*, at 14.

however, views EU-wide codes as having a role to play in converging expectations of professional diligence and reducing internal market barriers.[31]

The Commission invested a lot in the e-confidence initiative to try to promote codes of practice aimed at inspiring confidence in shopping on the Internet.[32] This resulted in the European Trustmark Requirements drafted jointly by BEUC and UNICE, but the Commission admits that the momentum behind the initiative has faded. It was unsuccessful in obtaining financial backing and there is no business plan for the long-term viability of such schemes.[33] In its contract law harmonisation the Commission wants to develop European-wide standard terms of contract.[34] This would open up the possibility that such standard contracts could have some of the features of codes incorporated into them. However, the Commission does not want to be the promoter of such standard contracts, but only the facilitator and, as with codes, there are few signs that there will be a major impetus to the development of European standard terms of contract so long as the Commission remains unwilling to be more active. Of course industry would really only be enthusiastic if it saw compliance with codes as forming a safer harbour. This would raise important policy implications and few consumer advocates would favour codes providing an automatic shield for traders.

This policy support for codes has been accompanied by provisions in several Directives seeking to promote then. Sometimes this support has been rather modest, as in the case of the Distance Selling Directive where the Member States were merely tasked, where it was appropriate, to encourage professional organisations to inform consumers of their codes of practice.[35] No actual obligation was included to encourage the development of codes at the national or European level. This had been the subject of an earlier non-binding Commission Recommendation 92/295/EEC of 7 April 1992 on codes of practice for the protection of consumers in respect of contracts negotiated at a distance (distance selling).[36]

In contrast the Electronic Commerce Directive is more explicit, imposing on both Member States and the Commission a number of obligations to encourage codes, including drawing up codes by trade, professional and consumer associations at the Community level, with particular mention being made of codes regarding the protection of minors and human dignity; the voluntary transmission of draft codes, both at the national and Community level, to the Commission; making these codes available in Community languages by electronic means and communication to Member States and the Commission by trade, professional and consumer associations of their assessment

---

31 Explanatory Memorandum to Proposal for Unfair Commercial Practices Directive: COM(2003) final 356.

32 See http://econfidence.jrc.it.

33 See Commission Staff Working Paper, *Consumer Confidence in E-Commerce: Lessons Learned from the E-confidence Initiative*, SEC(2004)1390.

34 *European Contract Law and the revision of the Acquis: the way forward*, COM(2004) final 651.

35 OJ L144/19 Article 16.

36 OJ 1992 L156/21.

of their application and impact.[37] That Directive also requires Member States and the Commission to encourage the involvement of consumer associations and organisations and where appropriate associations representing the visually impaired and disabled.

Another way in which Directives can promote codes and self-regulatory practices is by permitting Member States to require parties to rely upon such procedures before resorting to the law. This technique was used by the Misleading Advertising Directive to support the self-regulatory controls that were well established in the advertising sector.[38] This is one of the few express ways in which codes figure in the formal text of the Unfair Commercial Practices Directive. Although the Directive's provisions on codes are quite limited reforms the Commission noted the proposals in this area provoked the 'most questions and highest level of "don't knows"' from respondents and conjectured that this was because of their novelty and because they were only sketched out briefly.

The interest in codes may also be because it is recognised that in practice they will play a more important role than is formally prescribed for them. Towards the end of the chapter the relevance of codes to evaluations of trader conduct is considered. Although not formally stated as being relevant, compliance and non-compliance with codes is bound to have an impact on the assessment of trader conduct when courts assess the fairness of a practice. Finally we will note that whilst codes are only briefly mentioned in the text they are much debated in the policy work in this area. This debate will be assessed and the potential for codes to assist in promoting fair trading practices at the national and Community level will be explored.

### f. Code of Conduct – the Definition

The definition of a 'code of conduct' is important in various ways with respect to the Unfair Commercial Practices Directive. First, there is a specific provision regarding it as being misleading to undertake to be bound by a code and then fail to follow through on that commitment. Second, Annex I refers to certain practices relating to codes which are always considered unfair. Third, there are rules ensuring it is possible to have recourse to self-regulatory complaints procedures. These provisions will be studied after considering the Directive's definition of a code of conduct.

Article 2(f) defines a 'code of conduct' as 'an agreement or set of rules not imposed by law, regulation or administrative provision of a Member State which defines the behaviour of traders who undertake to be bound by the code in relation to one or more particular commercial practices or business sectors'.

This definition has four elements:

1. the need for an agreement or set of rules not imposed by law, regulation or administrative provision of a Member State;
2. which relates to the behaviour of traders;

---

37  OJ 2000 L178/1, Article 16.
38  OJ 1985 L250/20, Article 4(1) and 5.

3. whose scope covers one or more commercial practices or business sectors; and
4. which traders undertake to abide by.

### (i) Agreement or set of rules

Is the requirement for an agreement to be taken to impose a pre-condition that there be a meeting of minds in the contractual sense? Probably not. In competition law the requirement for an agreement is broadly construed. Likewise the policy in this area should be to give a broad construction. Agreement in this area is probably narrower than in the competition law context in so far as arrangements such as gentlemen's agreements and guidelines simply issued by one party and followed by others might not qualify; not so much because of the lack of an agreement, but rather because they would not satisfy the fourth criteria that the trader has undertaken to abide by them. The fact that no agreement in the contractual sense is required is made clear by the alternative that there be a set of rules that the trader undertakes to abide by.

On the face of it there would seem to be no legal requirement preventing the agreement for a code from being made orally, but that would be highly unusual and in this context a slightly bizarre interpretation. Indeed the word agreement, especially when juxtaposed alongside the even more formal concept of a 'set of rules', probably presumes that somewhere the rules are set down. In most cases this will be the case and if traders break oral understandings then they can probably be caught under the general misleading practices controls.

However, the trader does not have to have formally signed up to the code. It would be enough that he agreed to abide by an agreement that satisfies the other required characteristics of a code of conduct. Often traders will be bound to codes indirectly through their membership of a trade association and membership of such an association should be taken as agreement to abide by its rules and conditions of membership. These sets of rules might be the basis for a finding that there was a code of conduct which the trader undertook to abide by.

There is no need for all the traders who undertake to abide by a code to have been involved in its preparation. The traders commitment to the code will be assured by their undertaking to be bound by it. Of course it may be open to some code owners to impose conditions before traders can claim to abide by a code. For instance, a code might make it a condition that a trader use a particular redress scheme or pay a fee to an association before being able to claim to comply with a code. These will probably be drafted as integral parts of the code and therefore it will be misleading if a trader does not accept them and still claims to adhere to the code.

The agreement will often be developed by a trade association. Traders will often consult with consumers and sometimes consumer organisations might even propose code standards. A consortium of traders and consumers could develop a code and indeed the Dutch system for developing general conditions works on this basis,[39] as do some procedures for developing guidelines in the Nordic states. It is significant to note that the type of standardisation process, involving the use of standardisation bodies like CEN, that is common in relation to technical harmonisation has not developed in relation to codes. Indeed the attempts to foster this in relation to codes in the UK were rebutted.[40] This may have been because trade associations feared their loss of influence or because a system suited to scientific and technical questions is less well suited to developing business practice standards. One area where standardisation has been developed is in relation to complaints systems.[41] However, the process was not an easy one for the technically orientated procedures of the standardisation bodies did not work easily with the need to establish common understandings of what amounts to fair trading practices.

The term 'agreement' might signify that it refers to a private act rather than an act done by an organ of the state; although with new forms of regulations blending state and private actors such a sharp divide is perhaps best avoided. Nevertheless, the rules within the Directive are clearly aimed at codes that are drawn up by industry. There may be varying degrees of consultation and cooperation from consumers and the state, but the code should not have any legal force. The definition makes it clear that rules imposed by law, regulation or administrative provisions are excluded. There will often be some involvement of government, at least in the background encouraging the development of codes. The UK goes furthest and has a developed regime for giving its approval to codes.[42] These codes would still fall within the Directive's definition as the state approves rather than imposes the rules.

Excluded from the definition are those codes that have statutory force and provide guidance on how the law should be applied. Such codes usually seek to amplify what the laws mean. Thus a code of practice like that in the UK on price indications which was issued in 1988 under a specific statutory requirement[43] to provide guidance on how legislation should be interpreted would be outside the definition. Several countries have such ministerial guidelines. Indeed this practice is common in Scandinavia where the Ombudsmen lay down guidelines. These may have no legal force and yet still not fall within the Directive's definition as they are not agreed to by the trader. It could not be argued for these purposes that traders had by default or compliance undertaken to abide by what are in fact legal or quasi-legal obligations set down in guidelines. An interpretation of code that excluded

---

39  M. Radeideh and R. de Vrey, 'Netherlands', in *Marketing Practices Regulation and Consumer Protection in the EC Member States and the US*, H.-W. Micklitz and J. Kessler (eds), (Baden-Baden: Nomos, 2002).

40  See *Raising Standards of Consumer Care – Progressing Beyond Codes of Practice* (OFT, 1998); eventually the government settled on increasing the role of the Office of Fair Trading; see Section 8 Enterprise Act 2002.

41  See, for example, BSI ISO 10002:2004.

42  See G. Howells and S. Weatherill, *Consumer Protection Law* (2nd edn) (Aldershot: Ashgate, 2005) at 586–591.

43  Section 25 Consumer Protection Act 1987. A revised code came into force in 2005.

governmental guidance would be consistent with the definition of code owner which seems to be slanted towards private bodies.[44] However, if traders volunteer to abide by non-binding guidance then there would be nothing to prevent it coming within the scope of the definition of a code of conduct.

It will be a matter of national tradition whether standards are set down in legislative guidelines or codes. One side effect of a restrictive interpretation of code of conduct, excluding those backed by law, is that traders who claimed to be bound by binding state guidance and then did not comply would not be caught by the rule Article 6(2)(b) of the Directive on the basis of this holding out. However, in this situation there would usually be some other means of holding them to account, most likely under the general misleading practices provision in Article 6.

### (ii) Trader behaviour

Little need be said about this requirement. It simply makes it clear that the Directive only covers codes relating to the behaviour of traders; but one would hardly have occasion to consider other codes on this context. Trader is broadly defined.[45] It is worth noting that the term would not only catch the trader who works directly with the consumer. Thus codes governing advertising agencies or media organisations are potentially caught, although their claims to abide by codes will only be in issue if made in a consumer context.

### (iii) Commercial practice or business sectors

The code can relate to one or more particular commercial practices or business sectors. The reference to particular commercial practices means that it can cover codes that only deal with one aspect, for example, advertising, direct marketing, data protection or even something narrower like the sale of alcoholic beverages.

The wording, especially the use of the word 'particular', might suggest that it excludes general codes. However, this would be overly legalistic. It is submitted that it is intended to cover codes dealing with all types of commercial practices ranging from those that are narrowly focused through to general codes covering all commercial practices.

Although the wording is not very clear it should also be read as covering codes that cover one or more business sectors. This therefore includes codes related to particular industries. However, once again this should not be restrictively interpreted as it must have been intended to cover codes whose reach covers all industries; otherwise general advertising codes would not be covered.

---

44 See section g.
45 See Article 2(b).

*(iv) Trader undertaking*

Key to the definition is the requirement that the traders undertake to be bound by the code. This is reflected in the Directive's main substantive rule which is concerned with breaking this undertaking.[46]

### g. Code Owner

The Directive also provides a definition of who is a code owner. A 'code owner' is said to be 'any entity, including a trader or group of traders, which is responsible for the formulation and revision of a code of conduct and/or for monitoring compliance with the code by those who have undertaken to be bound by it'.[47]

The concept of code owner is important as Article 10 expressly uses this concept to define the bodies that can control trade practices other than by the judicial and administrative means prescribed by Article 11.

The concept is very broad. It applies to any entity. Thus it could be the state or an organ of the state, so long as the rules are not binding. For example, the Nordic Ombudsmen could be code owners. It might also be an industry regulator or a standardisation body. Most often, however, it will be a trade association. But the definition makes it clear that even a trader or group of traders may qualify. Code owners may be involved in all phases of a code's development – formulation, revision and monitoring compliance; or just in its formulation and revision or, alternatively, merely in monitoring compliance.

### h. Non-Compliance With a Code as Misleading Conduct

Article 6 sets out circumstances in which misleading actions will be controlled by the Directive. Article 6(1) sets out a general test, whereas Article 6(2) provides for two specific instances, one of them being misleading claims about following codes of conduct. It might be questioned why Article 6(2) should focus on two specific instances of misleading conduct. The answer is probably a desire to clarify that they are to be treated as misleading practices because of their novelty or uncertainty in the pre-existing law of some of the Member States. Nevertheless it remains a peculiar testament to the process of European law-making that these provisions are inserted into Article 6 rather than being added to the list of commercial practices that in all circumstances shall be regarded as unfair. Possibly this drafting choice can be justified because there are some circumstances in which these practices can be defended as not being unfair, but at least as regards Article 6(2)(b), once the strict criteria have been met for the provision to be invoked it would be hard to see how the practice could be otherwise than misleading.

---

46  See section h.
47  Article 2(g).

Article 6(2) provides that:

> A commercial practice shall also be regarded as misleading if, in its factual context, taking account of all its features and circumstances, it causes or is likely to cause the average consumer to take a transactional decision he would not have taken otherwise, and it involves …

> (b) non-compliance by the trader with commitments contained in codes of conduct by which the trader has undertaken to be bound, where

> (i) the commitment is not aspirational but is firm and capable of being verified; and

> (ii) the trader indicates in a commercial practice that he is bound by the code.

This provision regards as misleading non-compliance by traders with commitments contained in codes of conduct to which the trader has undertaken to be bound. Herein lies a potential gap, for if a trader claims to be bound by a code which he has not signed up for there would appear to be no breach of Article 6(2)(b) which only covers situations where the trader has undertaken to be bound. It covers situations where a trader fails to live up to his commitments, not situations where he simply lies about his participation in codes. This latter situation is actually covered by Item 1 of Annex I which renders unfair in all circumstances claiming to be a signatory to a code of conduct when the trader is not.

Article 6(2)(b) was controversial for it could be seen as threatening the voluntary basis of codes of conduct if non-compliance is to be the basis of a legal sanction. Indeed 28 out of 35 business associations and companies who expressed a view on this proposal opposed it, with 55 expressing no view.[48] In fact it need not be viewed as upsetting the voluntary nature of codes. Traders remain free to decide whether they will be bound, but simply cannot mislead consumers by claiming to be bound and not actually complying with the code. It does mean that once traders have signed up to a code they are no longer free to decide whether to honour their obligations.

This provision is quite narrow in scope. It is not concerned with whether there are legal means for ensuring compliance with codes, nor with whether non-compliance with a code can be treated as unfair or misleading conduct. If the trader did not claim to be complying in a commercial practice then this provision would not bite. It is simply concerned with the situation where a trader claims to be abiding by a code and then does not do so. Strict criteria have to be met before Article 6(2)(b) can be invoked so that the trader can be regarded as having been misleading on the basis of this provision. However, as worded it does not seem to be limited to situations where the trader intended not to comply. Mere noncompliance would be enough, So in theory if a trader misjudged his obligations and did not comply, because he thought he was genuinely under no obligation, he would still be in breach of Article 6(2)(b). But the measure was not intended or likely to be used where there is debate about

---

48 *Follow–up Communication on EU Consumer Law*, COM(2002) final 531 at 5.

the scope of the obligations. It is aimed at the trader who deliberately fails to live up to the commitments he has entered into.

The provisions in Article 6(2) contain some features which are common to all misleading actions and that have been considered in depth elsewhere in this book.[49] Thus non-compliance with an undertaking to be bound to a code will be regarded as misleading if it thereby causes or is likely to cause the average consumer to take a transactional decision that he would not have taken otherwise. Thus it uses the 'average consumer' and 'transactional decision' concepts found in the main misleading actions provision. There is, however, a difference in the way the relevant circumstances to be taken into account are expressed. This provision talks about assessing the practice in 'its factual context, taking account of all its features and circumstances'. The main test does not specify these factors, but they would usually be implicit in any assessment. Nevertheless it is strange that they only appear in Article 6(2).

Before noncompliance with an undertaking is regarded as misleading, certain conditions need to be satisfied. These relate to both the nature of the commitment in the code and the circumstances in which the trader purportedly bound himself to the code. The commitment must be (1) not aspirational, (2) firm, (3) verifiable and (4) the trader must indicate in a commercial practice that he is bound by the code.

*(i) Not aspirational*

The commitment in the code must not be aspirational. The *Follow-up Communication to the Green Paper* distinguished between a firm commitment to undertake certain 'good practices' and the aspirational commitment to use 'best efforts'.[50] This is not an entirely satisfactory distinction for much will turn on how the commitments to follow 'good practices' are framed to determine whether they are aspirational or firm. Nevertheless, it seems clear that statements like 'will use best endeavours', 'hope to be able to', 'will strive to' are unlikely to suffice in order to invoke Article 6(2)(b). Equally 'mission statement' objectives such as 'intending to provide a first class service' are likely to be classed as aspirational. In fact many clauses in codes are written in exactly this aspirational style and so the value of this provision is immediately less than might be suggested on a casual reading. It is a moot point whether obligations framed in terms like 'to despatch goods as soon as possible' are aspirational in this sense or in fact can form the basis of a firm promise.

*(ii) Firm*

The only commitments that can be the basis of a misleading practice based on non-compliance with an undertaking to be bound are those that are firm and verifiable. Firmness seems to have two aspects. First, it is a positive counter to the aspirational

---

49  See Chapter 5.
50  COM(2002) final 289 at 11.

test and emphasises that the commitment is one for which a binding undertaking was given. Thus 'we will deliver within seven days' would be a firm commitment, whereas 'we will use our best endeavours to deliver within seven days' would not be. Second, it must also be clear exactly what has been promised. If there is any discretion left to the trader about what is being promised, then it will not be a firm commitment. Of course there must be some sense of proportion to avoid traders too easily arguing that their promises were not intended to be firm. Thus a promise 'to exchange goods subject to availability' would seem to be a firm commitment, for although there may be no obligation to exchange if replacements are not available, there is a firm commitment to exchange if they are available. Treating the caveat as rendering it not a firm commitment would undermine the provision. Given the general wording of most codes, there is likely to be a good deal of debate in many cases about just how firm the commitments are and some sense of reality has to be introduced to prevent traders jumping on to any ambiguity or caveat to evade liability for failing to meet up to their obligations. Otherwise the provision can be emptied of any force.

## (iii) Verifiable

The additional requirement that the commitment be capable of being verified also requires a sensible interpretation if the provision is not to be undermined. Some obligations will be easily verifiable as they require traders to undertake practical obligations, for example, deliver goods within 28 days. It will be relatively straightforward to verify whether time limitations have been respected or the trader has used the prescribed means of communication. Thus commitments to provide specified information, provide the information in a specified form or by a certain means of communication or within a certain time period will be relatively easily verifiable. However, the provision does not limit its scope to commitments that are easily verifiable; a commitment merely has to be capable of verification.

Aspirational commitments are outside the scope of the provision. However, the text seems to suggest there are some obligations that are not aspirational and yet because they are not verifiable should still not fall within the provision. Commitments related to the quality of goods or the service provided should in principle be considered capable of being verified. After all courts constantly verify, with the assistance of expert witnesses, whether goods conform to the contract or work has been carried out with due skill and care. This caveat of verifiability might affect subjective standards such as 'carrying out work as fast as reasonably practical' if these are not deemed to be aspirational. What about a commitment to be 'punctual and reliable'? Presumably punctuality can be tested. We do it for train companies all the time. But is reliability too subjective a concept to be verifiable?

Treating subjective criteria as non-verifiable would reflect a desire to exclude from review those commitments that the courts will have problems in determining whether there has been compliance. For example, it might be suggested that a commitment 'to deal with all customers politely' is not capable of being verified, for perceptions of politeness are inherently subjective. It is of course arguable about the extent to which concepts have a settled meaning so that conduct can be tested against the standard to verify compliance. It would have been useful if the rationale for imposing these conditions had been more openly addressed during the preparation of the Directive.

### (iv) Indication in a commercial practice

Once a firm, verifiable, non-aspirational commitment can be established, there is one more condition that has to be met before a trader's non-compliance can be regarded as misleading. Article 6(2)(b)(ii) requires that the trader indicates in a commercial practice that he is bound by the code. Commercial practice is broadly defined in Article 2(d) to mean 'any act, omission, course of conduct or representation, commercial communication including advertising and marketing, by a trader, directly connected with the promotion, sale or supply of a product to consumers'. Thus statements claiming to abide by a code in advertisements, notices in shops or the use of a symbol connected to compliance with a code will all be caught as would an oral statement made to a customer.

Article 6(2)(b)(ii) will bite to exclude situations where the indication is not made in circumstances related to the consumer. Thus a statement in a trade journal that a company follows a code, or in answer to an inquiry by a regulator or in the trader's annual report aimed at shareholders would not be an indication in the course of a commercial practice. The definition of trader might include advertising or media agencies. However, for them to be liable for a false claim to abide by a code of conduct they must make the claim in the course of a commercial practice.

The scope of Article 6(2) is therefore limited by a number of conditions that have to be satisfied before non-compliance with an undertaking to be bound by a code is regarded as misleading. The question then arises as to whether a practice that does not meet all the criteria of Article 6(2) could nevertheless be misleading under Article 6(1) or unfair under Article 5. One line of argument is that since the legislator has specifically considered the circumstances in which such a practice will be regarded as being misleading all the conditions set out in Article 6(2) must be complied with and it would be wrong to apply the general misleading test to practices that do not fulfil those criteria. That is probably correct so far as the assessment of whether something is misleading goes, but it would be undesirable if the practice could not be reviewed under the general unfairness test. It might for instance be thought unfair to make aspirational statements that there was no intention to seek to achieve, even if this did not fit within the meaning of misleading; although the courts are likely to be cautious about extending control beyond the circumstances prescribed by Article 6(2).

### i. Unfair Practices in All Circumstances

Annex I of the Directive lists practices that are unfair in all circumstances. The first three items in this list under the heading of misleading practices are relevant to codes. They are:

1. Claiming to be a signatory to a code of conduct when the trader is not.
2. Displaying a trust mark, quality mark or equivalent without having obtained the necessary authorisation.
3. Claiming that a code of conduct has an endorsement from a public or other body which it does not have.

### j. Encouraging Reliance on Codes

Article 10 is entitled 'Codes of conduct' and is concerned with how codes can be encouraged in a legal regime which is premised on enforcement through the courts or administrative bodies. That said on the face of it the provision is not overly friendly towards codes. It states that Member States may encourage control of unfair commercial practices by code owners.[51] Such control is not excluded by the Directive. However, this stops short of requiring Member States to encourage the development of codes. By contrast Article 16 of the Electronic Commerce Directive requires that both Member States and the Commission shall encourage the drawing up of codes at the Community level.[52]

Control by code owners is very much viewed as supplementary to control by courts or administrative authorities. Article 10 makes it clear that such controls are allowed so long as they are additional rights and indeed spells out that recourse to such control bodies shall never be deemed equivalent to foregoing judicial or administrative appeal as set out in Article 11. Thus even if a consumer complains to a code owner, they must still have the right to go to court or an administrative authority if they are not satisfied with the outcome.

The real scope for encouraging reliance is actually found in Article 11(1) which gives Member States the discretion to enable courts or administrative authorities to require prior recourse to other established means of dealing with complaints, including those referred to in Article 10, that is, codes of conduct. There is a similarly worded provision in Article 4(1) of the Misleading Advertising Directive.[53] This was implemented in the United Kingdom by giving a right of complaint to the Director General of Fair Trading, but allowing him to require that a reasonable opportunity be given to establish means of dealing with complaints about advertising before he is prepared to consider the complaint.[54] In practice this means that the Office

---

51 Article 10.
52 OJ 2000 L178/1.
53 OJ 1984 L250/17.
54 Control of Misleading Advertisements Regulations 1988, S.I. 1988/915.

of Fair Trading is only involved after the Advertising Standards Authority has failed to satisfy a complainant. Similar filters that encourage the use of complaints schemes run by code owners can be introduced under the Unfair Commercial Practices Directive. However, courts and administrative authorities cannot be forced to refer a matter to a code complaints scheme. Equally Member States can decide not to give them any power to require referral. What Member States can do is give courts and administrative bodies the possibility of requiring prior recourse to such a scheme. They would, however, be free to not demand that referral and hear the matter directly, although in systems where such procedures were well established it would be anticipated that, save in exceptional or urgent circumstances, such a referral would usually be the expected norm.

### k. Codes and Standards of Fairness

One of the criticisms of general clauses is that they are ambiguous and leave consumers and traders uncertain as to the content of the obligations. This criticism has been voiced most strongly from some within common law countries where they are less accustomed to dealing with general clauses.[55] Indeed it was a major reason why the United Kingdom did not adopt a general duty to trade fairly after having debated it in the 1980s.[56] Naturally in looking to flesh out the general clause decision-makers will be keen to catch on to anything that helps concretise the standards and any codes of conduct will be an obvious starting point.[57]

Although the Commission had earlier talked about compliance with codes of conduct as possibly providing a 'presumption of conformity',[58] this was dropped and the Directive does not foresee any express link between codes of conduct and the assessment of the general clauses. Nevertheless the Explanatory Memorandum to the first proposal does suggest that codes can be taken into account by Member States in assessing whether there has been a breach.[59] In discussing the still to be realised EU codes of conduct it cryptically suggests that the way they could operate would depend on the needs and circumstances of different sectors. It is difficult to make much sense out of such a comment about institutions that do not yet even exist to any significant extent.

---

55 Although for an argument that such clauses are not too alien to the common law, see R. Bradgate, R. Brownsword and C. Twigg-Flesner *The Impact of Adopting a Duty to Trade Fairly* (Department of Trade and Industry, 2003) available at http://www.dti.gov.uk/ccp/topics1/pdf1/unfairreport.pdf.

56 *A General Duty To Trade Fairly* (Office of Fair Trading, 1986) and *Trading Malpractices* (Office of Fair Trading, 1990).

57 Indeed the Office of Fair Trading's report *A General Duty to Trade Fairly* had expressly foreseen a significant role for codes in fleshing out the general standard.

58 See *Follow-up Communication, op.cit.*, at 11.

59 *Op.cit.*, at 16.

Nevertheless, codes of conduct can be viewed as relevant for an assessment of 'honest market practices' or the 'general principle of good faith' that forms part of the professional diligence concept. The professional diligence concept is relevant to the unfairness test which will only rarely have to be relied upon. However, in practice compliance or non-compliance with codes of conduct will be important aspects of the assessment of trader conduct whether under the unfair, misleading or aggressive practices standard. For shorthand the issue will be expressed as whether a breach of a code of conduct can be equated with being contrary to professional diligence, for lack of professional diligence is implicit in finding a practice to be misleading or aggressive. In making this assessment it will be possible to consider codes, even if they fall outside the Directive's definition of a code of conduct, that is, all forms of self-regulation can inform the debate.

Compliance with codes of conduct will obviously be at issue where a trader adheres to a code. Article 6(2)(b) covers this situation, but even in cases where a trader does not undertake to be bound by a code, the code can serve as a reference point for what amounts to professional diligence. Indeed cases may involve comparisons between the provisions of different codes to see which best reflects the minimum standards of professional diligence. It is important to remember that the Directive only mandates minimum standards. Codes may well exceed that level of protection and that in itself suggests a cautionary note when mapping the contents of codes onto the legislative regime.

Two situations need to be distinguished. First, where non-compliance with a code is used as evidence that a practice is unfair, and secondly, where a trader seeks to use compliance as evidence of fairness. Codes are more useful in proving unfairness than in providing traders with a safe harbour. This is because, whilst traders can set minimum standards which inform consumers' minimum legitimate expectations about what they are entitled to expect, it would be wrong for them to also be able to set a cap on what the law expects. Nevertheless in both circumstances codes will have some role to play.

It is likely that failure to follow any widely established code would be presumed to be contrary to professional diligence. The wider the support there is for a code, the stronger the presumption would be that it represented the expected standard of professional diligence. This may be an incentive for trade associations to seek endorsement for their code in order to argue that this shows that it reflects the minimum standard expected and its rules should also be applied by analogy to non-members.

Such endorsement might come from international bodies, but to the extent this was merely endorsement from a federation of trade associations to which the national organisation belonged, this would not add much. Compliance with principles set down by a well-respected body like the International Chamber of Commerce would be more convincing and compliance with guidance set down by a governmental body such as the Organisation for Economic Co-operation and

Development (OECD) would be even more influential.[60] Involving stakeholders in the development of codes might be another way to show that the codes reflect generally expected standards. The credibility of codes is probably highest when they have been drawn up in consultation with governmental bodies, like the guidelines of the Nordic ombudsmen, or have been approved by a government agency as in the case of Office of Fair Trading approval in the United Kingdom.

It must of course always be possible for a trader to argue that he had been professionally diligent, despite failing to comply with a code. Otherwise there would be a danger that codes had anti-competitive effects.[61] Indeed sectors may have different trade associations with different conceptions of professional diligence and it would be wrong to bind traders always to follow the most demanding standards, so long as the standards they followed fulfilled the demands of professional diligence. Moreover, it will be necessary to distinguish between those aspects of the code that accord with the minimum professional diligence required by the Directive and those rules that go beyond that to reflect superior quality service offered by subscribers to the code. Codes are often promoted as a superior form of regulation precisely because they encourage traders to offer consumers protection above and beyond that mandated by the law. It would therefore be wrong to turn this extra protection into the legally protected minimum expected and to condemn as unfair a practice simply on the basis that it breached a code.

Non-compliance with a code is not therefore conclusive proof of lack of professional diligence, but in many circumstances it can be highly persuasive. The converse is not necessarily the case, that is, compliance with the code is not as strong evidence of satisfying the requirement of professional diligence. The business community desires such a safe harbour and often feels frustrated that they are not given the security of such a provision. The rationale for defeating the understandable wishes of the business community is that whilst traders can through codes help foster minimum expectations of professional diligence, they should not be allowed to set the maximum expectations for themselves. Professional diligence, unfairness, misleading and aggressive practices are normative concepts that are set by the legislator. The fact that there may be different codes operating in the same sector illustrates why compliance with a code cannot be an automatic defence for the trader. The code must be scrutinised to establish whether it fulfils the professional diligence standard.

Naturally in assessing professional diligence there will be some inter-relationship with what standards are prevalent in the market, but these cannot undermine the core meaning that is determined by the legal system. Obviously, however, compliance with codes will have an evidential value, and particularly where there has been the involvement of stakeholders in setting the standards, there will probably need to be

---

60 See, for instance, *OECD Guidelines for Consumer Protection in the Context of Electronic Commerce* (1999).

61 The danger of EU-wide codes preventing, restricting or distorting competition is noted by the Commission in Explanatory Memorandum, *op.cit.*, at 16.

good reasons for imposing stricter standards. This will be the more so the greater degree of consensus there is surrounding the code. This should provide further incentives for trade associations to involve stakeholders and seek endorsements or approvals for their codes. Nevertheless one could imagine sectors with competing codes reflecting different views of professional diligence and it must be the role of the courts to determine which conception accords with the minimum expectations of the Directive.

## I. Policy

Codes have long played an important role in some Member States. The EU wishes to encourage their development, but outside the specific field of e-commerce has done little to galvanise the process. In particular the development of EU-wide codes has been slow.

The Directive restricts itself to prohibiting certain practices in relation to codes of conduct that are always considered unfair; treating non-compliance with an undertaking to be bound to a code of conduct as a misleading practice; and allowing Member States to encourage matters to first be resolved under code complaints procedures. The bigger question is the extent to which codes will inform the content of the general test in the Directive. The Commission backed away from a scheme of approving codes or treating them as providing a 'presumption of conformity'. In states where codes are well developed it is likely that they will often be crucial in making assessments about commercial practices. Without some Community approval scheme, or measure to encourage states to approve codes, there is likely to be a divided Europe. In a few states codes will be the main driver of fair trading rules; in the remainder court practice will determine the content of the general clauses. Whilst codes should not be able to usurp the legal standard, they can be useful mechanisms for ratcheting up expectations. The Community could usefully foster a more consistent and central role for codes across Europe, even if the goal of EU-wide standards remains a distant aspiration. The difficulty is that it may be problematic for codes to be taken seriously in some legal cultures.

# Chapter 8

# Legal Redress

## Hans-W. Micklitz

## a. Regulation of Enforcement Under the Unfair Commercial Practices Directive: Some Introductory Remarks

The regulation of enforcement at the EC level involves complicated matters of power sharing. The European legal order is based on the assumption that Member States remain, in principle, free to decide how they enforce EC law as long as the measures taken by Member States guarantee that they give full effect to European law, and grant those parties who have been given standing to sue effective legal protection.[1] Accordingly, the European Court of Justice's (ECJ) rulings put emphasis on the Member States' responsibility, but do not tell the Member States precisely how they should act – although the ECJ has steadily encroached upon Member States' autonomy.[2] The concept of power sharing between EC law and national law results from the fact that the Treaty does not grant the European Community powers to adopt secondary Community law measures dealing with enforcement alone. However, from an early date, the European Commission started to use Article 95 as a basis to smuggle enforcement issues into the regulation of substantive law. This is what happened in the unfair commercial practices law. The overall purpose of such a policy, which has been accepted by the ECJ, is (whilst underlining Member States' autonomy) to define basic European standards on what national enforcement measures should look like.

### (i) The rules under the Unfair Commercial Practices Directive

This background might explain why the three articles, Articles 11, 12 and 13, in the Unfair Commercial Practices Directive dealing with enforcement are much more concrete than the ECJ's pronouncement of Member States' double obligation to give full effect to community law and to guarantee effective legal protection, but that these articles still leave much leeway to Member States. The articles often remain vague and are full of options, the importance of which is difficult to grasp.

---

1   This is the standard approach used by the ECJ; see, for a full account of the development of the case law, H.-W. Micklitz, § 29, in N. Reich and H.-W. Micklitz (eds), *Europäisches Verbraucherrecht* (Baden-Baden: Nomos-Verlag, 4th edn, 2003).

2   See Case 45/76 *Comet* [1976] ECR 2043; Case 33/76 *Rewe v Landwirtschaftskammer f. d. Saarland* [1976] ECR 1989; Case C–261/95 *Palmisani v INPS* [1997] ECR I–4025.

Article 11, entitled 'Enforcement', pursues five objectives: (1) it wants to make sure that the fairness or unfairness of commercial practices can be challenged in the courts; (2) to define who should be responsible for the enforcement, a public body, consumer or trade organisation; (3) to determine the remedies needed to set an end to unfair marketing practices by way of an injunction order, if necessary, by way of interim relief; (4) to invite Member States to introduce prior consultation mechanisms preceding litigation in the courts; and (5) to consider the publication of a final decision as well as a corrective statement. Under Article 13, Member States are obliged to lay down penalties for infringements of national provisions which must be effective, proportionate and dissuasive. Article 12 deals with substantiation of claims.

### (ii) The unanswered questions on enforcement

There are uncertainties throughout. Whilst Article 11 requires Member States to put the final responsibility on the decision concerning the fairness or unfairness of the commercial practice into the hands of the courts, it is not at all clear who should enforce the law – a public body, consumer or trade organisation. The traditions in the Member States differ considerably here. The majority of Member States have handed over enforcement to public authorities, whilst Germany and Austria rely on consumer and trade organisations to keep the market free from unfair commercial practices. The question is whether EC law obliges Member States to grant consumer and trade organisations legal standing to sue. Even if this is the case, does the Directive provide some guidance on what a consumer or trade organisation is and maybe even whether a public authority must fulfil some basic requirements in order to be regarded as a competent body in the meaning of the Directive?

Article 11 clearly refers to injunction orders and interim relief. However, the relationship between Article 11 and Article 13 is far from clear. Article 13 is entitled 'Penalties'; in German it is '*Sanktionen*', in French '*Sanctions*'. First of all it must be clarified whether Article 13 requires Member States to introduce measures reaching beyond injunction orders and interim relief or if Article 13 is meant to secure that injunction orders and interim relief must be 'effective', 'proportionate' and 'dissuasive'. Then there is the question of what sort of 'sanctions' the Directive has in mind? Are they penal sanctions, as the English version appears to indicate, or are civil law sanctions sufficient? Article 12 only indirectly deals with enforcement matters. However, the question here is whether the Directive shifts the burden of proof as to the accuracy of the factual claims onto the advertiser or whether the claimant must furnish evidence. The answer to that question is of utmost importance for each and any litigation in civil or administrative proceedings under Article 12.

The Directive purports to achieve full harmonisation. In theory its few articles must therefore be understood as a conclusive regulation on enforcement matters. The openness of the provisions and the vagueness of the wording, leaving so many important issues unclarified or subject to the discretion of Member States, make it difficult, however, to take full harmonisation seriously. At best, the Directive sets a broad framework which in no way differs from similar enforcement rules in related Directives on unfair commercial practices providing for only minimum harmonisation. That is why it might be more appropriate to understand that only the substantive law is fully harmonised – but not the matters of enforcement.

*(iii) The broader picture: individual and collective legal protection in unfair commercial practices law outside the Directive*

However, it is insufficient only to look into the Unfair Commercial Practices Directive to fully understand the enforcement policy enshrined in that particular piece of legislation. It is necessary to broaden the perspective by looking at similar pieces of secondary EC law where more or less identical issues on matters of enforcement have arisen. This presents the opportunity not only to enhance the role and function of collective legal protection in secondary Community law, but to look at the degree to which private individuals, consumers and competitors are granted legal standing under EC law to suppress unfair commercial practices.

The Commission has started dealing with collective legal protection at an early stage. This is particularly true in the Misleading Advertising Directive, which set the tone for the two other major pieces of EC unfair commercial practices law: the Comparative Advertising Directive 97/55/EC and the Unfair Commercial Practices Directive.[3] The above-mentioned rules have been taken as a blueprint for the shaping of Articles 11 to 13. Outside the core of EC unfair commercial practices rules, the development of matters on enforcement was enhanced by rather fringe areas of unfair commercial practices, namely the Distance Selling Directive, the Distance Selling of Financial Services Directive, and not least the Consumer Injunctions Directive.

In comparison, individual legal protection in unfair marketing practices law is more like a stepchild of European legal policy. One reason might be that legal actions taken by individuals will not be adequate in clearing the market of unfair advertising practices. Traders might be willing within limits to take legal actions against each other, if this is legally possible under the particular national legal order. The individual consumer will regularly only be concerned with the question of legal redress when he has entered into a contract as a result of unfair or misleading advertising. Often, the consumer will step back from the possibility of taking legal action as the damage is minor and the assertion of his rights is not worth its prosecution. However, it will be argued that the role and function of individual legal redress has increased over time and that secondary EC law appears to enhance the development of appropriate legal means at the national level.

*(iv) A connected issue: cross-border litigation and cross-border enforcement*

The ever denser integration of the European Community, more particularly the establishment of the internal market, has certainly contributed to 'Europeanise'

---

3    See section c on the role and function of collective legal redress under the Directive.

advertising and sales promotion practices. Larger companies at least are quite often no longer developing campaigns for particular national markets, but more and more for the internal market and even for the world market. These strategies necessarily reach across borders. Particular problems arise if advertising strategies originating from companies residing in Member State A affect consumers in Member State B. In 1998 the European Community adopted the Consumer Injunctions Directive. This Directive was meant to improve the enforcement of unfair commercial practices law across borders. It relied heavily on national consumer organisations to enforce consumer law rules in cross-border litigation before the courts of other Member States. This litigation-based approach did not really improve cross-border enforcement. That is why the European Community adopted, in 2004, the Enforcement Regulation 2004/2006[4] which is meant to resolve cross-border conflicts by way of cooperation between the competent national enforcement bodies. Whilst both pieces of EC law are not meant to deal in particular with unfair commercial practices, it seems fair to say that the European Commission had these sorts of conflicts in mind when it advocated the adoption of the Regulation on Consumer Protection Cooperation.

*(v) A disclaimer*

Whilst national courts have quite often referred questions under Article 234 on the interpretation of substantive EC unfair commercial practices law to the ECJ, no similar experience may be reported in matters of enforcement of the kind here at stake. EC rules on enforcement, in particular those laid down in secondary Community law, have not yet engaged the European Court of Justice. It appears as if the national courts tend to maintain Member States' autonomy in enforcement matters of all kind. That is why the interpretation of the enforcement rules in the Unfair Commercial Practices Directive necessarily lacks precision.

## b. Individual Legal Redress

All Directives dealing with unfair commercial practices[5] have the common feature that individual legal redress of competitors is only dealt with marginally, and that legal redress of consumers is not dealt with at all. The experience gained under Community law has shown that the ECJ has repeatedly granted the citizens of the Community individual rights which cannot be enforced horizontally in private legal disputes, but which possibly allow for compensation claims against their Member State if the latter fails to implement the provisions of the Directive in due course

---

4    Regulation (EC) No. 2004/2006 of the European Parliament and of the Council of 27 October 2004 on cooperation between national authorities responsible for the enforcement of consumer protection laws (the Regulation on Consumer Protection Cooperation) OJ 2004 L364/1.

5    Overview in section a(iii).

Legal Redress 221

or completely.[6] Case law on this subject is legendary. With the steadily increasing influence of 'unfair commercial practices law' on 'contract law',[7] the subject matter, that is the availability of individual rights, successively reaches those Directives which form part of European unfair commercial practices law as evidenced by the Unfair Commercial Practices Directive.

### (i) The individual legal redress of competitors

With regard to competitors the situation is comparatively straightforward. The relevant rule is contained in Article 4(1) of the Misleading Advertising Directive, according to which Member States shall ensure that adequate and effective means exist under which persons or organisations regarded under national law as having a legitimate interest in prohibiting misleading advertising may take legal action against misleading advertising. A similar provision is neither contained in the Distance Selling Directive nor in the Distance Selling of Financial Services Directive. 'Persons' are not determined as potential claimants. The same is true of the Consumer Injunctions Directive. The legal situation in Article 11(1) of the Unfair Commercial Practices Directive is unequivocal. The Common Position already clarified that competitors were allowed to bring legal actions.[8] In sum, the entitlement of competitors to sue each other is not disputed among Member States.

### (ii) Individual legal redress for the consumer

Theoretically it would be sensible to speculate over the term 'persons' in earlier Directives aiming at the protection of both consumers and traders. However, the Unfair Commercial Practices Directive has set an end to all such efforts by replacing the term 'persons' in Article 2(3) of the Misleading Advertising Directive with the term 'trader'.

The thorough preparatory works on the Unfair Commercial Practices Directive have caused the European Commission to raise the question of whether the Community should introduce a compensation claim to the benefit of individual consumers.[9] This idea did not pass through the legislative process, which led to the conclusion that the Unfair Commercial Practices Directive strives for collective protection – for

---

6    Cf. Micklitz, *op.cit.*

7    Chapter 3(f)(iii).

8    Cf. F. Henning-Bodewig, 'UWG–Reform und Richtlinienvorschlag' (2004) *Gewerblicher Rechtsschutz und Urheberrecht Internationaler Teil* 183, at 188; also H. Apostolopoulos, 'Neuere Entwicklungen im europäischen Lauterkeitsrecht: Problematische Aspekte und Vorschläge' (2004) *Wettbewerb in Recht und Praxis* 841, at 850.

9    COM(2002) 289 final 18; more detailed to the preparatory works of the Commission: J. Keßler and H.-W. Micklitz, *Die Harmonisierung des Lauterkeitsrechts in den Mitgliedstaaten der Europäischen Gemeinschaft und die Reform des UWG* (Baden-Baden: Nomos-Verlag, 2003) 115 *et seq.*

collective legal redress – of only the consumer interest.[10] That is why it depends on the Member States whether and to what extent they are willing to grant individual consumers the right to sue traders in order to combat unfair commercial practices.

## c. Collective Legal Redress Through Public Authorities, Consumer or Trade Organisations

*(i) Freedom of choice or limited choice?*

Since the adoption of the Misleading Advertising Directive, there is a longstanding discussion in the European Community about whether Member States are free to decide if they put the enforcement of the European commercial practices law into the hands of public authorities or whether the European commercial practices law obliges them to grant consumer organisations, and perhaps even trade organisations, legal standing. Behind this issue of choice, there is a more hidden second question. The point is whether EC commercial practices law defines standards independent of the responsible entities on how the enforcement must be organised in order to be regarded as 'legitimate' in the meaning of the Directive.

Enforcement mechanisms – be they public authorities, consumer or trade organisations – differ between Member States. Therefore the question raised concerns in Member States to a different degree. Those Member States which have chosen to control unfair commercial practices through public bodies have to face the question of whether they are under an EC law obligation to grant legal standing to consumer or trade organisations equally. This might sound strange for countries having a well-established public authority. But EC law might reach beyond an understanding of such bodies as purely private organisations; in particular consumer organisations have an active role to play in the building of the European legal order. Those Member States, for example Germany and Austria, who have implemented such a system for decades have to consider only whether and to what extent EC law sets standards on the way in which trader and consumer organisations must be organised in order to be regarded as 'legitimate' in the meaning of the Directives. This latter issue, however, is equally relevant to public authorities. They too may eventually have to be measured against European law standards.

Both sets of questions are clearly distinct from each other and have to be dealt with separately. First of all it is to be examined whether the choice is restricted or not, before it is possible to deal with the question of whether EC law lays down minimum requirements for the internal organisation of the enforcement bodies, be they public authorities, consumer or trade organisations.

---

10 H. Gamerith, 'Der Richtlinienvorschlag über unlautere Geschäftspraktiken – Möglichkeiten einer harmonischen Umsetzung' (2005) 51 *Wettbewerb in Recht und Praxis* 395, at 403, 404; see, on the collective nature of the Directive, Chapter 3(b).

## *(ii) The rules under Article 11 of the Unfair Commercial Practices Directive*

The rules in the Unfair Commercial Practices Directive seem to be clear, at least at a first glance:

> Article 11 (1) Member States shall ensure that adequate and effective means exist to combat unfair commercial practices in order to enforce compliance with the provisions of this Directive in the interest of consumers.
>
> Such means shall include legal provisions under which persons or organisations regarded under national law as having a legitimate interest in combating unfair commercial practices, including competitors, may;
>
> – take legal action against such unfair commercial practices; and or
>
> – bring such unfair commercial practices before an administrative authority competent either to decide on complaints or to initiate appropriate legal proceedings.
>
> It shall be for each Member State to decide which of these facilities shall be available.

Articles 11 (and 12) of the Directive correspond in content with Articles 4 and 6 respectively of the Misleading Advertising Directive. There are some minor differences though. The reference contained in Article 4(1) of the Misleading Advertising Directive to the interests of competitors and the public interest has been abandoned. Recital 21 of the Directive only refers to collective monitoring mechanisms in general terms and does not provide additional information.

In order to provide an answer to the question of whether Member States are free or not in shaping the enforcement structures, it will not be sufficient to examine the Unfair Commercial Practices Directive alone. Quite to the contrary – it is necessary to look into all relevant Directives in the context of European commercial practices law where a similar issue has already arisen. The different degree of harmonisation in the shaping of the enforcement bodies does not matter given the vague wording in all pieces of law at issue here.

## *(iii) Other Directives containing provisions on legal actions taken by associations*

*The Misleading Advertising Directive* The Misleading Advertising Directive pioneered the building up of collective legal protection. The Directive prohibits misleading advertising in the interest of the public, competitors and – since the adoption of the Unfair Commercial Practices Directive – consumers.[11] The Misleading Advertising Directive 84/450/EEC had already been amended by Directive 97/55/EC in order to include comparative advertising. Article 4(1) requires Member States to take adequate and effective means for the control of misleading advertising.

---

11 Cf. N. Reich, 'Rechtsprobleme grenzüberschreitender irreführender Werbung im Binnenmarkt' (1992) 56 *RabelsZeitschrift* 442, at 444 and 447.

Such means are to include legal provisions under which persons or organisations regarded under national law as having a legitimate interest in prohibiting misleading advertising may take legal action against such advertising (Article 4(1)(a)) or bring such advertising before an administrative authority (Article 4(1)(b)). Article 4(1) expressly states which Member States can decide which of these possibilities (judicial legal protection or administrative authority) shall be given.[12] The Proposal, from 1979, contained a right of consumer associations to sue, which was watered down in particular by virtue of British opposition. At the same time there were opinions which denied the Member State any discretion in the transposition process.[13] Nonetheless, given its history, Article 4 is to be interpreted in terms of minimum procedural protection in that the principle of effective, preventive and speedy legal protection and the principle of participation of consumer associations is recognised. The latter principle, however, is not constituted under Community law, but remains at the discretion of the Member States.[14]

*The Unfair Contract Terms Directive*   The Unfair Contract Terms Directive takes up the principal provisions as contained in the Misleading Advertising Directive. Read broadly, one may understand unfair contract terms as a form of commercial practice. Article 7 purports to create effective and supra-individual instruments to clear the market of unfair clauses. Article 7(1) requires Member States to ensure that adequate and effective means exist to prevent the continued use of unfair terms in contracts concluded with consumers by sellers or suppliers. Article 7(2) orders that these methods shall include provisions whereby persons or organisations, having a legitimate interest under national law in protecting consumers, may take action under national law before the courts or before competent administrative bodies for a decision as to whether contractual terms drawn up for general use are unfair, so that they can apply appropriate and effective means to prevent the continued use of such terms.[15] As the wording in the Misleading Advertising Directive and the Unfair Contract Terms Directive are not identical, the question arose as to whether consumer organisations must have standing.[16]

---

12  H.-W. Micklitz, *Fernabsatzrichtlinie A 3 No. 150* in E. Grabitz and M. Hilf (München: C.H. Beck Verlag, 15. Erg.Lieferung, 2000); for a different view: D. Hoffmann, *Consommation – Publicite et protection des consommateurs en droit europeen* (Paris: 1987) Fasc. 905 No. 46.

13  Hoffmann, *op.cit.*

14  Reich, *op.cit.*, 444, at 450 *et seq.*

15  H.-W. Micklitz, 'AGB-Gesetz und die Richtlinie über missbräuchliche Vertragsklauseln' (1993) 1 *Zeitschrift für Europäisches Privatrecht* 522, at 529; R. Damm, 'Europäisches Verbrauchervertragsrecht und AGB-Recht' (1994) *Juristenzeitung* 161, at 175.

16  T. Wilhelmsson, 'Public Interest Litigation on Unfair Terms', in H.-W. Micklitz and N. Reich (eds), *Public Interest Litigation before European Courts* (Baden-Baden: Nomos-Verlag, 1996) 385, at 387; as well as C. Willett, 'From Reindeers to Confident Consumers: UK Consumer Bodies and the Unfair Terms Directive', in Micklitz and Reich (eds), *Public Interest Litigation before European Courts* (Baden-Baden: Nomos-Verlag, 1996) at 403; J.

The English High Court referred the very same question to the ECJ at a relatively early stage.[17] After the election of the Labour government, the United Kingdom created a right of associations to take actions for injunction in the Unfair Terms in Consumer Contracts Regulations 1999[18] so that the claim brought by the Consumers' Association (now Which? Limited) was rendered obsolete. Unfortunately, the ECJ has had no chance to clarify the issue.

*The Distance Selling Directive and the Distance Selling of Financial Services Directive*   The Distance Selling Directive regulates very precisely individual and collective redress. Article 11(1) reiterates the obligation of Member States to ensure that adequate and effective means exist to ensure compliance with the Directive which aims primarily at the protection of the interests of consumers. Article 11(2) contains a collective remedy for consumers and professional organisations. During the legislative process of the Distance Selling Directive it remained open whether the remedies to be introduced should be obligatory or optional. However, in the mediation committee the European Parliament and Council agreed that the remedies should be obligatory.[19] The final wording leaves no doubt that Member States are obliged to grant consumer associations the power to take legal actions as an adequate and effective means of control. As the provisions of the Distance Selling Directive and the Distance Selling for Financial Services Directive are identical, the same consequences apply to the distance marketing of financial services.

*The Consumer Injunctions Directive*   The Consumer Injunctions Directive contains minimum standards concerning the right of foreign-registered associations to take legal actions and governs the procedural aspects.[20] Article 1 clarifies that it is the purpose of the Directive to approximate the laws, regulations and administrative provisions of Member States relating to actions for an injunction aimed at the protection of the collective interests of consumers included in the (consumer-) Directives listed in the Annex, with a view to ensuring the smooth functioning of the internal market. Pursuant to Article 2 Member States are obliged to designate the

---

Dickie, 'Article 7 of the Unfair Terms in Consumer Contracts Directive' (1996) 4 *Consumer Law Journal* 112; H.-W. Micklitz, 'Verbandsklage und Richtlinie 93/13 über mißbräuchliche Klauseln' (1998) *Zeitschrift für Wirtschafts- und Insolvenzpraxis* 937, at 943.

17 The question was: 'Does Article 7 Abs. 2 of the Directive 13/93 impose obligations on Member States to ensure that national law, (1) states criteria to identify private persons or organisations having a legitimate interest in protecting consumers, and (2) allows such private persons or organisations to take action before the courts or before competent administrative bodies for a decision as to whether contractual terms drawn up for use are unfair?', quoted in Dickie, *op.cit.*, 112.

18 SI 1999/2083.

19 In detail: Micklitz, *op.cit.*, No. 149.

20 In detail: P. Rott, 'The Protection of Consumers' Interests after the Implementation of the EC Injunctions Directive into German and English Law' (2001) *Journal of Consumer Policy* 401.

courts or administrative authorities competent to rule on proceedings commenced by qualified entities, which are defined in Article 3 as any body or organisation which, being properly constituted according to the law of a Member State, has a legitimate interest in ensuring the protection of the collective interests of the consumers. Professional organisations are therefore excluded.[21] This wording is very much in line with Article 4 of the Misleading Advertising Directive.

*(iv) Standing to sue as an EC obligation*

The six Directives are in no way coherent. There are the two Distance Selling and Distance Selling for Financial Services Directives, which may support a reading under which Member States are obliged to guarantee standing to private bodies. Such a reading may be backed, at least to some extent, by the Unfair Contract Terms Directive. The remaining three, the Misleading and Comparative Advertising Directives, the Consumer Injunctions Directive and last, but not least, the Unfair Commercial Practices Directive, seem to leave more leeway to Member States in their choice of the appropriate enforcement body.

The six Directives also differ considerably in the way in which they either affect the standing of consumer organisations only, or they cover also trade organisations. The Misleading Advertising Directive, the Distance Selling Directive, the Distance Selling for Financial Services Directive and the Unfair Commercial Practices Directive address consumer *and* trade associations. Such a conclusion has been challenged with regard to the latter, given its limited scope of application. However, Article 11(1) of the Unfair Commercial Practices Directive explicitly names competitors as having a legitimate interest. Then it appears irrational to exclude trade associations from taking actions in the interest of consumers. Pursuant to the soft wording of Article 11(1), which does not explicitly refer to trade associations, but which equally does not exclude them either, those organisations shall be entitled to take legal actions in business-to-consumer relations.[22] It appears necessary therefore to draw a distinction between the role and function that consumer organisations and trade organisations have to play in the enforcement.

Over the years, the European Community has continuously strengthened the position of consumer associations. On this basis it is possible to conclude that Member States are obliged to grant consumer organisations standing. Pursuant to Article 10 EC Treaty, Member States are obliged to take all appropriate measures, whether general or particular, to ensure fulfilment of the obligations arising out of the Treaty provided they are sufficiently clear and concrete. The regulation of collective consumer protection must be seen in connection with consumer policy

---

21 D. Baetge, 'Das Recht der Verbandsklage auf neuen Wegen – Zu den Auswirkungen der EG-Richtlinie über Unterlassungsklagen zum Schutz der Verbraucherinteressen auf die Verbandsklage in Deutschland' (1999) 112 *Zeitschrift für Zivilprozeß* 329, at 336.

22 Also M. Röttinger, 'Verfahrensrechtliche Aspekte des Richtlinien-Vorschlages über unlautere Geschäftspraktiken' (2004) *ecolex* 78.

of the Community which directly results from Article 153 EC Treaty. Collective consumer protection and legal standing have long been the subject matter of numerous position papers and action plans of the Community organs. Insofar as they are soft law they are not directly binding; however, their practical relevance should not be underestimated as the ECJ has held that national courts must consider them in their decision-making.[23]

Article 153 EC Treaty incorporates collective rights in a more concrete and precise form than its predecessor. It expressly constitutes the right of consumers 'to organise themselves in order to safeguard their interests' as an objective of the Community. According to Article 153 (1) EC Treaty the Community shall contribute to promoting the right to form consumer organisations. The Member States, as the 'masters of the treaties', clearly proceeded from the extant (minimum) level of protection (under Community law). Taken together with access to justice, understood as a human right, the suggested interpretation of Article 153 EC Treaty becomes more dynamic. As a result it can safely be argued that consumer organisations must be granted standing.

The legal position on trade organisations is less clear cut. Primary Community law provides no point of reference for a general right of trade organisations to play an active role in the building of the European legal order. Secondary Community law is divided. Under such circumstances, consumer and trade organisations cannot be put on an equal footing.

### (v) Minimum requirements for enforcement bodies

The second question is independent from the first. Even if the ECJ were to reject the idea that European law bears an obligation to introduce standing in the favour of consumer organisations, the point remains whether and to what extent EC law lays down basic requirements on the internal structure of enforcement bodies. Again looking into the Unfair Commercial Practices Directive alone is insufficient.

*Public bodies* Article 4(1) of the Misleading Advertising Directive as well as Article 7(2) of the Unfair Contract Terms Directive and Article 14(1) of the Unfair Commercial Practices Directive refer to 'competent administrative authority' or 'administrative authority'; Article 11(2) of the Distance Selling Directive as well as Article 13 of the Unfair Commercial Practices Directive classifies the competent administrative authorities as 'public bodies'. Whilst the terminology differs, the basic meaning appears to be the same. The idea is that there is a public body. Much more interesting are early efforts in secondary Community law to specify the character of the 'public body'. Article 4 of the Misleading Advertising Directive requires administrative authorities to be impartial, have adequate powers and normally give reasons for their decisions. Such bodies can either bring or decide complaints. The

---

23 ECJ C–322/88 *Grimaldi/Fonds des Maladies Professionnelles* [1989] ECR 4407; on the significance of soft law: F. Snyder, 'The Effectiveness of European Community Laws: Institutions, Processes, Tools, Techniques' (1993) 56 *Modern Law Review* 19, at 31 *et seq.*

very same wording is reiterated in Article 11(3) of the Unfair Commercial Practices Directive. The Consumer Injunctions Directive refers to 'independent public bodies' which are specifically responsible for protecting 'the collective interests of consumers'.

Therefore, taking the Directives as a whole, Member States are obliged, if they lay the control into the hands of a public authority, to put them into a position so that they can fulfil their mandate in a qualified and competent manner. The competent body must be free and independent, that is, it must be an administrative body which is not involved with other administrative tasks.

*Consumer associations*   It appears that all Directives, including the Unfair Commercial Practices Directive, only require of Member States that they grant consumer associations a right to take legal actions; however, they seem not to get involved with the discussion of competence issues as illustrated by the wording 'under national law'. Such a reading suggests that it is at the discretion of Member States to determine which organisation qualifies as a consumer organisation. This is opposed to Article 153 EC Treaty which Europeanises the power to define consumer associations. Regardless of the fact that legal standing is not mentioned in Article 153 EC Treaty, it is still necessary to set up general criteria for consumer organisations which are equally binding on all Member States. For this reason consumer organisations, in terms of EC law, are only those organisations which fulfil certain minimum requirements,[24] that is a stable organisational structure with an established place of business, a certain minimum size, long-term activity, and statutes defining the field of activity which has been generally agreed on. It appears that independence from the business sector is another requirement which must be met. These rules may be deduced from Article 153 EC Treaty in combination with the here-discussed Directives under which consumer organisations must be 'legitimate'.

*Trade associations*   The minimum requirements for consumer associations can be transferred *cum grano salis* to trade associations. Like consumer associations, trade associations should have a stable organisational structure with an established place of business, be of a certain minimum size, pursue a long term activity, and have articles recording a consumer policy field of activity which has been generally agreed on. They should also be independent from the consumer sector.

### d. Procedure and Remedies

*(i) Prior consultation*

The most important provisions on prior consultation are rooted in the Misleading Advertising Directive. According to its Articles 4(1)–(2) it shall be for each Member

---

24  Also T. Pfeiffer, *Mißbräuchliche Vertragskluseln, A 5 Article 7 No. 17 et seq.*, in E. Grabitz and M. Hilf (München: C.H. Beck-Verlag, 1999).

State to decide whether, prior to the commencement of legal proceeding or addressing a competent administrative authority, to require recourse to 'other established means of dealing with complaints'. Despite the fact that the terminology slightly differs in the other Directives and also in Article 11(1) of the Unfair Commercial Practices Directive, the major issue is the same. Community law grants Member States an option to introduce prior consultation in the control of unfair commercial practices. They can make formal proceedings dependent on the complainant first invoking a form of out of court procedure; however, they are not obliged to do so.

*(ii) Interim relief*

Interim relief in commercial practices-related Directives belongs to the *acquis communautaire*. Again, this was first introduced in Article 4(2) of the Misleading Advertising Directive and reappears in Article 11(2) of the Unfair Commercial Practices Directive. No such competence is found in the Distance Selling Directive, the Distance Selling of Financial Services Directive and the Unfair Contract Terms Directive. However, the remaining gap might be closed with reference to the well-established case law of the ECJ rooted in *Factortame*,[25] where it held that interim relief might be an indispensable means to secure the effective enforcement of EC legal rights.

*(iii) Injunction*

Article 12(2) of the Unfair Commercial Practices Directive obliges Member States to grant the competent courts or administrative authorities powers enabling them, in cases where they deem such measures to be necessary, taking into account all the interests involved and in particular the public interest:

- to order the cessation of, or to institute appropriate legal proceedings for an order for the cessation of, unfair commercial practices, or,
- if the unfair commercial practice has not yet been carried out but is imminent to order the prohibition of the practice, or to institute appropriate legal proceedings for an order for the prohibition of the practice, without proof of actual loss or damage or intention or negligence on the part of the trader.

Article 12(2) derives from Article 4(2) of the Misleading Advertising Directive with which it is in substance, if not literally, identical. The other Directives at issue here are equally referring to an action for injunction as the sole means to put an end to all sorts of unfair commercial practices, including the use of unfair contract terms in consumer contracts.

In essence, Member States are obliged to introduce an action for injunction, be it to put an end to existing unfair commercial practices or to prevent their realisation.

---

25  Case C–213/89 [1990] ECR 2433 at 21.

The action for injunction is not bound to further prerequisites. Traders are strictly responsible for unfair commercial practices and have to cease them independent of fault and damage.

### (iv) Penalties, sanctions and compensation for damages

According to Article 13 of the Unfair Commercial Practices Directive, Member States shall set out penalties for infringements of national provisions adopted in application of the Directive and shall take all necessary measures to ensure that these are enforced. These penalties must be effective, proportionate and dissuasive. The same wording goes back to the ECJ and has made its way since then into the codification of EC consumer law.[26] It has not yet been introduced in the Misleading Advertising Directive, however. It has already been said that there is some confusion over what 'penalties' means.[27] The unspecific wording allows for a broad understanding, which might cover civil sanctions as well as penal sanctions. However, it remains to be clarified what sort of national provisions should be 'sanctioned'. It is not clear which sanctions Member States are obliged to introduce under the Directive. Is it merely the action for injunction or those which the Member States have taken without being obliged to do so, such as group actions for compensation?

From the context of Article 13 it is clear that Member States must provide for a procedure which allows the execution of an injunction order sentenced by the court. They are not obliged, however, to provide, for example, for penal sanctions which are quite common in the Romanic legal systems. The much more complicated question is whether even those remedies which Member States voluntarily adopt may be measured against the requirement in Article 13 that sanctions be effective, proportionate and dissuasive. This might be possible to the extent that Member States make use of the option foreseen in Article 11(2)(a) and (b) to require the publication of a final decision or a corrective statement. In that case, Member States are under an obligation to make sure that the publication is done effectively and persuasively. However, if Member States introduce collection actions for compensation, as is more and more the case,[28] these procedures remain outside the scope of the Directive. These remedies cannot fall under the regime of EC law.

---

26 The first Directive here at issue where the formula has been introduced was the Distance Selling of Financial Services Directive.

27 The first judgment of the ECJ concerning penal sanctions is of no use, as it was clear from the Directive at issue that penal sanctions in the proper meaning of the word were meant: Case C–176/03 *Commission v Council* [2005] (ECR I-7879).

28 See, for a full account of the discussion, H.-W. Micklitz and A. Stadler (authors and editors), *Das Verbandsklagerecht in der Informations- und Dienstleistungsgesellschaft* (Münster: Landwirtschaftsverlag, 2005).

*(v) Substantiation of claims*

In principle, Member States remain free to regulate the burden of proof. Article 6(1) of the first proposal of the Unfair Commercial Practices Directive provided for a reversal of the burden of proof for claims about the product which the trader cannot substantiate.[29] However, this rule was dropped in the final version of the Directive. All that remains is Article 12 of the Unfair Commercial Practices Directive, according to which Member States shall confer upon the courts or administrative authorities powers:

a) to require the trader to furnish evidence as to the accuracy of factual claims in relation to a commercial practice if, taking into account the legitimate interest of the trader and any other party to the proceedings, such a requirement appears appropriate on the basis of the circumstances of the particular case,

b) to consider factual claims as inaccurate if the evidence demanded in accordance with (a) is not furnished or is deemed insufficient by the court or administrative authority.

Article 12 is identical to Article 6 of the Misleading Advertising Directive. Article 6 has always been understood to mean that the trader must furnish evidence only under quite particular circumstances, but that in general the enforcement body has to show the inaccuracy of the commercial transactions. The message of Article 12 becomes clearer in Recital 21: 'While it is for national law to determine the burden of proof, it is appropriate to enable courts and administrative authorities to require traders to produce evidence as to the accuracy of factual claims they have made'. However, if one compares Recital 21 with Recital 16 of the Misleading Advertising Directive, it becomes clear that the margin of appreciation left to Member States has been narrowed down. Recital 16 reads as follows: 'Whereas the advertiser should be able to prove, by appropriate means, the material accuracy of the factual claims he makes in his advertising, and may in appropriate cases be required to do so by the court or administrative authorities.' The language in the Unfair Commercial Practices Directive is much more straightforward. The perspective of the regulator has been turned upside down. Recital 21 puts the emphasis on the competences of enforcement bodies, which must have the right to request evidence; the restriction 'by appropriate means' has been abandoned.

---

29  See paragraph 69 of the Explanatory Memorandum, COM(2003) 356 final.

### e. Enforcement of Collective Consumer Interests in Conflicts Across National Borders

Only the Consumer Injunctions Directive deals with legal enforcement across national borders. However, it merely regulates the mutual recognition of the right to take action (in German *Klagebefugnis*, in French *qualité d'agir*). The right to take action means the right granted by the legislator by which qualified entities – public authorities and consumer organisations – are entitled to file an action. The right to take action must be distinguished from the question of whether the right to take action exists under the given circumstances of the case at issue. At least the German (*Rechtsschutzinteresse*) and the French (*intérêt d'agir*) legal systems draw a clear and in practice very important distinction between the general right to sue and the right to sue in the given case. The Consumer Injunctions Directive does not deal with the legitimate right to take action – *Rechtsschutzinteresse* or the *intérêt d'agir*; it leaves the decision about the applicability of national law to national private international law and does not touch upon the question of international jurisdiction either.

### (i) Problems and experiences with legal enforcement across national borders

To date, advertising across national borders and the use of general terms and conditions across national borders has been the focus of most interest. In a number of test cases, German and French consumers' associations had revealed the deficiencies of legal enforcement across national borders. They were concerned about the conduct of advertising by firms in the mail order business with a seat in Germany who, from Germany, approached French consumers using sweepstakes as means to attract the attention of consumers.[30] The point at stake was the question of whether the German consumer organisation, which has the right to take action (*Klagebefugnis*), is entitled to make use of this right in Germany to protect French consumers (*Rechtsschutzinteresse*). The right to take action, in German understanding, is a procedural prerequisite and must be defined in accordance with German procedural law if the case is being brought before a German court (*lex fori*). In essence, German associations were found to be competent only to protect German consumers or non-German consumers resident in Germany. This *Distant shopping* (this is the name of the mail order company) experience triggered off and legitimated the adoption of the Consumer Injunctions Directive, which, however, harmonises only the right to take action.

---

30 The story is recounted in H.-W. Micklitz, 'Cross-Border Consumer Conflicts – A French-German Experience' (1993) 16 *Journal of Consumer Policy Special Issue – European Consumer Policy After Maastricht* 411.

*(ii) International jurisdiction for actions against cross-border injunctions*

International jurisdiction in respect of unlawful advertising measures across national borders is determined by Regulation 44/2001 on Jurisdiction and the Recognition and Enforcement of Judgments,[31] if a 'civil and commercial matter' for the purposes of Article 1(1) is established. In cases of wide-ranging violations against consumer protection provisions, a 'tort, delict' or 'quasi-delict' in accordance with Article 5(3) of the Regulation on Jurisdiction and the Recognition and Enforcement of Judgments may exist, which provides for a special jurisdiction in the place where the harmful event occurred.[32] In this respect, there has been no change as compared to the Brussels Convention. The same applies to civil law actions for compensation which are connected to criminal proceedings against the wrongdoer.[33] This combination of civil law actions for compensation and criminal proceedings in the field of unfair commercial practices law is characteristic, for example, for France. Thus, the courts both in the place of action as well as the place where the event occurs have jurisdiction. This, in principle, allows for 'forum shopping'.

The Court of Appeal of Bremen[34] had, in a decision of 17 October 1991, still refused the international jurisdiction of the German courts in the case of injunctive relief, given the fact that the 'harmful event' had not yet occurred in accordance with Article 5(3) of the Brussels Convention, which is now Article 5(3) of the Regulation on Jurisdiction and the Recognition and Enforcement of Judgments. The mere fear of a tort (or delict) being committed was said to be inadequate in establishing the special jurisdiction of Article 5(3) of the Brussels Convention. This uncertainty has. been removed in the Regulation on Jurisdiction and the Recognition and Enforcement of Judgments as it is sufficient that the event 'may occur'. Hence, in light of the clear wording, injunctive relief comes under Article 5(3). However, the ECJ had already corrected the narrow interpretation of the OLG Bremen already under the Brussels Convention.[35]

*(iii) The right to take action and the legitimate interest to take legal action*

The Consumer Injunctions Directive, following French law, creates a twofold distinction in the right to take action. The first is the question of the right to take action (*qualité d'agir*), to which the determination of the *lex fori* applies. Here, the Consumer Injunctions Directive brings clarity by providing for a mutual recognition of the national organisations which have a right of action. The second is the legitimate

---

31 Council Regulation (EC) No 44/2001 of 22 December 2000 on Jurisdiction and the Recognition and Enforcement of Judgments in Civil and Commercial Matters: OJ 2001 L12/1.

32 Reich, *op.cit.*, 460 *et seq.*

33 ECJ, Case C–172/91 *Sonntag* [1993] ECR I–1963.

34 (1992) Recht der internationalen Wirtschaft 232.

35 ECJ Case C–167/00 *Henkel* [2002] ECR I–8111 at 33 .

interest to take action (*intérêt pour agir*), which is determined by the *lex fori delicti*, given the nature – as regards the law of tort (or delict) or the law of quasi-delict – of actions by associations concerning unfair commercial practices.

*The right to take action*    The aim of the Consumer Injunctions Directive is to establish, in respect of infringements across national borders within the Community, the principle of mutual recognition for entities qualified to bring an action. Member States are required, following application by their national entities, to inform the Commission of the name and purpose of the national authorities which, in its country, have a right to take action. This list is published in the Official Journal. Article 2(1) leaves it to Member States to designate the so called 'qualified entities', which is used as a synonym for public authorities and consumer organisations. New legal remedies are not created through the Directive. Article 4 obliges Member States to take all measures necessary to ensure that, in the event of an infringement originating in that Member State, any qualified entity from another Member State where the interests protected by that qualified entity are affected by the infringement, may seize the court or administrative authority referred to in Article 2, on presentation of the list provided for in paragraph 3. According to this, Member States' courts are obliged to regard the entities mentioned in the list as being qualified to bring an action. However, Member States' courts retain the right to examine whether the purpose of the qualified entity justifies its taking action in a particular case (Article 4(1)). The Directive allows the control of an abuse of the right to take action.[36]

*Legitimate interest to take action*    The Consumer Injunctions Directive does not make a statement in respect of standing to sue; it neither defines concrete requirements on the legitimate interest to take legal action, nor does it make arrangements about the applicable law. Hence, in case of conflict the solution is to be found under national law. The starting point is the legal nature of the claim to compel someone to refrain from doing something, which, based on Community law, is to be classified as falling under tort (or delict) or quasi-delict. If one puts both types of action on the same level, the way of determining the applicable law appears to be designated. Since a harmonisation of the international law of tort (or delict) has not yet taken place – it is underway in Rome II[37] – the national rules of private international law would have to be established and applied. Many countries refer to the applicable law as the one in which the incriminated commercial practice affects the market (*Marktwirkungsregel*). The applicable law is then to be inferred from the *lex loci delicti*. This could often be the receiving country.

One may wonder, however, whether this understanding needs to be revised under existing Community law. The starting point is the country of origin principle,

36   Cf. ECJ Case C–45/90 *Paletta and others v Brennet AG* [1992] ECR I–4323; Case C–206/94 *Paletta II* [1996] ECR I–2357.

37   Proposal for a Council Regulation on the Law applicable to Non-Contractual Obligations (Rome II) COM(2003) 427 final.

which guarantees free access in the internal market to all products and services which have 'lawfully' been placed onto that market.[38] The privilege of access fails to apply where the product or service has been placed upon the market unlawfully. The Member State, and this is the crucial conclusion of the interplay between lawful and unlawful, incurs responsibility for unlawful activities which emanate from its territory.[39] As a result of the country of origin principle, the country of origin must ensure that there are no risks originating in its territory which endanger the citizens in the other Member States. However, such a reading has not yet been confirmed by the European Court of Justice.

### (iv) The determination of the law applicable under EC private international law

Once it has been decided, with the help of the modified '*Marktwirkungsregel*'[40] whether the association has a legitimate interest to take action, then, according to the prevailing understanding, it has also been decided which law is applicable – namely the law of the state in which the offending action has been carried out.

Legal doctrine extensively discusses the consequences of defining the applicable law with the help of – national – international private law rules. So far, Rome II has not been adopted. It would, however, not contain any particular rules on commercial practices, but allow them to be treated as tort (or delict) or quasi-delict. That is why the '*Marktwirkungsregel*' could still apply. It would usually lead to the application of the law where the commercial transaction has taken place. This is not necessarily the country from where the commercial transaction originates, but where it affects the consumer in the market.

It might be preferable, however, to start from a different premise. If the transborder litigation is within the sphere of application of harmonised laws (meaning the Directives listed in the Annex to the Consumer Injunctions Directive), then it can make no difference whether the conflict of laws rules of the *lex fori* refers to its own law or to the law of another Member State. The basis, that is the reference point, is the same, one of the listed Directives. The counter-arguments are well-known. Most of the listed Directives provide for minimum harmonisation only, which is not the case in the Unfair Commercial Practices Directive. Here there are maximum standards. This is the common platform which the European Commission intended to create via the Directive.[41] It is true that the Directive must be implemented and it will be done in different ways. There are exemptions from the scope of application and there are uncertainties on the concept of fairness. However, it might be worthwhile

---

38 Cf. particularly clearly in ECJ Case 120/78 *Rewe v Bundesmonopolverwaltung für Branntwein* [1979] ECR 649 at 14, and ECJ Case 178/84 *Commission v Germany 'breach of contract'* [1987] ECR 1227 at 52.

39 Cf. Reich, *op.cit.*, at 509 more carefully about the extra-territorial extension of competence; W.-H. Roth, 'Der Einfluss des Europäischen Gemeinschaftsrechts auf das Internationale Privatrecht' (1991) 55 *Rabels Zeitschrift* 623, at 667.

40 See section e(iii).

41 See Chapter 2(c).

to reconsider, in the light of the intense harmonisation in matters of EC commercial practices law, the appropriateness and the feasibility of international private law as the appropriate reference point. The major argument in favour of using a common European platform is to be found in the supremacy of Community law. Even a possible regulation on the Law Applicable to Non-Contractual Obligations (Rome II) must be compatible with secondary Community law, as enshrined in the listed Directives. The ECJ has provided a conclusive argument in its case law on the verdict of indirect discrimination under Article 6 EC.[42] Where conflict of laws rules lead to, for example, German consumers in EC foreign territory losing the protection due to them under Community law – although the action originated in Germany and consumers resident in Germany enjoy protection under German law – such a refusal of protection is contrary to the prohibition against discrimination. It is obvious that the level of protection should be the same when the case at issue comes under the scope of application of harmonised and transposed national law. The ECJ, however, has not yet had any occasion to test its own arguments in international private law matters.

Such an understanding complies with the Consumer Injunctions Directive, which does not affect the common ground of Community law. The final version of that Directive, unlike the preceding drafts, does not contain a statement on applicable law. According to Recital 6, the Directive applies without prejudice to private international law and the Rome Conventions. This aim has been expressed in Article 2(2) which says: 'This Directive shall be without prejudice to the rules of private international law, with respect to the applicable law, thus leading normally to the application of either the law of the Member State where the infringement originated or the law of the Member State where the infringement has its effects.' The wording appears to leave Member States free choice, whether they determine the applicable law under reference to country of origin or country of designation principle. Recitals 3 and 4, which emphasise the risks connected to the effect of an infringement in the country of designation, speak against such free choice. For this reason, for example, the German law requires consideration of the country of origin principle in determining the applicable law within the sphere of harmonised law.

## (v) Execution of a judgment

Injunctive decisions of the courts, to the extent that the opposing party could be heard, are capable of being mutually recognised under the Regulation on Jurisdiction and the Recognition and Enforcement of Judgments as well as the Brussels Convention.[43] Payments in the form of a penalty can be enforced in accordance with Article 49 of

---

42  ECJ Case 398/92 *Firma Mund & Fester v Firma Hatrex International Transport* [1994] ECR I–467, and ECJ Case 323/95 *David Charles Hayes and Jeanette Karen Hayes v Kronenberger GmbH* [1997] ECR I–1711.

43  ECJ Case 125/79 *Denilauler* [1980] ECR 1553.

the Regulation on Jurisdiction and the Recognition and Enforcement of Judgments.[44] The provision reads: 'A foreign judgment which orders a periodic payment by way of penalty shall be enforceable in the Member States in which the enforcement is sought only if the amount of the payment has been finally determined by the courts of the Member State of origin.'

However, decisions reaching beyond this penalty, such as the publication of the judgment or an 'advertisement of corrective character', cannot be recognised. These rules allow for the execution of injunctive decisions across national borders through the competent national authorities and national consumer organisations. If one follows the reading of the Directive as outlined here, actions could be brought both in the state of origin as well as in the state where the infringement has its effect. Practical experience must be developed through test cases. Since the adoption of the Consumer Injunctions Directive, there is only one piece of transborder litigation to be reported. This concerned a Belgian advertisement that affected British consumers.[45]

### f. The Regulation (EC) No 2006/2004 on Consumer Protection Cooperation

Whilst the Consumer Injunctions Directive aimed at strengthening private enforcement mainly through consumer organisations, the Regulation on Consumer Protection Cooperation relies on cooperation between competent authorities. To 'significantly improve' the protection of the legal interests of the consumer in cross-border transactions and thus to increase the 'efficiency of the internal market' the Commission wants to have appointed central authorities in Member States which prevent-cross border infringements by way of mutual cooperation. The International Marketing Supervision Network as founded by the OECD, and which was recently renamed the International Consumer Protection Enforcement Network, served as a model for the Commission. For more than 20 years this informal body has been made up of representatives of authorities and organisations from the OECD countries. It meets twice a year to discuss problems which arise in connection with unfair commercial practices. The Regulation is based on the principle of international cooperation. At the same time, the Commission seeks to respond to insufficient cross-border law enforcement. The idea had already been mentioned in the Green Book on Consumer Protection.[46] It has passed through the legislative process smoothly. From the Austrian and the German point of view there is one notable exception. Austria and Germany have been opposed to the 'nationalisation' of law enforcement. As a result, both countries may delegate the rights and duties under the Regulation to consumer and trade associations.

---

44 O. Remien, *Rechtsverwirklichung durch Zwangsgeld – Vergleich – Vereinheitlichung – Kollisionsrecht* (Tübingen: Mohr Siebeck, 1992) at 317 *et seq.*

45 http://www.oft.gov.uk/news/press+release/2004/208–04.htm.

46 J. Glöckner, *Introduction B. No. 199 et seq.*, in H. Harte-Bavendamm and F. Henning-Bodewig, *Gesetz gegen den unlauteren Wettbewerb* (München: Verlag C.H. Beck, 2004).

*(i) The objective and contents of the Regulation*

The Regulation will come into effect on 29 December 2005. However, administrative cooperation has been postponed to 29 December 2006. This might be due to the fact that the Commission and Member States must take numerous measures to ensure the functioning of cross-border cooperation in practice.

*Objectives*   The Regulation does not purport to establish new authorities, or to replace controlling structures with new ones. Nor does it purport to take away the competence from Member States and to give it to the Commission. It relies on the possibility of further developing existing control structures in a way that cooperation and cross-border law enforcement can be improved. Therefore, the Regulation on Consumer Protection Cooperation does not interfere with the Consumer Injunctions Directive, which focuses extensively on consumer associations. To this extent the Commission purports to establish parallel structures. By this, the Commission avoids conflicts on the necessity of a unification of control structures within the EC.[47]

*The scope of application*   The Regulation only extends to economic consumer protection as defined in Annex 1, which lists the relevant consumer law Directives. Article 16 of the Unfair Commercial Practices Directive provides for an amendment of the Annex so as to include unfair commercial practices. The list already included the Distance Selling and the Distance Selling on Financial Services Directives. The list is as exhaustive as that in the Consumer Injunctions Directive.

*The competent authority and its power to act*   The Regulation is based on the concept that Member States name competent authorities which will cooperate in case of a cross-border violation of the law (Article 3(c)). This approach proceeds from the assumption that such authorities exist which have the investigation and enforcement powers necessary for the application of the Regulation and shall exercise them in conformity with national law (Article 4(1)(3)). This wording could become particularly relevant if Member States were only to take symbolic actions without providing the necessary resources for cross-border cooperation.

The Regulation establishes a number of minimum powers which Member States must grant to the competent authorities to allow them effectively to establish reasonable grounds for suspicion of a violation of the law. The Commission had in mind, as is evident in the preparatory works, the possibility of applying for an injunction to prevent legal infringements. Remedies, such as compensation for injury which consumers individually or collectively have suffered, are not provided for.

*Organisation of administrative cooperation*   The Regulation distinguishes between the exchange of information with and without request in Articles 6 and 9 and the

---

47  COM(2001) 531 final.

request for enforcement measures. Articles 8 to 15 regulate the details of the request for information or the request for enforcement measures which can be made by the authority, under what circumstances it may do so, which measures may be taken to keep data confidential and which measures can be taken by the requesting authority. Cooperation is based on the principle of confidentiality. The rules provided for are not meant to put the requesting authority in a position to compel the authority addressed to act, and not even to provide information. For this reason there are no provisions in case the authority addressed improperly declines to accede to the request to provide information or even to take appropriate measures to prevent violation of the law. The requesting authority may refer conflicts on the legitimacy of the request to the Commission, but is not obliged to do so.

Theoretically, the committee procedure in Article 19 is the focus of this interest. Despite the fact that the Regulation on Consumer Protection Cooperation uses 'comitology', the crucial difference is that the committee procedure is not automatically triggered in case of conflict, but only if a Member State asks for a formal decision on the legitimacy of a request under Articles 5 and 7 of Decision 1999/468/EC. The draft Regulation had contained the possibility of inviting so-called 'qualified bodies' under the Consumer Injunctions Directive, which means authorised or competent organisations, to participate in the decisionmaking process. This passage is not contained in the final version.

*The role of the Commission*   Even if the Commission formally has no powers, it is still the 'spider in the cobweb'. Under Article 10, its task is to build up a database which saves all information and enforcement requests and their consequences. Every second year, Member States have to provide a report to the Commission in compliance with a detailed catalogue, Article 21(3)(a) to (f). These reports will be made available to the public by the Commission.

*(ii) The significance of the Regulation with regard to the organisation of law enforcement*

The Regulation covers the entire spectrum of contractually relevant consumer law Directives, including the Unfair Commercial Practices Directive; it touches upon legal actions brought in the field of unfair commercial practices. The strong reliance on public control authorities affects Austrian and German consumer and trade organisations to which the enforcement of the unfair commercial practices law is entrusted. The centre of the conflicts, therefore, was Article 4(2) taken with Article 8(3), according to which Austria and Germany have to designate a competent authority. Given the compromise, these might be the established consumer and trade organisations. However, the Regulation does not release Member States from the obligation to designate one competent statutory body, which must supervise consumer and trade organisations to which the rights and duties under the regulation are delegated. To this end the designated Member State's authorities retain a residual control competence, Article 8(3). This authority must be given powers to file an

# Chapter 9

# Conclusions

Thomas Wilhelmsson

## a. A Directive of Legal and Practical Importance

The description and analysis of the Unfair Commercial Practices Directive in the previous chapters reveal the picture of a Directive that is designed to be important. It will certainly be a significant tool for converging the laws of the Member States in the process of building the internal market. The importance of the Directive stems from several features that distinguish this piece of EU legislation from many other consumer protection Directives.

First, as shown in Chapter 3, the scope of the Directive is very broad. It covers all kinds of business-to-consumer commercial practices, with very few limitations. Both pre-contractual and post-contractual practices are within the scope of the Directive and it covers both commercial communications and other acts, omissions and courses of conduct. Potentially, the Directive could be applied to almost anything a trader does that affects its consumer clients, and even the core of its scope is wide.

Secondly, in addition to its broad scope, the Directive confers extensive powers to those applying the Directive. As described in Chapter 4, it is based on a general clause outlawing 'unfair' commercial practices. Even though the Directive attempts to clarify its content with the help of the more elaborate provisions on misleading and aggressive practices in Articles 6–8, as well as by the examples in Annex I, it still leaves a very broad discretion to the decision-maker. As shown in Chapters 5 and 6, the provisions on misleading and aggressive practices at least partially resemble general clauses, and even outside the scope of these provisions the general clause remains open-ended anyway. Even the relationship, in principle, between the particular provisions and the general clause is unclear. Should the general clause be treated as a very important main rule, or rather as a relatively exceptionally used 'safety net' for situations where the provisions on misleading and aggressive practices fail to offer proper protection? Arguments in both directions can easily be made.[1] One may assume, for example, that jurisdictions feeling less comfortable with general clauses, like the United Kingdom, will tend to play down the importance of the general clause.

Thirdly, as discussed in Chapter 2, the Directive is the first important expression of the shift of EU consumer policy from a minimum to a maximum harmonisation approach. The Directive therefore does not only attempt to achieve a minimum level

---

1   Compare above, Chapter 4(h) and Chapter 5(a).

of consumer protection that would apply throughout the Union. It affects the legal orders of the Member States in a more thorough manner, as it becomes a device for outlawing more far-reaching consumer protection measures of the Member States as well. The potential importance of this mechanism is enhanced by its combination with the Directive's above-mentioned broad scope and the wide discretion conferred on decision-makers. These three features together give the European Court of Justice an instrument for intervening in national regulation of business behaviour whenever it considers it inappropriate.

The legal importance of the Directive is, in other words, plain. In addition, when one notes that the issues regulated by the Directive belong to the core areas of business activity, one should not have any doubts concerning the practical importance of the Directive. It will almost certainly become one of the key Directives in the EU system of consumer protection.

Importance is not, however, the same as success. Having stated that the Directive will obviously affect both Member States' laws and European business behaviour in many ways, it remains to be assessed whether these effects should be described in a predominantly positive or negative way.

## b. The Measure of Assessment: The Purposes of the Directive

For the assessment of the Directive one needs a system of measurement. One possible measure is the purpose of the Directive: can and does the Directive achieve what it aimed to do? In this chapter the Directive will be assessed mainly from this perspective. Below the main purposes of the Directive are spelt out, and the assessment in the following sections relate to these purposes. An assessment related to purpose is not, however, the only possible approach. One might want to criticise the purpose or to assess the Directive from a point of view that is not related to its purpose. Such a broader perspective is set out, in particular, in the last section of this chapter.

The purpose of the Directive is directly related to the creation of the internal market. As described in Chapter 1, the internal market perspective is made clear in two ways. On the one hand the Directive aims at strengthening consumer confidence in the internal market and thereby facilitating the consumer's access to cross-border shopping. It is assumed that a consumer who trusts that the rules on unfair commercial practices are the same throughout the Union is more likely to engage in cross-border shopping and, through this activity, contribute to increased competition and efficiency within the internal market.[2] On the other hand, the internal market

---

2    The Directive here reflects the recent general policy shift favouring full harmonisation instead of minimum harmonisation. According to the Consumer Policy Strategy 2002–2006, COM(2002) 208 final 7: 'It is also important that consumers have comparable opportunities to benefit fully from the potential of the internal market in terms of choice, lower prices, and the affordability and availability of essential services. Barriers to cross-border trade should therefore be overcome in order that the consumer dimension of the internal market can

perspective incorporates a business perspective. Similar rules on unfair commercial practices are supposed to remove perceived obstacles to cross-border trade and to diminish the transaction costs of traders engaging in such trade. The purpose of the Directive could, in other words, be expressed by the following two slogans: *more consumer confidence* and *less business transaction costs* (or more generally, less perceptible obstacles to trade).

Some substantive aims have also been cited as reasons for the Directive. These aims are, to some extent, related to the above-mentioned internal market goals, but they are also partially independent. This is true for the stated goal of reaching a high level of consumer protection within the Union; according to the Preamble of the Directive, 'the Community is to contribute to the attainment of a high level of consumer protection'.[3] This is a goal in its own right, given that the Treaty in its present form obliges the legislature to strive in this direction. At the same time this goal is, of course, closely interlinked with the internal market-based consumer confidence argument.

A similar position has the Directive's aim of enhancing legal certainty. Legal certainty must be considered a virtue in a Union based on the rule of law. At the same time it most certainly affects the confidence of the actors in the market. As the Unfair Commercial Practices Directive primarily regulates business behaviour, legal certainty in this area is crucial for business. Legal uncertainty may manifest itself as a barrier to trade, or as something that increases the transaction costs.

So, when assessing the Directive in the light of its aims one might use the following criteria:

– the Directive should increase consumer confidence in the internal market;
– it should achieve a high level of consumer protection;
– it should minimise transaction costs and obstacles to trade by unifying rules; and
– it should increase legal certainty in this area.

Even if one can agree on these purposes, this does not necessarily lead to agreement as to how the Directive should be assessed. Clearly, the economic and political backgrounds (in a broad sense) of those making the assessment will heavily influence the outcome. In addition, the general feeling concerning the advantages and disadvantages of the Directive to some extent will be coloured by the national legal background of the assessor. As mentioned already in the Preface, the fact that the present authors represent three different legal families, with different approaches both to consumer protection and to legal methodology in general, is visible in both content and style of the various chapters. Therefore, even though the authors share

---

develop in parallel with its business dimension. EU consumer policy therefore aims at setting a coherent and common environment ensuring that consumers are confident in shopping across borders throughout the EU.'

3    Recital 1.

a basic positive attitude towards the need for consumer protection, their assessment of the Directive is not identical either. A Nordic writer may perceive a threat towards the fairly successful Consumer Ombudsman-driven system of fairness control; a German may feel the need for fresh winds from Europe blowing in the relatively petrified area of unfair competition law; and a British person may feel uneasy about the legislative technique employed in the Directive. Yet on the most basic conclusion below – criticism of the choice of the maximum harmonisation approach[4] – there is no disagreement between the present authors. Indeed it is this feature which causes the concern about the impact of their national traditions.

It is interesting in this context to note how one's legal background even affects one's assessment of the quality of drafting. For a continental lawyer, the Directive as a whole, even though there are many problems in details, appears relatively well structured and accessible, at least in comparison with many of the other consumer law Directives. The threefold structure[5] is logical and easy to understand. A common lawyer, with a natural scepticism against general clauses, might judge the vagueness of the rules of the Directive as a sign of very poor drafting.[6] In relation to the present Directive, this argument does gain some force from the fact that the maximum harmonisation approach was chosen. Maximum Directives require better drafting than minimum Directives, as the national legislators have much lesser leeway for improving drafting errors in the former.

### c. Consumer Confidence

At the outset, consumer confidence reasoning appears to have at least some merits. Consumers may indeed be reluctant to acquire goods and services abroad because of a lack of confidence in the protection offered to them in foreign markets. There is some empirical evidence according to which consumers do not buy from other Member States because of difficulties relating to the exchange or repair of the goods or the settlement of disputes.[7] Such evidence was gathered when preparing the Unfair Commercial Practices Directive. According to this survey, 76 per cent of consumers who felt less confident buying from another EU country cited as a very or fairly important factor a lack of trust in foreign sellers and a perceived greater risk of

---

4   On this choice, see above, Chapter 2.

5   See above, Chapter 4(b)(i).

6   As examples of poor drafting one could mention the uncertainty concerning the scope of the detailed rules on the average consumer test in Article 5, in relation to Articles 6 and 7 (see above Chapter 5(b)(iii)), and the way the items in Annex I are grouped under the headings misleading and aggressive practices (see Chapter 5(d)(i)).

7   See, for example, L. Gibson, 'Access to Justice and Consumer Redress Within a Single Market' (1992) 15 *Journal of Consumer Policy* 407, 409, and Proposal for a European Parliament and Council Directive on the sale of consumer goods and associated guarantees, COM(95) 520 final 3–4.

fraud or deception.[8] However, looking more closely at the reasons offered in studies such as these, they primarily appear to relate to problems of procedure and access – the consumer refrains from shopping abroad because of fear of practical problems related to the access to the other party and problems of access to justice resulting from the fact that the consumer and the seller are located in different countries – rather than to lack of confidence in the substantive law.[9]

The Unfair Commercial Practices Directive primarily attempts to harmonise substantive law. Related to substantive harmonisation, the consumer confidence argument is not as convincing as in the context of procedural remedies facilitating redress against foreign sellers. To overplay the importance of the argument in relation to substantive harmonisation is at odds with self-evident knowledge about how consumers act in the marketplace. There are good grounds to believe that most consumers are not familiar with the content of their own legal system. However, this lack of awareness as such does not deter them from shopping in their national surroundings. It is hard to assume then that their lack of knowledge about the substantive law of other Member States would be an important deterrent to making use of the marketplace in those states.[10] Admittedly, in some sectors of high value, such as the credit sector, consumers may have acquired a practical knowledge which they suspect lacks value in other Member States.[11] If this is true, however, it only supports harmonisation measures within these specific sectors. It does not make consumer confidence a sufficient argument for more general harmonisation.

To this argument one may reply that the knowledge of the law is not the important matter with respect to confidence, but rather beliefs concerning the relevant level of protection. Consumers (like lawyers) may have a 'nationalistic' belief that their own system of protection is more advanced than that of other Member States, and therefore refrain from making full use of the internal market. A general understanding that the systems are substantively similar could therefore support attitudes which are

---

8 COM(2003) 356 final 4, citing from the Extended Impact Assessment, SEC(2003) 724, 6.

9 According to a survey, 68 per cent of those consumers who felt less confident in buying from another Member State said perceived lower standards of consumer protection laws were a very or fairly important reason for this (see SEC(2003) 724, 6 and COM(2003) 356 final 4). However, this does not necessarily relate to differences in substantive law, but can also reflect the trust in the working of the protection system as a whole.

10 The fact that in the above-cited survey 79 per cent of those consumers who felt less confident in buying from another Member State cited as a very or fairly important obstacle the uncertainty concerning the consumer protection provided (SEC(2003) 724, 6 and COM(2003) 356 final 5) does not necessarily indicate that uncertainty regarding the detailed content of substantive law is an important factor. It may just as well reflect uncertainty regarding the overall working of the consumer protection system in other countries.

11 In the consumer organisation responses referred to in the Action Plan for a more coherent European contract law, the only example mentioned in which disparities in national laws would create uncertainty for consumers was in relation to credit law, COM(2003) 68 final 31.

favourable to cross-border shopping. Indeed, according to empirical evidence, in very general terms the consumers of the internal market do appear to believe that their own protection systems are better than those of their neighbours.[12] However, if one looks at the attitudes of consumers in different Member States, the picture becomes much more complex. Consumers of some countries, especially in the south of Europe, such as Italy, Greece and Portugal, appear to trust foreign systems better than their own, whilst, for example, German, Swedish and Danish consumers have a reversed pattern of expectations.[13] There are strong reasons to believe that the list of countries in which consumers have more confidence in foreign protection systems than in their own has become longer after the accession of the new Member States in 2004. So even though the argument concerning 'nationalist' consumer beliefs may have some weight, it is clearly limited to consumers of some (predominantly northern) countries only.

This is not to say that the consumer confidence argument would lack relevance altogether. If, for example, business practices that are generally considered to be clearly unfair were allowed in some Member States this might indeed cause problems of confidence, especially if cases of this kind were reported and noted by a larger public. The Unfair Commercial Practices Directive can most certainly contribute to diminishing the risk of such occurrences that may bring disrepute to the idea of the common internal market. The extent to which it can do so is connected with the level of protection adopted, which is commented upon in the next section of this chapter. If a high level of protection is the target, as required by the Treaty, the Directive can have more effects of this kind.

The issuing of the Directive, in connection with the media coverage that has accompanied its enactment and that will probably accompany its national implementation, may increase the knowledge of consumers concerning EU law on fair trading. Despite the existence of detailed secondary EU law on fair business behaviour in several areas – such that some are ready to speak about the emergence of a general principle of fair trading in EU law[14] –consumer awareness of EU requirements on fair trading is probably still low.[15] The Directive may contribute to consumer confidence by enhancing such awareness.

There is, in other words, some, but not much, force in the arguments that consumer confidence requires a Directive in this area. These arguments, however, at best support the creation of a minimum safety net for consumers in order to diminish the risk that cross-border consumers would experience strongly unfair

---

12 In a European survey – Flash Eurobarometer 117, *Consumers Survey*, Results and comments (January 2002) – 31.5 per cent of the respondents thought that their consumer rights would be well or very well protected in a dispute with a seller or manufacturer in another Member State, whilst 55.6 per cent thought the same about a dispute in their own country.

13 See *Consumers Survey* 2002, *op.cit.*, 33–7.

14 M. Radeideh, *Fair Trading in EC Law* (Groningen: Europa Law Publishing, 2005) Chapter 3.

15 For this reason M. Radeideh, *op.cit.*, 286, argued for the adoption of a Directive.

treatment leading to well-publicised crises of confidence. These arguments do not appear to offer any reason for the choice of the maximum harmonisation approach. If consumers do not know exactly the content of their own law, it cannot be relevant for them to know that the law of another Member State is more or less identical to their own. It is sufficient for consumers to know that there is a minimum set of protection rules in force throughout the Union. The creation of consumer awareness of the EU principle of fair trading does not require maximum harmonisation instead of minimum harmonisation.

Concerning what is known about consumers and their behaviour, the consumer confidence argument, as a reason for the maximum harmonisation approach of the Unfair Commercial Practices Directive, is not convincing.[16] The argument appears to be used in a normative rather than empirical fashion. European consumers should be confident, since the European legislator has issued the Directive. It is possible that such a normative argument could be used in legal decision-making, reflecting the purpose of the legislation. Yet as a legal policy argument, concerning the need for the new legislation and for its maximum character, it has little force.

### d. The Level of Protection

According to its Preamble,[17] the Directive strives to achieve a high level of consumer protection in the area regulated, as required by the present wording of the Treaty. Yet does it fulfil its promises?

An assessment of the level of protection depends on what one compares the Directive to. In comparison to previously existent secondary EU law, the Directive is clearly a step forward. By introducing a general principle forbidding unfair commercial practices it fills many lacunae between the more specific enactments introduced in EU law to date. By greatly broadening the scope of the consumer protection offered by EU legislation, it raises the level of the protection that exists throughout the EU. As the new Directive is essentially in line with the existing particular Directives, and as those particular Directives still remain in force, the new Directive does not lower the protection from previous levels, even within the particular areas in which there already exist EU rules.

It is, however, rather a truism that the Directive raises the level of consumer protection in EU law. All new consumer protection Directives that do not abolish previous ones or amend them in a less demanding direction do precisely that. When assessing the level of consumer protection offered by the new Directive, the correct object of comparison is therefore not previously existing EU law, but rather national law in the Member States. In this respect the impression of the Directive becomes more multi-faceted.

---

16 See, in more detail, T. Wilhelmsson, 'The Abuse of the "Confident Consumer" as a Justification for EC Consumer Law' (2004) 27 *Journal of Consumer Policy* 317.

17 Recitals 1 and 5.

On the one hand, the Directive certainly entails a rising level of consumer protection in many Member States. In some it has even meant the introduction of a general principle against unfair commercial practices that did not exist previously. In the United Kingdom, the change can be considered fairly dramatic, since the enactment of a broad general clause here is a certainly a novel innovation. Also, in parts of Southern Europe and among the new Member States, such general improvements are discernible. And, obviously, in all Member States the Directive contains at least some details that are more consumerfriendly than the previous national law.

For many commentators, one of the most important advances in consumer rights lies in the express provisions on precontractual disclosure. In the United Kingdom, for example, the provisions on precontractual disclosure of material information have been mentioned as one of the cases in which the Directive envisages 'control over commercial practices not readily tamed under existing English law'.[18] As mentioned above, the provision on misleading omissions in the Directive has largely been understood as containing an information duty that goes further than was previously accepted in many Member States.[19] It can even be argued that the main strength of the Directive is its attempt to improve market communication.

The improvements will probably not be limited to substantive law only, despite the fact that issues of enforcement are largely left to national law. The European character of the rules, and the European elements of the enforcement mechanism, may add pressure to make the enforcement of these rules more efficient in Member States in which enforcement of consumer unfair commercial practices law so far has not been considered important and has been under-resourced. The need for efficient enforcement is in many ways underlined in the Directive.[20] The Directive may also, despite the fact that it does not directly apply to individual claims,[21] in some jurisdictions indirectly increase the availability of the remedy of damages.

On the other hand, it is also easy to indicate solutions in the Directive which appear to be less protective than the corresponding rules in certain national laws. The paradigmatic example relates to the basic understanding of how consumers behave, and ought to behave, in the marketplace. The images of the consumer that guide the application of the consumer protection rules in various Member States vary considerably. Even after the dropping of the definition of 'average consumer' as being 'reasonably circumspect' from the Articles of the Directive, it is obvious that the 'average consumer' approach adopted in the Directive gives traders more

---

18  G. Howells and S. Weatherill, *Consumer Protection Law* (Aldershot: Ashgate, 2005) 433.

19  See more closely, Chapter 5(c)(i).

20  See Chapter 8.

21  See Chapter 3(b).

leeway than in those countries in which the 'credulous consumer' was used as a benchmark.[22]

The provisions relating to the protection of children against unfair commercial practices illustrate the restrained manner in which the Directive deals with the needs of vulnerable groups. Even though the Directive admits the need to provide special protection to vulnerable groups, such as children, it most certainly does not go as far in this direction as, for example, Nordic marketing law.[23] In the latter one can find both outright bans against advertising to children[24] as well as strict limits on measures that are allowed in this context.[25]

Of course, in a Union of 25 Member States, it would be virtually impossible to create any kind of coherent consumer protection measure that would not in any respect be less consumerfriendly than the position in any national law. It is hard to criticise the Directive because it does not, in every detail, reach the highest level of protection achieved in every Member State. If the Directive had been a minimum Directive, this would rather be the normal and acceptable approach. The problems from a consumer perspective are connected with the fact that the Directive is made a maximum harmonisation Directive and therefore forces some Member States to lower their level of protection from that reached prior to the adoption of the Directive. The aim of achieving a high level of consumer protection is overruled by the business-oriented, internal market purpose of the Directive that emphasises the importance of having identical rules throughout the Union.

As long as this impact on national laws relates to more or less technical details, a formal lowering of the level of protection would not be problematic from a

---

22  A. Bakardjieva Engelbrekt, Fair Trading Law in Flux? National Legacies, Institutional Choice and the Process of Europeanisation (Dissertation: Stockholm, 2003) 623, sees the Directive as directly targeting the relatively strict German requirements based on the UWG, in this and other respects. The Directive 'may be seen as one collective attempt to shake the UWG at its foundations'. For the UK the approach adopted by the courts seems compatible with the concept of 'average consumer', see the report by C. Twigg-Flesner, D. Parry, G. Howells and A. Nordhausen, An Analysis Of The Application And Scope Of The Unfair Commercial Practices Directive, A report for the Department of Trade and Industry, 18 May 2005 (published on http://www.dti.gov.uk/ccp/consultpdf/final_report180505.pdf) 30. However, even for UK law, it has been claimed that the reference to the 'average consumer' could lower the level of protection if it spills over to the common law doctrines of duress and undue influence, see C. Twigg-Flesner, 'Deep Impact? The EC Directive on Unfair Commercial Practices and Domestic Consumer Law' (2005) 121 *Law Quarterly Review* 386, 387.

23  See also on the high level of protection in the Nordic Member States, R. Schulze and H. Schulte-Nölke (eds), *Analysis of National Fairness Laws Aimed at Protecting Consumers in Relation to Commercial Practices*, June 2003 (published on http://europa.eu.int/comm/consumers/cons_int/safe_shop/fair_bus_pract/green_pap_comm/studies/unfair_practices_en.pdf) 98–9.

24  On the Swedish ban, see Chapter 3(d)(ii).

25  The Finnish Market Court has, for example, expressly stated that marketing to children should not be suggestive (1984:11) and should avoid emotional devices such as reference to children's loneliness and need of friends (1990:16).

consumer point of view. In fact, the multitude of detailed consumer protection rules on business practices in the Member States is not necessarily in all cases dictated by genuine concerns regarding the consumer interest. They may relate to attempts to distort competition as well. However, the examples above show that the potentially 'negative' (from a consumer point of view) impact of the Directive is not limited to such 'technical' issues. The Directive may also, in some cases, lower consumer protection in ways that are at odds with central policy choices within national systems of consumer protection. The need to amend national approaches to consumer images, as well as to the protection of children, offers examples of such effects.

The limitations of the scope of the Directive may, in some Member States, highlight the problematic consequences of the maximum character of the Directive for national legal policy concerning the level of protection. In particular, the limitation of the scope to business-to-consumer relationships in combination with the maximum approach may produce irritating anomalies within the national systems. As the Directive designates a maximum standard for the protection of consumers, but not traders, it may in some countries and in some situations lead to consumer buyers having less protection than commercial buyers, as the latter may still be protected by the – possibly more favourable – national general rules of the Member State. With regard to the general starting points of consumer policy this would not be acceptable.

Irrespective of the level of protection adopted in the Directive, it may also be subject to criticism for being rather static and not allowing for sufficiently rapid reactions to the quickly emerging new problems at the national level. Of course, the flexibility of the general clause as such offers the national courts and supervising authorities some space for intervention in new and unacceptable commercial practices. It is worth noting, however, that the Directive does not contain any 'safeguard clause' that would give the national authorities a right to deal with new phenomena not covered by the Directive. Despite the fact that some other Directives contain such safeguard clauses,[26] it was not deemed necessary in this context. Rather, the Commission 'was confident of its law'.[27]

### e. Traders' Costs and Risks

As it seems difficult to regard the Directive – based on a maximum harmonisation approach – as an adequate response to consumer needs and expectations, its purposes of removing barriers to trade and diminishing transaction costs in cross-border trade come to the fore. In fact, these goals seem to be the main objective of the Directive. Needless to say, the removal of barriers and reduction of transaction costs may indirectly benefit consumers as well, through greater choice and lower prices.

---

26  See, for example, the Electronic Commerce Directive Article 3.

27  G. Howells, 'The Rise of European Consumer Law – Whither National Consumer Law?' *Sydney Law Review* forthcoming.

The variation in national laws is seen as an obstacle to pan-European marketing strategies and campaigns.[28] The Directive attempts to make it easier for traders to approach the internal market in a much more comprehensive way.

The most convenient solution for traders would obviously have been the inclusion of a fully-fledged country of origin provision in the Directive. In terms of costs and risks, for traders it would have been ideal to have to comply with just one set of rules and only one type of administrative control. The proposed express country of origin provision was, however – for good reasons that relate to the variations in needs and expectations of consumers in various parts of the Union – dropped during the final stages of preparing the Directive. The legal effects of the remaining part of Article 4 are unclear.[29] The advantages of the Directive for traders' costs and risks therefore have to be judged rather in terms of its maximum harmonisation approach.

The problems for traders in the pre-Directive state of affairs were of both a substantive and informational nature. Substantively, the wide variations in the level of consumer protection, as well as the numerous differences in detail, made it very difficult for traders to develop cost-saving pan-European marketing strategies. In information terms, an additional difficulty – and perhaps the most important – related to the lack of transparency concerning the variations in national laws. A trader who wanted to adhere to the national laws concerning commercial practices faced problems in first finding out the content of the appropriate law.

In precisely this area the problems have been exacerbated by the vagueness and variations of the structures and locations of the national rules in question.[30] Some rules in certain Member States have been located within the sphere of private law, whilst others have appeared in various sectors of public law. Even though compilations of rules concerning unfair commercial practices did exist in some Member States, in others the rules have been spread over a large variety of legal instruments. Member States used general clauses and specific legislation in various combinations, and the amount and accessibility of practice concerning the use made of general clauses varied. In some Member States codes of conduct are important; in others their role is less central. A key issue is whether, as a consequence of the Directive, 'this cacophonic mixture of institutional traditions, historical legacies and procedural designs' will 'fuse into a harmonious polyphony of different laws and policies'.[31]

Both in terms of the substantive, as well as informational problems, it appears clear that the Directive can bring some relief. Being a maximum harmonisation Directive it at least to some extent approximates the levels of consumer protection in the various Member States. This being the case, it also somewhat alleviates the information problem: the trader, as a rule, should be able to rely on the acceptability of a measure that fulfils the demands of the Directive and therefore should not

---

28  R. Schulze and H. Schulte-Nölke, *op.cit.*, 95.

29  See above Chapter 2(e).

30  See R. Schulze and H. Schulte-Nölke, *op.cit.*, 94.

31  A. Bakardjieva Engelbrekt, *Fair Trading Law in Flux?*, *op.cit.*, 609.

have to check the content of national laws. Even though the difficulties in getting information on the content of national laws are not necessarily completely removed by the Directive (given that the implementation of the Directive may be accomplished by differing legislative instruments and in various branches of law), the information gathered in connection with implementation naturally makes the task of finding the right provisions in respective national laws much easier. The Directive, in other words, can be assumed to have effects that contribute to its purpose to diminish transaction costs and obstacles to trade for traders in Europe.

Despite its maximum character the Directive does not, however, completely remove the need for acquiring knowledge concerning national laws. This is the case for several reasons.

First, the Directive contains limitations of scope that may leave important national provisions concerning business practices unaffected by the attempts to harmonise in this area. These have been analysed more closely in Chapter 3. Potentially broad areas of national law are left outside the sphere of application of the Directive by, for example, the focus on collective protection that leaves room for national rules on damages and other private law remedies containing stricter requirements on business behaviour than those of the Directive; the consumer interest perspective that leaves potentially large areas of regulation of taste and decency matters, as well as protection of other societal interests unharmonised; the exception related to protection of health and safety; and the exception concerning regulated professions that accepts particular and detailed national provisions in many specific areas of activity.

When one adds to these limitations the fact that the Directive, as a consumer protection measure, does not deal with problems that the trader may face in relation to other traders – be they transaction partners or competitors – it is obvious that the trader cannot act in such a legally safe way in foreign Member States as the Directive at the outset appears to promise.

Secondly, as the Directive is – and necessarily has to be – vague in its wording, one cannot assume that it will be interpreted in the same way in all actual situations in the Member States. On the contrary, it is easy to predict that the previous experiences and traditions of each Member State will be reflected in the emerging practice within each country. The obligation to apply the rules in a harmonised manner, supervised by the European Court of Justice, can only to a limited extent remove such differences. Practically speaking, only a very small proportion of the cases can be referred to the Court, and the Court will most certainly acknowledge this by restricting its decisions to matters of principle.[32]

In addition, both the Directive itself and previous decisions from the Court emphasise the necessity of allowing, to some extent, national and local variations. The concrete assessment of the fairness of commercial practices should take into

---

32  See, in relation to the Unfair Contract Terms Directive, Case C–237/02 *Freiburger Kommunalbauten GmbH Baugesellschaft & Co. KG v Ludger Hofstetter et Ulrike Hofstetter* [2004] ECR I–3403.

account relevant 'social, cultural or linguistic factors'.[33] The 'average consumer' test, offering the basic measure for assessment, is partly culture-bound.

The need to take into account social, cultural and linguistic factors has already been observed in several contexts. For example, the relation between information, emotional assessments and legitimate commercial exaggeration must be related to national cultural patterns and to cultural codes on how one understands communication in different societies.[34] The impact of information on consumers' likely transactional decisions is also, to some extent, related to national habits and expectations,[35] and the question of whether information should be considered as ambiguous is partly related to cultural predispositions.[36] In addition, the information needs of consumers are culturally relative.[37] It is, of course, a matter of debate how culturally relative these assessments are – and should be.[38]

Both the limitations of scope and the variations in application are at odds with the stated purpose of the Directive to remove obstacles and costs related to national differences in the regulation of unfair commercial practices. It has been said that the Directive, rather than replacing 25 national laws with one unified system, 'forms only another layer of regulation, parallel to persisting Member States' regulatory models'.[39] This should not, however, be understood as a criticism of the remaining variations. On the contrary, as will be discussed below, most of these can be very well defended from both a consumer and societal point of view.

The criticism – if the remaining variations should be seen as a matter of criticism at all – should rather be targeted at the fact that the Directive promises something that it cannot and should not deliver, except to only a very partial extent. By choosing a maximum harmonisation approach that, as has been shown above, has many drawbacks, it creates the impression of similarity that will not be fully achieved. In fact, it may be sometimes more dangerous to have rules that appear harmonised but contain hidden traps for the traders operating across borders, than to have rules that all actors know are different.[40]

---

33 See Chapter 4(c)(v) and Chapter 5(b)(iii).

34 Chapter 5(b)(ii).

35 Chapter 5(b)(iv).

36 Chapter 5(c)(ii).

37 Chapter 5(c)(iii).

38 Compare above, the more harmonising approach related to the concept of professional diligence, Chapter 4(d)(ii).

39 A. Bakardjieva Engelbrekt, *Fair Trading Law in Flux?*, *op.cit.*, 624.

40 Compare H. Beale, 'Finding the Remaining Traps Instead of Unifying Contract Law', in S. Grundmann and J. Stuyck (eds), *An Academic Green Paper on European Contract Law* (The Hague: Kluwer Law International, 2002) 67, who sees the removing of such traps to be the main purpose of the harmonisation work (which can therefore be limited).

## f. Legal Certainty

The Directive does not, on good grounds, fully reach its goals of harmonisation. The legal certainty related to the replacement of 25 sets of rules with a European one is only partially offered to traders. In addition, the Directive may, because of its approach, even create some new issues of uncertainty in addition to those already in existence.

As demonstrated in several contexts, the Directive is open-ended and leaves very broad discretion to the decision-maker. Its general clause obviously cannot offer the same kind of predictability that specific and detailed rules may do. However, it is not even completely clear what the basic philosophy of the general clause is in relation to the competing values of internal market considerations versus moral values.[41] Even the more specific provisions on misleading and aggressive practices are general clauses that give only some guidance to those applying the Directive. In particular, the concept of aggressive practices is underdeveloped in the Directive and needs further refinement in practice.[42]

The initial hope that codes of conduct could be a useful method of relieving the uncertainty also appears to have vanished, probably because of the poor prospects of having functioning pan-European codes in this area. The encouragement of the use of codes of conduct in the finalised Directive is very modest.[43]

However, the uncertainty related to the general clause method of the Directive should not be a target of criticism as such. The regulation of the complex field of commercial practices – a field in constant flux with new methods and approaches continuously being invented and tested – cannot be done efficiently without the help of broad general clauses. Member States' laws in this area have traditionally often made use of such regulatory measures.

However, in the context of the Unfair Commercial Practices Directive the problem of uncertainty related to the extensive use of general clauses is made much more serious because of two other features of the Directive, already mentioned at the beginning of this chapter.

First, the broad and, as demonstrated in Chapter 3, vague and unclear scope of the Directive makes it very difficult to foresee the possible effects of the general clause. This is particularly true concerning problems outside the core area of the Directive concerned with advertising and other pre-contractual commercial communications. One cannot with any degree of certainty foresee how the Directive might be applied, if at all, to various kinds of commercial activities outside of this core area.

Secondly, the problem is made more serious as a result of the maximum character of the Directive. In other words, the difficulties can be said to relate to 'the contradictory status of the UCPD of being an act of full harmonisation and at

---

41  A strong internal market perspective is defended above, in Chapter 4(c).
42  Chapter 6(a)(iii).
43  See Chapter 7(j).

the same time remaining a framework directive'.[44] The maximum harmonisation approach, in combination with the vague content of the general clause-based Directive, and with the considerable uncertainty concerning its potentially very broad scope, creates a new kind of uncertainty on the level of national law. Even pieces of national legislation that previously have been very precise and certain in their application easily become uncertain when confronted with the maximum harmonisation requirements of the vague Directive.

Both features together leave wide open the question of where to draw the line between the permitted and the forbidden. The Directive can, in a very surprising way, like a jack-in-the-box,[45] affect both detailed and general legislation and case law of the Member States. It is very difficult to foresee what pieces of concrete national legislation will be deemed unacceptable in the light of the Directive. This is because the maximum approach not only requires the Member States to have similar general clauses, but may in principle also affect all kinds of particular legislation that give the consumer better protection than the general clause (as it is understood by the European Court of Justice). The situation is particularly obscure, for example, in relation to sector-specific provisions of various kinds, as the limitations of scope concerning health and safety, as well as regulated professions, only partially – and in an unclear way – regulate the relationship between the Directive and national sector-specific legislation. Needless to say, the very general definition of unfair commercial practices, that can include almost anything, adds to the uncertainty. As noted in Chapter 3, the Directive covers 'any act, omission, course of conduct or representation, commercial communication ... by a trader, directly connected with the promotion, sale or supply of a product to consumers', including activities both before and after the consumer transaction. As the Directive is given such a broad scope, it is practically impossible to foresee what national rules it may make illegal or at least legally doubtful. It presents an enormous task for the national authorities in charge of legislation, if they take the Directive seriously, to go through the current national rules and check that the protection they offer does not exceed the level accepted by the Directive.[46]

Traditionally, consumer protection Directives have been implemented in various ways. In some countries, they have simply relied on existing general private law or public law rules that have not been amended; sometimes they have led to a development of the general rules; and sometimes specific rules on consumer relations have been adopted. The minimum harmonisation approach of most Directives to date has made

---

44 A. Bakardjieva Engelbrekt, *EU and Marketing Practices Law in the Nordic Countries – Consequences of a Directive on Unfair Business-to-Consumer Commercial Practices* (Report for the Nordic Council of Ministers Committee on Consumer Affairs, 2005, published on http://www.norden.org/konsum/sk/rappdownload.asp) 81.

45 A similar effect as the Treaty may have, see T. Wilhelmsson, 'Jack-in-the-Box Theory of European Community Law', in L. Krämer, H.-W. Micklitz and K. Tonner (eds), *Law and Diffuse Interests in the European Legal Order* (Baden-Baden: Nomos, 1997) 177.

46 See, on UK law, the voluminous report by C. Twigg-Flesner, D. Parry, G. Howells and A. Nordhausen, *op.cit.*

it possible to accommodate such variations. The Directives have been easier to adapt to national law than maximum harmonisation Directives, since rules and principles of the existing national background legislation that in certain situations might lead to better protection for the consumers have not posed a problem. By contrast, the chosen strategy of maximum harmonisation makes the legal situation much more difficult to navigate. In principle, it requires a clear delimitation of the scope of the maximalist rule in the Directive from the scope of other rules and this is in practice often very difficult to achieve.[47] This problem, however, has largely been ignored by the European institutions in the debate on the choice of approach to harmonisation of the Unfair Commercial Practices Directive.

### g. United in Diversity

The maximum harmonisation policy of the Directive is primarily based on the needs and expectations of traders. Although the promotion of the access of traders to the internal market may, under certain conditions, indirectly benefit consumers as well, the assessment of the relationship between maximalism and minimalism becomes quite different when looked at from a consumer's point of view. There is much localism in consumers' needs and expectations that is not well served by fully harmonised rules.

The legal environment obviously also plays a role in determining the needs and expectations of consumers. EU consumer law is not implemented in a legal vacuum, but incorporated into national legal orders of very diverging natures. This environment partially defines the problems to which consumer law may offer a solution[48] and also the expectations as to what the law can offer. For example, it

---

47 One can just imagine the problems of a similar kind that would arise, if, for example, the Consumer Sales Directive were a total harmonisation Directive. In fact, the Commission has recently announced that it will review the minimum nature of this Directive, COM(2004) 651 final 3. Any general rules of contract law affecting the understanding of conformity, or of the use of the remedies that would put the buyer into a better position than the Directive, would have to be disregarded in consumer relations, but not in businessto-business relations. What about (general) rules that would give the consumers additional remedies than those offered by the Directive? Would the Directive rule out a national right to withhold payment or a right to some form of liquidated or punitive damages, as used in some US consumer statutes, or could these rights be allowed, as in any event the list of remedies of the Directive is not complete, with the issue of damages excluded? What about the rules of some Member States concerning the liability of the producer, as this issue was dealt with but was not included in the Directive?

48 In this context one may also again refer to the judgment of the ECJ in Case C–237/02 *Freiburger Kommunalbauten GmbH Baugesellschaft & Co. KG v Ludger Hofstetter et Ulrike Hofstetter* [2004] ECR I–3403, in which the Court expressly emphasised that the unfairness of a term, when applying the Unfair Contract Terms Directive, has to be assessed with reference to 'the consequences of the term under the law applicable to the contract' and that '[t]his requires that consideration be given to the national law'.

is well known that in English law and business practice a party has a more limited obligation to inform the other party about negative circumstances when the contract is concluded than according to many systems of Continental law.[49] One may on good grounds assume that the expectations connected with basic approaches such as this may to some extent shape and influence the perceptions and consequences of the information and transparency policies embodied in EU consumer law and in the Unfair Commercial Practices Directive.

This example illustrates one of many possible variations of consumer expectations within the consumer cultures prevailing in different Member States. Many other matters unrelated to the legal environment, but rather to the social, cultural and linguistic context of the consumers, provide such a pluralist shape to Europe that they are difficult to combine with the maximum harmonisation approach of the Directive. The cultural environment (*senso largu*) affects the consumers' needs and expectations in differing ways in the various Member States.

To this one may reply that European consumption culture is today so homogeneous that variations in consumer expectations relate to details that can be safely dealt with by making the European rules sufficiently flexible, and that basic consumer expectations are sufficiently similar in Europe to be well served by European consumer law measures based on the principle of maximum harmonisation. Indeed, in comparison, for example, with the USA – not to mention more culturally distant parts of the world – there appears to exist a specific European consumer culture and set of consumer expectations.[50] European consumers appear to expect the state to safeguard their position in the marketplace much more than their American counterparts, who rather tend to trust in the recourse to collective consumer activism. However, looking more closely at Europe, this culture of trust in a regulated market does not appear as particularly homogeneous. Trust is invested in various ways in the regulation and in the actors in the marketplace. The claim has been put forward that in Northern Europe consumers normally expect to be protected at the level of institutions and programmes, whilst the expectations at the level of personal contact predominates in Southern Europe.[51] There is empirical evidence supporting this variation: in some Member States consumers believe very strongly in their own system of consumer protection through law – with Finnish consumers being the most trusting – whilst others are very sceptical concerning their protection at home – with the Greeks and the Portuguese being the leading sceptics. The gap between

---

49 See, for example, the comparison made by J.H.M. van Erp, 'The Pre-Contractual Stage', in A. Hartkamp *et al* (eds), *Towards a European Civil Code* (The Hague: Kluwer Law International, 3rd edn, 2004) 363, 369.

50 See in detail G. Howells and T. Wilhelmsson, 'EC and US Approaches to Consumer Protection – Should the Gap Be Bridged?' *Yearbook of European Law 1997* (Oxford: Clarendon Press, 1998) 207.

51 V. Gessner, 'Europas holprige Rechtswege – die rechtskulturellen Schranken der Rechtsverfolgung im Binnenmarkt', in L. Krämer, H.-W. Micklitz and K. Tonner (eds), *Law and Diffuse Interests in the European Legal Order* (Baden-Baden: Nomos, 1997) 163, 174.

these poles is wide.[52] One may reasonably expect that the variation has become still considerably larger through the inclusion of former socialist countries in the Union.[53] It seems clear that if consumers have such different expectations concerning their legal protection, they will also have very different expectations concerning how cautiously they must behave when acting on the consumer market. A European legislation based on maximum harmonisation cannot easily be adapted to such great variations in expectations without leading to considerable losses to consumers left with 'false' expectations.

As consumers do most of their contracting locally, one cannot presume that there will be an inevitable emergence of a Europeanised shopping culture, even among those consumers who take active advantage of the internal market. The growing use of the international virtual marketplace may contribute to a gradual convergence of virtual shopping cultures,[54] but from this possible convergence (in a sector that still represents only a small part of the total consumer expenditure) one can hardly (yet) draw any conclusions concerning the expectations which consumers have in relation to their daily shopping activities in their physical environment. The level of harmonisation that may be defended in electronic shopping – where consumers can be assumed to have different expectations on the level of protection than in traditional ways of contracting – is not necessarily suitable for traditional markets.

Some of the variations in needs and expectations of consumers in different Member States can be properly responded to by making the European rules sufficiently flexible. As mentioned earlier, the European Court of Justice has expressly noted the necessity of taking into account 'social, cultural or linguistic factors' in determining whether there is a risk of consumers being misled. This expression is also imported into the official understanding of the Directive through the recitals. In the present work, many issues have been identified, in connection with which this formula could offer a useful tool for adapting the application of the Directive to local consumer needs and expectations.[55]

However, the differences between consumer cultures within the EU do not appear to relate only to those details that can be dealt with by using flexible legislation, but also to the basic approaches of the systems of protection.[56] Despite efforts to cater for the variations in needs and expectations by the use of flexible provisions, there may be a justifiable fear that a maximum harmonisation Directive cannot sufficiently respond to such basic diversity without unduly sacrificing the interests of many

---

52  Eighty-two per cent of the Finns feel themselves to be well protected, whereas only 21 per cent of Greek and Portuguese do so, *Consumers Survey* 2002, *op.cit.*, 32–3.

53  See many of the interesting papers in the volume H.-W. Micklitz (ed.), *Rechtseinheit oder Rechtsvielfalt in Europa? Rolle und Funktion des Verbraucherrechts in der EG und den MOE–Staaten* (Baden-Baden: Nomos, 1996).

54  And accordingly of the protection techniques, see G.-P. Calliess, 'Transnationales Verbrauchervertragsrecht', (2004) 68 *Rabels Zeitschrift für ausländisches und internationales Privatrecht* 244.

55  Above, section e.

56  See, in particular, examples mentioned above in section d.

consumers. Although regulation through general clauses can be very useful in terms of specific details, it offers only a partial answer to the local variations in consumer needs and expectations.

Cultural autonomy of European nations is an important piece of the emerging European architecture. The proposed European Constitutional Treaty, in the provision on the Union's objectives, expressly emphasised that '[t]he Union shall respect its rich cultural and linguistic diversity'.[57] Therefore the European legislator should take seriously the idea of a Europe 'united in its diversity' as expressed in the Treaty.[58]

The maximum harmonisation approach of the Directive is problematic in this sense. However, as the Directive has been adopted in this form, one must live with it and make the best of the situation. Those who apply the Directive should be sufficiently sensitive to cultural, social and linguistic variations in Europe.

---

57 Draft Treaty Establishing a Constitution for Europe, adopted by consensus by the European Convention on 13 June and 10 July 2003, Article 3.

58 Draft Treaty Establishing a Constitution for Europe, Preamble.

# Appendix

**DIRECTIVE 2005/29/EC OF THE EUROPEAN PARLIAMENT AND OF THE COUNCIL of 11 May 2005 concerning unfair business-to-consumer commercial practices in the internal market and amending Council Directive 84/450/EEC, Directives 97/7/EC, 98/27/EC and 2002/65/EC of the European Parliament and of the Council and Regulation (EC) No 2006/2004 of the European Parliament and of the Council ('Unfair Commercial Practices Directive') (Text with EEA relevance)**

THE EUROPEAN PARLIAMENT AND THE COUNCIL OF THE EUROPEAN UNION,
Having regard to the Treaty establishing the European Community, and in particular Article 95 thereof,
Having regard to the proposal from the Commission,
Having regard to the opinion of the European Economic and Social Committee(¹),
Acting in accordance with the procedure laid down in Article 251 of the Treaty(²),
Whereas:

(1) Article 153(1) and (3)(a) of the Treaty provides that the Community is to contribute to the attainment of a high level of consumer protection by the measures it adopts pursuant to Article 95 thereof.

(2) In accordance with Article 14(2) of the Treaty, the internal market comprises an area without internal frontiers in which the free movement of goods and services and freedom of establishment are ensured. The development of fair commercial practices within the area without internal frontiers is vital for the promotion of the development of cross border activities.

(3) The laws of the Member States relating to unfair commercial practices show marked differences which can generate appreciable distortions of competition and obstacles to the smooth functioning of the internal market. In the field of advertising,

---

1   OJ C 108, 30.4.2004, p. 81.

2   Opinion of the European Parliament of 20 April 2004 (OJ C 104 E, 30.4.2004, p. 260), Council Common Position of 15 November 2004 (OJ C 38 E, 15.2.2005, p. 1), Position of the European Parliament of 24 February 2005 (not yet published in the Official Journal) and Council Decision of 12 April 2005.

Council Directive 84/450/EEC of 10 September 1984 concerning misleading and comparative advertising([3]) establishes minimum criteria for harmonising legislation on misleading advertising, but does not prevent the Member States from retaining or adopting measures which provide more extensive protection for consumers. As a result, Member States' provisions on misleading advertising diverge significantly.

(4) These disparities cause uncertainty as to which national rules apply to unfair commercial practices harming consumers' economic interests and create many barriers affecting business and consumers. These barriers increase the cost to business of exercising internal market freedoms, in particular when businesses wish to engage in cross border marketing, advertising campaigns and sales promotions. Such barriers also make consumers uncertain of their rights and undermine their confidence in the internal market.

(5) In the absence of uniform rules at Community level, obstacles to the free movement of services and goods across borders or the freedom of establishment could be justified in the light of the case-law of the Court of Justice of the European Communities as long as they seek to protect recognised public interest objectives and are proportionate to those objectives. In view of the Community's objectives, as set out in the provisions of the Treaty and in secondary Community law relating to freedom of movement, and in accordance with the Commission's policy on commercial communications as indicated in the Communication from the Commission entitled 'The follow-up to the Green Paper on Commercial Communications in the Internal Market', such obstacles should be eliminated. These obstacles can only be eliminated by establishing uniform rules at Community level which establish a high level of consumer protection and by clarifying certain legal concepts at Community level to the extent necessary for the proper functioning of the internal market and to meet the requirement of legal certainty.

(6) This Directive therefore approximates the laws of the Member States on unfair commercial practices, including unfair advertising, which directly harm consumers' economic interests and thereby indirectly harm the economic interests of legitimate competitors. In line with the principle of proportionality, this Directive protects consumers from the consequences of such unfair commercial practices where they are material but recognises that in some cases the impact on consumers may be negligible. It neither covers nor affects the national laws on unfair commercial practices which harm only competitors' economic interests or which relate to a transaction between traders; taking full account of the principle of subsidiarity, Member States will continue to be able to regulate such practices, in conformity with Community law, if they choose to do so. Nor does this Directive cover or affect the provisions of Directive 84/450/EEC on advertising which misleads business but

---

3   OJ L 250, 19.9.1984, p. 17. Directive as amended by Directive 97/55/EC of the European Parliament and of the Council (UJ L 290, 23.10.1997, p. 18).

which is not misleading for consumers and on comparative advertising. Further, this Directive does not affect accepted advertising and marketing practices, such as legitimate product placement, brand differentiation or the offering of incentives which may legitimately affect consumers' perceptions of products and influence their behaviour without impairing the consumer's ability to make an informed decision.

(7) This Directive addresses commercial practices directly related to influencing consumers' transactional decisions in relation to products. It does not address commercial practices carried out primarily for other purposes, including for example commercial communication aimed at investors, such as annual reports and corporate promotional literature. It does not address legal requirements related to taste and decency which vary widely among the Member States. Commercial practices such as, for example, commercial solicitation in the streets, may be undesirable in Member States for cultural reasons. Member States should accordingly be able to continue to ban commercial practices in their territory, in conformity with Community law, for reasons of taste and decency even where such practices do not limit consumers' freedom of choice. Full account should be taken of the context of the individual case concerned in applying this Directive, in particular the general clauses thereof.

(8) This Directive directly protects consumer economic interests from unfair business-to-consumer commercial practices. Thereby, it also indirectly protects legitimate businesses from their competitors who do not play by the rules in this Directive and thus guarantees fair competition in fields coordinated by it. It is understood that there are other commercial practices which, although not harming consumers, may hurt competitors and business customers. The Commission should carefully examine the need for Community action in the field of unfair competition beyond the remit of this Directive and, if necessary, make a legislative proposal to cover these other aspects of unfair competition.

(9) This Directive is without prejudice to individual actions brought by those who have been harmed by an unfair commercial practice. It is also without prejudice to Community and national rules on contract law, on intellectual property rights, on the health and safety aspects of products, on conditions of establishment and authorisation regimes, including those rules which, in conformity with Community law, relate to gambling activities, and to Community competition rules and the national provisions implementing them. The Member States will thus be able to retain or introduce restrictions and prohibitions of commercial practices on grounds of the protection of the health and safety of consumers in their territory wherever the trader is based, for example in relation to alcohol, tobacco or pharmaceuticals. Financial services and immovable property, by reason of their complexity and inherent serious risks, necessitate detailed requirements, including positive obligations on traders. For this reason, in the field of financial services and immovable property, this Directive is without prejudice to the right of Member States to go beyond its provisions to

protect the economic interests of consumers. It is not appropriate to regulate here the certification and indication of the standard of fineness of articles of precious metal.

(10) It is necessary to ensure that the relationship between this Directive and existing Community law is coherent, particularly where detailed provisions on unfair commercial practices apply to specific sectors. This Directive therefore amends Directive 84/450/EEC, Directive 97/7/EC of the European Parliament and of the Council of 20 May 1997 on the protection of consumers in respect of distance contracts([4]), Directive 98/27/EC of the European Parliament and of the Council of 19 May 1998 on injunctions for the protection of consumers' interests([5]) and Directive 2002/65/EC of the European Parliament and of the Council of 23 September 2002 concerning the distance marketing of consumer financial services([6]). This Directive accordingly applies only in so far as there are no specific Community law provisions regulating specific aspects of unfair commercial practices, such as information requirements and rules on the way the information is presented to the consumer. It provides protection for consumers where there is no specific sectoral legislation at Community level and prohibits traders from creating a false impression of the nature of products. This is particularly important for complex products with high levels of risk to consumers, such as certain financial services products. This Directive consequently complements the Community *acquis*, which is applicable to commercial practices harming consumers' economic interests.

(11) The high level of convergence achieved by the approximation of national provisions through this Directive creates a high common level of consumer protection. This Directive establishes a single general prohibition of those unfair commercial practices distorting consumers' economic behaviour. It also sets rules on aggressive commercial practices, which are currently not regulated at Community level.

(12) Harmonisation will considerably increase legal certainty for both consumers and business. Both consumers and business will be able to rely on a single regulatory framework based on clearly defined legal concepts regulating all aspects of unfair commercial practices across the EU. The effect will be to eliminate the barriers stemming from the fragmentation of the rules on unfair commercial practices harming consumer economic interests and to enable the internal market to be achieved in this area.

(13) In order to achieve the Community's objectives through the removal of internal market barriers, it is necessary to replace Member States' existing, divergent general clauses and legal principles. The single, common general prohibition established by

---

4   OJ L 144, 4.6.1997, p. 19. Directive as amended by Directive 2002/65/EC (OJ L 271, 9.10.2002, p. 16).

5   OJ L 166, 11.6.1998, p. 51. Directive as last amended by Directive 2002/65/EC.

6   L 271, 9.10.2002, p. 16.

this Directive therefore covers unfair commercial practices distorting consumers' economic behaviour. In order to support consumer confidence the general prohibition should apply equally to unfair commercial practices which occur outside any contractual relationship between a trader and a consumer or following the conclusion of a contract and during its execution. The general prohibition is elaborated by rules on the two types of commercial practices which are by far the most common, namely misleading commercial practices and aggressive commercial practices.

(14) It is desirable that misleading commercial practices cover those practices, including misleading advertising, which by deceiving the consumer prevent him from making an informed and thus efficient choice. In conformity with the laws and practices of Member States on misleading advertising, this Directive classifies misleading practices into misleading actions and misleading omissions. In respect of omissions, this Directive sets out a limited number of key items of information which the consumer needs to make an informed transactional decision. Such information will not have to be disclosed in all advertisements, but only where the trader makes an invitation to purchase, which is a concept clearly defined in this Directive. The full harmonisation approach adopted in this Directive does not preclude the Member States from specifying in national law the main characteristics of particular products such as, for example, collectors' items or electrical goods, the omission of which would be material when an invitation to purchase is made. It is not the intention of this Directive to reduce consumer choice by prohibiting the promotion of products which look similar to other products unless this similarity confuses consumers as to the commercial origin of the product and is therefore misleading. This Directive should be without prejudice to existing Community law which expressly affords Member States the choice between several regulatory options for the protection of consumers in the field of commercial practices. In particular, this Directive should be without prejudice to Article 13(3) of Directive 2002/58/EC of the European Parliament and of the Council of 12 July 2002 concerning the processing of personal data and the protection of privacy in the electronic communications sector([7]).

(15) Where Community law sets out information requirements in relation to commercial communication, advertising and marketing that information is considered as material under this Directive. Member States will be able to retain or add information requirements relating to contract law and having contract law consequences where this is allowed by the minimum clauses in the existing Community law instruments. A non-exhaustive list of such information requirements in the *acquis* is contained in Annex II. Given the full harmonisation introduced by this Directive only the information required in Community law is considered as material for the purpose of Article 7(5) thereof. Where Member States have introduced information requirements over and above what is specified in Community law, on the basis of minimum clauses, the omission of that extra information will not

---

7   OJ L 201, 31.7.2002, p. 37.

constitute a misleading omission under this Directive. By contrast Member States will be able, when allowed by the minimum clauses in Community law, to maintain or introduce more stringent provisions in conformity with Community law so as to ensure a higher level of protection of consumers' individual contractual rights.

(16) The provisions on aggressive commercial practices should cover those practices which significantly impair the consumer's freedom of choice. Those are practices using harassment, coercion, including the use of physical force, and undue influence.

(17) It is desirable that those commercial practices which are in all circumstances unfair be identified to provide greater legal certainty. Annex I therefore contains the full list of all such practices. These are the only commercial practices which can be deemed to be unfair without a case-by-case assessment against the provisions of Articles 5 to 9. The list may only be modified by revision of the Directive.

(18) It is appropriate to protect all consumers from unfair commercial practices; however the Court of Justice has found it necessary in adjudicating on advertising cases since the enactment of Directive 84/450/EEC to examine the effect on a notional, typical consumer. In line with the principle of proportionality, and to permit the effective application of the protections contained in it, this Directive takes as a benchmark the average consumer, who is reasonably well informed and reasonably observant and circumspect, taking into account social, cultural and linguistic factors, as interpreted by the Court of Justice, but also contains provisions aimed at preventing the exploitation of consumers whose characteristics make them particularly vulnerable to unfair commercial practices. Where a commercial practice is specifically aimed at a particular group of consumers, such as children, it is desirable that the impact of the commercial practice be assessed from the perspective of the average member of that group. It is therefore appropriate to include in the list of practices which are in all circumstances unfair a provision which, without imposing an outright ban on advertising directed at children, protects them from direct exhortations to purchase. The average consumer test is not a statistical test. National courts and authorities will have to exercise their own faculty of judgement, having regard to the case-law of the Court of Justice, to determine the typical reaction of the average consumer in a given case.

(19) Where certain characteristics such as age, physical or mental infirmity or credulity make consumers particularly susceptible to a commercial practice or to the underlying product and the economic behaviour only of such consumers is likely to be distorted by the practice in a way that the trader can reasonably foresee, it is appropriate to ensure that they are adequately protected by assessing the practice from the perspective of the average member of that group.

(20) It is appropriate to provide a role for codes of conduct, which enable traders to apply the principles of this Directive effectively in specific economic fields. In sectors where there are specific mandatory requirements regulating the behaviour of traders, it is appropriate that these will also provide evidence as to the requirements of professional diligence in that sector. The control exercised by code owners at national or Community level to eliminate unfair commercial practices may avoid the need for recourse to administrative or judicial action and should therefore be encouraged. With the aim of pursuing a high level of consumer protection, consumers' organisations could be informed and involved in the drafting of codes of conduct.

(21) Persons or organisations regarded under national law as having a legitimate interest in the matter must have legal remedies for initiating proceedings against unfair commercial practices, either before a court or before an administrative authority which is competent to decide upon complaints or to initiate appropriate legal proceedings. While it is for national law to determine the burden of proof, it is appropriate to enable courts and administrative authorities to require traders to produce evidence as to the accuracy of factual claims they have made.

(22) It is necessary that Member States lay down penalties for infringements of the provisions of this Directive and they must ensure that these are enforced. The penalties must be effective, proportionate and dissuasive.

(23) Since the objectives of this Directive, namely to eliminate the barriers to the functioning of the internal market represented by national laws on unfair commercial practices and to provide a high common level of consumer protection, by approximating the laws, regulations and administrative provisions of the Member States on unfair commercial practices, cannot be sufficiently achieved by the Member States and can therefore be better achieved at Community level, the Community may adopt measures, in accordance with the principle of subsidiarity as set out in Article 5 of the Treaty. In accordance with the principle of proportionality, as set out in that Article, this Directive does not go beyond what is necessary in order to eliminate the internal market barriers and achieve a high common level of consumer protection.

(24) It is appropriate to review this Directive to ensure that barriers to the internal market have been addressed and a high level of consumer protection achieved. The review could lead to a Commission proposal to amend this Directive, which may include a limited extension to the derogation in Article 3(5), and/or amendments to other consumer protection legislation reflecting the Commission's Consumer Policy Strategy commitment to review the existing *acquis* in order to achieve a high, common level of consumer protection.

(25) This Directive respects the fundamental rights and observes the principles recognised in particular by the Charter of Fundamental Rights of the European Union,

HAVE ADOPTED THIS DIRECTIVE:

## CHAPTER 1
## GENERAL PROVISIONS

*Article 1*
**Purpose**

The purpose of this Directive is to contribute to the proper functioning of the internal market and achieve a high level of consumer protection by approximating the laws, regulations and administrative provisions of the Member States on unfair commercial practices harming consumers' economic interests.

*Article 2*
**Definitions**

For the purposes of this Directive:

(a) 'consumer' means any natural person who, in commercial practices covered by this Directive, is acting for purposes which are outside his trade, business, craft or profession;

(b) 'trader' means any natural or legal person who, in commercial practices covered by this Directive, is acting for purposes relating to his trade, business, craft or profession and anyone acting in the name of or on behalf of a trader;

(c) 'product' means any goods or service including immovable property, rights and obligations;

(d) 'business-to-consumer commercial practices' (hereinafter also referred to as commercial practices) means any act, omission, course of conduct or representation, commercial communication including advertising and marketing, by a trader, directly connected with the promotion, sale or supply of a product to consumers;

(e) 'to materially distort the economic behaviour of consumers' means using a commercial practice to appreciably impair the consumer's ability to make an informed decision, thereby causing the consumer to take a transactional decision that he would not have taken otherwise;

(f) 'code of conduct' means an agreement or set of rules not imposed by law, regulation or administrative provision of a Member State which defines the behaviour of traders who undertake to be bound by the code in relation to one or more particular commercial practices or business sectors;

(g) 'code owner' means any entity, including a trader or group of traders, which is responsible for the formulation and revision of a code of conduct and/or for monitoring compliance with the code by those who have undertaken to be bound by it;

(h) 'professional diligence' means the standard of special skill and care which a trader may reasonably be expected to exercise towards consumers, commensurate with honest market practice and/or the general principle of good faith in the trader's field of activity;

(i) 'invitation to purchase' means a commercial communication which indicates characteristics of the product and the price in a way appropriate to the means of the commercial communication used and thereby enables the consumer to make a purchase;

(j) 'undue influence' means exploiting a position of power in relation to the consumer so as to apply pressure, even without using or threatening to use physical force, in a way which significantly limits the consumer's ability to make an informed decision;

(k) 'transactional decision' means any decision taken by a consumer concerning whether, how and on what terms to purchase, make payment in whole or in part for, retain or dispose of a product or to exercise a contractual right in relation to the product, whether the consumer decides to act or to refrain from acting;

(l) 'regulated profession' means a professional activity or a group of professional activities, access to which or the pursuit of which, or one of the modes of pursuing which, is conditional, directly or indirectly, upon possession of specific professional qualifications, pursuant to laws, regulations or administrative provisions.

*Article 3*
**Scope**

1. This Directive shall apply to unfair business-to-consumer commercial practices, as laid down in Article 5, before, during and after a commercial transaction in relation to a product.

2. This Directive is without prejudice to contract law and, in particular, to the rules on the validity, formation or effect of a contract.

3. This Directive is without prejudice to Community or national rules relating to the health and safety aspects of products.

4. In the case of conflict between the provisions of this Directive and other Community rules regulating specific aspects of unfair commercial practices, the latter shall prevail and apply to those specific aspects.

5. For a period of six years from 12 June 2007, Member States shall be able to continue to apply national provisions within the field approximated by this Directive which are more restrictive or prescriptive than this Directive and which implement directives containing minimum harmonisation clauses. These measures must be essential to ensure that consumers are adequately protected against unfair commercial practices and must be proportionate to the attainment of this objective. The review referred to in Article 18 may, if considered appropriate, include a proposal to prolong this derogation for a further limited period.

6. Member States shall notify the Commission without delay of any national provisions applied on the basis of paragraph 5.

7. This Directive is without prejudice to the rules determining the jurisdiction of the courts.

8. This Directive is without prejudice to any conditions of establishment or of authorisation regimes, or to the deontological codes of conduct or other specific rules governing regulated professions in order to uphold high standards of integrity on the part of the professional, which Member States may, in conformity with Community law, impose on professionals.

9. In relation to 'financial services', as defined in Directive 2002/65/EC, and immovable property, Member States may impose requirements which are more restrictive or prescriptive than this Directive in the field which it approximates.

10. This Directive shall not apply to the application of the laws, regulations and administrative provisions of Member States relating to the certification and indication of the standard of fineness of articles of precious metal.

*Article 4*
**Internal market**

Member States shall neither restrict the freedom to provide services nor restrict the free movement of goods for reasons falling within the field approximated by this Directive.

CHAPTER 2
**UNFAIR COMMERCIAL PRACTICES**

*Article 5*

**Prohibition of unfair commercial practices**

1. Unfair commercial practices shall be prohibited.

2. A commercial practice shall be unfair if:

(a) it is contrary to the requirements of professional diligence,

and

(b) it materially distorts or is likely to materially distort the economic behaviour with regard to the product of the average consumer whom it reaches or to whom it is addressed, or of the average member of the group when a commercial practice is directed to a particular group of consumers.

3. Commercial practices which are likely to materially distort the economic behaviour only of a clearly identifiable group of consumers who are particularly vulnerable to the practice or the underlying product because of their mental or physical infirmity, age or credulity in a way which the trader could reasonably be expected to foresee, shall be assessed from the perspective of the average member of that group. This is without prejudice to the common and legitimate advertising practice of making exaggerated statements or statements which are not meant to be taken literally.

4. In particular, commercial practices shall be unfair which:

(a) are misleading as set out in Articles 6 and 7,

or

(b) are aggressive as set out in Articles 8 and 9.

5. Annex I contains the list of those commercial practices which shall in all circumstances be regarded as unfair. The same single list shall apply in all Member States and may only be modified by revision of this Directive.

*Section 1*
**Misleading commercial practices**

*Article 6*
**Misleading actions**

1. A commercial practice shall be regarded as misleading if it contains false information and is therefore untruthful or in any way, including overall presentation, deceives or is likely to deceive the average consumer, even if the information is

factually correct, in relation to one or more of the following elements, and in either case causes or is likely to cause him to take a transactional decision that he would not have taken otherwise:

(a) the existence or nature of the product;

(b) the main characteristics of the product, such as its availability, benefits, risks, execution, composition, accessories, after-sale customer assistance and complaint handling, method and date of manufacture or provision, delivery, fitness for purpose, usage, quantity, specification, geographical or commercial origin or the results to be expected from its use, or the results and material features of tests or checks carried out on the product;

(c) the extent of the trader's commitments, the motives for the commercial practice and the nature of the sales process, any statement or symbol in relation to direct or indirect sponsorship or approval of the trader or the product;

(d) the price or the manner in which the price is calculated, or the existence of a specific price advantage;

(e) the need for a service, part, replacement or repair;

(f) the nature, attributes and rights of the trader or his agent, such as his identity and assets, his qualifications, status, approval, affiliation or connection and ownership of industrial, commercial or intellectual property rights or his awards and distinctions;

(g) the consumer's rights, including the right to replacement or reimbursement under Directive 1999/44/EC of the European Parliament and of the Council of 25 May 1999 on certain aspects of the sale of consumer goods and associated guarantees([8]), or the risks he may face.

2. A commercial practice shall also be regarded as misleading if, in its factual context, taking account of all its features and circumstances, it causes or is likely to cause the average consumer to take a transactional decision that he would not have taken otherwise, and it involves:

(a) any marketing of a product, including comparative advertising, which creates confusion with any products, trade marks, trade names or other distinguishing marks of a competitor;

(b) non-compliance by the trader with commitments contained in codes of conduct by which the trader has undertaken to be bound, where:

---

8    OJ L 171, 7.7.1999, p. 12.

(i) the commitment is not aspirational but is firm and is capable of being verified,

and

(ii) the trader indicates in a commercial practice that he is bound by the code.

## *Article 7*
## **Misleading omissions**

1. A commercial practice shall be regarded as misleading if, in its factual context, taking account of all its features and circumstances and the limitations of the communication medium, it omits material information that the average consumer needs, according to the context, to take an informed transactional decision and thereby causes or is likely to cause the average consumer to take a transactional decision that he would not have taken otherwise.

2. It shall also be regarded as a misleading omission when, taking account of the matters described in paragraph 1, a trader hides or provides in an unclear, unintelligible, ambiguous or untimely manner such material information as referred to in that paragraph or fails to identify the commercial intent of the commercial practice if not already apparent from the context, and where, in either case, this causes or is likely to cause the average consumer to take a transactional decision that he would not have taken otherwise.

3. Where the medium used to communicate the commercial practice imposes limitations of space or time, these limitations and any measures taken by the trader to make the information available to consumers by other means shall be taken into account in deciding whether information has been omitted.

4. In the case of an invitation to purchase, the following information shall be regarded as material, if not already apparent from the context:

(a) the main characteristics of the product, to an extent appropriate to the medium and the product;

(b) the geographical address and the identity of the trader, such as his trading name and, where applicable, the geographical address and the identity of the trader on whose behalf he is acting;

(c) the price inclusive of taxes, or where the nature of the product means that the price cannot reasonably be calculated in advance, the manner in which the price is calculated, as well as, where appropriate, all additional freight, delivery or postal charges or, where these charges cannot reasonably be calculated in advance, the fact that such additional charges may be payable;

(d) the arrangements for payment, delivery, performance and the complaint handling policy, if they depart from the requirements of professional diligence;

(e) for products and transactions involving a right of withdrawal or cancellation, the existence of such a right.

5. Information requirements established by Community law in relation to commercial communication including advertising or marketing, a non-exhaustive list of which is contained in Annex II, shall be regarded as material.

*Section 2*
**Aggressive commercial practices**

*Article 8*
**Aggressive commercial practices**

A commercial practice shall be regarded as aggressive if, in its factual context, taking account of all its features and circumstances, by harassment, coercion, including the use of physical force, or undue influence, it significantly impairs or is likely to significantly impair the average consumer's freedom of choice or conduct with regard to the product and thereby causes him or is likely to cause him to take a transactional decision that he would not have taken otherwise.

*Article 9*
**Use of harassment, coercion and undue influence**

In determining whether a commercial practice uses harassment, coercion, including the use of physical force, or undue influence, account shall be taken of:

(a) its timing, location, nature or persistence;

(b) the use of threatening or abusive language or behaviour;

(c) the exploitation by the trader of any specific misfortune or circumstance of such gravity as to impair the consumer's judgement, of which the trader is aware, to influence the consumer's decision with regard to the product;

(d) any onerous or disproportionate non-contractual barriers imposed by the trader where a consumer wishes to exercise rights under the contract, including rights to terminate a contract or to switch to another product or another trader;

(e) any threat to take any action that cannot legally be taken.

## CHAPTER 3
## CODES OF CONDUCT

*Article 10*
### Codes of conduct

This Directive does not exclude the control, which Member States may encourage, of unfair commercial practices by code owners and recourse to such bodies by the persons or organisations referred to in Article 11 if proceedings before such bodies are in addition to the court or administrative proceedings referred to in that Article.

Recourse to such control bodies shall never be deemed the equivalent of foregoing a means of judicial or administrative recourse as provided for in Article 11.

## CHAPTER 4
## FINAL PROVISIONS

*Article 11*
### Enforcement

1. Member States shall ensure that adequate and effective means exist to combat unfair commercial practices in order to enforce compliance with the provisions of this Directive in the interest of consumers.

Such means shall include legal provisions under which persons or organisations regarded under national law as having a legitimate interest in combating unfair commercial practices, including competitors, may:

(a) take legal action against such unfair commercial practices;

and/or

(b) bring such unfair commercial practices before an administrative authority competent either to decide on complaints or to initiate appropriate legal proceedings.

It shall be for each Member State to decide which of these facilities shall be available and whether to enable the courts or administrative authorities to require prior recourse to other established means of dealing with complaints, including those referred to in Article 10. These facilities shall be available regardless of whether the consumers affected are in the territory of the Member State where the trader is located or in another Member State.

It shall be for each Member State to decide:

(a) whether these legal facilities may be directed separately or jointly against a number of traders from the same economic sector;

and

(b) whether these legal facilities may be directed against a code owner where the relevant code promotes non-compliance with legal requirements.

2. Under the legal provisions referred to in paragraph 1, Member States shall confer upon the courts or administrative authorities powers enabling them, in cases where they deem such measures to be necessary taking into account all the interests involved and in particular the public interest:

(a) to order the cessation of, or to institute appropriate legal proceedings for an order for the cessation of, unfair commercial practices;

or

(b) if the unfair commercial practice has not yet been carried out but is imminent, to order the prohibition of the practice, or to institute appropriate legal proceedings for an order for the prohibition of the practice, even without proof of actual loss or damage or of intention or negligence on the part of the trader.

Member States shall also make provision for the measures referred to in the first subparagraph to be taken under an accelerated procedure:

— either with interim effect,

or

— with definitive effect,

on the understanding that it is for each Member State to decide which of the two options to select.

Furthermore, Member States may confer upon the courts or administrative authorities powers enabling them, with a view to eliminating the continuing effects of unfair commercial practices the cessation of which has been ordered by a final decision:

(a) to require publication of that decision in full or in part and in such form as they deem adequate;

(b) to require in addition the publication of a corrective statement.

3. The administrative authorities referred to in paragraph 1 must:

(a) be composed so as not to cast doubt on their impartiality;

(b) have adequate powers, where they decide on complaints, to monitor and enforce the observance of their decisions effectively;

(c) normally give reasons for their decisions.

Where the powers referred to in paragraph 2 are exercised exclusively by an administrative authority, reasons for its decisions shall always be given. Furthermore, in this case, provision must be made for procedures whereby improper or unreasonable exercise of its powers by the administrative authority or improper or unreasonable failure to exercise the said powers can be the subject of judicial review.

## *Article 12*
## Courts and administrative authorities: substantiation of claims

Member States shall confer upon the courts or administrative authorities powers enabling them in the civil or administrative proceedings provided for in Article 11:

(a) to require the trader to furnish evidence as to the accuracy of factual claims in relation to a commercial practice if, taking into account the legitimate interest of the trader and any other party to the proceedings, such a requirement appears appropriate on the basis of the circumstances of the particular case;

and

(b) to consider factual claims as inaccurate if the evidence demanded in accordance with (a) is not furnished or is deemed insufficient by the court or administrative authority.

## *Article 13*
## Penalties

Member States shall lay down penalties for infringements of national provisions adopted in application of this Directive and shall take all necessary measures to ensure that these are enforced. These penalties must be effective, proportionate and dissuasive.

## *Article 14*
## Amendments to Directive 84/450/EEC

Directive 84/450/EEC is hereby amended as follows:

1. Article 1 shall be replaced by the following:

'*Article 1*

The purpose of this Directive is to protect traders against misleading advertising and the unfair consequences thereof and to lay down the conditions under which comparative advertising is permitted.';

2. in Article 2:

— point 3 shall be replaced by the following:

'3. "trader" means any natural or legal person who is acting for purposes relating to his trade, craft, business or profession and any one acting in the name of or on behalf of a trader.',

— the following point shall be added:

'4. "code owner" means any entity, including a trader or group of traders, which is responsible for the formulation and revision of a code of conduct and/or for monitoring compliance with the code by those who have undertaken to be bound by it.';

3. Article 3a shall be replaced by the following:

'Article 3a

1. Comparative advertising shall, as far as the comparison is concerned, be permitted when the following conditions are met:

(a) it is not misleading within the meaning of Articles 2(2), 3 and 7(1) of this Directive or Articles 6 and 7 of Directive 2005/29/EC of the European Parliament and of the Council of 11 May 2005 concerning unfair business-to-consumer commercial practices in the internal market([9]);

(b) it compares goods or services meeting the same needs or intended for the same purpose;

(c) it objectively compares one or more material, relevant, verifiable and representative features of those goods and services, which may include price;

---

9   OJ L 149, 11.6.2005, p. 22.';

(d) it does not discredit or denigrate the trade marks, trade names, other distinguishing marks, goods, services, activities, or circumstances of a competitor;

(e) for products with designation of origin, it relates in each case to products with the same designation;

(f) it does not take unfair advantage of the reputation of a trade mark, trade name or other distinguishing marks of a competitor or of the designation of origin of competing products;

(g) it does not present goods or services as imitations or replicas of goods or services bearing a protected trade mark or trade name;

(h) it does not create confusion among traders, between the advertiser and a competitor or between the advertiser's trade marks, trade names, other distinguishing marks, goods or services and those of a competitor.

4. Article 4(1) shall be replaced by the following:

'1. Member States shall ensure that adequate and effective means exist to combat misleading advertising in order to enforce compliance with the provisions on comparative advertising in the interest of traders and competitors. Such means shall include legal provisions under which persons or organisations regarded under national law as having a legitimate interest in combating misleading advertising or regulating comparative advertising may:

(a) take legal action against such advertising;

or

(b) bring such advertising before an administrative authority competent either to decide on complaints or to initiate appropriate legal proceedings.

It shall be for each Member State to decide which of these facilities shall be available and whether to enable the courts or administrative authorities to require prior recourse to other established means of dealing with complaints, including those referred to in Article 5.

It shall be for each Member State to decide:

(a) whether these legal facilities may be directed separately or jointly against a number of traders from the same economic sector;

and

(b) whether these legal facilities may be directed against a code owner where the relevant code promotes non-compliance with legal requirements.';

5. Article 7(1) shall be replaced by the following:

'1. This Directive shall not preclude Member States from retaining or adopting provisions with a view to ensuring more extensive protection, with regard to misleading advertising, for traders and competitors.'

*Article 15*
**Amendments to Directives 97/7/EC and 2002/65/EC**

1. Article 9 of Directive 97/7/EC shall be replaced by the following:

'*Article 9*
**Inertia selling**

Given the prohibition of inertia selling practices laid down in Directive 2005/29/EC of 11 May 2005 of the European Parliament and of the Council concerning unfair business-to-consumer commercial practices in the internal market ([10]), Member States shall take the measures necessary to exempt the consumer from the provision of any consideration in cases of unsolicited supply, the absence of a response not constituting consent.

2. Article 9 of Directive 2002/65/EC shall be replaced by the following:

'*Article 9*

Given the prohibition of inertia selling practices laid down in Directive 2005/29/EC of 11 May 2005 of the European Parliament and of the Council concerning unfair business-to-consumer commercial practices in the internal market ([11]) and without prejudice to the provisions of Member States' legislation on the tacit renewal of distance contracts, when such rules permit tacit renewal, Member States shall take measures to exempt the consumer from any obligation in the event of unsolicited supplies, the absence of a reply not constituting consent.

*Article 16*
**Amendments to Directive 98/27/EC and Regulation (EC) No 2006/2004**

1. In the Annex to Directive 98/27/EC, point 1 shall be replaced by the following:

---

10  OJ L 149, 11.6.2005, p. 22.';
11  OJ L 149, 11.6.2005, p. 22.'

'1. Directive 2005/29/EC of the European Parliament and of the Council of 11 May 2005 concerning unfair business-to-consumer commercial practices in the internal market (OJ L 149, 11.6.2005, p. 22).'

2. In the Annex to Regulation (EC) No 2006/2004 of the European Parliament and of the Council of 27 October 2004 on cooperation between national authorities responsible for the enforcement of the consumer protection law (the Regulation on consumer protection cooperation)([12]) the following point shall be added:

'16. Directive 2005/29/EC of the European Parliament and of the Council of 11 May 2005 concerning unfair business-to-consumer commercial practices in the internal market (OJ L 149, 11.6.2005, p. 22).'

*Article 17*
**Information**

Member States shall take appropriate measures to inform consumers of the national law transposing this Directive and shall, where appropriate, encourage traders and code owners to inform consumers of their codes of conduct.

*Article 18*
**Review**

1. By 12 June 2011 the Commission shall submit to the European Parliament and the Council a comprehensive report on the application of this Directive, in particular of Articles 3(9) and 4 and Annex I, on the scope for further harmonisation and simplification of Community law relating to consumer protection, and, having regard to Article 3(5), on any measures that need to be taken at Community level to ensure that appropriate levels of consumer protection are maintained. The report shall be accompanied, if necessary, by a proposal to revise this Directive or other relevant parts of Community law.

2. The European Parliament and the Council shall endeavour to act, in accordance with the Treaty, within two years of the presentation by the Commission of any proposal submitted under paragraph 1.

*Article 19*
**Transposition**

Member States shall adopt and publish the laws, regulations and administrative provisions necessary to comply with this Directive by 12 June 2007. They shall

---

12  OJ L 364, 9.12.2004, p. 1.

forthwith inform the Commission thereof and inform the Commission of any subsequent amendments without delay.

They shall apply those measures by 12 December 2007. When Member States adopt those measures, they shall contain a reference to this Directive or be accompanied by such a reference on the occasion of their official publication. Member States shall determine how such reference is to be made.

*Article 20*
**Entry into force**

This Directive shall enter into force on the day following its publication in the Official Journal of the European Union.

*Article 21*
**Addressees**

This Directive is addressed to the Member States.

Done at Strasbourg, 11 May 2005.

For the European Parliament
The President
J. P. BORRELL FONTELLES

For the Council
The President
N. SCHMIT

ANNEX I

## COMMERCIAL PRACTICES WHICH ARE IN ALL CIRCUMSTANCES CONSIDERED UNFAIR

Misleading commercial practices

1. Claiming to be a signatory to a code of conduct when the trader is not.

2. Displaying a trust mark, quality mark or equivalent without having obtained the necessary authorisation.

3. Claiming that a code of conduct has an endorsement from a public or other body which it does not have.

4. Claiming that a trader (including his commercial practices) or a product has been approved, endorsed or authorised by a public or private body when he/it has not or making such a claim without complying with the terms of the approval, endorsement or authorisation.

5. Making an invitation to purchase products at a specified price without disclosing the existence of any reasonable grounds the trader may have for believing that he will not be able to offer for supply or to procure another trader to supply, those products or equivalent products at that price for a period that is, and in quantities that are, reasonable having regard to the product, the scale of advertising of the product and the price offered (bait advertising).

6. Making an invitation to purchase products at a specified price and then:

(a) refusing to show the advertised item to consumers;

or

(b) refusing to take orders for it or deliver it within a reasonable time;

or

(c) demonstrating a defective sample of it, with the intention of promoting a different product (bait and switch)

7. Falsely stating that a product will only be available for a very limited time, or that it will only be available on particular terms for a very limited time, in order to elicit an immediate decision and deprive consumers of sufficient opportunity or time to make an informed choice.

8. Undertaking to provide after-sales service to consumers with whom the trader has communicated prior to a transaction in a language which is not an official language of the Member State where the trader is located and then making such service available only in another language without clearly disclosing this to the consumer before the consumer is committed to the transaction.

9. Stating or otherwise creating the impression that a product can legally be sold when it cannot.

10. Presenting rights given to consumers in law as a distinctive feature of the trader's offer.

11. Using editorial content in the media to promote a product where a trader has paid for the promotion without making that clear in the content or by images or sounds clearly identifiable by the consumer (advertorial). This is without prejudice to Council Directive 89/552/EEC([13]).

12. Making a materially inaccurate claim concerning the nature and extent of the risk to the personal security of the consumer or his family if the consumer does not purchase the product.

13. Promoting a product similar to a product made by a particular manufacturer in such a manner as deliberately to mislead the consumer into believing that the product is made by that same manufacturer when it is not.

14. Establishing, operating or promoting a pyramid promotional scheme where a consumer gives consideration for the opportunity to receive compensation that is derived primarily from the introduction of other consumers into the scheme rather than from the sale or consumption of products.

15. Claiming that the trader is about to cease trading or move premises when he is not.

16. Claiming that products are able to facilitate winning in games of chance.

17. Falsely claiming that a product is able to cure illnesses, dysfunction or malformations.

---

13 Council Directive 89/552/EEC of 3 October 1989 on the coordination of certain provisions laid down by Law, Regulation or Administrative Action in Member States concerning the pursuit of television broadcasting activities (OJ L 298, 17.10.1989, p. 23). Directive as amended by Directive 97/36/EC of the European Parliament and of the Council (OJ L 202, 30.7.1997, p. 60).

18. Passing on materially inaccurate information on market conditions or on the possibility of finding the product with the intention of inducing the consumer to acquire the product at conditions less favourable than normal market conditions.

19. Claiming in a commercial practice to offer a competition or prize promotion without awarding the prizes described or a reasonable equivalent.

20. Describing a product as 'gratis', 'free', 'without charge' or similar if the consumer has to pay anything other than the unavoidable cost of responding to the commercial practice and collecting or paying for delivery of the item.

21. Including in marketing material an invoice or similar document seeking payment which gives the consumer the impression that he has already ordered the marketed product when he has not.

22. Falsely claiming or creating the impression that the trader is not acting for purposes relating to his trade, business, craft or profession, or falsely representing oneself as a consumer.

23. Creating the false impression that after-sales service in relation to a product is available in a Member State other than the one in which the product is sold.

Aggressive commercial practices

24. Creating the impression that the consumer cannot leave the premises until a contract is formed.

25. Conducting personal visits to the consumer's home ignoring the consumer's request to leave or not to return except in circumstances and to the extent justified, under national law, to enforce a contractual obligation.

26. Making persistent and unwanted solicitations by telephone, fax, e-mail or other remote media except in circumstances and to the extent justified under national law to enforce a contractual obligation. This is without prejudice to Article 10 of Directive 97/7/EC and Directives 95/46/EC($^{14}$) and 2002/58/EC.

27. Requiring a consumer who wishes to claim on an insurance policy to produce documents which could not reasonably be considered relevant as to whether the

---

14 Directive 95/46/EC of the European Parliament and of the Council of 24 October 1995 on the protection of individuals with regard to the processing of personal data and on the free movement of such data (OJ L 281, 23.11.1995, p. 31). Directive as amended by Regulation (EC) No 1882/2003 (OJ L 284, 31.10.2003, p. 1).

claim was valid, or failing systematically to respond to pertinent correspondence, in order to dissuade a consumer from exercising his contractual rights.

28. Including in an advertisement a direct exhortation to children to buy advertised products or persuade their parents or other adults to buy advertised products for them. This provision is without prejudice to Article 16 of Directive 89/552/EEC on television broadcasting.

29. Demanding immediate or deferred payment for or the return or safekeeping of products supplied by the trader, but not solicited by the consumer except where the product is a substitute supplied in conformity with Article 7(3) of Directive 97/7/EC (inertia selling).

30. Explicitly informing a consumer that if he does not buy the product or service, the trader's job or livelihood will be in jeopardy.

31. Creating the false impression that the consumer has already won, will win, or will on doing a particular act win, a prize or other equivalent benefit, when in fact either:

— there is no prize or other equivalent benefit,

or

— taking any action in relation to claiming the prize or other equivalent benefit is subject to the consumer paying money or incurring a cost.

## ANNEX II

## COMMUNITY LAW PROVISIONS SETTING OUT RULES FOR ADVERTISING AND COMMERCIAL COMMUNICATION

Articles 4 and 5 of Directive 97/7/EC

Article 3 of Council Directive 90/314/EEC of 13 June 1990 on package travel, package holidays and package tours([15])

Article 3(3) of Directive 94/47/EC of the European Parliament and of the Council of 26 October 1994 on the protection of purchasers in respect of certain aspects of contracts relating to the purchase of a right to use immovable properties on a timeshare basis([16])

Article 3(4) of Directive 98/6/EC of the European Parliament and of the Council of 16 February 1998 on consumer protection in the indication of the prices of products offered to consumers([17])

Articles 86 to 100 of Directive 2001/83/EC of the European Parliament and of the Council of 6 November 2001 on the Community code relating to medicinal products for human use([18])

Articles 5 and 6 of Directive 2000/31/EC of the European Parliament and of the Council of 8 June 2000 on certain legal aspects of information society services, in particular electronic commerce, in the Internal Market (Directive on electronic commerce)([19])

Article 1(d) of Directive 98/7/EC of the European Parliament and of the Council of 16 February 1998 amending Council Directive 87/102/EEC for the approximation of the laws, regulations and administrative provisions of the Member States concerning consumer credit([20])

Articles 3 and 4 of Directive 2002/65/EC

---

15  OJ L 158, 23.6.1990, p. 59.

16  OJ L 280, 29.10.1994, p. 83.

17  OJ L 80, 18.3.1998, p. 27.

18  OJ L 311, 28.11.2001, p. 67. Directive as last amended by Directive 2004/27/EC (OJ L 136, 30.4.2004, p. 34).

19  OJ L 178, 17.7.2000, p. 1.

20  OJ L 101, 1.4.1998, p. 17.

Article 1(9) of Directive 2001/107/EC of the European Parliament and of the Council of 21 January 2002 amending Council Directive 85/611/EEC on the coordination of laws, regulations and administrative provisions relating to undertakings for collective investment in transferable securities (UCITS) with a view to regulating management companies and simplified prospectuses ([21])

Articles 12 and 13 of Directive 2002/92/EC of the European Parliament and of the Council of 9 December 2002 on insurance mediation([22])

Article 36 of Directive 2002/83/EC of the European Parliament and of the Council of 5 November 2002 concerning life assurance([23])

Article 19 of Directive 2004/39/EC of the European Parliament and of the Council of 21 April 2004 on markets in financial instruments([24])

Articles 31 and 43 of Council Directive 92/49/EEC of 18 June 1992 on the coordination of laws, regulations and administrative provisions relating to direct insurance other than life assurance([25]) (third non-life insurance Directive)

Articles 5, 7 and 8 of Directive 2003/71/EC of the European Parliament and of the Council of 4 November 2003 on the prospectus to be published when securities are offered to the public or admitted to trading([26])

---

21  OJ L 41, 13.2.2002, p. 20.

22  OJ L 9, 15.1.2003, p. 3.

23  OJ L 345, 19.12.2002, p. 1. Directive as amended by Council Directive 2004/66/EC. (OJ L 168, 1.5.2004, p. 35).

24  OJ L 145, 30.4.2004, p. 1.

25  OJ L 228, 11.8.1992, p. 1. Directive as last amended by Directive 2002/87/EC of the European Parliament and of the Council (OJ L 35, 11.2.2003, p. 1).

26  OJ L 345, 31.12.2003, p. 64.

# Index